DONNA HOWELL & ALLIE HENSON

DARK COVENANT

How the Masses Are Being Groomed to Embrace the
Unthinkable While the Leaders of Organized Religion Make

A DEAL WITH THE DEVIL

DEFENDER

CRANE, MO

DARK COVENANT: How the Masses Are Being Groomed to Embrace the Unthinkable While the Leaders of Organized Religion Make a Deal with the Devil
by Donna Howell and Allie Henson

Defender Publishing
Crane, MO 65633
© 2021 Donna Howell and Allie Henson
All Rights Reserved. Published 2021.
Printed in the United States of America.

ISBN: 978-1-948014-42-7

A CIP catalog record of this book is available from the Library of Congress.

Cover design by Jeffrey Mardis.

All Scripture quoted is from the King James Version unless otherwise noted.

This book is first and foremost dedicated to God. I hope and pray that this work stirs His people and glorifies His name. Also, to my amazing husband who has been by my side for going on a gloriously happy fifteen years; to my mind-bogglingly intelligent and mature "little scholars" at home who are studying the Word every day (and who make their mama *so* proud!); to the rest of my family who have continuously loved and supported me in every phase of life; and to *all the true believers* out there whose walk with Christ manifests into more than Sunday-morning cameo appearances on the pews.

~Donna Howell

∾

To Randy, John, Karol, Gwyneth, Kat, Reagan, and Ian. May you always have eyes to see and ears to hear (Matthew 13:16), so that your world might be a better place.

~Allie Henson

CONTENTS

{ I }

ARE YOU AWAKE?

A Glimpse of the Public's Discernment

The year was 1998. I (Allie Henson) had made the short drive to a rural location to attend the meeting all townspeople had been made aware of. The small, makeshift room was filled with people who gazed curiously at the displays on the snap-together plywood walls. Folding metal chairs made up several rows in the middle of the room, where those gathered for the informational meeting were soon to be seated. Charts and laboratory photographs lined the walls of this temporary, portable building. It had the feel of a traveling carnival's funhouse: room corners, held together by folding hinges, could be spotted by the careful observer, and one could somewhat effectively track where the collapsible structure's joints would fold flat once the assembly was over and it was time to take the nomadic production to the next town. But, unlike any carnival that's anticipated and voluntarily attended, this was a mandatory meeting for all registered residents of the tiny town. The government had sent out notice that all citizens were to be here to witness the unveiling of the military's new, revolutionary super-weapon…

A bald, thin man wearing glasses and a lab coat called attention to those who were milling about the room; as he did, people agreeably sat down, expectant smiles across their faces. A modest team of qualified, professional-looking people then began to introduce the groundbreaking technology that had been genetically designed in a laboratory to guarantee victory against all enemies in what would likely be all future warfare.

A small door on the left side of the room opened, revealing a sign indicating that all attendees were to line up, single file, and prepare to walk through to the other side. As it swung open, the man in the lab coat announced proudly, "Ladies and gentlemen, I give you…the Splicer."

A hush fell over the audience members as they craned their necks to try to see what was in the next room. When I got through the door, I realized that the makeshift nature of the presentation seemed to have elevated. This wasn't just one portable room, but rather was one of many connected into a small labyrinth of cheap plywood walls posing as a transportable government office. I began to get the feeling that we were somehow being toyed with, but the wowed expressions on faces around me told me I was alone in my suspicion. We were then ushered into little circus-like cars, much like the kind a carnival ride would sport, which then took us on a "moving display": We were taken through a series of rooms filled with photographs, posters, and charts—and there was even an audio file that played the voice of a man narrating various facts about the Splicer's development. As we sat in these mini cars, we were carried from room to room, and in each one, we were given another portion of the Splicer's story to cover its conception, its visionary scientists, and the series of pioneering methods by which the weapon had been designed.

Once again, I looked at the people around me. Each smiled with fascination, gleeful in advance of possessing such a powerful military tool. I wondered at their blissful acceptance of this and wished I could celebrate with them. But something wasn't right. In fact, several things weren't right. First, the makeshift nature of the building we were in lacked the quality that such cutting-edge military development would seem to deserve. Second, there was a kindergarten-like quality in the sound of the audio narrative played over the portable loudspeakers that sat in each improvised room. The narrator's tone and the "chinsy, brink-dink" quality of musical interludes between commentaries had the likeness of every book-and-cassette story set I had enjoyed as a small child (you know, the ones that explain at the beginning that the child is to listen for a bell cue, then turn the page). Further, this nomadic-campaign-style reveal of cutting-edge warfare technology didn't seem characteristic of the military at all, which I found suspicious—*especially* when information about most truly ominous means of warfare is kept highly classified. And, I wondered why the meeting's leaders were talking to us as though we were toddlers; they fronted larger-than-life smiles such as those a parent displays when attempting to get a small child to take a spoon full of medicine, while using sing-song vocal tones. Worse, I wondered why no one else seemed to notice anything strange.

As the car I was in entered one of the final rooms of the exhibit, the methodology of the Splicer was finally revealed. Its tactic was brutish and simple. It was made to kill people, but strategically. It would identify and capture a person's scent, then hunt for that person until it found and killed him or her, or until it came upon his or her corpse, which would allow the monster's "kill mode" to disengage. (At this time, it would find its way back to headquarters for a new assignment.) These "beasts," the narrator explained, were engineered to "live" for many days without food or water, never wavering from their mission. In times of war, one could merely turn them loose on the enemy with the right scent cues, and they would pursue relentlessly until they fatally conquered their prey. The whole thing was unbelievable, really; no animal within creation has such capabilities. But that, we were assured, was the beauty of lab-designed bioweaponry. The impossible becomes the possible.

As we entered the next room, what I saw horrified me. It was a giant cage, and displayed inside were several of these Splicer creations. My first instinct was to look intently at the cage, hoping its construction bore better integrity than that of the temporary building we had been touring. It did appear to be strong, which was good, since the snarling beasts were growling at passersby, charging at the cage walls, and attempting to break through its bars. The creatures' fangs were enormous and sharp, their frames looking something like an overgrown, spiky hyena with deranged eyes boring into the souls of the individuals they glared at hungrily. They were formidable foes indeed, and I wondered why we civilians were being shown these monstrosities. Worse, I wondered *still* why nobody else seemed to find the entire display amiss.

Then, I got my answer. With a downward "whirring" sound, the cars all wound to a stop. Concerned-looking officials approached each car, instructing passengers to disembark and meet in another room. Clearly something had gone wrong. We were seated in more rows of folding chairs in similar fashion to those in the first room where we had met, and the man in the lab coat who had originally addressed the crowd walked to the front of the room and began to nervously address the assembly.

"Ladies and gentlemen," he began, "there has been a problem."

A low murmur spread across the crowd.

"Two of the Splicers have escaped…" He paused, fidgeting with his hands while looking down nervously. "The fact that they have moved from their cages indicates that each one has triggered on someone's scent and has already begun pursuit. Understand that this is an ultimate threat. At least two of you are in grave danger. They are masters at stealth, will stop at nothing, and will continue their hunt—even if they're wounded. We have no way of knowing which people here are in danger, but we do know that these weapons are extremely dangerous, they are very hard to kill—impossible for a civilian, in fact—and they'll remain committed to their endeavor until they successfully find and kill their target."

The voices across the room began to sound panicked. People looked around at one another, as if hoping for a visual cue that could indicate danger. The speaker raised a finger so he could continue addressing the crowd, and the wave of voices finally fell again.

"Fortunately, such complications were considered in advance of bringing these informational meetings to each community, and we have come prepared with a remedy. In order to guarantee the protection of everyone here, we must implement this solution immediately."

A woman, presumably a nurse or other type of medical personnel, came into the room pushing a medical supply cart. Across its stainless steel top shelf, a countless number of small syringes, preloaded and still capped, sat next to a package of individually wrapped alcohol wipes and a few other medical-looking materials. This all seemed far too "convenient," and the skepticism I had felt since arriving reached an all-time high. Glancing at those around me, however, I saw relieved faces. People were smiling again, and many were whispering things like, "I'm so glad they came prepared," and "Oh, what a relief!"

"Ladies and gentlemen," the man again addressed the crowd, silencing them, "allow me to present what we call SMART-DNA. The contents of these syringes contain a solution that, while completely safe in every way, will make such subtle changes to your DNA that your body's chemistry will adjust, altering the scent it releases. By allowing us to administer this solution, each of you will be guaranteed that the Splicer will not be tracking your scent. I'm afraid it's for this reason that nobody will be allowed to leave today until the SMART-DNA inoculations have been administered. However, it is a simple and painless procedure, and will only take a moment of your time. Then, rest assured, the Splicers will disengage from the altered scents, and all will be well."

I looked around in disbelief. I had a million questions. *None* of this added up. Why had they *really* brought us here? The military never goes from town to town showing off its most recent form of warfare, so this display did not make sense to me in the first place. Then, there was the sheer irresponsibility involved in exposing civilians to such beasts that could potentially target single individuals of the general public. How had they lacked the foresight to realize that such creatures should be kept under top-notch security, but then somehow had the anticipation to arrive with enough DNA-altering vaccinations to inoculate *all* attendees? I also wondered what was in the vaccine that would be powerful enough to change one's DNA, yet was still somehow supposedly safe? How did the "scientists" behind this know the substance wouldn't alter other functions of the body besides just the scent it put out?

And, *why* were these people *still* talking to us as though we were five years old?!

As I looked around incredulously, attempting to put into words my first of many protests, I was dumbfounded by the pleasant expressions on everyone's faces. They had been scared for a minute, but now each person only looked relieved that the powers that be had brought a solution; *never mind* that they had been the ones who had brought the *problem* in the first place! As attendees were directed to line up, single file, in front of the stainless steel cart, the nurse-appearing woman began to administer SMART-DNA inoculations (the acronym SMART was never explained).

I walked, stunned, amidst the crowd, looking for anyone else who seemed to be disturbed by this suspicious turn of events. I found no one. Not one individual seemed to be angry about the setup, hesitant about receiving the syringe's contents, or otherwise wary of any aspect of all these circumstances. Everyone just seemed to be glad the problem was about to be solved, as each person sequentially lined up to receive the SMART-DNA injection.

~

"Mommmm…" I was jolted back into reality by my two-year-old son waking me up, looking for his breakfast. "Mom…are you awake?"

In 1998, I was too young and immature to appreciate the many layers of irony in his question. Was I awake? Not yet. Up to that moment, I had been absorbed in all the machinations of a young adult's life, paying no attention to the direction of world politics, let alone to any discussion about the end times. (At that moment, I had one job: be a responsible young adult, and in many ways I wasn't yet "rocking" the *one* role I had.)

Yet, as hard as I tried over the next several days to shake off the haunting quality of the dream, I wasn't able to stop thinking about it. As years passed, in fact, the dream's significance to me increased as I watched the powder keg that is modern society come closer and closer to its boiling point. As the powers that be progressively manipulate and shape the masses, my mind repeatedly and frequently drifts back to that "brink-dink" quality of the music that played over the kindergarten-quality voice of the narrator as he spoke of the military's newest and fiercest weapon.

As I said, I had that dream in 1998. I was twenty-three years old. Today, such rudimentary phrases as "Splicer" and "SMART-DNA" seem childish or sophomoric in comparison with the high-tech terms that might be used in a similar situation in current-day labs. That was, however, years before such phrases as "smartphone," "smart cities," or "smart home" had become household terminology. It was as though there was a predictive element to my dream, although I never believed it to be a vision and won't begin to claim it as such now. But, the nature of the crowd-control and manipulation tactics used in the dream weren't the type I had—at that time—been alerted to or seen on a large scale. It was as though God showed me some identifying factors I should look for while observing our everyday society. In many cases, people are subconsciously aware that something isn't right, but they struggle to put their finger on the source of what makes them wary.

We live in a society filled with evil. The master puppeteers are already at work in manipulating society to embrace Antichrist and usher in end-time events. Many people will placidly acknowledge this, but unfortunately they're often spread too thin because of daily obligations; they're politically disenchanted and exhausted (thus feel powerless); or they're so busy trying to survive their own circumstances that studying the large-scale shape of the culture around them is an indulgence they don't have the time or the energy for. Worse, it's easy for many to relinquish the obligation of contributing to cultural changes to a church that *appears* to stand at the ready, but that is so "asleep" that it has become ineffective. As the evil that seeks to devour all of mankind pushes its final pieces into place, the fruitless modern church congratulates itself on having all the answers, while a lost and dying population hangs in the balance. The reference to a wayward culture may draw images of depraved individuals in the minds of many churchgoers, but the sad truth is that many of those who have gone astray are attendees of the local church who once *promised* that they would make a difference when this terrible day came upon us.

The world is in trouble, the world needs a Savior, and the Church needs to wake up.

The truth is, many manipulation tactics are used on individual and large-scale levels each day, shaping society to embrace the unthinkable. There are no longer "safe zones" into which humanity will not venture. Seemingly impossible or unspeakable things that haunted the horror and science-fiction genre of our grandparents' nightmares are either happening on a societal level or have migrated dangerously close. And, as the populace becomes increasingly conditioned to embrace such atrocities, every passing day brings us one day closer to the time of the Man of Sin.

Whether we realize it or not, our society is being groomed to embrace End-Times events. And much of the Church is blissfully unaware that this is occurring beneath its nose. The tools being used to influence culture are recognizable tactics, each of which has a name. Once we are aware of their existence, they become impossible to ignore. And when we—as individuals or as the Church—understand the strategies of the enemy, we can begin to contemplate how to engage a counterstrategy. We are no longer shadow-boxing with an invisible enemy in a darkened room, but are empowered to action.

If you believe society is being primed to legalize and embrace unspeakable and heinous deeds, you're correct. If you perceive culture as being groomed to usher in End-Times events, you're not imagining things. And, if you are wondering why the Church seems to lack power in this urgent day and age, your concerns are well-founded.

If you feel that something isn't right—in the secular world *or* the religious institution—you are not imagining it. The crowds are being controlled. The masses are inviting the end of days. The Church is missing its opportunity.

"Mommm, are you awake?"

I am now.

Are you?

A Glimpse of the Church's Discernment

I (Donna Howell) was sitting on the edge of a hospital bed. My friend, David, was receiving treatment for a longstanding medical condition. Nita Horn was with me, though she stood a little farther off in the corner of the room. All three of us were afraid.

"Something isn't right," David said, shaking his head with worry and clutching at his bedcovers. "This facility. My treatment. Something is wrong here, and I mean *spiritually*."

We had little to go on, save for a feeling. "Something" was a vague word, but it was strangely accurate in describing a common enemy around us that threatened our very lives while smiling nurses and doctors looked straight past it. The color scheme wasn't typical of a hospital's usual stark-white, "sanitary hues" decor. The cupboards that lined the walls all the way around the room were stained dark, more like what would be found in a funeral parlor than in a cheerful recovery room. The walls were muddy-brown wood paneling characteristic of the 1970s, and the carpet was a sickening, burnt-urine yellow. Even the cream-colored phone on the wall looked aged and dingy, sun-bleached of its vitality in some spots and stained in other spots from the oil residue left after years of fingertips pressing on and around the numbered buttons. These environs made the fresh, snow-colored pillows on David's bed look bombarding and out of place, as if they would be infected with disease by mere exposure to the atmosphere.

Yet, the eerie ring of danger that pulsed and throbbed in the room with every heartbeat warned of a kind of attack that has nothing to do with exposure to viruses or sickness. David was right about that. *Something* was pure evil here, and we needed to get out immediately.

Suddenly, I saw six orbs of light appear down the hallway in front of me. Their flight path was erratic and nervous, like hummingbirds: zoom, hover, dip, stop; zoom hover, dip, stop... I pointed in excitement and shouted "Angels!" as the lights jerked their way around to the bed.

For a split second, the light faded, revealing six peculiar flies of some sort. But they were unlike any fly I had ever seen: They were blondish, almost silvery, in color, like moths with a "mother of pearl" iridescence on the surface of their wings; their heads and bodies were furry in texture, as if covered in the tiniest of cream-colored feathers; and they were the size of a housefly, every one of them. I was the only one who saw them in this form, as I was between them and Nita when it happened, and David was scrambling in the other direction to get out of bed. By the time Nita and David had arrived at my side, the "flies" had become orbs of light again.

At the center of each glowing orb was a small bird, roundish in shape, like a baby chick, but solid white outside of the tiny, light-orange, perfect-v beak.

Doves, I thought, *like the Holy Spirit.*

Then rapidly, though the main body of the birds remained unchanging, from their backs grew large, majestic, wings like those you would expect to see in a Renaissance painting. The wings continued to expand until David, Nita, and I had to back away and give them room.

Wings? Hmm... Doves have wings, but angels don't.

I reflected for a moment, remembering the theology from my and Allie Henson's previous work, *Encounters*, wherein we illustrated the difference between God's throne-room guardians, the seraphim and cheru-bim, who do have wings, and His messengers, angels, who do not. As I considered this, the birds morphed into scarlet-red hearts attached to the top of the wings and covered in crimson feathers, like fancy chocolate boxes on Valentine's Day.

I gasped and looked down. The necklace I wore around my neck was a white pair of wings with a feathery red heart layered on top—a "winged heart." I glanced excitedly at Nita, who wore the same necklace. I remembered that I had bought us matching jewelry earlier in the week as a friendship gesture.

These angels must be choosing to appear to us in a way that's personal, familiar, and comforting. How great God is to send us messengers like these who can bring reassurance in such a dark place! I cannot wait to hear what message from God they've come to bring!

Nita wasn't convinced. I saw the doubt in her action as she took just the slightest step backward, away from the figures that were, once again, transforming.

The brightest light yet radiated from the large wings, so dazzling and intense that we shielded our eyes for a few moments until it began to fade. When it did, six muscular men in clean, white robes were attached to them, standing, smiling, arms outstretched. Their skin was the light-est peachy pink, their hair the color of sand, and, from the way their robes hung on their frames, I could tell they were as muscular and fit as Olympic athletes.

David beat me to them. He had, at some point in all of this, begun to cry, and now his sobs flowed freely, heaving from his chest as he ran to the arms of the angels, greeting the first two in short order with tears of joy and a collection of words in an emotional, unintelligible string that I was sure only a spirit could comprehend. I ran to the messenger nearest me and embraced him as well.

It felt nice. Casual. Natural, you might say.

Odd, I thought to myself. *The angels in the Bible were fearsome and formidable creatures. They often appeared with a "Fear not!" greeting to ease the panic of those they approached...yet here I am, hugging one like a brother?*

In response to David's increased weeping, each of the two angels around him took one of his arms, as if to brace him with consoling strength, and led him to the far corner chair so he could sit. I felt so happy for David, after spending such a long time in the shadows of this spiritually sinister facility, to be receiving ministering spirits from our Lord, who would undoubtedly provide direction.

Some hushed conversational exchanges behind me caused me to turn. I saw Nita walking behind three of the angels as they began to lead her down a hallway off the opposite end from David. She looked over her shoulder and locked eyes with me.

Well, clearly Nita's afraid. Why aren't David and I? And why didn't her messengers tell her to "fear not"?

The last angel, the one I had hugged, smiled and held out his strong, robed arm, indicating that I was to follow Nita and the others.

"Where are we going?" Nita, a few feet ahead of me, asked as I, too, walked a length of the hall.

Their voices were low, so I only caught pieces of the answer, but I gathered that they needed to separate us just a little to give us each our own message, and they needed our full attention. We would be within sight of each other the whole time, so it wasn't a true separation. It seemed legitimate and reasonable to me, so I continued to follow them until my angel stopped short and pointed to two chairs facing each other in a nook of the hall. Nita's angels stopped a little farther down, but from where I stood, I could still see her, as well as David, right where we left him.

David was sobbing tears of relief and happiness. The two other figures continued to pat him on the back and grip his shoulders like ministering brothers in a prayer circle as he poured his heart out to them about how much his health had taken its toll upon him and his family in recent years. I smiled, still believing he was about to receive a touch from the Lord.

"I remember those mortal days," my angel said as I turned to face our designated table. "Those times were *tough*." He looked down the hall toward David with a sympathetic nod.

For a moment, I thought I had misunderstood. I contemplated his features and allowed myself a minute to consider his countenance before reacting right away. He looked physically flawless on the outside and, though the light was largely faded now, his skin, hair, and robe shone as one who had just been made of light…like the glass of a lightbulb that still retains a glow for a moment after you extinguish the illumination currents within. He regarded my hesitation, and his perfect head tilted slightly to one side. His eyebrows raised, as if he was wondering what I was waiting for, what I was staring at. Yet, for the first time since the six angels had arrived, I was only just then coming down from the high of the initial excitement to think about what I was actually seeing.

I couldn't put my finger on it, but the being's expression and demeanor seemed uncharacteristic of how I imagined a messenger of God would have presented himself. That slight Brad-Pitt-, Justin-Bieber-like celebrity smirk that was appearing at the edge of his mouth came across as a little…conceited. Cocky, perhaps. His eyebrows arched a little farther up. He looked impatient, maybe even a trifle annoyed, at my reluctance.

"Wait a minute," I said. "You *remember* those 'mortal days'? What do you mean by that? You're an angel, aren't you?" Once again, recent memories of being on radio and television with Allie Henson flashed through my mind. We had written all about the theology of angels, not as culture or the New Age described them, but as they were taught about in the Bible. Through promotional efforts for the book, we had repeated some details over and over, inadvertently committing them to memory. If it hadn't have transpired that way, I might not have been sure. I may have wondered if I was wrong about what the Bible says. But I *was* sure.

"I thought angels were *created beings*," I said, "not saints who had once lived mortal lives and 'turned into' angels after death."

"Oh, you're absolutely right," my messenger said without missing a beat. He sat down with his back and wings to me in one of the two chairs, held his hand out to gesture me toward the empty one facing him, and jovially said, "Please, have a seat. We have much to discuss."

It rubbed me the wrong way that he acknowledged I was correct, but didn't acknowledge how his words apparently contradicted that which was correct. Why would he say he had once been mortal?

…Was it because he wanted to come across as wise and experienced? If so, it was an outright *lie*. But maybe there was another explanation? God *had* sent these spirits, didn't He? Maybe it was a misunderstanding.

I regarded the angel sitting before me.

What was up with my lack of reverent fear? Why didn't their arrival affect me at all the way that it did those men and women in the Bible who had to be told there was no reason to be afraid? Why did it feel like I was chilling with a frat boy whom I could high five and pull into dude-bro hugs?

It occurred to me: Why *did* they separate us? It's not as if we wouldn't have paid attention had we been together; in fact, wouldn't Nita, David, and I have been able to receive the message in a stronger way as a whole unit with each other to witness the same words and remember them together?

Suddenly, the number six—the number of man and eventually the number of the Beast (Antichrist)—was standing out to me as being bizarre. Why were there six of them?

And those wings. They weren't supposed to be there… Only guardians of the throne room had those, and if he was a guardian of the throne room, then why was he *here*? Like a messenger?

…And what message was he about to give me? What would he tell me to do?

I started to feel nervousness creeping in and pushing away my confidence. I didn't know what to do. On one hand, these beings didn't appear to line up with what I knew Scripture said about angels. On the other, if I was wrong, if I had misinterpreted Scripture, then rejecting their help would be rejecting God's provision. Either way, there was nothing I could do to know for sure. There was no way to be certain whether—

Yes there is. It dawned on me abruptly. *The "test of the spirits" from 1 John 4!*

"Hey, I have a question," I said to the back of my angel as I started to circle toward his front.

"Shoot!" he said cheerfully, glancing up to meet my gaze with a confident grin. As I stepped around, I chanced a quick glance down the hallway to David, who was now on his knees in front of his two angels, hands clasped together prayerfully. I remembered the angel John at Patmos tried to worship (Revelation 19:10; 22:8) told him to stop, identifying himself as a fellow servant. He had told John to worship God, only. Here, it looked like David was worshiping the angels, and they didn't appear to be stopping him.

Another misunderstanding?

I swallowed my trepidation to finish what I had started.

"Who do you say Jesus is?" I asked, arriving to stand beside my appointed chair.

The being held his hands out coolly to his sides, tilted his head, and condescendingly smirked, unimpressed. If his expression and body language could have spoken aloud, it would have said: "Pah-lease. *This* old test again? Come on, already. Everybody knows He's the Son of God. Hit me with a harder one. Next!"

What terrified me was not that he didn't appear to know who Jesus was, as his "Duh!" reaction was now revealing he did; what terrified me was that he *wouldn't* answer my question.

A true angel of God would have.

Oh no... I thought, feeling the blood drain from my face. *We need to get out of here, now!*

Over my shoulder, I could see that David remained on his knees, and I was now convinced he *was* worshiping these entities, just as it had appeared moments prior. The angels were standing before him, a soft, warm smile on each of their faces as they accepted the incoming praise.

Down at the other end of the hallway, Nita was looking right at me in alarm. Her three companions were attempting to get her attention gently, and their faraway tones sounded like they were trying to reason with her. Nothing they said was making much difference. Nita had a gut feeling about them, as had been obvious from the beginning. I saw now that her fear was not the reverent kind that springs from recognizing the overwhelmingly immense presence of God's power; it was of someone recognizing evil. She was afraid to even be near them, but she was also afraid to run.

This is why they separated us, I deliberated. *We're vulnerable now. What do I do? Dear Lord, what do I do!?*

I faltered for a moment, trying to hold it together on the outside so as not to draw suspicion. I didn't want to provoke the being, yet I was so scared now that I couldn't look at him. My thoughts were racing.

Do I scream the name of Jesus? Do I tell my "messenger" that I will be right back and go whisper in David's ear that these are not angels of the Lord? Do I—

Gasp!

I opened my eyes and looked at the ceiling, the walls, the makeshift sheet "curtain" I had tacked around the window above the bed…I was safe at home. *Thank God.*

Literally, thank God.

The mattress was hot under me, and my nightgown was damp with sweat. My face was covered in tears, and my blankets were twisted about. I was panting. I knew I had awakened from something that had held me more deeply in sleep than normal, and I've learned to pay attention when that happens.

"Jesus, Jesus, Jesus," I whispered aloud repeatedly. Taking several calming breaths, I looked to see that it was just after 4 o'clock in the morning. All of my back and neck ached, and I turned to lie on my side for some relief. *"Jesus… Jesus…"*

The sound of the Name being spoken softly for a couple of minutes straight settled me like it always does, and I stared at my wall in contemplation. The usual questions went through my mind: Was this just a silly dream? Or was God trying to show me something?

That was rare, but it had happened before, so it was *possible.* Usually I could tell, because those dreams, unlike most I envision in the night, tend to be deeply theological and make consistent sense throughout. A typical, Donna-nonsense dream would have been one where I would have done something stupid, like offer to take the angels out for lasagna or ask them if they would use their wings to take me on a ride flying above the city. Or, an element outside myself would have been absurd, like I would blink and everyone would be wearing a Santa suit and I would find myself jealous. My brain, left to its own devices and imaginings in the still of the night, tends to ride the fence on logic, and I know how to recognize rapid, unconscious thought-processing for what it is most often.

But once in a while, a dream I experience has too many layers of meaning and awareness, makes too much sense, and involves too much legitimate, cognitive logic. Those, I normally pay attention to—and this appeared to be one of those dreams.

If God *was* showing me something, though, what could it be? Was He merely confirming that His messengers would be what His Word said they would be? Or was there a warning hidden somewhere in there for Nita or David? Should I call them right away and see if it was supposed to be for one of *them*?

Before I could think too much about it in that particular hour, I drifted back to sleep. I had been stifled and shaken when I first awoke, but once I had freed myself from the tangles of my blankets and found a position that relieved my back, my body relaxed, my breathing slowed, and I was back to a dreamless, but restful, state.

Getting ready for work the next morning, I thought about the dream several times. Every step of my morning routine, I found myself shaking my head. It wasn't just nonsense. Something was prickling my spirit, and, strangely, I had managed to remember every detail of the dream without writing it down when I first woke, even though I had gone back to sleep for a few more hours. That was unusual. Many times in the past, I would have an experience in the middle of the night that I would take mental note of. If I went back to sleep right afterward, I would forget for a day or two, until the memory of the disturbance came back, and when it would, it came back fuzzy—parts clear, the majority forgotten. This time, not only could I remember everything, but the details wouldn't leave me alone. They were circling through my mind even as I started my car to drive to the office I share with Allie Henson.

I picked up my phone, scrolled to Allie's name, and hit the microphone-shaped "talk to text" button: "Running late. Body's wrecked. Weird night. Be there soon."

Fully awake now, with coffee coursing through my veins as I was headed down my driveway, one component of the story suddenly shocked me.

Flies? I questioned silently. *Doesn't the name Baalzebub mean "the Lord of the Flies"?*

This realization, atop the more obvious association of these pests as a plague upon Egypt, gave me the creeps. I had *hugged* one of these reviling creatures. Well, the Donna in my dream did. Yuck.

A few moments later, I was heading into the office. Allie, as sweet as ever, had a pot of coffee brewing. I knew we desperately needed to work on this book, because we had a deadline hovering over our heads, but Allie somehow knew better.

"Tell me everything. The book will get done," she said. "If you don't, it'll haunt you all day and you won't be able to get any writing done, anyway."

I knew she was right, so I threw my purse onto the counter and flopped into the entryway chair. I told her the whole dream, including precisely what the furry, moth-like flies looked like when they landed on the bed, as well as every other bizarre detail.

"So then, I'm in my car, just after texting you, and I remembered: Doesn't Baalzebub mean 'Lord of the Flies'?"

Allie nodded, and we sat in quiet reflection for a minute or two. Time was ticking, deadlines were looming, and if God *did* mean to give me a message through this dream that was relevant for this book, He would make that clear, we believed. Meanwhile, we needed to get to work.

We headed for our computers, each pouring a fresh cup of coffee and agreeing on the way that I probably wasn't supposed to immediately call Nita or David. As my computer was blinking to life, I glanced at my Logos Bible Software toolbar icon and got the idea to quickly look up "lord of the flies," just to be sure we were right about the name. When I did, I got *much* more of a lead than I could have hoped for.

"Allie, check it out... Baalzebub was so named not just for flies generically, but specifically for the species of flies that swarmed Palestinian territory in summer. These scholars on Logos are saying it's something with a long name I can't pronounce."

"Spell it," Allie said, immediately pulling up a new tab on her browser.

"Uh...p-s-y-c-h-o-d-i-d-a-e. This guy says it's otherwise called the 'drain fly,' because they hang around stagnant pools of water and breed bacteria, lay their eggs, and—ew, *gross*—they multiply to the point that they can clog the plumbing." I clicked another source. "Ugh, this is sickening, but part of the reason they are known as 'drain flies' is because their jaws are powerful enough to bite through the hair and sludge waste that builds up in drains."

"Wow," Allie said. "That's disgusting. I wonder what they—"

"—I wonder what they look like!" I interrupted.

We were both immediately clacking away at the keyboard for a second, spelling *psychodidae* into the Google search box to see what would come up in the photos. I was floored, and my heart quickened at what I saw… Every picture that flooded my screen in that first search was *exactly* what I had seen in my dream. The size of a housefly, but blondish in color, moth-like and furry, almost feathery in texture. Each time the *psychodidae* drain fly was captured at just the right angle of light in these pictures, its wings took on that "mother of pearl" iridescence they had in my dream when the light faded from them.

There was no way I could have depicted that specific pest to that detail and then "coincidentally" discover later on I was describing the very fly that Baalzebub was ruler over. Yet, when nobody else was looking, for a split second, I had seen these "angels" in the form they didn't want anyone to know about.

Psychodidae drain fly, over whom Baalzebub rules[1]

This was confirmation that whatever the message of this dream was, it had assuredly been from God; He allowed that to be known in spades through this one specific detail. The ruler of the "angels" in my dream—or was it a *vision?*—was not our Lord, but the dark lord who can, as the Bible acknowledges, "masquerade as an angel of light" (2 Corinthians 11:14).

Later, I looked up "doves." Despite what the Donna in the dream thought were "doves, like the Holy Spirit," the little "chick-like" birds that the angels had morphed into at one point were *not* doves. After pouring over hundreds of images on every birdwatching site I could access, there were a few possible matches (blackbird with albinism, white house sparrow, sparrow with albinism), all of which are extremely rare and ironically irregular—as if they *normally* appear in another form but "aberrant [a word that is synonymous with "deviant"] plumage" masks them as something else. At the same time, I looked up "winged heart." It's a common jewelry icon as well as a leading tattoo for many, who often place it along the lower back and bicep. In our culture, it has various "in love" and "freedom" associations, but as I dug a little deeper, I found that the winged heart is a *very* ancient symbol. It holds many historical ties with world religions (especially the Sufi order of Islam), frequently denoting a link between our soul or spirit and the physical world—a kind of transcendence, so to speak. Angels of the Lord I serve wouldn't have any purpose appearing as "aberrant plumage" birds *or* winged hearts. (At the time of this writing, I'm still looking into the many echelons of symbolism this dream revealed. It's developing and unraveling as I type…)

Two days after sharing all of this with Allie, I was at a meeting with the executives of SkyWatch TV and Defender Publishing, discussing the then-upcoming launch of the new studio and what content would be featured in the inaugural episodes. I was still reeling about "this fly thing," as Allie had heard me loop about, so I decided to share it with everyone present, including Nita, who was hearing it for the first time. Oddly, I did *not* tell anyone that I was still hoping for an interpretation of the dream; I just said it was bothering me, I had to get it off my chest, and I felt this was the time to do it. As I shared, Allie piped in and confirmed that I had described the flies to her, *and then* discovered the connection to Baalzebub.

Joe Ardis Horn offered a surprising interjection. Typically, Joe is never that "signs and wonders" guy, and he's not always looking for spiritual meaning under every rock, so I was shocked when he said what he did. Without skipping a beat, he articulated what rang true for all of us.

"I think the dream *is* from God, and I think it's quite obvious what it means," he began. "You, Nita, and David represent three kinds of people in the Church. We all love David," Joe said, speaking of the mutual friend, "but we know that he tends to accept what is told to him at face value sometimes." By "sometimes," Joe was being gracious and showing decorum. We have all seen this particular friend embrace one answer after another to his own detriment when unconditional reliance upon Scripture would have led him straight countless times in the past. "He is so desperate for spiritual answers that when someone comes along claiming to have them, he doesn't always think about whether the intervention is from the *Lord* or from the world, or even from somewhere darker in origin. You saw him off in one corner praising the angels because he represents a drastic lack of discernment in the Church. Nobody reads their Bibles anymore, so nobody can be counted on to recognize what is from God versus what isn't. David, at least *currently*, represents those who will embrace the Beast System."

We all nodded. It was, sadly, a valid observation.

"Nita represents that Christian who is so close to the Lord that the Holy Spirit blares warning signals when something isn't right. She knows the voice of God, and she hears from Him, so even when everything *looks* legitimate, if something is off, the Spirit within her can reach her with a warning. Nita may not be a theologian with three or four doctorates behind her name, and she may not therefore be the first one to lay out all the theological angles and layers of what is or is not an angel, but she has a far greater power. She reads the Word of God, which has taught her how the Lord speaks—and she prays without ceasing, which also has given her a *relationship* with God. So, even when she doesn't exactly understand *why* something is suspect the way a scholar would, she knows when the voice of God is warning her of danger."

Everyone nodded again. Nita is steadfast in her faith. That much was common knowledge. She has *many* times had that "gut feeling," that "Spidey-sense," as we all say, to recognize—*well before the rest of us*—when something "feels off." She has counseled Tom Horn on numerous occasions in the past about whether to sell a business, launch a major endeavor, move to a new place, take a ministerial position, and so on. Every last time, Tom has admitted later that, against his own judgment, Nita "was right." Her "I have a gut feeling" moments have spared everyone in that room from fatal or near-fatal disasters at some point, and on many occasions, her "don't do it" warnings have rescued us from bad relationships and terrible life decisions. The list goes on and on with her. Joe was right in saying that she represented the Remnant: the people who love the Lord and sincerely follow Him up to the End, who hear His voice louder than all the others as a result.

"You, Donna—" Joe turned to me. "Unlike Nita, who has had multiple decades of spiritual maturity to recognize the Lord's voice and have a sharpened 'Spidey-sense,' *you* represent those who are pouring into the Word of God. You know what the Word says, and you're dedicated to increasing that knowledge every day. You're thrilled when you figure out that a verse doesn't mean what culture thinks it does, and you continue to challenge those around you to dig into the Word in the same way. Nita follows the Lord with her heart and soul, and the mind follows. You follow the Lord with your mind, and your heart and soul follow. But regardless of the intellect-first approach, which looks initially like it will trip you up and have you hugging fly-angels, you eventually recognize when something is *not* what the Bible says it is, and you have the head knowledge to respond to that kind of warning."

"What bothers me," I interjected, "is that I didn't *start* with the test of the spirits or any other discernment exercises. What took me so long?"

"Yes, *but*," Joe said, "you recognized the evil before these beings ever had a chance to give you their message or tell you what to do."

Again, everyone nodded. It was humbling to hear him speak of me that way, but the others in the room had the same opinion. I may not "hear from the Lord" the way Nita does with that immediate, internal, divine detection, but a person *can absolutely* be led by God through His Word, which I have given my life over to studying.

"Bottom line—" Joe said, leaning forward in his chair; we all followed suit, interest piqued, leaning forward as well. "—you and Nita are the Remnant. The few."

Joe didn't realize it, but he was preaching this book you hold in your hands.

"When the Beast System arrives," Joe continued, "some Christians will recognize it because they intimately know the *voice* of God; others will recognize it because they intimately know the *Word* of God. The voice and the Word are from one and the same Source. The majority of Christians, tragically, will not recognize the Beast System for what it is, because they are accepting what they are spoon-fed about God and religion. When a doctrine comes along that is an affront to the God of the Bible, instead of consulting God or the Word, they will consult culture and the world to see what is societally acceptable. In the End, many Christians will be led astray by a religion that looks nothing like true Christianity."

"A syncretized religion..." I said, leaning back into my seat. My expression told Joe that something he had just said was significant... *Very* significant.

"What?" Joe said.

"Nothing," I responded, shaking my head. I didn't have the time it would take to tell Joe that he had just accidently prophesied—and therefore confirmed—the book Allie and I had been writing.

This book you hold, with everything we said about the Church, at that moment Joe completed his interpretation of my dream, *was already written…*

"For God speaketh once, yea twice…in a dream, in a vision…" (Job 33:14).

Something Wicked This Way *Unleashed*

The dream about angels I (again, Donna Howell) had wasn't the first time the Lord has rattled me lately. Another moment was equally radical, but it happened so fast—and while I was wide awake. It was unlike anything I had previously experienced, and it couldn't be chalked up to a dream or any kind of "imaginings" because of the speed at which it occurred and the multiple tiers of revelation it immediately brought.

It was about 7 o'clock in the evening. My husband, James, was talking about mowing the lawn. I was engaged in the conversation, which, for my part, involved trying to figure out who was going to watch the kids during work hours the next day so James could tend to our too-tall grass.

Without any warning whatsoever, from nowhere at all, absolutely right in the middle of a sentence about grass and childcare, my mind's eye was taken to the floor of a dark, murky, underwater place. Some kind of arm—I'm not sure if it was biological or mechanical—reached out and swept away a giant layer of mud from the surface of an enormous, transparent container. Within it, the face of a being was looking off to the left, eyes wide open and alert. The instant the muck was brushed aside, the being inside the container sensed the movement and snapped its attention forward, focusing its intense gaze upon me.

"…kids will be at the babysitters for a couple hours," my voice trailed back in.

"You okay?" James asked.

I nodded, and the conversation went on. I decided at that moment to keep to myself what had happened, because my "sensible" and "logical" side said I had in some way allowed my mind to wander, and that's all it was.

But that *wasn't* all it was.

I saw that face for what can only be described as a fraction of a second…but I will never forget it. For days, it haunted me. And, before my sentence to James about a babysitter even had a chance to end, there were, just like the angel dream, "layers" of meaning. Unlike the angel dream, the layers were unpacked within my understanding all at once, in that very instant. It was like my psyche had been involved in a file download, multitasking conversations about lawns and babysitters while the download carried on in the background, then the file opened in a pop-up window that showed me multiple angles of theological significance.

It—and I want to say "she," based on the gentility of the facial features—was immensely beautiful. She radiated something behind her bluish skin that trumps the glow enhanced by any beauty product our terrestrial scientists have ever created. Her eyes were such a vision that the English language denies a sufficient description: something like a flame to a moth, having the ability to draw in with a single look. She didn't have hair, but she wasn't bald, either; from her forehead back, a sort of skin-covered crown grew up from her skull, surrounded by what appeared to be two or three wavy, kelp-like hair tendrils. If I hadn't known any better, and this entity were to approach me on land—if I wasn't Donna Howell who knows Jesus as her personal Savior with the discernment and wisdom God gives His people through the Word—I would easily have worshiped it. Others who do *not* have spiritual discernment certainly would have as well. *That* is how commanding a single look was.

But there was something else.

In the eye contact, for the fraction of a second we held it, there was a vengeance…a thirst for blood. If there hadn't been unbreakable material between me and the being, it would have taken me down. And it had been ready for such a feast for ages. Nothing about it was sleepy. It didn't need to be awakened or stirred. This thing had been alive, awake, and alert for *thousands* of years, just waiting for the layers of muck to be removed and herald the dawn of its release. When it turned its eyes on me, the evil, supercharged retaliation of its imprisonment was evident in its piercing stare. It *hated* God and anyone who followed Him.

In an instant, when my thoughts cracked back into reality, I knew things about this being that I don't know how I knew. I have since explained it as "layers of knowing." Words can't express the "download" of information into my thoughts, but the moment I saw the being in the water, I just inherently recognized that it was an angel bound at the bottom of the Euphrates (Revelation 9:14).

Since seeing "her" for the first time and reflecting on what I actually saw that day, it has occurred to me that she looks like she could easily be a female attendant of Dagon's retinue, at least based on our cultural association to him as the god over the fish-people. With that in mind, she could have been Dagon, himself, in a form that we would recognize to be female, as those old-world gods are frequently known to appear as either male or female. Dagon was the prized Canaanite deity of Nineveh, the city to which God sent Jonah with a warning for its people as recorded in the book of the same name. The possible association between the entity I saw and the city God threatened to destroy in forty days if they didn't repent is not lost on me. Far more astounding, however, is Derek Gilbert's explanation that Dagon was the "chief god of the Amorite kingdoms in the middle-Euphrates region"![2] (Though, Derek went on to explain, Dagon wasn't actually the fish-god, as erroneously represented in history books.) Further, according to some Ugaritic temple remains, he was, at times, acknowledged as the father of *Baal*![3]

But whoever I saw—no, *whatever* I saw—it was a vile, corrupt, beastly evil just waiting to rise out of the sea and wreak havoc on land in apocalyptic proportions.

As with the later angel dream, Allie was the first person I told. After I recounted the details to her, she said, "It sounds like something very evil is about to be unleashed upon the earth."

Then, in a phone call I had with SkyWatch colleague Wes Faull later that day, in which I shared with him what I had seen, he responded with the same *exact* words as Allie: "It sounds like something very evil is about to be unleashed upon the earth."

"For God speaketh once, yea twice…in a dream, in a vision…"

I had, in my own thoughts, been reminded of the title of that old novel by Ray Bradbury, *Something Wicked This Way Comes*, about a malevolent carnival that arrives overnight in a small town, enticing and then trapping its victims with its evil rides and attractions. Allie had essentially responded with her own "something wicked this way comes" sentiment, followed by Wes Faull. Many since have done likewise.

The dream that Allie shared relayed a sense of warning regarding society's willingness to follow authority figures without discernment. Those within the Church assume that when the great day of evil is upon us, they will rise to the occasion and defend truth, recognize wickedness, and take a stand against the enemy. However, my dream reflects that the Church will be misled in that terrible day.

My vision of this entity at the bottom of the Euphrates illustrates that this "terrible day" might already be unleashed upon the earth. Both culture *and* the Church have a great deception coming. Only the Remnant will have eyes to see and ears to hear (Matthew 13:16–17).

So I come around to where Allie began: *Are you awake?*

{2}

THE CULT OF WESTERN
CHRISTIANITY

Wow… What a provocative, inflammatory title for such an early chapter of our book. What could we possibly be thinking? How could we—full-time authors and researchers dedicated to serving in a conservative Christian ministry—dare suggest that Christianity would in any way resemble a *cult*?

Right off the bat: A cult is "a system of religious beliefs and ritual;… a religion regarded as unorthodox or spurious; also: its body of adherents."[4] This is *precisely* what the Western Church has become, as we will endeavor to reveal throughout the following pages.

Before we dive in to begin our comparison of the cult to concerning trends in Western Christianity, we should take a brief moment to consider what it is we are actually comparing the Church *to*. Although our ultimate point of comparison will be to look at the word "cult" as it is defined by biblical values, if we want to proceed without confusion this early on, we need to dissociate from some popular thinking.

When we hear the word "cult," mental imagery that floods the mind tends to be a messy conglomeration of Manson Family members slaying pregnant Sharon Tate in the name of Helter Skelter; women and children trapped in burning buildings in Waco, Texas; or thirty-nine lifeless bodies, wearing brand-new Nike Decades tennis shoes, lying on cots in a posthumous journey behind the comet Hale-Bopp. Perhaps the memories aren't as local, and we think of almost a thousand bodies lying dead from drinking what many later thought to be poisoned Kool-Aid (it was Flavor Aid, in actuality) in Guyana, or the thirteen deaths and fifty-eight hundred injuries from a toxic nerve gas release on a Tokyo train line. Or, in an age when shocking shifts are rapidly taking place in the practices of human sex-trafficking and pedophilia, maybe what flashes through our heads is David Berg's blasphemous, objectifying, sexually explicit, and pedophilic artwork of *The Children of God* comic books…

Such concepts related to the word "cult" would understandably lead readers of this book to recoil against our assertion that Western Christianity "looks like" these examples. One might naturally offer the rebuttal: "No, our Sunday-morning gatherings do *not* lead to bloody crime scenes, gassed subway lines, poisoned drinks, or anything of the sort. We don't resemble that at all! How can you even dare to make that comparison?" In response to this and similar potential statements, questions, or retorts, we'll remind our readers of an ominous truth:

The Apostate Superchurch of the End Times will be the grandest, bloodiest cult in world history, and the "Christian Church" will be a huge part of it!

The beginning of every deviant cult looks polished, safe, doctrinally reasonable, and wholesome to its members, just as the Western Church appears to many today. A *vast* number of cult cases from English-speaking areas of the world started as Christian ministries based on Christ-centered doctrine, but they slowly drifted farther and farther off-track over time, usually because some manipulative leader is in it for his or her own wicked, narcissistic gain. If the enemy can do the same thing with the Christian Church across the globe, he can effectively set the stage for Antichrist to show up and assume leadership over a perverse Christianity, just as the Bible says he will do!

Based on what's described in apocalyptic Scripture, the Christian Church during the End Times will be split into two groups:

1. The Apostate Superchurch, which will be found guilty of twisting the Word of God with counterfeit scriptural interpretation that amounts to the ultimate blasphemy. This cult will remain out in the open and legal under the religio-political reign of the Man of Sin, and in order to appeal to everyone alive on the earth at the time, it will be a global super-religion combining key aspects of all faiths into one—including Christianity. Drs. George W. Westlake and David D. Duncan, in their college textbook *Daniel and Revelation*, acknowledge this, describing Antichrist's Church of the End Times as "many, many faiths and religions the superchurch has blended together to achieve [the] world unity"[5] necessary for him to be established as a worldwide leader, capable of making social and political decisions that complement every background, culture, and conviction.

2. The Remnant Church, made up of Christian disciples who are well-versed enough in the Bible to recognize Antichrist as the imitation he is. This group will be persecuted and driven underground or into hiding, and many of its members will be mercilessly executed.

The number of deaths resulting from Antichrist's rule while he is in leadership of the idolatrous Apostate Superchurch is literally going to be a worldwide, cultic massacre—a bloodbath unlike anything planet earth has ever witnessed on its own soil. Antichrist will demand *global* compliance with his religion, and anyone who refuses to submit to this Satan-in-the-flesh will be put to death (Revelation 13:7–8, 15).

Remember a few paragraphs ago, when it seemed nothing less than irrational to compare the Church to a "cult" like the Manson Family,

David Koresh and his followers in Waco, Texas, or the Peoples' Temple movement in Jonestown, Guyana?

Yeah… It is going to be much, *much* worse.

And right now, the institutional, public churches across the Western world are readying the stage for the Man of Sin to walk right in and take over, fooling folks of all religions, including Christianity and Judaism. The only way this *wouldn't* happen is if Christians lived like Christians ought…but they don't.

The "Apostate Superchurch" Cult of Antichrist

Let's compare words super quick:

> APOSTASY…. A public denial of a previously held religious belief and a distancing from the community that holds to it. The term is almost always applied pejoratively, carrying connotations of rebellion, betrayal, treachery, or faithlessness.[6]

In biblical eschatology studies related to the coming Apostate Superchurch—"the apostasy comes first, and [Antichrist] is revealed" (2 Thessalonians 2:3; NASB)—"apostasy" refers to "a great 'falling away' or 'rebellion' (*apostasia*) from the Christian faith before the day of Christ."[7] Even more simply put, from the *Dictionary of Latin Forms*, it refers to a "departure from one's religion, [or a] repudiation of one's faith."[8]

As the scholars and commentators acknowledge:

> Before that great day [the Tribulation] comes, Paul declared, the **rebellion** [*apostasia*] must occur…. [T]here will be a great denial, a deliberate turning away *by those who profess to belong to Christ* [Christians]. It will be a rebellion. *Having once allied themselves with Christ, they will abandon him.* Within the recognized church

there will come a time when people will forsake their faith. Throughout history there have been defections from the faith. But the apostasy about which he wrote to the Thessalonians would be of greater magnitude and would signal the coming of the end.[9]

In other words: A rebellion of the Christian Church from the inside out will happen, and then Antichrist will rise with his One-World-Order government and One-World Religion (his cult, the grandest deception of the world, which we, as you've likely noted by now, have coined "the Apostate Superchurch").

But what is a *cult*, exactly?

Contemporary dictionaries give some form of the following takeaway: "Cult: a system of religious beliefs and ritual…a religion regarded as unorthodox or spurious; also: its body of adherents."[10] (Truthfully, the word points directly to an Apostate-Superchurch agenda, as well as a modern, anti-Christ-spirited itinerary that normalizes and celebrates false religion. For now, it's only important to understand that the word "cult" used in this work will refer first to "an unorthodox/spurious religion," and, by extension, to Antichrist's *supremely* unorthodox/spurious "veiled Christianity" of the End Times. It may surprise you to read that, underneath all the convoluted semantics games, "apostasy" and "cult" mean the same thing…more on this later.)

By suggesting that an off-track Christianity precisely fulfills the definition of a cult, not only is that how most get started, but neither are we saying anything that God didn't say first: In the End, the Apostate Superchurch under Antichrist's reign is going to entice and deceive countless multitudes of people who *think* they're a part of the Remnant Church. They will absolutely be "religious," but Christ cannot authentically be their Lord.

Both of the End-Times churches just discussed will claim to be the Remnant Church, and by the time the Apostate Superchurch is well formed, it will—in the same pocket with Antichrist's One-World-Order government (Revelation 13:7)—surface as the answer to many challenges humanity faces today: world hunger, global strife, disease, racial inequality, class inequality, and *countless* other "quality of life" philanthropic and humanitarian efforts that a religiously, socially, and politically fragmented world has never been able to solve. It will be a One-World Church, a (phony) respecter of *all* religions on the planet at that time, that cleverly manages to convince everyone that "we have always known the path to God," though each culture/religion "calls it by another name" or "experiences it differently," and so on.

Dr. David R. Reagan—founder of Lamb & Lion Ministries; author of seventeen books related to prophecy; and host of his nationally broadcast weekly television program, *Christ in Prophecy*, which airs on eleven Christian networks plus DayStar—holds graduate degrees in international relations from Fletcher School of Law & Diplomacy at Tufts and Harvard University. Considering his education in international law, policies, history, and communications, *on top* of his long-developed expertise in biblical eschatology, we find his position on the Apostate Superchurch enlightening:

> The most popular apostasy in Christendom today is the teaching that God has revealed Himself in many different ways to different cultures and that, therefore, all religions worship the same god, but just use different names. From this viewpoint, the Allah of Islam is the same as the Yahweh of Judaism and both are the same as the Krishna of Hinduism. The natural conclusion that is drawn from this apostate idea is that there are many different paths to God, Jesus being only one of them. This has led liberal leaders of groups like The National Council of Churches in the United States and the World Council to condemn missionary activity as "arrogant" and "anti-cultural."[11]

Don't assume, as some have done, that the book of Revelation only foretells a sentence upon the Jews. Although the Last-Days, wrath-of-God events certainly weave around and circulate through the spiritual state of the Jews, their historical and contemporary rejection of Jesus as Messiah, as well as their accepting Antichrist to be "the Messiah they've waited for all along," it's not accurate or fair in a worldwide eschatological scenario that the Jews would be the only people held spiritually accountable. That would just be true if they were the only ones left on the earth in that day, and even in the case of a pre-Trib Rapture (the theology that the saints will be taken up to be with the Lord *before* the Tribulation), there would still be nonbelievers of other world religions left behind. This means that, regardless of the timing of the Rapture (pre-Trib, mid-Trib, pre-wrath, and so on), the grand deception *will* entice people of all faiths, including the false Christianity of that day. This is why it becomes crucial that wherever on earth the Remnant Church is thriving, both before and during the Tribulation (when the Remnant Church will be underground), strict adherence to true Christian tenets, practices, and doctrines must be maintained at all costs to distinguish it from the Apostate Superchurch.

Even if Antichrist himself were to be Jewish (a near certainty, according to many scholars), a twisted Christianity will be at the front of his agenda on the disastrous day he rises to the throne! World-renowned and highly respected scholars of Scripture have dedicated their lives to exposing this reality, as is clear to anyone that has taken time to look into who Antichrist is and what he will do in the (possibly near) future.

One of the most authoritative "Revelation theologians" alive on our planet today is professor of New Testament and Biblical Theology at Westminster Theological Seminary, Dr. Gregory K. Beale. He has written more than twenty-five groundbreaking works currently used in diverse universities and is considered by an enormous number of scholars to be "the" expert on the book of Revelation. Beale states directly:

"The Antichrist figure in Revelation 13 has both a pagan political-religious side *and a pseudo-Christian side*, both of which were associated together in the Danielic expectation of the end-time opponent of God."[12] Based on this, we can expect that Antichrist will stand as head over a Superchurch that is, at least in part, "pseudo-Christian."

Of course, true, Bible-reading Christians are aware that the syncretistic/polytheistic, One-World-Religion "Superchurch" endeavors are immediately and intrinsically incompatible with *real* Christianity, because there is only *one way* to the Father, only *one Name* that grants access, and that is Jesus (John 14:6). Though some of the Western world outside Christianity may not be able to quote this (or similar) Scriptures, Christianity's firm, monotheistic theology has been understood well enough that we would expect only a minority within the Church to quote the syncretic ideal, "All religions are true religions," or similar statements. Those who have proclaimed such ideas throughout history have had the hierarchy within Church to answer to, and the penalty for their heretical beliefs could mean anything from death to excommunication to social ostracization, depending on when and where in history such bold statements were declared. Nevertheless, something has happened since the 1950s, and Western culture has openly fostered an *extremely* syncretistic society where it's acceptable to discard portions of the Bible that we don't agree with and simply "hodgepodge" our own hybrid religion together with any other belief system we personally find beautiful. Add postmodernism to the heap, and it's already a miracle that the Remnant Church still exists at the time of this writing, let alone will be flourishing underground when the Apostate Superchurch is flaunting itself topside, in bed with the One-World Government, solving every malady of the human condition, unsuspectingly worshiping its satanic leader and praising his pet statue (Revelation 13:3–4, 15).

But still, the logical question remains: How will the entire world accept this? What matter of deception could be so great that we no longer distinguish a synagogue from a mosque, a temple from a church, the Bible from the Qur'an, or the Torah from the Vedas or the Tibetan Book of the Dead—even though the core doctrines behind these places of worship and sacred writings conflict? How do we find ourselves in the position where we've permanently erased the lines separating Buddhism from Catholicism, Islam from Hinduism…Christianity from *Satanism*!? As unbelievable as this religiously apocalyptic scenario might have sounded ten years ago, in 2020, it's almost "yesterday's news" that we will see these things come to pass soon. There are a number of reasons this is the case, and a thorough examination of the entire subject would require more space than we have here.

However, what we *can* take a few pages to address are the platforms Antichrist will use to develop the One-World Religion in a world like the one we're currently (and haphazardly) forming.

Resurrection/Miracles Platform

The first platform Antichrist will have to stand on when he promotes the Apostate Superchurch is the authority of his own resurrection and miracles. Though the Word is not completely clear about his head wound (Revelation 13:3–4, 14), it *does* stipulate that it's incurable. Theories and explanations in current academia don't agree on whether it's a literal or figurative wound, and scholars will likely hypothesize right up to the day it occurs about how much it has to do with the "serpent's bruised/crushed head" curse of Genesis 3:15. Regardless, anyone who is not a part of the Remnant Church (and therefore recognizes this event for what it is) will marvel at Antichrist's survival and think him to be an invincible god upon whom no other person can inflict harm: "and his [Antichrist's] deadly wound was healed: and all the world wondered after the beast. And they worshipped the dragon [Satan] which gave power unto the beast: and they worshipped the beast, saying, Who is like unto the beast? who is able to make war with him?" (Revelation 13:3–4, 12–14). Additionally, he will perform great, beneficial miracles that make him further appear to be genuinely benevolent and all-commanding (2 Thessalonians 2:9–10; Revelation 13:13); these signs and wonders will be so convincing that even Christians will accept his authority (Matthew 24:24). Many scholars see the similarities between this future reality and what the Egyptians must have felt when Pharaoh's evil sorcerers mimicked a few of the miracles God performed through Moses (Exodus 7:11).

If it plays out the way most Bible prophecy theologians suggest it will, Antichrist will live up to his title in every literal way. As the "anti" form of our Savior, Christ, the Man of Sin will parallel Jesus' death, Resurrection, and miracles, looking in every way to be the Messiah figure for all world religions and cultures across the globe: Jews will believe he is the promised Messiah they've waited for; misled Christians will believe it is the Second Coming of Christ; people belonging to other world religions will interpret him to be the fulfillment of other prophetic, redeeming, or delivering god-figures; and atheists will suddenly come to believe that there *is* a God—and that Antichrist fills that role.

With that in mind… How will Antichrist *not* have the ability to form a One-World Religion that doctrinally satisfies everyone's expectations? All he'll have to do is approach the pulpit and address every person in the world (technologically speaking, we're already there) and explain in short order that he is "the" god-man of all of their religions and philosophies. Any crossover theologies from one belief system to another that aren't compatible will be flagged as mere misinterpretation of the holy books that all point to him.

Also consider how much today's Church is arranging this framework at this very moment. Petty, irrelevant squabbling between Christian "trolls" (online or otherwise) doesn't impress anyone. When we "throw a verse" at someone we disagree with, even *if* it succeeds in silencing them (it typically doesn't), we don't prove anything except the idea that the Bible can represent a number of different things, depending on the interpreter. When "the" interpreter (Antichrist) arrives and deduces that it's all about *him*, many "Christians" will be too fragmented in their theology to stand firmly against his deception.

For certain, the Man of Sin will capitalize on the weaknesses the Church will have mounted upon herself. Why wouldn't he? He's the absolute epitome of blasphemy...which brings us to the next platform.

Intelligence/Blasphemy Platform

We've heard Christians use Revelation 13:6 as an argument *against* the idea that Christians will be deceived in the End Times: "And he opened his mouth in blasphemy against God, to blaspheme his name, and his tabernacle, and them that dwell in heaven." Wouldn't believers recognize Antichrist for who he is because of this verse? And doesn't this single passage of Scripture disprove that he could ever merge Christian theology with the One-World Religion? Try as he might to make himself "look like" Christ or make Christianity "look like" his religion, if he blasphemes the God of the Bible, that cancels itself out...so how could blasphemy be a means by which Antichrist ushers in his Apostate Superchurch, with himself as the head?

First, this would mean that Christians would be reading their Bibles well enough to recognize blasphemy when they hear/see it—and they're not. (Much more discussion on this topic in a later chapter.) It would likewise require that the Bible Christians are reading is the whole, complete, uncut Word of God, including *both* the Old and New Testaments. Before we offend anyone, let us clarify: This is not to insult those who carry around or distribute New Testament Bibles! It's simply a statement that the *entire* Word of God must be familiar to the Body of Christ in order for them to identify the moment when Antichrist does or says something that opposes it, and *that is especially true of an enemy scholars believe will position himself as an orthodox (i.e., Old Testament) Jew.*

Second, it seems incredibly unlikely that Antichrist's blasphemies would fit the cartoonish, clichéd, "fist-shake at God" imagery that first comes to mind. A deceiver would be far more convincing if he, like Satan, appeared as "an angel of light" (2 Corinthians 11:14) who respected God. Consider who we're talking about here… Antichrist will be a man, but he'll also be the "seed of the serpent" (Genesis 3:15). Just as Christ was (and is) the Son of God, Antichrist will be the son of Satan. Therefore, just as the Son of God exercises power from His Father in heaven (Matthew 9:6, 8; 21:23ff; 26:64; 28:18–19; Daniel 7:14), so, too, will Antichrist receive his power from his father in hell (Revelation 13:2, 4). Nothing about his intelligence will be limited to a single life-time or one mere man's powers of articulation. As he will be filled with the unbridled influence of all the authority in hell, Antichrist's capabilities of misleading the masses and appearing as an "angel of light" will result in his display of *ultimate*:

- **Speaking presence:** "There was given unto him a mouth speaking great things" (Revelation 13:5); "and a mouth speaking great things" (Daniel 7:8); and "a mouth that spake very great things" (Daniel 7:20).
- **Political power:** "Ten kings…shall give their power and strength unto the beast… and give their kingdom unto the beast" (Revelation 17:12–13, 17; cf. Daniel 9:27).
- **Military command:** "The beast, and the kings of the earth, and their armies, gathered together to make war" (Revelation 19:19).
- **Earthly wealth and extravagance:** "A god whom his fathers knew not shall he honour with gold, and silver, and with precious stones, and pleasant things" (Daniel 11:38).
- **Economic policies and organization:** "And the merchants of the earth are waxed rich through the abundance of [Antichrist's city, Babylon's] delicacies"; "The merchandise of gold, and silver, and precious stones, and of pearls, and fine linen, and purple, and silk, and scarlet, and all thyine wood, and all manner vessels of ivory, and all manner vessels of most precious wood, and of

brass, and iron, and marble, And cinnamon, and odours, and ointments, and frankincense, and wine, and oil, and fine flour, and wheat, and beasts, and sheep, and horses, and chariots, and slaves, and souls of men…[and involving] all things which were dainty and goodly…[and] ships…[and] trade by sea…[and] harpers, and musicians, and…pipers, and trumpeters…[and] craftsmen" (Revelation 18:3, 12–17, 22).

- **Persuasion in self-aggrandizement:** "And he shall exalt himself… and shall prosper" (Daniel 11:36).
- **Patient, successful oppression of God's people:** "And shall wear out the saints of the most High, and think to change times and laws: and they shall be given into his hand" (Daniel 7:25).

On top of all of this, he's going to be tremendously attractive, with features so appealing that the Word says he will be better looking than any of "his fellows" (Daniel 7:20).

When *that guy* blasphemes, it's probably not going to be in the too-obvious form of shaking fists upwards to the sky or dropping the "f-bomb" in a statement about Jesus. It will more likely be in the form of Scripture taken directly from the Word of God and just slightly altered (like a "new translation" or a contemporary rewording "for the sake of clarity") or misinterpreted (like we're already familiar with doing now whenever it suits our proof-text agendas). So long as the endgame is the intent to take the Word of God as He has spoken it to humanity and make it say the opposite of what it does, that's the *worst* kind of blasphemy—all the way up there with self-deification (claiming to *be* God, which Antichrist will also be guilty of; see 2 Thessalonians 2:4).

Some of the people who will line up to worship the Beast and take his Mark will do so *even knowing what the Bible says about him*. But he will be *so* convincing that he will fool people into believing that "his truth" is the "greater truth"—that what he says is "more true" than the Word of God. They will think back and remember the warnings of

Scripture, and they will get in line anyway, believing that his words and interpretations "replace" the Word of God as a spiritual ideology that simply makes more sense than the archaic God of that "old book."

In this thread of thought, Antichrist's blasphemies will not be a hindrance to his goal of establishing himself as world ruler and forming the Apostate Superchurch of all world religions. Much to the contrary, blasphemy is the very vehicle he will use to do it.

Technology Platform

Of course, identifying how all this is possible also partly relies on identifying how the human appetite has demanded the steps to be put in place for this. We stomp our feet for globalist conveniences and technology that puts us in touch with anyone on earth at the snap of a finger, instantaneous currency conversion, flights to anywhere in the world on any day of the year, individualistic consumer trends in international trade (including online shopping), language-translation apps that listen to and translate conversations as they're happening, media streaming across devices no matter where we are, user-uploaded entertainment and information trading…and on the list goes. However, we often lose sight that these "conveniences" are also laying the groundwork for a "One-World Everything" scenario, which is what Antichrist will use to come to power. He will be seen *everywhere*, and his words will be understood in *every* language. (Note: A counterargument can be made for how we can also "go global" with the Gospel in a way that hasn't been possible before. We realize this. Our aim in this illustration is not to preach against the tools, but to discuss how the evil messenger of the End Times will exploit them.)

Vulnerability Platform

Then, of course, there's the harsh stab of human vulnerability that will cause anyone with a weak faith to call out for the ultimate answer man.

Matthew 24:4–8 paints a picture of a day when "birthing pains" (war, famine, earthquakes, etc.) will reveal a plethora of false christs who position themselves as just that, and we will be all the more prepared to hail a more impressive hero when Antichrist parodies Jesus' Resurrection and raises himself from a fatal head wound through the power of Satan. Right now, COVID-19 and a string of other upsets through 2020 have already produced a *global* desperation for leaders to take us "back to normal" and "repair our cities." The devastation on the earth in the End Times will be so overwhelming that the fragility of human life will cause people of all walks of life—"small and great, rich and poor, free and bond"—to cooperate with an answer man out of panic, impulse, and fear (Revelation 13:16).

When life is good, people are naturally less susceptible to following a leader in a rush. We're intellectual beings who like to see multiple front runners vying for the same chair so we can weigh them against the other, tune into debates, and watch the playout of grand campaigns to see who most closely aligns with our own ideologies. But when this planet starts to experience the biblically prophetic "birthing pains," which will introduce woes unlike anything we've seen in the history of the world, many of us are going to forget whether the candidate taking the chair is "red" or "blue" or shares our views on political subcategories and legislative goals, and we'll look for the man who postulates "God" as the answer. When extreme tragedy hits, nonreligious people suddenly get very religious, very fast (9/11 is a major example of this), learning for themselves that the "God-shaped hole in everyone" that the Church talks about is real. When adherents of various faiths are shown the famous miracle worker who "is the one and only God over all world religions," as he will claim to be, they'll turn to him for answers to the natural calamities occurring all over the planet. The populations of the world will feel the instability and vulnerability of humanity and vote for, support, follow, and usher in *any* man who can effectively prove that his political and religious ideas will unite humanity in responding to these catastrophic

End-Time events (Matthew 24:11). This moment in time is what Paul described in 2 Thessalonians 2:3: "The apostasy comes first, and the man of lawlessness is revealed" (NASB).

What will "the answer" to everything be?

God.

Who will "God" be to most in that day?

Antichrist.

When Antichrist raises himself from the dead, many will believe he has a power that all the other "false christs" of Matthew 24:4–11 haven't had, and they will be ready to trust this "Messiah" when he announces that "there are many ways to God" just before he unites the Apostate Superchurch.

The Day All Religions Are Destroyed

When I (Donna Howell) first started to read the book of Revelation, I found myself slowly drinking it in and understanding it fairly well. But when I came to the part about the Beast devouring the Harlot, all of a sudden I thought, *Where did that come from? I thought* she, the Harlot, *was in control!*

Scholars and theologians have *long* acknowledged that the Harlot of Revelation represents both: a) the city of Babylon (most likely Rome, though a minority believes this to be the historic Babylon rebuilt), which includes the power and authority that this city will have over the earth (Antichrist's "system" and policies, etc.); and b) false (pagan) religions of the world. The former is taken from Revelation 17:18, where the Harlot is specifically referred to as "that great city, which reigneth over the kings of the earth." The latter requires an understanding of how, in biblical typography and symbolism, the Church is likened to a woman (1 Corinthians 11:1–2; Ephesians 5:23–32; Galatians 4:21–31; Revelation 19:7–8; 21:2). But, throughout the Bible, when we read that "woman"

(God's people) is unfaithful to God, "she" is a "harlot," like Gomer, the adulteress God told the prophet Hosea to marry as a symbol of the Israelites' idolatrous spiritual infidelity (Hosea 1:2ff). Elsewhere, the Apostle Paul clearly demonstrated that God will not "share" His people with the "harlot" called false religion. In a letter to the church at Corinth, in a verse that would have been a shocking string of words for that early culture, Paul challenged: "What? know ye not that he which is joined to an harlot is one body? for two, saith he, shall be one flesh. But he that is joined unto the Lord is one spirit" (1 Corinthians 6:16–17).

Therefore, the Harlot of the End Times is understandably interpreted to represent "false religion" and the unholy alliance that false religion has with the "kings" of the One-World Government (Revelation 17:1–2). Upon her very forehead is "a name written, Mystery, Babylon the Great, the Mother of Harlots and Abominations of the Earth" (Revelation 17:5).

In the beginning, as the Great Tribulation begins to unfold for the first three and a half years, approximately (according to the "forty-two-month" mathematics behind the "time, times, and half a time" prophecies [Daniel 7:25; 12:7; Revelation 12:14]), the Harlot is perched atop the Beast, riding him like a steed.

Many scholars interpret the woman to be in complete control over the Beast, as if to suggest that Antichrist is not yet powerful enough to take over. Others believe that, due to her seemingly instant downfall, Antichrist will have been strong enough to devour her all along but chooses instead to take advantage of her ability to draw people into false religion to further weaken resistance from real Christians. In either case, Antichrist will decide to play nice and share his toys with the Harlot while his rule strengthens in the background. When the Beast is through with the Harlot—when Antichrist has successfully built a "peaceful," "benevolent" rule with the help of all the "beautiful" religions and philanthropic economics she represents—he will "hate the whore, and shall make her desolate and naked, and shall eat her flesh, and burn her with fire" (Revelation 17:16) in the second "forty-two-month" (or three-and-a-half year) time slot of his command.

Nobody will have any further use for the archaic religions of their forefathers. Antichrist, in this moment, will "be God," or so the globe will acknowledge, and it will be as if all the religions of the world from the beginning of time never existed.

The destruction of all religions of the world...

Woe to Western Laodicea!

Why are we railing about Western Christianity, specifically? Why are we picking on our own area of the earth when the West undoubtedly is in the lead as far as what territories produce the most Gospel ministers, scholars, theologians, seminary graduates, and experts on Scripture? Shouldn't it be the other way around? We are apparently the world's center for scriptural training and missionary-sending, so why do these authors find the West to be more deserving of scrutiny and blame for humanity's sabotage under the Apostate Superchurch?

It's *because* we are the world's center for scriptural training that we are held more accountable for honoring the true Gospel message than are the other geographical areas of the world...and the Word agrees with this conclusion: "But he that knew not, and did commit things worthy of stripes, shall be beaten with few stripes. For unto whomsoever much is given, of him shall be much required" (Luke 12:48). The more we know about Jesus, the more responsibility we have to spread the Good News about Him and to *maintain the integrity of His Name!* Yet, despite the *ocean* of information and biblically sound training materials we have at our fingertips—ministerial training seminars, universities and seminaries of theology, Bible software programs, online and offline archives of nearly every extrabiblical writing of the ancients (including the historians and the apocrypha), Bible bookstores all over the place, and instant access to all of this and more online—our cultural approach to responsibility makes it perpetually "someone else's job" to know what the Word says. We simply "have things too good" to feel it when moral conviction about the depraved society around us presses in, so our pastors, preachers, teachers, and church staffers choose to do what the Laodiceans did and take another toke off that doobie called "spiritual anesthesia."

Laodicea was another site of extreme cultural prosperity. Its resident Christians were so spoiled to "the good life" that they overlooked their true responsibilities and were found by their Lord to be spiritually empty (Revelation 3:14–22). To them, following Christ was a popular lifestyle or trend, but where it counted, they didn't prioritize the Gospel as they had been commissioned. Consider what Christ says to them: "You say, 'I am rich; I have acquired wealth and do not need a thing!' But you do not realize that you are wretched, pitiful, poor, blind and naked" (Revelation 3:17; NIV). They were blind to their own spiritual bankruptcy.

As Revelation expert G. K. Beale acknowledges, these words from Christ are "to unbelievers who have prospered materially because of their willing intercourse with the ungodly world system ([Revelation] 6:15; 13:16; 18:3, 15, 19)."[13]

How humbling a rebuke from the Messiah, Himself, to a congregation that sounds much like our own…

Beale points out another interesting connection "which has been observed by many commentators," going on to quote the similar boast of Ephraim in the Masoretic Text of Hosea 12:8: "Surely *I have become rich, I have found wealth* for myself; in all my labors *they will find in me no iniquity, which would be sin.*"[14] Unlike He did with Laodicea, however, God didn't keep knocking on Ephraim's door. Much to the contrary, when the "cult of Ephraim"[15] could not be trusted to stop religiously syncretizing itself, whoring after idols and merging its own hybrid version of the One-World Religion of its day, God said, "Ephraim is joined to idols: let him alone" (Hosea 4:17).

47

Fast forward to the book of Revelation and the Laodiceans' Ephraim-esque reliance on the comforts of their own routines, which propagated a festering apathy in the matter of the Gospel, making them into a then-modern Ephraim. This, the Laodicean compromise, "made their witness to Christ impotent in its effect...they were on the verge of being considered an unbelieving community (cf. also [Revelation] 2:5; 3:1–3), no different from the rest of the pagan world."[16]

Fast forward again, this time to the contemporary West...

Our own witness of Christ is "impotent," and we, too, are "on the verge of being considered an unbelieving community...no different from the rest of the pagan world."

Oh, how akin we are to Laodicea! Yet, because the Western Church is too busy investing in fog machines and confetti cannons for the stages upon which we put on godless concerts—the one and the same platform where our scripturally deficit "inspirational speeches" are called "sermons"—we don't have time to look at what Jesus was really saying in His letter to the church of Laodicea. We don't know that the famous "lukewarm" reference is related to the temperature of the water supply the Laodiceans used, which came from a filthy aqueduct outside the city that collected heavy amounts of bacteria on its journey from Deni-zli to the south. Neither do we know that, when Christ implores the Laodiceans to buy their "eyesalve" from Him so that they might "see" again, He was rebuking the thriving local cosmetics trade that assisted in blinding them to their own spiritual depravity in the first place, or that, when He told them to clothe themselves in white robes, He was blasting them with an ironic juxtaposition of the Gospel message against their jingling purses, which brimmed with the gold they made on their specially bred, long-haired, black-sheep textile exports.[17]

We, here in the West, despite all the trained ministers we crank out from our region, know very little about the true message of God as contained in His Word! What a *grand* misuse of our time, money, and talent, when the average church on the corner here is still preaching that "lukewarm" means we're "not excited enough about God" (a message that has produced emotional phenomena leading to counterfeit revival).

Worst of all, we don't understand the most obvious part of Christ's message to that comfortably wealthy city—the description of Him standing outside the door and knocking. It's *not* that individualistic altar call summon we talk about in the West today, but the entreaty for the *collective Body* to open the door and allow their Messiah back into their church!

God, once the head of their people, instructed that Ephraim be left to idols, rendering the entire Northern Kingdom of Israel at the time a pagan cult without Yahweh as leader, because God will not share His people with a harlot. The Laodiceans made a similar decision, placing their congregation and city in a position where Christ has to stand outside and ask permission to be put back in His rightful place as the Head of their church, because He, too, refuses to occupy the harlot's place amidst His people.

Both Ephraim and Laodicea booted the God of the Bible out of their club and raised up a pagan central focus that misdirected their God-appointed purpose—Ephraim to Jeroboam's calf-worship and Ahab/Jezebel's Baal-worship, and Laodicea to Roman emperor-worship. Not surprisingly, both were also destroyed—Ephraim to the hands of Assyria and Laodicea to a terrible earthquake.

We cannot dine at the same table with Christ and with demons (1 Corinthians 10:21).

We, in the West, of all people, know that the genuine Church Jesus came to build was consecrated by the blood of the martyrs who were willingly tortured to death if it meant their lives pointed others to the One True Gospel of Yeshua.

We, in the West, of all people, know that the Church Jesus came to tear down was built on the hypocritical religious, pharisaic spirit that gladly dons holy robes in the square but holds the oral traditions of the day as being more authoritative than the Almighty Word of God.

Therefore, we, in the West, of all people, should recognize when we've forsaken the Church Jesus came to build in trade for today's oral-tradition Church of the Pharisees. If *we* have the world's majority of biblical universities, education and training programs, seminaries, and libraries of theological answer books—as well as the general prosperity, wealth, *and religious freedom* to use these resources—then *we* hold a majority of the fault when we corporately fail to show ourselves "approved unto God" as people who "needeth not to be ashamed, rightly dividing the word of truth" (2 Timothy 2:15).

If today's Church is guilty of getting off track (which we have)—and of lackadaisically remaining off track while we drift farther away from the truth (which we are)—then we are choosing to attempt to redress the powerful Name of Christ by adorning it in the clothing of Revelation's Harlot. When we are apathetic to the lives of martyrs who were slain to keep Jesus' mission pure, we are removing the white robe of innocence from our culture's perception of the cross and are choosing to join the Harlot while she gets drunk on the blood of the saints (Revelation 17:6). When we, Christ's ambassadors, sacrifice sound doctrines to embrace a wicked, liberal interpretation or "translation" of the Word that tickles itching ears and feeds the lust of proof-text, "lifestyle Christians" (2 Timothy 4:3), we're making the deliberate decision to be seduced by the Harlot's "purple and scarlet, and...gold and jewels and pearls" (Revelation 17:4). We willingly unite with her, trading our identity as Yeshua's sweet Bride into a whore worse than Hosea's Gomer.

We are absolutely, irrefutably guilty of turning the Church Christ built into the Church He came to tear down, and when "Christianity" becomes so mixed in the heretical, profane, blasphemous, idolatrous, and misleading doctrines that Antichrist will prize, we will have assisted in introducing our Harlot religion to the Beast that will turn on her and devour her when her pathetic role in his ascension to world power is over.

The window of time we have to stand up to fight against the Beast and maintain the purity of the message of the cross is closing. The

Church of Tickling Ears, that Apostate Superchurch, is already forming. We are deliberately sending out a signal to Antichrist, letting him know we're ready for him, we've already prepared a place for him, and he's welcome to rule here. A counterfeit Christianity that is beautiful and logical (by human standards) on the outside, but blasphemous and profane (by God's standards) on the inside, will be absolutely, positively *thriving* on the earth when Antichrist takes his throne. These authors personally believe that the Western Church is posturing itself to embrace, and then become, false religion—and false religion is unquestionably the doorway through which Antichrist will enter to arise and establish himself as the Messiah.

Our Controversial Prediction

Everything you've read so far is evidence that our forthcoming prediction is possible. What you are about to read in the coming pages has not yet been written in any previously published work, for who in their right minds would call the Christian Church a cult? However, it's a prediction that hit us with a power as unstoppable as a steam engine train ten feet from its unsuspecting victim…and on the very same day. Both of us— Allie Henson and Donna Howell—were involved in our own writing projects when, in a fortuitous conversation over breakfast at a local diner one morning, we revealed to each other details of what we were working on, only to discover we were both being obedient to a calling on the same book: Henson was working to address the failures of Western society through grooming a public to embrace the unthinkable while the Church was sleeping; Howell was working to address how the sleeping Western Church is largely at fault for the demoralization of society. However, Henson didn't know what to say to the Church; Howell didn't know what to say to society. When this conversation occurred organically, while our hardworking server kept our coffee mugs filled, there was *no* stopping the force of the epiphany that drove us to write this book, with the hope that the warning we feel compelled to issue may hit for the Remnant before the atrocity does.

We are aware that much of what is in this book will be considered provocative and inflammatory by readers in both the secular world and the Church. However, we believe without hesitation that this work contains an urgent message that God has spoken to each of us. Unfortunately, we realize that we won't likely make trainloads of new friends via the warm-and-fuzzy emotional appeal solicited in much religious nonfiction these days. This project is controversial; yet we believe that shying away from its delivery would be disobedient to God. In this way, we can offer only one comment as we proceed:

We're here to chew bubblegum and deliver the truth. And we're all out of bubblegum.[18]

We're referring to the grand-scale vulnerability of Westerners' psychological and spiritual wellbeing, both in the present and in the soon-approaching End Times. Not only do we predict that the Church will be persecuted, but we believe (as many Church Fathers and celebrated Church historians did in earlier centuries) that she will actually assist in reinforcing the enemy's eschatological plan. We're talking about the "Cult of Western Christianity"...as it has already unfolded on our soil, and as it will increase in the near future to pave the way for Jesus' prophecy of the greatest earthly deception as foretold in Revelation.

How?

We're glad you asked. Turn the page.

{3}

THE SCI-FI WE ARE LIVING

After opening this book with a hard look at the contemporary Church's shortcomings, you may have expected us to proceed by outlining how the religious institution should revamp itself to more fully reflect what God desires of His Churches. Not to worry—we *will* get there, but as mentioned in the introduction, this book is about more than just Western Christianity. This is a vital point, because modern culture is made up of more than just those who follow Jesus. In fact, a vast majority within our society today are unsaved. So if we speak only to the Church, we are "preaching to the choir." Furthermore, since many Christians have, in recent years, found it difficult to maintain relevance to secular culture, anything that isolates the religious institution as a topic fails to bridge the cultural and communicative gap when it comes to the world outside the Church. While we believe that God's transformative power has the means to change the world when people look to Him for direction, we also understand that God has allowed humanity to be agents of free will. As such, when we look for answers within the four walls of the church that would apply to the troubles that pillage the world outside, we often hit a disconnect. The transformative power of God accompanies the willing heart, and society is filled with those who aren't ready to surrender. Because of this single element, our biblical solutions are limited outside the Church or the Christian home. For the Church to become relevant to culture again, we have to understand where people are, and where they've come from.

In the meantime, we're able to see fairly accurate reflections of where our society is headed when we study the media. Movies, books, television shows, and other means of storytelling outline where society has previously projected itself to be, and how we have fared along the journey. When fiction writers construct a good story, they often imagine where mankind's depravity and technological advances will take us in the future. Then, based on their imaginings, they approximate a story they believe will be thrilling, scary, or engaging. At the time they're written, many of these speculations seem impossible; yet, the possibilities become more realistic as the years go on. In this chapter, we'll show only some of the many ways that we're currently living the sci-fi movies our grandparents were afraid of. Likewise, we'll reveal how dangerously close we are to living—in the not-so-distant future—the seemingly impossible entertainment that viewers take in today.

If we were to say that we're living in a horror or sci-fi movie, most folks would probably say, "No way." After all, such productions reach for the fantastical, while combining out-of-reach technology with an escalated and even dehumanized level of human depravity. The blend of such things, in the realm of entertainment, is what makes a great book or movie. In fact, the perfect balance of these elements is often what sets a work apart as *really* gripping or even *downright scary.* Yet, once a piece of media crosses over completely into the realm of what viewers perceive to be the impossible, it's no longer considered "scary," but mere "fantasy."

For example, a criminal in a Superman movie may kill many people and terrorize a city, but viewers—many of them children—never really experience fear. In fact, many moviegoers leave the theaters with smiles and laughter; they never believed they were in any kind of *real* danger.

On the other hand, those who take in a movie about a calculated serial killer often watch with intense facial expressions, sitting at the edge of the seat and even jumping at sudden, unexpected encounters with the antagonist. As these patrons exit the theater, they're often wide-eyed, discussing unforeseen plot-twists or the fearsome depravity of the murderer. Additionally, we would wager no small children will be seen exiting that particular film, even though far fewer deaths appear in the movie about the serial killer than in the superhero flick.

What, then, is the difference between these two types of movies? It's the notion of fantasy vs. reality: the *possible* vs. the *impossible*. Anyone watching a Superman movie feels secure in knowing that they won't ever see a day when a boy from another planet possessing special powers, including that of flight, will land on earth and fight global terrorists. They can explain to their children that the characters are a product of mere make-believe. On the other hand, serial killers *do* exist, and they *have* terrorized populations before. These individuals are real people, whose maladaptive minds are the places where *real* nightmares are made—and few is the number of parents who would expose their kids to such brutal reality (even on the big screen). There is nothing pretend about it. It is a completely possible scenario, which is why such films cross the line from *exhilarating* into *scary*.

When viewers walk away from a production saying "that would never happen," they usually report their experience in terms of whether or not they were entertained: "That was fun!" "An enjoyable movie, highly recommended!" When they've experienced a sense of threat, however, reports tend to be more emotional: "That was scary!" "I'm so freaked out right now!" They may even describe a physiological response: "I screamed when [insert frightening event here] happened" or "I was on the edge of my seat!"

Often, as mentioned previously, what makes such productions successful is the perceivable balance between the real and the possible. Truly successful sci-fi, thriller, and horror works take the audience to the height of suspense and fear by borrowing realistic notions from the real world, then launching them into the realm of what is barely speculative. For example, a film might portray something that *could* happen, then leave viewers with the exhilaration and relief that accompanies the return to the "safety" of the real world. The fear lingers beyond the close of the film, residually, based on how close to actuality a portrayed scenario comes. In a nutshell, the audience's response is determined by the thrill of fright incited by events that could *potentially* happen, while enjoying the security of knowing that cinematic events aren't currently occurring. While some productions and series such as *Star Wars* or *Superman* succeed on the mere fantastical and gather generations of loyal followers, others draw crowds who are titillated by the knowledge that the fearsome events on the screen aren't completely out of the question in real life. In these cases, there are often only two elements that bar the storyline from creeping into our daily reality: the advancement of technology and/or the depravity of mankind.

To say that today's movies and books could become tomorrow's reality may seem sensationalistic. Yet it has been mentioned, in many ways, that we are currently living the sci-fi our grandparents feared. Great minds of yesteryear who dared to imagine what the future would look like drew similar responses to their writings in their own time. They, as it turns out, were closer than even they might have expected to the future reality, which reinforces the notion that, should history repeat itself, the media often foreshadows our culture's future.

When we draw connections between the fiction works of yesteryear and today's reality, we're able to follow the shift in society's mentality over the past decades. And, we are left with a notion more frightening than anything in past movies or books that has come true: The pattern can, and likely will, repeat itself. If we're now living out scenarios that terrified and chilled past generations, then it seems reasonable that the Hollywood creations now showing post-apocalyptic, dystopian, or even post-Christian societies wherein the depravity of mankind runs rampant and unchecked could very well be the true scenarios of tomorrow. Could today's media be a tool for shaping the masses to embrace the unthinkable? It's not as unlikely as we might think. For those who still doubt the possibility of this statement being true, we ask you to join us as we look at a few examples of things that have already come to pass.

1984

In 1949, when George Orwell wrote *1984*, he depicted a world wherein one totalitarian leader, known as "Big Brother" (who, some say, is a predictive parallel to Antichrist), continually surveilled and controlled the entire population. People in this tale are subjects to the government through and through; their very emotions, ideas, and statements are legislated and monitored by the "Thought Police" and are constantly reminded that "Big Brother is [always] watching."[19] In addition to this nonstop, invasive monitoring, this speculated world is kept in a perpetual state of war. This condition best serves those in control of society by keeping resources sparse and personal ambitions minimal. All efforts and resources of the public are directed at the "war," despite the fact that there appears to be no resolution in sight. The livelihood and individuality of the population remains suspended toward political efforts, while liberties are surrendered in trade for safety. The controlled populace then surrenders their sovereign rights for what they're told is the protection of the population as a whole; thus, this submission holds the makings of a good citizen. Healing of the land is not a goal of those who are in control in *1984*. On the contrary, the state of war is suspended for an intentional purpose. Consider Orwell's seemingly prophetic words: "War, it will be seen, is now a purely internal affair. [Previously, when war had been built on international conflict,] the victor always plundered the vanquished. [Now, instead,] the war is waged by each ruling group against its own subjects, and the object of the war is not to make or prevent conquests of territory, but to keep the structure of society intact…. It would probably be accurate to say that by becoming continuous war has ceased to exist."[20] The truly spooky elements of the *1984* story rely on the same two elements mentioned previously: the notion that technology could ever evolve to this level of surveillance, and the idea that a government would become so controlling that it would dare to censor the actions, efforts, relationships, and even statements and thoughts of its civilians. Likewise, one of the dystopian elements of *1984* that lends a sense of "safety" to readers (thus balancing the negative components and allowing the audience to end the experience with exhilaration and resolve) is the idea that Americans would never be asked to submit to such controlling forces that there would be a place for the Thought Police. Likewise, many in 1949 never would have dreamed of a future wherein every action could be completely surveilled, because at that point, the necessary technology wasn't yet in place. But, seven decades later, we live in a place where accusations of "hate speech" and surveillance methods are a thriving, rampant, and even complacently accepted dynamic of censorship and governmental control (more on this in an upcoming chapter). In many ways, we are living a type of parallel to the world portrayed so long ago in *1984*.

Other Predictions

Some question whether modern technology would even exist without its fictional inspiration. Certainly this is a fair question. However, it reaches into the realm of other questions without answers, such as which came first between the chicken and the egg. This is ultimately beside the point, because mankind will go everywhere that technology and ethical boundaries allow. When people feel inhibited, they press the boundaries within one or both of these parameters until they've created more room to evolve. We see evidence of this even within our lifetime; our modern innovations are the products of the imaginings of the previously fantastical. Think about it: Since the creation of *The Jetsons, 2001: A Space Odyssey*, and *Dick Tracy*, inventions such as Skype and Facebook video chatting have been on the roster of things we hoped to progress to. The 1980 film, *Superman II,* starring Christopher Reed and Margot Kidder, visualized replayable video messages in hologram form, stored on crystal disk-type drives. The military drones of 1984's *The Terminator* seemed to predict the ones introduced in the early 2000s. Countless futuristic cartoons and movies such as the already-mentioned *The Jetsons, The Fifth Element, Blade Runner* and *Total Recall* predicted flying vehicles and self-driving cars. The 1960s series *Star Trek* inspired the invention of many new forms of technology, not the least of which was the first cell phone: Motorola's 1973 800 MHz.[21] Other movies and TV shows such as *2001: A Space Odyssey, Fahrenheit 451*, and *Star Trek* foretold devices like iPods, tablets, and earbuds.[22,23] *Star Wars* portrayed a world where lasers could be used for cutting and holograms could be seen as 3D visuals. *Back to the Future II* suggested interactive home devices such as automatic-entry ID via fingerprint, voice-command functions such as lights, flat-screened televisions, video chatting, voice-activated food delivery, and cars that run on recycled forms of energy rather than solely on gasoline.[24]

Movies portraying the concept of robots that both impersonate and serve mankind date back as far as 1927's silent movie, *Metropolis*, wherein the ethics of mass production, wealth-class distinction, and even the creation of a robot culminate in the predictive principle: "The mediator between the head and the hands must be the heart."[25] However, with this initially ethical approach toward the creation of robots seemingly abandoned, we now live with robots that serve and track us daily. For example, Apple's Siri can be programmed to wake us up, manage our finances or social media, run varieties of calculations, track our schedule, give us reminders, and even make schedule changes and reservations.[26] Amazon's Alexa/Echo technology boasts similar services, offering everything from meal suggestions and a newsfeed based on preferences, smart-home controls, fitness tracking, and even vocal-commands TV controls.[27]

Zeroing in one of the above-listed technologies, "smart home" features include an ever-growing list of amenities that seem to come straight out of sci-fi movies of previous generations, such as the aforementioned climate control, lighting control, surveillance, door-lock/unlock control, and home-security monitoring (many of these functions can be handled even from remote locations). Further, those who live in a "smart home" can "train" various devices to "communicate" for better efficiency or convenience, such as setting "the coffee machine to…[brew coffee] as you wake up…[or] automatically heating up dinner in a Crock-Pot as you roll into the driveway."[28] Motion sensors, proximity detection in key fobs, and tracking in smart phones can be integrated with automated home features to bring one's house to life—and production—without so much as the flip of a switch. Tracking apps on children's phones and devices placed in pet collars make it easy to check on family members from the office, while door alarms can alert parents at work if the kids at home enter an off-limits area, such as the garage, gun-safe room, or closet storage for chemical supplies.[29] Other safety measures include gas- or water-leak detection and security devices that can signal when there's a problem at home—and can even call for professional help and intervention if needed.[30]

In 2014, Japanese Professor Hiroshi Ishiguro introduced a robotic news anchor called Kodomoroid, a name formed from the combination of two Japanese words meaning "child" and "android." Ishiguro, director of the Intelligent Robotics Laboratory, said he desires to see artificial intelligence become more "clever," and he looks for such creations to become more readily available, eventually being sold for "price of a laptop computer."[31] Consequently, he has made a life-like, robotic copy of himself, which he sends traveling in his stead to his speaking engagements. While these robots look more like robots than humans during their demonstrations, it is clear to see that the gap between the appearance and mannerisms of the two is closing.

In the 1970s, a professor at the Tokyo Institute of Technology, Masahiro Mori, coined the term "uncanny valley," explaining that, as human-like robots become more realistic, there is a point at which they will lose their charm: "They are so lifelike and yet they are not 'right.'"[32] Those watching robots as they speak can see what he means, but we wonder how long this visible differentiation between the invented and the real human will exist.

In fact, that gap between the mechanical and biological forms narrows daily where digital humans are concerned. At the 2020 Consumer Electronics Show in Las Vegas, Nevada, Samsung unveiled its "Neon" line of video chatbots. These are on-screen digital, interactive humans created to provide online chat support, artificial-intelligence assistance, or customer-service exchanges. These avatars are completely convincing; because each is designed with unique styles, looks, and personalities, users may not realize that they're talking to a computer product.[33]

Heading farther back into history to 1865, Jules Verne wrote about the potential of mankind making a trip to the moon in his work *De la Terre à la Lune* ("From the Earth to the Moon"). The parallels between his imaginings and twenty-first-century space-travel innovations almost need no mention. However, it's worthwhile to note that beyond merely going to space and landing on the moon, the 1990s television series *Babylon 5* depicted a self-contained, interplanetary space city filled with "humans and aliens wrapped in 2,500,000 tons of spinning metal; all alone in the night."[34] That series also presented many of the other advances listed in this chapter, but most notably predicted the use of deepfake technology in an episode wherein a main character was told that if he didn't publicly confess to crimes he didn't commit, he would be executed, with a posthumous confession artificially created to deface his memory.[35] The setting of this encapsulated, galactic city also bears a striking similarity to the International Space Station (ISS), which NASA is now opening up to commercial companies for "producing, marketing, or testing their products," along with "filming commercials or movies against the backdrop of space."[36] Certainly, anyone who can shell out the thirty-five thousand dollars per day/per person cost of staying on the station probably won't expect to share amenities with aliens from non-human races, but that may soon be one of the few distinctions between Babylon 5 and NASA's ISS.[37]

The invisible plane of the *Wonder Woman* series, as well as the wholly transparent vehicles in *Star Trek IV: The Voyage Home* and James Bond's *Die Another Day*, showed a futuristic world wherein cloaking devices could render objects invisible. This technology is now closer to reality with "active camouflage," which is a mainstream pursuit for militaries around the world.[38] Similarly, fabrics with "retro-reflective projection" (RPT) allow wearers to blend in with their surroundings, offering fluid camouflage that results in near invisibility.[39] *Star Trek: The Next Generation*'s "holodeck" was only one of many portrayals of a world where participants can engage in the virtual reality (VR) that they imagine and desire. Now, VR technology exists—and is rapidly improving—to create an interactive experience for users in settings ranging from video-gaming to simulated, hands-on training such as surgery.[40] Like Orwell's *1984*, 1998's *Enemy of the State* alluded to extreme levels of surveillance we may someday be subjected to, and few would argue that these fore-shadows of what's developing have become fairly accurate (more on this in an upcoming chapter).

Demon Seed

The 1977 film *Demon Seed* begins with the successful creation of artificial intelligence: a computer called Proteus, which can "think with the power and a precision that will make obsolete many of the functions of the human brain."[41] Similarly, Proteus' creator's home is equivalent to what would still be considered a futuristic "smart home," served by an artificial intelligence unit called "Alfred." (In fact, these homeowners interact with this unit in similar fashion to users of Amazon's modern-day Alexa.) Upon request, the house opens and closes shutters over windows, locks and unlocks doors, pours drinks, makes breakfast, adjusts climate control, answers the door, and even creates a video likeness of its residents to communicate with the outside world. The problem begins when Proteus asks when he will be let out of his "box"; his creator responds by laughing and saying that he will not. Simultaneously, the unit begins to argue ethical positions with his maker, refusing to do certain jobs that they attempt to program him for. Proteus then takes matters into his own hands; he relocates himself to the nearby home served by the computer called Alfred and overtakes the home's residential AI service. Proteus then locks the lady of the house inside, manipulating the home's features to torment her—with tactics that include limiting water and sunlight and keeping the heat so high it makes her ill—until she agrees to bear him a child so that he can achieve freedom outside his "box." (When outsiders arrive at the home to check on the woman's well-being, Proteus merely conjures her image, which tells the visitors that all is well.) The movie ends with the birth of a half-human, half-computer child who declares in a robotic voice that she is "alive."

While innovations in this "smart home" in *Demon Seed* were futuristic and impossible when the movie was made, we now see them as being believable for the not-too-distant future. As for the concern regarding a computer's ability to create an offspring with a human being, scientists are even now working on such endeavors, and many claim that it's much closer than people realize.[42] In fact, technology currently exists that allows a computer to intake DNA, analyze it, then "blend" it with its own digital properties while the synthetic embryo grows in a lab setting. While this process isn't packaged for consumer purchase as of yet, some say it will be widely available at major retailer outlets sooner than we think.[43]

Logan's Run

The 1976 film *Logan's Run* shocked its viewers with the notion of a utopian society in a self-contained city where residents are mandated to die when they reach the age of thirty. Set in the year 2274, people in this location are free to pursue creativity and self-indulgence. However, the world outside has been ravaged and can no longer support all of humanity for the full life span. Thus, population balance is maintained by the "carousel," the rite by which those who have reached their expiration age—the time for their "renewal"—will be put to death.

Many would say that such a scenario could never happen, and it's possible that we'll never see a day and age when mere thirty-year olds will be mandatorily exterminated, but there are places in the world where euthanasia is legal now, and there are those arguing for its cause in America. Further, many of the deaths aren't of the elderly, but are the legal terminations of people as young as seventeen.[44] When such atrocities become permissible, what barriers keep them from becoming law? Could such legislation ever pass, or would ethical blockades protect our population? Many would make the case that euthanasia is a humane way to solve the problem of suffering for some people. If such stances take hold and become the verbiage by which this practice gains a foothold in society, would it then ever become compulsory for certain suffering citizens? This isn't completely far-fetched, and we'll address these questions in an upcoming chapter.

They Live

In 1988, "Rowdy" Roddy Piper appeared in the sci-fi movie *They Live*, wherein alien forces have invaded and overtaken earth's society. While this plot may place the movie outside the realm of believability for many (these authors included), it's the tactics these forces use over the population that we want to note here. In the film, the tired, impoverished masses live a seemingly dreary existence, not suspecting that there is a strategy behind their deprivation. Everything changes for construction worker Nada, who finds a pair of seemingly ordinary sunglasses. However, when he puts them on, his vision of the world around him changes. Signs that previously boasted ad campaigns for foods, services, or other consumables changed, their subliminal message revealed by Nada's new shades; he now saw that they issued such orders as "obey," "stay asleep," "consume," and worse, "submit," and "submit to authority."[45] At the same time, the ruling aliens are revealed as the ugly creatures they are, and Nada responds by fighting. Through a series of events, he—of course—saves the planet, but not before declaring war on the aliens by stating, "I have come here to chew bubble gum and kick [rear-ends]. And I'm all outta bubblegum."[46]

Aliens and shoot-'em-ups aside, there is a profound sense of reality to this movie, considering the consumer-driven thrust of society. And, when people's finances are spread as thin as they are today, with folks buying things they don't need (but believe they do), prioritizing status or possessions in attempt to keep up with the Joneses, or even collecting worldly goods as a means to find spiritual satisfaction or inner peace, one wonders what outside forces influence this materialism. While many realize that there are people around the world who are in dire need of such basics as food, clean drinking water, and access to basic medical care, they often do little or nothing about it because the material wealth of their own society presents itself as a "need" that keeps them financially distracted from being the force for good they could be. Additionally, more than a few folks find themselves entrapped by buying more than what they need and accruing debt in the process. The ensuing financial strain becomes a type of enslavement that contributes to the lifestyle portrayed in the earlier portions of this movie: People are tired, over-worked, and impoverished.

The Island

In another work of science fiction, the 2005 film *The Island* depicts a large, self-contained city wherein residents are told that they are survivors of a "contamination" that killed the rest of society and rendered the outside world unlivable. Individuals living in this city are continually monitored by computers that give readings on their vital signs, sleep patterns, nutrition levels, emotional outbursts, and even their proximity to others who are standing too close. The population is fed in common food lines, and its average mental maturity seems to be about age fifteen.

Through a series of events, the protagonist, called Lincoln Six Echo, witnesses the murder of a peer who has just delivered her baby. The newborn is immediately taken down a hallway and placed in the arms of the apparent *real* mother, who strangely appears identical to the child's recently deceased birth mother. Later, viewers learn that the self-contained city is actually a cloning center: People living on the outside contract the cloning of themselves to harvest their organs, and they delegate tasks such as childbirth to the "copies," who are unaware that they are clones—and are terminated after serving their purpose. The movie's plot follows Lincoln Six Echo's efforts to escape with comrade Jordan Two Delta, and mildly probes the ethical dilemma of such business ventures.

While initial conversations about this movie might center on its suspense and even on the ethics of such practices, many will respond dismissively to speculation once the screen has gone dark, because the technology—and mankind's depravity, for that matter—hasn't escalated to this position in our reality, *yet*. However, many who find the premise of the movie interesting are unaware of just how closely we currently parallel the scenarios. To say that mankind would never cross such a technological and ethical threshold can't be accurate, when fetal-tissue harvesting has reached such wide acceptance. Many people are surprised to learn that the tissue of aborted babies is often bought by biomedical companies that use it for research and other purposes,[47] such as cure-seeking for Alzheimer's disease, spinal-cord conditions, HIV, Parkinson's disease, and other stem-cell study, to name a few.[48] However, many claim that abortion procedures have been altered to procure a live fetus—unbeknownst to the terminating parent. In fact, according to former abortionist Dr. Forrest Smith, techniques have, at times, been altered at increased risk to the mother and resulting in the live birth of the fetus to "obtain, fresher, more intact organs."[49] While legislature continues to conduct ethical review and rewording of the legislation to avoid loopholes that allow for harvesting and selling fetal tissue and organs, the industry accrues big money. In 2018, the National Institute of Health "spent $115 million on grants involving human fetal tissue research and is estimated to spend $120 million in FY [fiscal year] 2019,"[50] while another project that utilizes aborted fetal liver, bone marrow, intestinal matter, and thymus has to date held a contract of at least $13,799,501.[51] In 2017, abortion claimed more than 850,000 lives; that total was even greater in 2016, when numbers exceeded 925,000.[52]

If *The Island's* premise ever elevates to scientific possibility (and we are headed in that direction), it provides some realistic ways the ethics might be justified. For example, the clones are unaware of their status as "copies." They live in a self-contained city where they are employed, housed, and fed under the guise of the outside world being "unavailable." They're told of a beautiful place called "the Island," where only a select few are able to go and live. (Those fortunate enough to be relocated to the Island, of course, are those who have served their purpose and are thus terminated). It is a happy enough existence lived without fear, and their impending expiration is never brought to their attention. They leave for the Island joyfully, as the lucky winners of a lottery promising a beautiful life across the water. It is perceivable that this might be considered a humane and ethical strategy should the movie's proposition ever reflect reality. And it seems apparent that desperate people will be quick to justify such an industry, as stated toward the end of the movie: "The only thing you can count on is that people will do anything to survive. I want to live, and I don't care how."[53] If this sentiment represents most of mankind (and it likely does), then it can become the mantra for so many of these events. In addition, as stated previously, such movies often predict conditions that are only held back by two elements of society: technological advancements and mankind's depravity. Since we're able to depersonalize and kill our unborn, harvesting their body parts for research, then it's feasible that we will eventually be able to embrace the logic of using clones in a way that would make *The Island* prophetic. The only thing we're waiting for is the technology…

So how close are we to cloning a person? While several early reports of success in fully cloning human embryos turned out to be fraudulent, scientists have asserted that they have had this capability for seven years now. While most sources report that these haven't resulted in live births of humans, cloning sheep and primates has been successful.[54] Despite that human cloning is still theoretical, many countries have already created legislation outlawing the practice, should it become mainstream. As for whether legalization would ensure that anyone would actually participate in cloning, we suppose time will tell. Beyond moral issues such as who would "own" the clones and what purposes would qualify one for approval to use the technology, the rights of clones, their uses, and their termination and disposal would need to be clearly defined legally. The implications in reference to malevolent individuals are concerning as well: Guidelines and limitations would need to be in place to prevent those with deviant minds from cloning people for sadistic purposes and pleasures.

Since public knowledge currently maintains that the notion of cloning a human being is technically possible but has not—as of yet—become a perfected science, most of us can feel a (false) sense of safety that widespread realization of this practice is not imminent, and thus maintain detachment from the likelihood that elements of *The Island's* plotline will come to pass. Yet perhaps such events lie in the near future.

There is the possibility that it would take no more than a nudge in the direction of technology and/or man's depravity to see the premise of *The Island*, like that of *1984*, become reality.

(Note that a similar dystopian idea was depicted in the book *Cloud Atlas*, as well as the subsequent film by the same name starring Tom Hanks. A central theme throughout part of the narrative shows young, female human clones, servers at a futuristic restaurant called Papa Song's, awaiting the day they will earn their release into Xultation, a utopian paradise promised to those who serve faithfully for a designated time. Each of these women is fitted with a slave collar that houses hidden technology to execute her if she exercises free will in any way, fails to comply with the rules of her servant position, or doesn't succeed in completely pleasing every Papa Song patron during her shift (regardless of what abuses or humiliation a patron might inflict upon her). The narrative follows one of these women, a faithful servant at the end of her slave contract, as she is led into a back room. She has been told she will be redressed, relieved of her collar, and released into Xultation. Excited for the paradise beyond, she smiles and cooperatively leans back, allowing mysterious men and women wearing "nurse-like," red garbs to lower an apparatus around her head, listening as they reassure her in soothing tones that the machine will remove her collar. The device instead activates the execution, killing the girl instantly, without a sound, and without even the slightest reaction from its victim. Her lifeless body is then placed on a conveyor belt and taken to the recycle room, where her organs will be harvested and turned into the food that subsequent generations of the cloned human slaves will unsuspectingly consume as their regular sustenance rations. (The organic material will also serve as bio-matter for the womb tanks that grow the clones. If cloning ever becomes a reality for us, then *feeding* the clones will be an issue as well, and film plots like this might be unthinkable now, but they illustrate that depraved minds can come up with an answer if they are ever confronted by inconvenient, inquiring clone-people...)

For each small step in progress man takes, a trade is made. With each technological stride, he becomes more certain of himself, more confident in his own ways, more the master of all he surveys. We're not saying that technological or scientific progress is sinful by its own right, but often each successful innovation is met by man taking another step farther away from his Creator. With this in mind, one might wonder if the future will become so filled with man's achievements that there will no longer be room for God at all.

Aggression in Media

For many, a relationship between media and culture is undeniable. Yet, it's often easy to overlook just how deeply and intricately the two are inter-twined—the immediacy and severity of the condition. When research defines the relationship in solid numbers, it can be a wake-up call, espe-cially considering the prevalence of aggression depicted in media. In fact, research shows that, typically, American children witness eight thousand killings and more than one hundred thousand other types of violent acts—all while they're still in elementary school.[55] Multitudes of studies have shown connections between violence in media and the willingness to act aggressively toward peers,[56] the types of media aggression and sub-sequent criminal activity and conviction,[57] and the volume of violence in media taken in and later-life infractions,[58] as well as concluding that, in general "exposure to violence makes violent thoughts and emotions more accessible."[59]

Video games equally encourage hostile behavior, which is no big surprise, since they literally make players participants in violence. Usu-ally, games are designed so that such acts are rewarded, which is positive reinforcement for aggression. Research has shown a correlation between teenagers engaging in risky, delinquent, or violent behaviors while play-ing video games and their willingness to take similar actions in real life.[60]

Additionally, with the upsurge in popularity of VR (virtual reality) gaming, young minds are trained not only to enact violence such as shooting at enemies appearing on a screen, but also to carry out that activity toward someone standing right next to them. The more realistic this type of gaming becomes (and, for readers who haven't experienced VR technology, it's scary how realistic it is!), the easier it will be to initiate violence toward people *in real life*. Think about it: Players have the benefit of much practice in using weaponry, with only rewards and none of the catastrophic consequences that the correlating real-life action brings. In fact, for impressionable minds, they are merely having to do what they must to survive (within the game's context). The convincing vulnerability they feel while engaging in such gaming, followed by rehearsing multiple homicides or other gruesome acts, provides the perfect training ground—and desensitization—for future, real-life performances. Furthermore, our young suffer increased distance from their fellow man (which is exacerbated by the social-distancing practices ushered in during 2020). In essence, real-life peers become depersonalized as those in the virtual realm become more lifelike. Even worse, these authors won't even *begin* to discuss how detrimental VR technology can be for the young mind who uses it in conjunction with pornography.

Regardless of whether one is willing to believe that seeing an excessive amount of violence on screen causes a person to act out, there is also the fact that what takes place on screen is implanted into the minds of our youth. Usually, people don't think of heinous things to do unless the idea has been placed there by some form of entertainment. Consider the following observation of Jerry M. Burger:

> In May, 1981, John Hinckley tried to assassinate President Ronald Reagan.... Hinckley had viewed the motion picture *Taxi Driver* several times before the shooting...subsequent investigation discovered that Hinckley also had a strong attraction to Jodie Foster [who takes similar action in the film]. In July 1991, the motion picture *Boyz n the Hood* opened around the

country. Although calm was the norm at most of the theaters, some became the setting for real-life violence, including several shootings. Thirty-five people were reported wounded or injured for the first night the movie was shown. A man in Chicago was killed. In December 1997, a 14-year-old boy entered his Kentucky high school carrying five guns. The boy opened fire on classmates who had gathered for a prayer meeting, and three students were killed. Later, the boy said he was acting out a scene from the movie *The Basketball Diaries*. On May 25, 2009, a 17-year-old set off a bomb outside a Manhattan Starbucks. When arrested weeks later, the boy confessed to plans for a series of similar attacks. He explained that he was just imitating Brad Pitt's character in his favorite movie, *Fight Club*. The list goes on and on.[61]

Some arguments assert that the violence level in media is determined by those who are more aggressive, thus, an individual's propensity toward violence is not fed by the selection, but rather feeds it.[62] Others point to the masses who have watched plenty of violence in television shows and movies yet have never—nor would they ever—hurt anyone. These are fair arguments, and research abounds for curious readers who want more information on this topic. Suffice it to say here that when we see a culture riddled with spikes in nearly every sort of crime—theft, cybercrimes, hate crimes, physical and sexual assaults, homicides, child abuse and neglect, sexual exploitation and human trafficking, brutality toward and by people in authority—not to mention the burning, raiding, and looting of our cities, it's not a stretch to suggest that increasing violence in media could be shaping the behavior of our population (more on that shaping in a later chapter).

For folks who already show a greater propensity to carry out acts of violence—especially those whose inner predator appears manageable and dormant until something or someone pushes them past the tipping point—exposure to this kind of media *could* be the catalyst that creates the killer. One sci-fi/horror anthology film illustrates this concept profoundly: A concerned eye doctor discovers that one of his female patients is being physically abused by her boyfriend, and he decides to intervene. Using futuristic technology and medicine, he creates an injection that will induce a barrage of rapid, violent images upon contact with the eyeball. His idea and intent is that, even when the eye is closed, the bombardment of bloody, gory, violent, and disturbing pictures will flash in view for a temporary time in the abuser's view to "scare him straight" so the violence against the woman will stop. Luring the abuser into his clinic under the guise of a free eye exam, the doctor administers his serum to the unsuspecting boyfriend, and it succeeds in generating the inescapable volley of horror into his mind. The violent man flees the clinic and returns home in a panic. However, minutes later, the audience discovers that the serum backfired tragically, resulting in the gruesome murder of the female patient. The man returns to the doctor after the dose has worn off, informing him of the irony:

> You think heaping a pile of murderous images and abuse on *my* brain was gonna make *me* think, "Oh, God, oh God, what a bad man I am. I repent." You know, you may be an okay eye doctor...but you're a crap psychologist, Doc. You don't know a *thing* about me—my life, what I've seen....
>
> [He laughs.] You thought this would help me? You *turbocharged* me! Who knows? Maybe if you'd loaded my head full of images of cute, cuddly kittens, I would have straightened out right as rain, you know? But *you* messed up! *You* killed her, Doc.[63]

A fight ensues between them in which the doctor prevails, but not without having first received a shot of his own serum. Unable to withstand the flood of sadistic imagery that suddenly appears across his vision, he plucks out his eye to make it stop. The drastic measure appears to work for a moment, but when it resumes a moment later, the doctor ends his life as a final escape.

Some might see a twofold moral to the story: Through the influence of this (currently fictional but futuristically predictive) technology, via the same violent-image induction, bad men release inner killers; good men can be tortured to the point of death.

Will We Reach a Point of No Return?

Midsommar

Of a slightly different flavor, the 2019 film *Midsommar* may seem to be mistakenly classified under the "folk horror" genre, since, at first glance, it seems more "weird" than "scary." Upon deeper investigation, though, it would seem that perhaps, for this film, the truly fearsome elements lurk, hidden in plain sight.

Midsommar begins with the double homicide and suicide of the main character's parents and sister. In a search to find peace, the girl joins her boyfriend and several acquaintances as they travel to Sweden with an earth-worshipping cult to attend a festival that only occurs every ninety years. Filled with symbolism, this film subtly presents a shift in futuristic culture, where luciferian worship, human sacrifice, imitative- and sex-magick, and ancient religion lead a cultish, post-Christian society. In a setting laced throughout with what director Ari Aster later admitted was occult runes, this commune embraces orgiastic worship, mind-altering drugs/hallucinogens, human sacrifice, witchcraft, and even euthanasia in its pursuit of the perfect harmonious, utopian society. Parodies of Christianity, such as a mimicry of the language of tongues, are on display throughout the film. The lead male character—ironically (and likely, *intentionally*) named Christian—is a self-serving, dishonest personality who thinks only of himself (unfortunately, this is how much of the secular world views Christians). He takes no stand on principle throughout the movie, does what feels good despite whether it's right or wrong, and gives no support to those he claims to care for. The movie's dialogue and scenes revealing his shortcomings are laden with inferences of the failures of Christianity, as illustrated by a futuristic, utopian familial way of approaching life as traditional Christian lifestyles are left behind and newer, modern, and idealistic ways are embraced.

The film portrays a crude level of singularity via the ability of the entire community to experience the emotions or experiences of an individual. For example, when one woman cries in devastation after learning that her boyfriend (Christian) has been unfaithful, other women gather around her and scream in agony, as though they also feel her pain. As the scene depicting the ritual of human sacrifice approaches and closes the film, we see Christian dressed in the fresh, still-bloody skins of a recently killed bear (which symbolizes communication with the spirit world), and scapegoat-type rites (those placing iniquities upon the sacrificial individual for the purging of communities' wrongdoings) are read over him as he and eight others are burned alive; this is the way villagers are "purged" of all negativity and guilt. There are multiple layers of symbolism throughout the production, but the overall point of the film is summed up in a hidden-in-plain-sight observation regarding where society is portrayed to be headed: A post-Christian nation embraces New Age practices such as earth-worshiping pantheism amongst an ancient, pagan religion. This society features singularity, utopia, selective breeding, orgiastic fertility rituals, spirit-channeling, and cremation of care (the placing of one's wrongs upon a sacrifice or effigy for purging). In trade, ancient rites of magic and human sacrifice replace "outdated" Christian values.[64] Ultimately, the symbolism leaves viewers to decide whether they will embrace the coming resurgence of ancient religion or adhere to the outdated notions of Christianity, which will soon disappear. (Due to the graphic nature of this film, including nudity and sexual content, we suggest that, if you'd like more information on this movie, you watch the documentary *Midsommar: Initiation into the Ancient Religion of the Future* produced by Truthstream Media, 2019, rather than the film itself).

Santa Clarita Diet

1973 sci-fi/thriller *Soylent Green* depicted a horrific future wherein the world is devoid of sustenance and people live on prepackaged rations. Only the older members of society recall a variety of fresh, unprocessed foods being a part of their diet. In this dystopian society characterized by euthanasia and assisted suicide, a series of events reveals that the food staple distributed to citizens and known ambiguously as "Soylent Green" is made of recycled human remains. While this plot twist was intended to disturb viewers and leave them unsettled, newer movies and television series have used a different approach to the subject of cannibalism. For example, no longer villainizing the notion, shows such as *iZombie* and *Santa Clarita Diet* make light of it.

The latter, *Santa Clarita Diet*, unapologetically attempts to blend comedy with disgusting crudities such as projectile vomit and physical mutilation, not to mention brutal and repulsive cannibalism and sex between the living and the undead. This series attempts to condition its audience to find cannibalism nonsensical and humorous rather than threatening and satanic. The production features a suburban family involved in real estate and keeping up with the Joneses. The leading female character, played by Drew Barrymore, finds that she has somehow turned undead and craves human flesh. As her husband, played by Timothy Olyphant, becomes an accomplice in her murderous feedings, the family tries to maintain a "normal" image for their neighbors and acquaintances—while keeping Barrymore's character fed. Their gruesome antics involve eating cadavers, making smoothies from dead flesh, hiding body parts in freezers, engaging in extramarital affairs, and disfiguring undead bodies as they slowly decompose and fall apart, among many other repulsive activities. While many may say that the series is all silliness and would never represent reality, again, these authors find that there are current parallels in the real world that only await depravity and technology to bring to fruition these imaginings...

What if you could request lab-raised meat based on a celebrity's DNA, which could then be blended with other meats, fruits, and vegetables, cured into salami and shipped to your house for your eating pleasure? Sound disgusting? Believe it or not, Bitelabs is a company that since 2014 has been campaigning to do this very thing (unless it is involved in one of the most complex and long-lived hoaxes society has seen to date). Celebrities this organization is currently attempting to harvest DNA from include Kanye West, Ellen DeGeneres, Jennifer Lawrence, and James Franco.[65] We know what you must be thinking: This seems so outlandish that it *absolutely* must be a hoax, right? While it's possible (and seems like the rational explanation), efforts to confirm it have, up to this point, come up empty.

A researcher at *Time* magazine attempted to verify the claims regarding Bitelabs, and someone who identified himself as the CEO of the company stated that the company's ability to carry the project out would "depend on...[their] ability to generate public enthusiasm," and that an additional aim the company had was to "prompt widespread discussion about bioethics, lab-grown meats, and celebrity culture... treating it as a cultural precursor for when our product eventually hits production."[66] While *Time's* take-away from this contact was that Bitelabs' emphasis was more on fueling conversation regarding lab-raised meats in general, the ambiguity of the lab's position never cleared up. The CEO completely avoided stating that their efforts were in any way aligned with pretense.

Additionally, when Brian Merchant of *The Vice* reached out to Bitelabs, expecting a tongue-in-cheek reply to what he presumed was a humorous attempt at disgusting satire, he received a "series of lengthy, sincere responses...that didn't appear to be mocking it."[67] The emails

Merchant received explained that a staff of five full-time workers wished to start a discussion about their project, and said that "making celebrity meat a reality from there will all depend on our ability to build a user-base." The emails outlined some specific details of their plan, including the percentage of celebrity meat vs. animal meat. Interestingly, the full names of Bitelabs' staff members were protected in communication with both *Time* and Merchant, apparently to maintain anonymity in light of the scandalous nature of their work. However, after being offered multiple opportunities to confess that the project is a hoax, Bitelabs continued to say that they are interested in seeing what type of marketability may exist for both lab-raised animal meats and for celebrity meat, along with "pushing the boundaries of tech and society."[68]

While these authors still hope that this is somehow a joke, further digging yields no confirmation that it is. On the other hand, if it is a hoax, then the Bitelabs folks have certainly remained stubborn about seeing it through. As yet, there has been no hint of anything other than sincerity from them, and their ongoing wish to remain anonymous makes us wonder if there really is something to this project. With television shows such as *iZombie* and *Santa Clarita Diet* trivializing the notion of cannibalism, the possibility certainly could exist.

Cuties

When Netflix announced its newest film title to be *Cuties*, an English-dubbed version of the French award-winning movie from Sundance Film Festival, they may have been surprised (or perhaps not, as we'll discuss in the next chapter) to see that the public response was to rage against the production. Memes and Facebook posts everywhere boasted such slogans as "Cancel Netflix," and, for a moment, even the word "Netflix" itself seemed synonymous with the acceptance of pedophilia. All in all, Netflix saw a spike in the number of views of this title, but reported a plummet in revenue as subscription cancellations mounted to more than nine million.[69] Why? Because the public saw the movie as a production that promotes blatant acceptance of the sexuality of too-young girls who dress in scant clothes, wear lots of makeup, and move their bodies as though conducting a strip-tease years before such a show would even be legal for their under-developed bodies.

Cuties begins with eleven-year-old Amy (short for Aminata) moving to a new housing development with her mother and brother, expecting her father to join them in their new location soon. Amy discovers that when her dad does arrive, he'll be bringing a second wife into the existing family; a segment of the film seems to address the family members' emotional adjustments to this anticipated newcomer. As a preteen, Amy becomes fascinated by the provocative dancing of a group called "Cuties" in her new neighborhood. She joins them, adopting their fashion of dress and dance, but keeps her activities—and her wardrobe—hidden from her family, who would be offended due to their conservative Muslim beliefs. Over the course of the movie, Amy's clothing becomes more and more seductive and her actions become more daring; her search for her identity somewhere between promiscuity and traditionalism is followed as her look—along with her dance flair—becomes more sensual, revealing, and mature.

On a stolen cell phone, the girl watches a clip of adult women doing strip-tease-style dancing, and she begins to emulate their looks, body language, and wardrobe choices. Using the same phone, she and her friends also flirt and chat online with older boys and attempt to film a young man's anatomy as he urinates in the boys' restroom. Amy even posts a naked picture of her own genitalia on social media.

Her crowning moment of peer acceptance comes when the other Cuties find that, by watching the provocative dances and mastering the moves, Amy brings a new line-up of salacious moves to the group's repertoire: gyrating in a variety of positions, booty-bouncing, swatting and bumping of each other's buttocks, shaking their buttocks near others' faces, adopting extremely suggestive hand gestures, and much more.

The girls add to their graphic moves the facial portrayal of innocence. Coy, wide-eyed expressions paired with a single finger placed at the corner of the mouth and other such child-like touches serve as alluring counterpoints to the maturity of their scandalous gestures and attire. All this, presented via camera shots filmed in close-up range to such brazen positions as the spread-eagle, create a scandalous dance scene that justifiably outraged viewers.

While the movie—especially the final dance scene—has become notorious online, those who haven't seen the entire film may not realize that it features an even more alarming element. The worst thing *Cuties* offers is not the in-your-face sexualization of these preteen girls, although that is extremely disturbing. Even worse is what takes place at the end of the final dance scene, when the onlooking crowd's reaction is mixed: some parents cover their children's eyes and some bystanders show expressions of shock, while still others bob their heads to the rhythm. Some men watch, wide-eyed with intrigue and arousal. Amy, however, freezes mid step, hearing in the back of her mind the traditional music of her family's heritage. Tears fill her eyes and she runs off stage, then returns home to make amends with her mother, don age-appropriate clothing, and walk outside to join other girls her age as they jump rope to an innocent and peaceful tune. The camera zooms in, showing her hair whisking across her face as the wind whips through her curls with every ascent and descent. Amy smiles joyously into the lens, signaling to the audience that she has at last found peace with herself and returned to innocence.

These moments illustrate a conditioning tactic called "foot in the door," which we'll explain at more length in an upcoming chapter. For now, we'll just say that it's a method that introduces an idea, then backs off, leaving the idea to simmer. In this movie, it went like this: The oversexual behavior of a confused young girl is introduced, then is dialed back, yet is reinforced with the subtle suggestion that this behavior will "iron itself out" if allowed to run its course and the teen is given space.

Unfortunately, in the real world, behaviors like the ones this girl engaged in are a cry for help; ignoring them only means the problem will escalate, not resolve itself. To put it another way, the movie subliminally communicates that young people who are dabbling in sexual activity, being exposed to pornography or strip-tease dancing online, posting inappropriate pictures of their anatomy on social media, abandoning their family's conservative values, lashing out, sneaking out, dressing inappropriately, and otherwise acting in salacious ways will have a sudden moment of clarity, after which they can reclaim their joyful innocence without further consequences, baggage, or ado. Additionally, by cuing the film's viewers in on the mixed reactions of the audience at the girls' dance—from the shock to the interest—producers seem to be acknowledging that sexualizing our youth will also be met with a variety of reactions. Yet it also seems to answer these attitudes preemptively, as if to say, "Yes, we know it's shocking, but hang in there; these young people will be fine. There is no need for you to intervene." Those who hide this message in plain sight expect the masses to generalize this resignation into real life, where little girls are behaving sexually far older than their years.

After watching the film, these authors discussed its implications and general message. Howell mentioned that just a minor tweak of the ending would have rendered it to be a completely different kind of movie. For example, if these girls had been taken into sex trafficking, it could easily be a film asserting the exploitive or even mortal dangers of sexual grooming amongst our youth. Had Amy's "moment of clarity" come after a passionate and compelling intervention from a trusted adult in her life, it could have been a message to parents and guardians to be watchful and involved in their young ones' lives—a reassurance that their intuition matters and that they are empowered to act; they're not just being "overprotective." The list of possibilities that *would have* shifted this movie's message to one of activism rather than acceptance (and even to an embracing) of the sexualization of our youth is endless.

All it would have taken would have been a statement at the end wherein the "moral of the story" or a "plan of necessary action" would compel viewers to intercede for the sake of our young people, and the entire movie would have been received differently. (Had they done so, it's still likely that viewers would have been justifiably upset at the scandalous dance scene.)

However, the film did no such thing. As we have stated, the movie sends the message that troubled waters are normal for our youth, and they'll eventually calm down on their own—no intervention needed.

Netflix's response to all the backlash about *Cuties* was to *claim* the movie was an attempt to raise awareness about the over-sexualization of our youth—not to add to the problem. The organization's co-CEO, Ted Sarandos, released a statement defending the film, saying the response to the production had been both "surprising" and the result of a cultural misinterpretation, citing the many locations in Europe where the movie met public acceptance.[70]

However, Sarandos claimed that American reaction had been unlike that of the rest of the world—even "unique" in its outrage.[71] Immediately following its September 9, 2020, release, the production company saw such protests as a letter from Missouri Senator Josh Hawley demanding a reply no later than September 18, 2020. In the correspondence, the senator asked questions including: "Did Netflix…take measures to ensure the protection of the physical, mental, and emotional health of child actors made to perform simulated sex acts and filmed in sexual or sexually suggestive ways?"[72] In consideration of Netflix's representation of Cuties as a "'social commentary' against the sexualization of young children,"[73] Hawley's questions make a series of valid points. Other of his inquiries included a demand to know why a movie that features "a range of issues including religion, culture, and social media" was marketed with "a poster solely depicting scantily clad preteens in sexually suggestive positions."[74] Interestingly, as Netflix asserted that the film had been played in other countries with acceptance, one may find it interesting that Hawley insisted on an answer for why Netflix chose "to market this film with a poster different from the French original, which depicts children throwing confetti into the street."[75]

Good question, Senator. Perhaps the answer lies in the fact that there is an attempt to shape the public toward accepting the pedophilia occurring in the States, and the agenda that has either created or adopted this film has procured a new tool via its visibility. The buzz that has surrounded the movie, in addition to its scandalous content, has created a breeding ground allowing the conversation of pedophilia to polarize. It fosters several types of manipulation tactics geared toward bringing acceptance of such content to the center of mainstream media, which will incite impassioned arguments for both sides of the issue (more on this in the next chapter).

In October of 2020, the state of Texas brought child pornography charges against Netflix, indicting the company for the "promotion of lewd visual material" of girls under the age of eighteen, due to the graphic and intentional "exhibition of pubic area of a clothed or partially clothed child."[76] Some may wonder how the film provoked such specific charges, when so many forms of media objectify children. The *Washington Times'* elaboration of the scenes shed light on the matter by describing the movie's graphic scenes as including "group twerks, mouth gestures, ground humping...hip grinding...and other sexualized moves that the girls are sometimes depicted as only half-understanding."[77]

More on this matter will be discussed in subsequent chapters, as the long-term aspect of this issue points to the populace being groomed to accept pedophilia. As we've stated, if the glimpses of the future captured in movies and television programs of the past are at all comparable to events and circumstances of our present lives (and we believe this is often true), then what we consider mere entertainment *now* has the potential of giving us a look at our own future. For this reason, it's important for us to scrutinize and vet the content of present-day movies, books, television shows, magazines, and even marketing campaigns in order to protect our future generations.

Indirect Exposure to Porn

While we're on the subject of inappropriate content and messages hidden in plain sight, let's talk about pornography. Did you know it's now being hidden in television shows that claim to be of a different genre? For example, the 2019 Amazon production, *The Boys*, which is categorized as an action, comedy, and crime film, is only one of many recent shows that include pornography. The characters in this series blatantly view pornography; in fact, during any given episode, porn scenes are allowed to play in the background—or even in the forefront. Many scenes show fully nude men and women engaging in intercourse or the exchange of sexual dialogue between same-gender couples and groups (also including nudity). At one point, a superhero on the rooftop of a New York City skyscraper pleasures himself while repeating variations of the phrase, "I can do whatever I want."[78] These authors aren't the only ones who find the sexual content of this series out of line; even liberal media outlets have cited their objections. *Cosmopolitan* author Hannah Chambers, for example, wrote an article entitled, "Uh…Can We Talk About All the Weird Sex Stuff Happening on 'The Boys'?" In it, she states that her "eyelids are now singed [on the inside] with all the insane sex scenes from this ridiculous show," and makes the tongue-in-cheek comment that she now categorizes her life into two segments: "before and after *The Boys* scarred…[her] memory."[79] The article also reveals other *secular* sources in which viewers have made similar comments, and Chambers highlights the most disturbing of their sexual content— which these authors cannot bring ourselves to elaborate upon.

The alarming issue about the pornographic subplots in this show is the deception in how it's marketed. When allowing their kids (especially young boys) to watch a superhero series (which, in this case, you'll remember, is listed in the category of action, comedy, and crime), they have no idea that they're introducing their kids to this type of content. Because exposure to pornography grooms children to tolerate many other exploitive situations and taints their ability to form their own identity in a healthy way, conditioning and normalizing sex amongst our minors is a major way the population is undoubtedly being groomed to embrace the unthinkable (pedophilia).

What Does the Future Hold?

We live in a world whose very media has turned against the population viewing it (as we will show in upcoming chapters) and serves to divide, indoctrinate, and strip our youngsters of their innocence while feeding them an agenda their minds aren't ready to process—and which God never wants these little ones to see. When we add this reality to the fact that we are living amid the sci-fi technology and developments our grandparents were afraid of, we find that our own future could become quite scary. As stated previously, the only things that keep us from living the scenes we see played out on television are the level of depravity of mankind and technological advancements. If and when these two elements were to catch up to what we see portrayed—if mankind becomes depraved enough and technology advances enough—we must wonder what will keep our world safe, our youths innocent, our minds guarded, and even our bodies fully human. What unthinkable things could the public be conditioned to embrace as technology continues to open doors to myriad possibilities?

For example, in 1987's *The Running Man*, Arnold Schwarzenegger finds himself as a contestant in a game show wherein the public savagely watches people fight to the death for entertainment. You may say that would never happen, but if you did, you'd have to make a case for why it would never happen *again*, since previous cultures have already done this very thing with Christians and others in the coliseums of centuries past. This is only one of many cases where people may think such things would never happen, but they don't realize mankind has already proven that it has the depravity necessary for engaging in such a practice. If history truly repeats itself, then the perception that this is an impossible scenario could be borne out of false sense of security.

On another sinister note, *The Terminator* predicted artificial intelligence so advanced that it would eventually surpass the intellect of its makers, waging war on humankind. What other plotlines in current fictional fantasy could point toward our society's future? Could generalizing sexual behavior in minors lead to the mainstream acceptance of pedophilia? Will euthanasia as portrayed in such movies as *Logan's Run* eventually be embraced, and even enforced? Is Bitelabs' "celebrity meat" endeavor merely a hoax, or is the day coming when someone can order the edible, lab-grown clone-meat of another human being? Will technology foster innovations such as a digital economy, paving way for the Mark of the Beast?

While the science behind many unspeakable activities lingers on the horizon, most of us take consolation (founded or unfounded) in the notion that these scenarios may never be reality. But what makes us so sure? We're so quick to place our hopes in the concept that mankind will draw and adhere to certain ethical lines, yet when previously faced with opportunities to cross such barriers, our track record gives us reason to doubt. As we've emphasized throughout this chapter, the advancements and accomplishments featured in many sci-fi movies are evident in our daily practices already. We've already established that activities such as harvesting fetal tissue aren't efforts we seem to ethically oppose. We've tolerated and even embraced being surveilled and having our location monitored for years now. Euthanasia is already legally occurring in some places of the world, while the US becomes increasingly open-minded about it. Considering what *is* already possible and allowed, who can say that we won't embrace even worse monstrosities?

In the midst of all these questions, the hands of society's sculptors are at work. Our culture, by and large, reflects the work of a mastermind manipulator, carefully crafting for centuries to bring mankind to a point of wreckage, loss, and self-destruction. His culpability is often anonymous, and his very existence is denied by many who unwittingly follow him. His agents work diligently to foster within the populace the readiness to adopt his manifestations. It is a global, large-scale shaping for the acceptance of monstrosities like those that are foretold in the book of Revelation. It is crowd control: how the masses are being groomed to embrace the unthinkable amidst a post-Christian nation.

{4}

THE STRATEGIES
SHAPING SOCIETY

Naming the Manipulation Methods

There are many ways people try to control others. It's easy to unwittingly be influenced by them—whether out of willful or unintentional ignorance. These methods of manipulation aren't necessarily random and uncoordinated; in fact, in many cases, they're secretly puzzle-pieced together by either evil influences or the powers that be (or both) for a greater impact upon society's thinking, condition, or well-being.

As we've said, many manipulation tactics go unnoticed. This isn't always, by the way, a reflection of the public's intelligence, because the craftsmen behind the deception are clever indeed; often, it's highly educated intellectuals who are inserting manipulative concepts into the public sphere. However, once we identify and explain these strategies for shaping the public's thoughts and behavior—many of which are formulas that have long been used in advertising and marketing—they'll be easy to recognize as common threads running through society's mainstream communication. With this in mind, and under the heading that "knowledge is power," we present these methods of manipulation here by name. It's time to call them what they are and show how they're are being used to shape our culture's mentality.

The Tactics

Conditioning

Russian psychologist Ivan Pavlov, as many remember from high school psychology class, trained his dogs to salivate on demand by associating the sound of a tuning fork with their food.[80] In essence, his experience proved that, by applying the stimulus (the tone), the conditioned response (salivating) becomes a predictable reaction.[81] We see this stimulus-response concept play out in myriad avenues in our day-to-day lives, including marketing, sales, and even education. For example, have you ever thought that you weren't hungry…until you walked into a restaurant and smelled the aroma of food cooking? Surely, the scent in a floral shop or a spray of perfume wouldn't prompt the same hunger response—despite the fact that those also stimulate the sense of smell. Or have you ever found that, after spending a stressful day at work where the phone rings a lot, you cringe when you arrive home and your cell phone rings? In yet another example, consider an energy-drink ad that portrays a beautiful, tan, scantily clad woman. Guys want to date her and girls want to *be* her. Of course, the ad is designed to make both genders feel a little closer to this goal, as long as they partake of *this* particular energy drink. The list goes on and on. While these are simple examples, the truth is that conditioning occurs in the background of society's landscape, and when we're aware and looking, we can see it everywhere.

Shaping

The concept of shaping is simple and can be used for both good *and* evil. Generally speaking, it is the slow coaxing of an individual or group from one type of behavior or stance into another. To put it more academically, it's when "successive approximations of the desired behavior are reinforced."[82] For example, a teenager balks about being asked to clean the entire house on a Saturday. So parents might start small and offer a reward, allowing the teen to visit friends later—*after* making sure the kitchen is clean or the living room is vacuumed. As the youth gets more used to doing chores and learns to take care of them more thoroughly and with a better attitude, the parents add new responsibilities to the list. Eventually, the teenager will be (rightfully) shaped to recognize the importance of keeping a tidy house, which will serve him or her well as an independent adult. In contrast, when we study how far today's Church has drifted from the leadership of devout, prayerful, theologically inclined saints of generations past, we see that an increasingly lackadaisical attitude, reinforced by the conveniences and leisure of the world's offering, it's certainly no stretch of the imagination to see that our Body of believers has been reshaped in a negative manner. And not just in the Church, but throughout our entire society, we are seeing results of the shaping that has occurred throughout generations.

Selective Exposure/Omission

A little more than a year ago, my (Allie Henson's) husband and I stopped in on a local bookstore in a small town we were traveling through. We noticed that the bumper stickers on cars, political signs in yards, and messages in local businesses all seemed to have an anti-conservative flavor. In fact, that's putting it mildly, as some of the statements we were seeing even had slightly hostile wording. As we were driving out of the town, my husband mentioned that the shop we had visited only had books on the liberal agenda displayed. There seemed to be a lack of balance in the presentation of media in that town.

Of course.

One of the simplest ways that groups of people are groomed to embrace a certain point of view is by selective exposure. When the masses don't hear both sides of an issue, the one that's regularly argued becomes familiar. Over time, senses warm to this position, and a large percentage of people tend to push against anything that would challenge that position. It is no secret that people are afraid of what they don't know, they fear change, and they tend to be closed-minded about anything that contradicts the building blocks of their comfort zone. Thus, the shape of their foundation can be manipulated by filling their proximity with only a certain agenda. When the Church's core beliefs come to be labeled as "hate speech" (which will be discussed later), then they begin to disappear from mainstream public view, because they're no longer accepted as politically correct. Additionally, what little Scripture the public may be hearing and seeing is either taken out of context and twisted in a negative light or presented as archaic, old-fashioned, and outdated. Thus, the community is sanitized of all godly messages for the sake of political correctness, and Christianity is removed from the public eye in general. At that point, reasserting scriptural values is perceived as threatening rather than foundational.

Of course, there are times when selective exposure is appropriate. For example, a four-year-old doesn't need to know where the keys to the gun safe are or how to open it. The omission of this info is both expected and responsible, until the child has developed the appropriate level of maturity. So, in no way are we saying that every minute fact should be given to every individual all of the time. Our point is that, as we look at what types of subject matter, propaganda, and even news reports the masses are being exposed to, we can see a spike in the promotion of certain agendas and a diminishment in the advancement of others. We see this played out, for example, when it becomes trendy to hate a certain politician or celebrity. From that moment on, the target's every wrong move is overpublicized, while his or her redeeming acts are ignored. Such tactics in the realm of public media have extreme shaping power in our society.

Door-in-the-Face/Foot-in-the-Door

These two manipulation tactics are similar, but each has certain elements that occur in different order. In studying both group and individual conformity/compliance in the school of social psychology, we see these techniques emerge in the world every day to influence the majority. Additionally, we see hints of these approaches nearly everywhere, once we've learned to recognize them. When successfully carried out, they often produce the desired results: The masses accept a concept they previously rejected, or they come to regard something that may have seemed irregular before as commonplace.

The "foot-in-the-door technique" involves introducing an idea or request on a small scale to prevent immediate rejection, and it builds from there. For example, in 1966, a number of people were asked to sign a safe-driving petition. Many agreed to do so, because it was only a simple signature toward indicating support of a good cause. Two weeks later, the members of this group, along with others, were asked to place "a large, ugly sign" in their yards instructing those on the road to drive carefully.[83] The majority of those who had signed the petition agreed to post the sign as well, but most of those who *hadn't* been involved in the petition part of the social experiment refused to place the sign. By starting small—just a "foot in the door," a signature, but a statement the signer could personally connect to and remember for two weeks before the bar was raised—people became more open-minded about participating in the safe-driving cause on another level.[84]

In today's media, we see this strategy used regularly. When carried out on a collective level, the "support" is measured by our lack of protest. This can be done by briefly including something potentially controversial in the background of a song, book, or movie, or it can emerge in other areas of culture in small, isolated, and seemingly harmless increments. Once the debatable issue has become generally accepted as a piece of the background, it is slowly brought to the forefront and presented in a more overt fashion. At this point, any protests are met with the reminder that the matter "has been around for a long time." Furthermore, since it will have likely been conditioned over a period of years, those who recall a time without it will likely be pointing to a distant period gone by, making the protest now seem old-fashioned and out-of-touch. Those who have been successfully conditioned to embrace the element will often support their stance with phrases such as "this is [insert current year]" or "get over it."

To take one example, in 1962's black-and-white film *What Ever Happened to Baby Jane?* starring Bette Davis and Joan Crawford, Davis' character is ragingly jealous of Crawford's. In frustration, the former utters the words "you miserable—" then she performs the lip movement to form an expletive (rhyming with "witch") that can't be heard because of the timely sound of a buzzer in the background (a part of the movie's plot).[85] To the audience, it appears as though Davis' character speaks the entire phrase. Such language hadn't yet been accepted into filmmaking when the movie was released, yet, the profanity took place with diminished impact on the audience because it was communicated without being *heard.* Slipping in curse words in this manner was the only strategy many filmmakers dared to use at that time. However, as moviegoers grew more accustomed to vulgarity via this type of exposure, actors were allowed to utter such words and phrases fully, uncensored, out loud. Fast-forward to today, and we now hear profanity in movies and television programs, on magazine covers, and even in brand names and logos on product packaging, t-shirts, bumper stickers, and more. Foul language is simply everywhere these days, and that's because, decades ago, the public was slowly prepared to accept it. The same type of conditioning can be seen regarding such issues as nudity, sexual content, violence, sexualization of minors, devaluation of human life, illicit subject matter, and political agendas.

Absolutely without doubt, those who wish to drive an anti-Christian agenda would, and have, used this tactic by hinting that Christians are incompetent, unfair, money-hungry, hypocritical, shallow, selfish, judgmental, and so on. And as those concepts become acceptable (with any disproof omitted by selective exposure), the accusations increase to a greater indictment of Christians' moral fiber. Then, every time the name of a believer—or a belief—is dragged through the media mud, the concept is further solidified.

Even sneakier than the "foot-in-the-door" technique of conditioning is called "door-in-the-face," because it comes from the opposite direction and tends to be unexpected. This method provides the false sense of security that comes with believing we have overcome a situation, when really, we've been duped into letting our guard down. The process is simple: A real request is hidden behind one that will be rejected. The way this plays out is simple, as in the following example:

Betty wants to borrow Jane's brand-new, leather, high-heeled shoes. She knows Jane spent about $100 on this addition to her wardrobe, and is certain that she will say no to this request, since she has damaged items Jane has loaned her in the past. She goes to talk to Jane, but instead of asking for the shoes outright, she recalls an expensive handbag that cost Jane nearly $300. Instead of asking to borrow the heels, she asks to use the purse. As expected, Jane refuses. Acting hurt, or maybe disappointed, Betty leaves. The next day, she returns to ask Jane if she can borrow the shoes. Jane, feeling bad for turning down Betty's initial request, gives in. After all, the shoes have a lower replacement value than the handbag, and she's already turned Betty down once recently. Jane's conscience feels a boost (after she felt guilty for not loaning her friend the heels), and Betty leaves with the very item she originally wanted. "The success of the door-in-the-face technique is probably due to our tendency toward mutual reciprocity, making mutual concessions," explains psychologist and author Richard Griggs. "The person making the requests appears to have made a concession by moving to the much smaller request [the individual being manipulated feels obligated to make a concession as well]."[86] In this case, both Betty and Jane are happy, but Jane has no idea that she's been played.

Maybe this scenario will seem more familiar: Your teenaged daughter wants to go shopping at the mall on Saturday with her friends—and she wants you to give her a hundred dollars to spend while she's there. Instead, she asks if she can go on an overnight trip with her friends—an excursion that will cost four hundred dollars. When, for whatever reason, you say no to that, she responds, "Okay...Daddy—" [insert eye-batting here] "—then can I have...?"

You see where this is going; parents fall for this strategy every day!

Although the scheme appears unabashedly manipulative and controlling, its common use in society is no more controversial than the sales pitch used to move the latest new car off the Ford lot or sell the last oil painting to the highest bidder at an auction house. And, just like the foot-in-the-door method, its sister technique, door-in-the-face, can be (and often is) practiced upon the public to incite a cultural change in our attitudes.

People presented with the first idea have time to refute it and identify why it's not practical. Meanwhile, in the pursuit of "slamming the door shut" on that, they're also required to think about the grander picture presented to them, even if only momentarily considering how the proposed idea *could* work, hypothetically. Still putting this together?

Taking the example about Betty borrowing Jane's three-hundred-dollar handbag, Jane had to entertain the "what-if" idea that she *might* loan it to Betty before she could identify the reasons she ultimately would not. Just visiting the possibility imprinted it on her memory as a notion that, even subconsciously, continued to be considered. Rehearsed conversations with Betty play out in Jane's head as her resolve strengthens; she prepares for future confrontation about the issue, should there be hard feelings. Every time she sees her handbag hanging in her closet, she reminds herself of how she feels about the answer she gave Betty—whether the reflection is one of regret or relief. The more Jane's subconscious thoughts and hypothetical-scenario "memories" solidify in the back of her mind, the more her cognitive, conscious mind revisits and accepts the idea that it *could* happen. Having played and replayed myriad potential scenarios in her mind, Jane is relieved when Betty returns, *only* asking for her shoes.

So, when this strategy is used for large groups or even entire populations, it begins with something grand, unreasonable, perhaps even abrasive. For example, consider the over-the-top manner of illicitly cruel behavior depicted of those who follow (and twist) the Bible in *The Handmaid's Tale* (more on this in an upcoming chapter). The series introduces concepts of extreme, ritualistic, sexual abuse being committed by these individuals, but because it is done in the realms of entertainment, the "accusation" is tapered down to a hypothetical for the viewer's mind to process and ponder. The result is seedlings of factional polarity between Christians and non-Christians. A suggested scenario is presented, but under the guise of a premise so outrageous that people don't even have to refuse it; after all, it's complete fiction. Yet the idea is then a set of hypotheticals planted in the back of people's minds, and even seeded deep into their subconscious, asking seemingly unrealistic but severe questions like "Christians: What if it's ever 'us' or 'them'"? As the brain plays with all the directions a fictional scenario such as that in *The Handmaid's Tale* could go, people begin to watch Christians differently in the real world as well: Anything the Church does that looks awry is met with suspicion, those who claim to believe and follow the Gospel but turn out to be hypocrites solidify this wariness, once-respected biblical principles are relabeled as "hate speech," and in general, the public begins to see the Church more as a threat than as a force for good in the world.

Create a Problem...Present the Solution

I (Allie Henson) will never forget when, late in 2007, the price of wheat, rice, and barley spiked. Stories speculating the arrival of crisis-level food shortages were featured on the news. There was talk of super-inflation and food rationing, and I heard people quoting Revelation 6:6 not only in church, but in public settings: "A measure of wheat for a penny, and three measures of barley for a penny." It was an economically unstable time, and all types of conjecture riddled conversations in workplaces, grocery stores, and bank lines—especially among Christians.

I had heard that local grocery stores had begun to limit the number of certain grain and rice products a customer could purchase at a time, but when I experienced the rationing firsthand, it still threw me. Somehow, the gravity of the situation was driven home in that single moment, and I immediately believed the reports of the food-supply shortage were valid. I remember seeing those around me give way to fear; many began stocking up food and supplies. I'll admit that, during that season, I kept a *very* well-stocked pantry. To be sure, there's a hunger problem throughout America and the rest of the world, and it's prudent to be prepared. Yet, I eventually realized that those driving the panic were far removed from the problem itself. And while the shortages of certain foods were real, other groceries remained in healthy supply. But they weren't brought into focus as an alternative—which would have helped reduce public panic (via utilization of the omission tactic). At least, not at first...

Then it happened: In January of 2008, the FDA announced that it had approved animal cloning for use in food-livestock resources. As we talked about earlier in the book, cloning had been a highly debated subject that met with much resistance, and its approval was worded in vague language. The administration's response to consumer concern was dismissive and unspecific: "'The milk and meat for cattle, swine and goat clones are as safe to eat as the food we eat every day,' said Randall Lutter of the FDA."[87]

For some, cloning *anything* brought moral questions to the forefront of discussion. However, setting aside the issue of ethics and morality, most people were simply "weirded out" by the idea of eating something that hadn't been naturally bred. Those who opposed the approval of cloning also pointed out that lab-raised animals use the same amount of resources as naturally bred ones—on top of the additional costs involved in the cloning process. Thus, many questioned the true motives of the practice. They stated that cloning to create food was gratuitous and out-landish—not *at all* cost effective, and insisted that breeding healthy live-stock would always be more practical than lab-generating any meat, for any reason. Add to this the ambiguity of the FDA's guidelines regarding the process, and many of those watching were alarmed. A number of qualified, outspoken—but largely unheeded—critics called it a "huge, uncontrolled experiment on the American people," for which there could potentially be "consequent effects the FDA has not yet looked at that could impact human health."[88] While some opponents of cloning arose, others were simply happy to see the headlines drift away from the topic of food shortage, hyper-inflation, and potential hunger-related riots. They were just glad "they" had found a way to feed us all again.

Do you see what happened there? Imagine strolling through the aisles of a grocery store and seeing labels that boast, "New, improved, lab-grown, cloned beef!" on display in the meat section. *Gross.* Few people would ever buy that. So what changed? A desperate time had fostered panic for many, causing them to consider an idea that previously hadn't met their high standards. And, for those promoting the practice of cloning meat for the masses, this "crisis" provided a place and time to seize the moment and affirm their itinerary. While much of the population was hunkering down in fear, getting ready to "ride out the disaster" of the looming foot shortage, an opening presented itself through which those with dubious intentions could advance their alternate agendas. And, by the time this mind-job had taken place, many were relieved to see the *very thing* that they previously would not have accepted.

This is a recurring theme in society's trends: When an idea meets adversity, it is withdrawn for a time, then reintroduced when it can be presented as the answer to a dire problem. (This will likely be a tactic utilized when the Mark of the Beast is implemented; more on this in a future chapter). The makers of the problem and solution are often one and the same, with the fear factor as their key selling point. You may have heard the adage that "some people make their own storms and then get mad when it rains."[89] There's a lot of truth to that. But, what about those who create rainfall, then come out to sell their umbrellas? We should be on watch for such sinister peddlers.

Gaslighting

Gaslighting is one of the most subversive of all the forms of manipulation, because its victims usually begin to doubt their own perception of reality. Despite their instincts to the contrary, they usually feel powerless because of their self-disbelief. Gaslighting involves a great deal of lying—but the deceit is subtle and is easily twisted to look like truth.

The term "gaslight" originates from the 1940 and 1944 films by the same name that have similar plots: A man planning to murder his wife first makes her believe that she is losing her mind or having a nervous breakdown. Items are moved around, the gas-fed lights seemingly adjust on their own, and other strange incidents occur; the young bride can't account for these oddities, but feels she must be responsible. Her husband is behind these actions, but he feigns innocence. Reminding the young woman that mental illness runs in her family, he suggests that perhaps she is succumbing to similar weakness. At one point, he removes a painting from the wall, hides it, then insinuates that his bride has intentionally hidden it and forgotten it—a manipulation (among many others) that causes her to doubt her reality, her memory, and her sanity. It's not until, with the help of a trusted friend, the young woman discovers her husband's scheme and finally realizes that she is *not* losing her grip on reality.

This type of manipulation is very common in abusive relationships, as well as in bullying. It often develops over time, with the perpetrator, early on, lavishing praise and compliments on the future victim. The positive affirmations, however, slowly but steadily become infected with "a snide comment every so often...and then it starts ramping up. Even the brightest, most self-aware people can be sucked into gaslighting—it is that effective."[90] If the strategy is allowed to escalate, eventually the perpetrator can even assert that the one being duped hasn't seen something the person *knows* he or she saw, and the latter will acquiesce, believing himself or herself to be confused.

Perhaps you've known someone who speaks to you condescendingly—for example, a smooth-talking bully at work—but, when you attempt to recall precisely *what* the person said or did that was so offensive, you can't pinpoint it. Gaslighters are sometimes so smooth that they can demean a family member or coworker in a room *filled* with other people, yet the jab can go unrecognized.

In talking about gaslighters, their victims often make statements such as, "It wasn't *what* he said, it was really more *how* he said it." Folks who tend to believe the best in people are inclined to be particularly vulnerable to this type of manipulation, because their propensity to give the benefit of the doubt immobilizes them; they become their own worst enemy. In fact, the power behind this strategy relies on the notion that the victims will question their certainty of reality, and they'll even begin to perceive that *they* themselves are at the root of the problem. Using the example of an interaction with a condescending person, a target of this method may begin to wonder, "Maybe he wasn't that way at all; maybe it's *me* who is the problem. Maybe I'm judgmental. Maybe I need to work on self-improvement." See how quickly this approach can morph from a situation of bullying to one of the attacked person resorting to self-blame? (This dynamic is rampant in situations of domestic abuse; often, one partner accepts the blame for aggravating the other's temper, "causing" the other to lash out physically.)

In addition to the reality-questioning element of this approach is the fact that it often occurs slowly, over a period of time, and is mixed with positive reinforcement, which further incites confusion. For example, perhaps the condescending individual we've talked about earlier also pays you gratuitous compliments now and again. Considering the sometimes-disdainful words spoken by this person, these flattering statements will likely make you feel very good—a nice reprieve from all the negatives. This, in turn, fortifies the self-doubt: "He's not such a bad guy; perhaps I *am* the problem…" For many, the result is an elevated effort to please the person out of the desire to rectify the problem and in hopes of finally gaining the gaslighter's approval. Unfortunately, this response often feeds a narcissistic or self-gratifying aspect of their own personality; thus, attempts to please the other person meet even higher (although still subtle) demands—and peace in the relationship is never found.

For example, a man might, in a disgusted tone, tell his wife in the privacy of their bedroom, "You need some new dresses. You've gained so much weight since having the baby that none of those look good on you anymore." Likely, his wife would rightfully feel insulted. Later, however, in a gathering such as a party, the man might smile and say, "I was just telling Lily I'd like to take her dress shopping this week." Of course, this comment—out of context and presented differently than earlier—draws gleeful and even jealous smiles from Lily's friends. But this isn't how she is struck by the comment. For her, it's a public reminder of the cruel reality that her husband has told her, in so many words, that she isn't as attractive to him as she used to be. However, if she shows offense in front of their friends, he'll feign innocence and say, "I'm just trying to spoil you, honey. After all, you deserve it, with all the work you've put in since the baby was born." (This is the most common type of lying that occurs in gaslighting: spinning the truth to prevent victims from being able to back their own argument).

Then those at the gathering will no doubt tell Lily how very lucky she is to have a husband who cares about her enough to spoil her, and they'll remark on how *especially* fortunate she is that he, unlike their own spouses, is willing to go shopping *with* her. However, later that week, when her husband takes her on that shopping trip, she is miserable, she feels fat or ugly in everything she tries on, and she doesn't choose clothes based on her own preferences. Rather, she looks for something—anything—that *he* thinks she's pretty in, hoping to finally meet his approval and fix the problems in their relationship. Likely she'll see her own physical, post-baby body as the issue; she may respond to that by self-criticizing—a misdirected effort to get relief. Instead of seeing the gaslighting for what it is, she may turn to diet and exercise for help, but she could also even begin a dangerous venture into behaviors that lead to eating disorders.

On a large scale, gaslighting occurs in our society every day, although it can look a little different than the husband/wife example given here. When we discuss how it plays out across the populace, the first major symptom of gaslighting is that culture seems suspended in a state of constant questioning regarding reality. For example, nearly anyone these days will admit—even *laughingly*—that they're not sure what news is true versus what's fake. But this is no joking matter. Think about the implications of a population that's become so accustomed to being lied to that even public news outlets are perceived as knowingly giving false information, and this is passively accepted. Consider the fact that, in 2016, candidate Hillary Clinton was *simultaneously* potentially headed for either prison or the presidency! How had we arrived at a world where the same person could be facing both possible futures at once? Our population no longer knows what's real and what's not. Elections of all types feel, to many, like charades put on to placate a public who will never *really* control the outcome. Selective omission of details in news reports cause us to wonder if events occurring or charges/accusations against public servants are truly represented. And, caught in the middle are the masses—who attempt to decipher what in the world around them is *truly happening.*

News broadcasters lie, and we take it in stride. Officials fib, and we accept it with resignation. We hear of organizational corruption and we shrug, unsurprised. Bankers operate shady dealings at our expense, yet we shake our heads and go about our day. We *expect* falsehoods from politicians of all ranks. Teachers, and, sadly, even a lot of preachers talk out of both sides of their mouths, and the wary population has grown mindful that when it comes to the public arena, nothing can be perceived as real.

As we touched on in the example of the husband gaslighting his wife, this type of manipulation often results in the victim's willingness to self-improve in order to remedy the issue. Gaslighting plays out a little differently, however, when used on the masses. One reason is that there is no single entity to appease and gain the approval of (until the manifestation of Antichrist; more on that later). So those who mistrust nearly all the powers that be begin to shift their attention away from politicians, organizations, institutions, rulers, and—sadly, for those who've been let down by religious leaders—even God, and refocus it on *causes*. After all, people will let you down, right? But *causes* are worthy. To fix what is broken, many folks look to a world in need of help and search for a place to sow good seeds.

Understand that this *can* be a good thing. Our desire to make things better—whether in our relationships or in the world around us—is a reflection of the fact that we are made in the image of God. When He gave Adam dominion over the earth and when He ordered the first couple to be fruitful and multiply (Genesis 1:26–28), He invited mankind to replicate the creative and nurturing process He had initiated during the first six days of Creation (Genesis 2:2). Our desire to "fix" what is wrong in the world is God-given and ordained. In fact, this innate, driving need is ultimately the desire for redemption; we want to find the missing part of our souls that allows us to be drawn to God.

Unfortunately, just as in the example of the gaslighting man and his wife, this yearning can be exploited, and it often is. Many give their hearts, hands, time, and resources to causes they deem worthy, but that ultimately exploit them. In such cases, passionate, earnest folks may begin the search for truth, justice, and world improvement with a wide-eyed, open-hearted zeal. Then, sadly, the enthusiasm of activism sometimes overrides discernment, and, depending on the cause, unwary people may find themselves on a bandwagon heading for a destructive destination.

Polarize the Crowd via "Causes"

All of us, whether or not we'll admit it, have the deep-seeded need to believe that our lives have purpose and meaning. As stated previously, in a world where truth is hard to find, many engage their efforts and resources in *causes* to try to meet this need. This is a simple, under-standable, and even healthy concept that needs no elaboration. How-ever, also as noted earlier, a compulsion toward activism can be exploited and abused. Sadly, when this occurs, those who have given their all to a movement are often left with little to show for their sacrifice. How can a motivation that starts out healthy become destructive? This occurs when the "cause" becomes the label by which people expend their energy, yet their connections with others are cut off. This may seem contradictory, but subtleties reveal when a cause is more destructive than it is good. Allow us to explain.

Many avenues of activism are based on a desire to help people. Obviously, lots of folks join up with this in mind. However, they may soon realize that it isn't the "cause" itself that's motivating them; it's the fact that they want to help others. For example, if I (Allie Henson) join an effort to raise awareness regarding human equality, my compulsion isn't about bolstering the words "human equality," which are touted in numerous arenas every day. Rather, it's about the fact that I have com-passion on those who don't yet enjoy equality in all of its fullness, and I want to help remedy that. Essentially, my motivation for participating in the movement is my concern for *people*, not for the cause itself. As such, the program I join is merely a vehicle I use to take me to my goal regarding people.

Unfortunately, this simple line is often blurred; as a result, people who serve in movements that occupy similar spaces but who don't see eye to eye often begin to see each other as enemies. This happens often, and is a sad exploitation of the energies of those who became activists so they could *help* people. Sadly, it divides them *against* their neighbors. In these cases, the movement itself hijacks the passions of those involved, and the connection to fellow humanity they sought—what motivated them to begin with—is unwittingly traded for loyalty to a faction.

The danger of a society that becomes heavily involved in pursuing causes is easily seen when it becomes divided against itself, which we see in spades during this current tumultuous time. Rather than having a population that unites to make the world a better place, many are at war with one another over issues such as methods, political correctness, and expenditures of resources. Soon, the good intentions behind the movement's original goals are buried in division that turns the very individuals who joined to improve society *against* each other on the basis of technicalities.

Unfortunately, an added danger in activism is that, at the administrative and structural levels, causes are susceptible to being seized by individuals who have self-serving or ulterior motives. Considering the current state of events in our country, it's easy to see that many organizations founded with good intentions have transformed into entities far different from what their original founders had in mind. This is the case with political movements, charities, philanthropic efforts, and, sadly, even religious institutions. Many of these were built upon the compassion, resources, dreams and visions, energy, blood, sweat, and tears of their originators, but subsequently, they evolved into something that more closely resembles a corporate machine.

Endeavors that begin with good intentions can become the means by which people are exploited, but we see it happen every day. Many of the movements that our young generations are caught up in are highly divisive—even when they operate under the heading of "equality." Those who disagree with a particular worldview are considered enemies or radicals who should be feared, their statements even labeled "hate speech." In such cases, those who once viewed the world as a place where all should be lovingly accepted soon find that they, themselves, cannot accept another because of these clashing perspectives.

Here is the crux of the issue: "Causes" are not people, and those who serve in them but lose sight of surrounding humanity are misled. Additionally, those who become detached from the original dream of these crusades' founders can quickly realize they are passengers on a machine that has captured and derailed their original passions. Activism is only a vehicle by which one's desire to connect with other human beings manifests. When it separates rather than unites people, the participants' motives are exploited. Because of this, no one can find fulfillment by serving a movement, because the link with other human beings can perpetually be severed in the process. When the group is separated, it's a type of sociocultural civil war (this is what we saw in our cities in 2020). In this way, movements that masquerade as the glue holding people together actually divide them, tying up resources, energy, and time. The sad cost is that the population—comprised of many who earnestly strive to make the world a better place in their own way—loses hope, feels defeated, and feels farther removed from finding *truth* (exacerbating the large-scale gaslighting going on). That which promises supporters a place of belonging and the pride of accomplishment only reveals rifts with fellow man. In this way, social and political causes *can* be (but aren't always) the secular world's counterfeit substitute for the camaraderie Jesus intended when He brought the Church Body together to bring light to the world. When they fall into this category, they always leave followers empty.

Learned Helplessness

Learned helplessness is a method of manipulation based on the premise that people, subjected to an undesirable element outside their control, eventually lose the power to remove it. For example, a man may finally resign himself to the fact that he'll keep hearing the neighbor's barking dog because his efforts to silence the animal have failed and the pet's owner doesn't respond to requests for action. A parent stops fighting with school administrators regarding "required" sex-ed classes she doesn't want her daughter attending; she's given up because it feels as though nobody is listening and her protests aren't getting her anywhere. An elderly man in a care facility experiences a loss of vitality; as a result, he becomes inactive, relinquishing his independence and trusting the medical staff to care for his needs.[91] Again, this type of manipulation stems from the response to a situation—more specifically, it depends on a person's sense of empowerment.

Here's a quick illustration of how this works, using a financial analogy. Let's say that two people—we'll call them Judy and Steve—are given identical budgets, and are observed to see whether they are able save any money. Judy regards saving money as hard; she won't be able to make it work. On the other hand, Steve thinks that it's always possible to save money, regardless of how tight the funds. When financial hardships are placed on both to impede their ability to reserve any funds, each will respond by either feeling powerless and giving up or by realizing that he/she can control his/her own destiny and thus trying even harder to reach the savings goals.

Ultimately, it's likely that Judy won't have set anything aside—perhaps she'll even have spent money that she *could have* saved. In fact, she probably thought she might as well enjoy any extra pennies, since saving them wouldn't amount to much, anyway. The bottom line: Judy, the unempowered money manager, won't even try. For people with this disposition, learned helplessness can be triggered by additional hardships or by making things easy enough for them that the attitude "why try?" is fostered.

At the end of the day—or the fiscal year—Steve, however, will likely have money set aside. That's simply because his perception of his own power over the situation compels him to *create* opportunities for saving. He doesn't reach his goals because it's easy, but by pinching pennies, making sacrifices, cutting corners, clipping coupons, and practicing other forms of fiscal ingenuity. For Steve, the empowerment he feels fuels his motivation to create his own strategic opportunities.

However, the world is full of people who aren't fully aware of their own abilities, or whose willingness to make the effort reduces over time because of resistance. For these folks, the more obstacles they face in meeting their goals, the more likely they are to stop trying. Worse, when complacency is rewarded, it serves a double whammy against their motivation to take power over their situation.

The way we most often see this manipulation method at work in today's society can be summed up in the old adage, "Nice guys finish last." Many who try to act nobly or with moral integrity face lots of opposition. For instance, consider the way many tax laws financially favor couples who are living together instead of those who are legally married. As another example, think about those who believe abortion is morally wrong but quietly accept that it's an established practice now, because fights against its legalization and practice have been so regularly lost. In the same vein, most people are aware that child abuse is a rampant problem, but because they feel powerless to keep it from happening, they do nothing. Via these and many other ways that our culture has been shaped, low moral standards have been fostered and reinforced across the populace.

Another case can be seen in those who attempt to improve their situations by working full-time jobs or starting businesses. Often, despite tight finances, they don't qualify for certain types of public assistance that would help them greatly when added to their existing—albeit inadequate—income. However, with *no* money coming in, they're eligible for a larger level of economic help and thus they experience less financial stress. At this point, some may say that public assistance is *where* learned helplessness comes from, but it isn't quite as simple as that. When our civic, socioeconomic structure is aligned in such a way that those who *attempt* to improve their situations are at less of an advantage than those who don't, then the lack of effort becomes a positively reinforced behavior—and entrapment. Unfortunately, over a generation, children are raised believing that they, like their adult examples, aren't powerful enough to improve their situations. When they try, taking on that first, entry-level job, they forfeit the assistance that would otherwise be available if they weren't working at all. Without any post-high school education, minimum-wage-paying jobs are most likely all they're qualified to obtain. Yet again, if they attempt to improve the situation by attending college or technical school, they'll probably be overwhelmed by scholastic and employment duties, alongside being financially strapped. This, then, reinforces the notion that it's easier to relinquish personal power in trade for being taken care of.

In the meantime, we lavish esteem upon the government we look to for our needs—the benevolent "they" that makes our laws, collects tax money, provides public amenities, and holds increasing sovereignty over the people in order to provide protection of and care for the masses. For those who suffer from learned helplessness, there's no reason to challenge this entity, nor would they have the means. This is the trade that's made when relying on a higher force to meet one's needs: submission to that authority.

The best assistance that can be implemented in the public sphere is the kind that empowers citizens to become responsible for themselves again in every way. Merely allocating resources to people, assuming full care for their needs but never teaching them how to take charge of their own situation, ultimately disempowers those they claim to be helping.

Complicate Truth

Now let's take a look at the spiritual aspect that exists when a crowd is manipulated into misconceptions regarding truth. In the beginning, God presented absolute truths that came attached to moral values. As time progresses, mankind has migrated farther away from those boundaries, trading them in for more palatable ones. Surely, the last few centuries have transformed the kernels of modernism into the full-scale rewriting of reality through what is now termed "postmodernism."

Before the Renaissance, cultures were homogenized, and one's role in society was predefined and predictable. But the Renaissance ushered in intellectual, cultural, religious, and economic changes that prompted people to begin searching for deeper meaning in the weighty matters of life, including philosophy and even personal depth, meaning, fulfillment, and liberty. Humanism sparked the intrigue of those who began to see the individual as "the center of his or her own universe and... personal achievement...[as] the noblest of pursuits."[92] With the individual as the center of focus and personal fulfillment as the measure of success, mankind hit a new level of self-awareness. When the Gutenberg press was invented in 1450,[93] these ideas were further propagated in two ways: 1) Reading material became available to everyone, not just to the wealthy elite or the scholarly; and 2) Publishing was more readily available to those who wished to circulate new and radical ideas. Mainstream authorship began its slow migration away from traditional and biblical perspectives and began to indulge the "new" and "enlightened" ways of thinking. While many wonderful innovations came out of this time, the Renaissance also became the historical hinge upon which the ultimate authority of Scripture began to see competition from media that offered the idea that there are other ways than God for pursuing righteousness, fulfillment, and even entry to heaven. Each trail of thought flourished to the point that, after fast-forwarding hundreds of years, we entered the modern era—which in turn has grown into postmodernism. The differences between these periods and worldviews are many, but the one that best serves our study is the fact that the Renaissance opened a search for more elaborate realities humans could find, while the most recent age, the postmodern era, seeks to redefine that which is and carve it into that which we would have it to be. As Douglas Groothuis explains: "Modernism began with the attempt to discern objective reality without recourse to divine revelation or religious tradition, which it dismissed as merely culturally contingent and ultimately superstitious.... Postmodernists affirm relativism even at the level of language itself."[94] In other words, our communication has changed to the point that we now define truth as being anything we perceive it to be. Truncating what could be chapters of elaboration, we land at such a simple assessment as this: It's the shifting of "*the* truth" into "*my* truth." The distinction looks and sounds small, but the repercussions are enormous.

When we refer to "*the* truth," we assume there is a solid, universal, absolute truth that everyone shares: The sun is hot; rain makes the ground wet; cows are large animals.

When we begin to refer to "*my* truth," we no longer have the common, reliable certainties that are known by all. Here's what happens when we apply that idea to earlier truths we listed:

- "The sun is hot." *My* (Allie Henson's) truth is that it is snowing outside, and I am cold, so the sun is not nearly hot enough.
- "Rain makes the ground wet." I (Allie Henson) spent a lot of my adult life in Oregon. Thus, I have seen a lot of rain in my time, so *my* truth is that after a light drizzle, the ground can barely be considered wet.
- "Cows are large animals." A cow may be large, but it is vastly outranked by hippopotami, elephants, and rhinos, so *my* truth is that cows are, at best, medium-sized animals.

Certainly, these statements are subjective, allowing for differing opinions as to an individual's truth. The problem comes in when interpreting "one's own truth" impedes our perception of absolute truth. Here's what we mean: Show a crowd of people a brick, and they could see any number of things, such as the start of a building, a weapon, an innovation that changed the world around 7000 BC,[95] or even, if dropped, a broken toe. Yet, none of these impressions alters the fact that everyone in the group likely sees a concrete rectangle. So, where is the disconnect between each person's truth and the fact that the brick is an inanimate, concrete block? It's this: Everyone's "truth" is actually his or her own perception of the brick's potential based on his or her experience with the object; it's *not* a property of the item itself.

I (Allie Henson) can say that "my truth" calls this brick a person—I can even give it a name and paint a face on it. However, the brick will never form a relationship with me. I can decide that it will be the heir to all my worldly goods, but it can certainly never spend or enjoy the money. I can call it a piece of my future house, but all it will really be is one foundational element that *I* will be responsible to place and build upon. Even regarding its connection to innovations in construction practices that occurred in 7000 BC, unless I'm holding one of the *actual* ancient bricks (which, technically, would be made of different material), I still only have a *representation* of that innovation. Essentially, as stated earlier, I hold a concrete rectangle, nothing more.

Some things are absolute, universal truths—whether we like it or not.

In the postmodern world we live in, the concept of reliable, fundamental truths has simply gone out of style. It is the prerogative of all people to dissect each morsel of reality under the lens of what they perceive to be *their own truth*; for many, it's become an outlet for expressing individualism and/or creativity. Redefining truth with more profoundness or ingenuity than one's predecessors becomes a challenge that, if successful, draws accolades of having the "more enlightened mind" that sees the most unique and progressive version of reality. The secularization of society has taken God, His supremacy, and His law from the center of focus and placed man in the position of the final authority by which our own standards of morality and fulfillment come. As this revolution has occurred, mankind has placed himself on his own throne of deity, and those who still believe in and follow God are seen as old-fashioned, unevolved, stuck in their ways, and hateful. Eventually, their statements (and even their faith) are at risk of being labeled as hate speech, censored, and legislated.

Having abandoned common belief in a God who imposes absolute truth/moral law, we no longer have a common thread of right and wrong to unite us. See the following excerpt from *Unscrambling the Millennial Paradox*:

> If there is no God, there is no standard by which morality is required to be measured. And if morality is left completely up to individual preferences [filtered through such subjectivities as "*my truth*"], then we can decide that acts previously considered sinful or even heinous are no longer immoral based upon personal enjoyment. [We can see this progression through the evolution of depravity portrayed on movies and media in comparison with increased conservatism of decades past]. Some individuals even escalate this philosophy by believing that God is a mere state of mind or other attribute found in each of us. Beyond this, people then were given a path by which they could literally choose their own reality, free of judgment from others.[96]

It has taken years for us to get here, but know one thing: Complicating truthful perspectives *will* be a tool used to groom the masses to embrace unthinkable deeds.

Skew the Perspective on Love

Despite the fact that many people would like to assert their autonomy apart from God, a recurrent theme throughout history says that mankind wants to be connected to a divine authority. Those who study human nature throughout the ages often draw the common conclusion that mankind, of his own accord, consistently comes up with a religious system that involves such powers as good, evil, and hierarchies of entities embracing both factions.[97] Other than the modern Western culture, few civilizations have evolved to become free of religious belief. Some have even claimed that there is such a thing as a "God gene:...the need for God [which] may be a crucial trait stamped deeper and deeper into our genome with every passing generation."[98] This is reinforced by anthropologists who repeatedly discover "tribes living in remote areas [who] come up with a concept of God as readily as nations living shoulder to shoulder...[which makes] a fairly strong indication that the idea is preloaded in the genome rather than picked up on the fly."[99]

In addition to cultural studies linking various civilizations to the compulsion toward religion, we see that when people are is separated from the notion of a Higher Power, they often feel listless, depressed, lost, or without purpose. While many assert themselves to be the center of their own universe, they often experience an emptiness that's hard to account for in a postmodern, "enlightened" state of mind. Yet, many are surprised to learn that, following the Renaissance, a sweeping melancholy brushed across much of the population. Termed the "Renaissance Melancholy," it was the depressed and directionless aftermath of "enlightenment" many experienced when they realized that the exchange they made for their illumination was the stability and absolute reality that came with believing in a Higher Power. (Maybe most people haven't heard about this because of selective omission?)

We read in one article about this period that "human action was [no longer] judged in terms of right and wrong or good and evil...but in... concrete validity, effectiveness, and beauty...once the unity of design had lost its authority, certainty about the final value of human actions was no longer...found."[100]

Studies on this subject abound, and curious readers will find that we've only scratched the tip of the iceberg. Suffice it to say, it's more than believable theory that something deep inside each of us desires to be connected to God. After all, we were created to live in community with Him and with each other, in a beautiful garden setting where all our needs were provided. Unfortunately, at the Fall of Man, we lost access to that environment wherein we were created to live, and since then, our plight has been to try to recreate and reenter this type of utopia. Equally unfortunate is the fact that we can never reproduce the ideal conditions our Maker originally assigned for us. (This is why every attempt to create heaven on earth ends in a lackluster, troubled version of communal living, often under the authority of a sometimes-crazed leader who likely has a skewed sense of authority or religion.)

Since the human race was removed from the Garden, we've compensated for the loss by polarizing between two pursuits: chasing God relentlessly and trying to narrow the gap between ourselves and the Almighty. The second—which, sadly, occurs more often—involves running farther from God, denying our need for Him, and filling the resulting breach with other attempts to numb the pain and fill in the empty place. When all efforts to satiate the desire for a connection to the Supreme come up short, we attempt to "repress...[our] desire for love because...[this unmet need] leaves us vulnerable to being hurt."[101] God is aware of this aching in the human soul and meets this need by offering the remedy in the two most important commandments He gave: 1) that we have no other Gods before Him (Exodus 20:3) and 2) that we love Him with all of our heart, soul, and mind, and love our neighbors as ourselves (Matthew 22:37–39). These instructions are first in God's eyes because He knows the level of destruction that is caused when our capacity for and understanding of love are tampered with. By prioritizing these commandments, He shows us that the *first* thing He wants to do when we surrender to Him is heal that vital aspect of our injured souls.

When our comprehension of love is skewed, our desires fall out of alignment and our affections are at risk of being hijacked by counterfeit contenders that invade our lives and mislead us. When our love is first for God and secondly for one another as He intends, we avoid many of the pitfalls that so easily befall us because of the way we vet our every action. If we don't keep these "love priorities" as our guiding principles, we're at risk of forming attachments that captivate our passions but lead us into dark territories. This may seem like an oversimplified strategy of manipulation in a chapter that outlines other, more technical methods, yet this one likely is the most subversive and difficult to arm ourselves against, because *it* tangles the heart instead of the mind. When we become fixated on and infatuated with pursuits God hasn't ordained for us, the attachment becomes "nailed, to specific behaviors, objects, or people…[and becomes] the process that enslaves desire and creates the state of addiction."[102] (The author in that reference is referring to any unhealthy compulsion that commandeers our passions and drives us to engage in unhealthy habits, friendships, or activities. Much more is on the line than substance addiction.) Collectively, a skewed understanding of love is a dangerous trait. What, as a society, are people passionate about? These authors observe many behaviors and activities that have been mistaken and even substituted for love—and always with destructive consequences. For example, sex is often mistaken for love, which causes many seeking love to become intimate with countless people. Yet, they yet remain unfulfilled and keep searching, because the thing they desperately seek—again, love—cannot be found in physical gratification. Similarly, some use food as a replacement for love, which has contributed to such health epidemics as obesity and diabetes. As we look to find and exchange love in a world that is increasingly detached from the very definition of the word, we find ourselves facing a paradox: If it's true that "whatever we are ultimately concerned with is God for us,"[103] then, when we look at what captivates and preoccupies our society, we see what this culture's gods are. What/who are these gods? On the dark end of the spectrum, they are fear, loneliness, depression, isolation, and abuse. On the other extreme, these emotions are channeled into the search for love by manifesting in the desire to join a cause, to engage in something worth fighting for, to gain validation of our human reasoning, and to follow a "truth" that all can agree upon and accept, once and for all. Do these sound like the pursuits that demand the attention of modern society? We believe they are a clear summation.

We can see how closely these efforts reflect a large-scale need for God. The dark emotions experienced by today's society express the need for a Savior. The participation in positive activities—causes—shows a generation looking for righteous undertakings. Yet, these efforts are exploited by the gods of this world that distract us from the underlying pain of separation from our Maker with superficial exploits that pretend, momentarily, to fill the void but leave us empty. Ultimately, through this confusion about love, what it is, where we find it, and where we should direct it, we've become our own gods, preoccupied with our own reason, and the powers that be are perfectly willing to sit back and watch members of society destroy themselves, at their own expense, in the search for love and spiritual fulfillment.

The Enemy Is Patient

The manipulation tactics currently at work shaping society all have one thing in common: They're the handiwork of an enemy who seeks to destroy mankind. Certainly, we can *see* each of these at work in the physical realm, but their visible manifestations are the result of a spiritual war being waged in hidden places (Ephesians 6:12). Ultimately, the enemy is not one of flesh and blood, but is "the dragon, that old serpent, which is the Devil" (Revelation 20:2). Perhaps the best manipulation tactic the enemy and his agents employ is the fact that he is *patient*. He has had, literally, all the time in the world to culminate his plan. Understand that while his aim is to destroy every soul over the course of time, he is playing with an end-game strategy in mind. This means that we must be vigilant, and we must teach our children to be so as well. Each generation serves as the watchmen for the next. What *we* allow to slide will escalate in subsequent years; what our children see us regarding complacently will be viewed as acceptable and soon become the norm. It's vital that we avoid laziness regarding the ways the masses will be deceived. Complacency in such circumstances is similar to what we're told will lead us to poverty: "Yet a little sleep, a little slumber, a little folding of the hands to sleep: So shall they poverty come as one that travelleth; and thy want as an armed man" (Proverbs 24:33–34).

Conditioning is often allowed to simmer in the background for many years before its damage comes to fruition. Consider what we mentioned earlier about postmodernism. We've only seen the full impact of the changes it's made to our thinking over the last several decades, but the seeds have been germinating for hundreds of years. We may think nothing bad will happen "on our watch." However, when we ignore what's going on in the background or fail to address the peripheral conditioning we're subjected to, we can almost guarantee that something bad *will* happen on our children's watch. This is only part of the reason it's so important for us to "train up" our kids "in the way [they] should go…[so that] when [they are] old, [they] will not depart from it" (Proverbs 22:6). They are the guardians for future generations.

One morning, while getting ready to begin my research for the day, I (Allie Henson) received an email from a digital-coupon company that advertises local businesses running discount deals. The offer boasted 90 percent off the tuition of an online course that teaches witchcraft, magick, curses, and spells—with many of these "skills" specifically tied to hurting or attracting other people. Highlights of the courses included chakra healing, interacting with spirit guides, astral projection, and polarizing energy, and the promotion piece placed great emphasis on using rituals to impact sexual energy, and vice versa. All this, and all for only nineteen dollars! In world of people who lack discernment regarding the powers of evil, our children can dabble in such occult activity without purchasing so much as an Ouija board. Things like this are available all around them, while the reality of precisely *who* they're dabbling with is blurred.

For example, the television series *Lucifer* humanizes Satan, painting him as a guy who got tired of "ruling hell," so he came to earth for a break, whereupon he assumes the human form and the name Lucifer Morningstar. In this portrayal, he's just a regular guy who isn't necessarily bad. In fact, he helps people, is capable of sympathy, and is generally more morally inclined than many humans. He's characterized as being a weary but necessary component in the grand-scale plan of God (whom he refers to as "my father" throughout the series)—an essential antagonist without whom God's story of good vs. evil can be allowed to play out. In general, the series depicts Satan as a guy who received a bad rap thousands of years ago, who is tired of being pigeonholed into his hellish role, and who is largely misunderstood. Further, the tortures of hell are downplayed in this program. This is a great example of one of the sneakiest tactics of all: asserting that Satan either doesn't exist or that, even if he does, he's not alive and working in our current world—*today*. And sadly, the strategy is working...

I (Allie Henson) learned about this show's portrayal of Satan while talking with a couple of teenagers who, after watching it, were having a discussion about who Satan is. One asserted that since Lucifer was an angel of light before he was the devil, it was likely that he actually wasn't all bad. The other maintained that he was indeed evil. What really bothered me about this particular conversation was the fact that these were both church-going teens. Regardless of whether the church leaders hadn't addressed this issue or whether the teen who seemed confused about Lucifer's evil nature had simply missed that sermon (or hadn't paid attention if he had been present), we can't speculate. Suffice it to say, there are likely teens in *your* church as well who think that Satan is a fable.

At the same time, the world is conditioned to hold a humorous or dismissive stance about the devil's existence entirely. After all, if "my truth" says that he doesn't exist, then anything perceived as evil must be the manifestation of someone's guilt, self-proclaimed moral compass, or even the gap between conflicting ethical boundaries. And since these are subjective topics, revealing moral shortcomings or sinful acts becomes quickly classified as matters others need to "just deal with" or "get over."

Simultaneously, while many deny that he even exists, Satan somehow manages to keep enough personhood about him that he continues to be a subject of religious fascination. Many see him as a source of power, a place to point the finger to escape culpability ("the devil made me do it"), or a somewhat fantastical being who might be capable of evil deeds, but who isn't present in any relevant way—here and now—impacting humanity's everyday lives. In the meantime, dabbling in interactions with him is trivialized and normalized.

Putting It Together

Cuties Revisited

By now, you're familiar with many of the manipulation tactics used regularly on a large scale. The agendas behind such tactics range from selling products to promoting acceptance of ideas and policies that should incite outrage. By carefully shaping the mindset of the masses, matters that were once unspeakable become commonplace.

The mass response to the movie *Cuties*, as outlined in the previous chapter, is encouraging, in that we see that there are a number of individuals who will stand against the sexualization of our youth. However, we also see that the sensationalism it attracted serves as its own type of conditioning. After all, the conversation about sexualizing our youth isn't just taking place in religious circles and the objections haven't come solely from conservative Christians; it's the focus of much discussion among many members of broader segments of society who represent all perspectives—including those with a more liberal worldview. However, such blatant, eroticism regarding minors, alongside the film's lack of resolution or conviction toward solution, has the potential to leave the public confused regarding the *real* motivation behind this movie. (This is part of the perpetual mind games played on the populace we've discussed in this chapter.)

Because of the filmmakers' stated position of advocating for young people, some may eventually question their own outrage as they begin to wonder who the "good guys" *really* are (gaslighting). They may even sympathize with the film's producers, assuming that if their intentions were pure, they deserve the benefit of the doubt (as mentioned, humans are wired toward reconciliation and thus feel obligated to compromise). At this, they may find the subsequent "attack" on filmmakers by righteous individuals justified, yet, still somehow regrettable. In a careful study of all that's gone on with the film, we can see that it started as an example of foot-in-the-door manipulation: An attempt was made to introduce the idea of sexualizing minors with the expectation that it would simmer in the backs of the viewers' mind and eventually become accepted as a part of society. Because of the public's outrage, this film likewise has properties of door-in-the-face manipulation: It drew a heightened response that, after fostering sympathy, leads to a smaller "dose" of the controversial subject matter being accepted. In future instances, the sexualization might be less blatant, but the reaction should be comparative relief rather than outrage.

All the while, the conversation lingers around the filmmakers' *real* intentions—whether they meant to behaviorally condition our public to embrace the sexual exploitation of minors or motivate them to whistle-blow on the loss of our youth's innocence—our populace becomes more accepting of it. Understand that these authors are *not* saying the conversation shouldn't happen, nor are we stating that awareness is a bad idea (it's *vital!*). We *are*, however, saying that whenever new mindfulness is wrought upon a public, we must be watching for smaller concessions regarding the same topic that may be in the periphery. After all, the movie itself derived much notoriety from the scandal, and there is *much* power involved with controversy. As all arguments regarding the issue become polished by the sensationalism provided by *Cuties*, human wiring toward compromise could cause some to question the credibility of the outrage itself.

This is where we must remember the original issues that drove the debate in the first place. There are clues that reveal the true motives behind the release of this film. First of all, the close-up, spread-eagle camera shots and partial nudity of both over- and under-aged females shown were not necessary, if the film's point was in fact to raise consciousness about sexual exploitation. Second, the trailer and promotion of the film presented it as a "coming-of-age" story; nothing was mentioned to let the viewing audience know *Cuties* was an effort to raise awareness about the sexualization of our youth. Additionally, the conclusion of the movie was quite the opposite of how a "whistle-blowing" movie would have ended (as these authors have explained). Further, many more than just extreme conservatives found this production exploitive. As we said earlier, if the ending of the movie had motivated its audience to take problem-solving action, offered a moral lesson, or even fostered feelings of outrage toward the *problem*, it could then appropriately claim intentions of raising awareness. But since the movie's conclusion leaves viewers with the impression that the young characters will—on their own—suddenly regain innocence, its message is clear: This sexually charged behavior among teens is normal, will run its course, and will require no parental intervention. In this case, it's not a stretch to conclude that there could be an agenda behind the production *and* surrounding controversy. (The normalization of pedophilia will be discussed in a later chapter).

This Is Happening Now

As we've said, the manipulation strategies we've described are playing out in society at this very moment. Though many are unable to see it, each method is being employed to drive our culture into directions that—until now—only science fiction or other media has dared to go. If you look at the world around you and feel as though we are moving toward the End Times quickly, it's not your imagination. The hands that shape the attitudes and behaviors of the population are fiercely at work behind the scenes, making great strides every day toward ushering in the destruction of mankind. When we examine the events that tore potentially irreparable holes in our culture during 2020, we recall a year of lockdowns, riots, and global disruption of all types. Were these events random, or were they the consequences of a calculated plan that has spread a web of deception across all nations as a push to bring in a global governmental regime? These are questions we'll take a closer look at in the upcoming pages.

{5}

CALCULATED CHAOS

On May 25, 2020, an employee of a convenience store phoned 911 to report an individual who had allegedly purchased cigarettes with a fake twenty-dollar bill. When police arrived, their maneuvers manifested in "a series of actions that violated the policies of the Minneapolis Police Department [which] turned fatal, leaving the perpetrator unable to breathe."[104] In only a matter of minutes after the emergency call, the man, George Floyd, was dead. Despite the fact that the Minneapolis Police Department dismissed the officers involved from their employment and filed a series of murder charges against Derek Chauvin, the officer who was most culpable, public outcry was, understandably, immediate and passionate.[105] The same day, protests against police brutality began to upsurge in major cities across the nation. As political unrest swelled, it collected and propelled the fury. But the rage of the crowd had been stirring for a while before this tragic event. And when the impassioned masses met a justified cause, the population exploded...

The Powder Keg

In addition to the understandable outrage regarding George Floyd's death, another issue was brewing beneath the surface of society's demeanor. For months prior, the country had been experiencing government-mandated shutdowns and quarantines due to the spread of the virus COVID-19, causing economic stagnation, unemployment, and financial strain for countless numbers of families across the nation. The government offered several types of relief efforts—including a first round of $1,200 stimulus checks going to qualified citizens, with rumors that there would be a second round.[106] Despite this assistance, the population became a powder keg—ready to blow at the first spark. The strain on individuals was immense: financial hardship, the lockdown of many business and most social activities, extreme isolation, disruption of public schools, fears about the future, and grocery and supply shortages—and the list doesn't even include the threat of contracting the virus itself. Many lost their jobs and businesses. A great number of folks became angry at the government for how it was handling the crisis. These and many other issues constitute only a small portion of the anxieties felt daily by people who found themselves stuck at home, twenty-four-seven.

During this time, workers deemed "essential" were allowed to continue employment and were thus exempt from parts of the mandated "stay-home orders," but their liberty wasn't always something to be jealous of, because their ability to continue working equated to increased risks of exposure to the virus. These laborers faced fears of being coughed or sneezed upon, sometimes intentionally,[107] of being assaulted and beaten,[108] or of leaving work to find their tires slashed or vehicle vandalized.[109] All this risk was in addition to increased exposure to the virus, a shortage of protective materials, and extra pressure at work to implement new sanitation policies while learning and enforcing emerging guidelines for social-distancing procedures.

Because schools, workplaces, and other community entities were shut down during this time, children, spouses, and domestic partners in abusive situations were stuck at home with their perpetrators, and hospitals saw a dramatic increase in the number of child-abuse-related deaths.[110] For many children, the trusted adults in their lives are those they interact with at school. Without access to these protectors, children were isolated, without help. Additionally, abusers who may have otherwise kept their actions in check for fear of being discovered at school through a child's demeanor or injury were free of accountability, thanks to the knowledge that it would be months before the victims would be reunited with their primary advocates.

Many cities across the nation not only saw a spike in the number of domestic abuse incidents, but they reported that cases were also more severe. Thomas Manion of the Montgomery County Family Justice Center remarked that, despite the fact that their facility had not treated *additional* cases of violence, it had seen a "massive increase" in situations that had escalated to much more severe levels of threat, such as "cases involving strangulation, cases involving firearms…[and/or] other weapons."[111] Economists at Brigham Young University conducted a study comparing the number of emergency calls to police in 2020 with the number of calls placed in other years, and results showed a 7.5 percent increase during the months correlating with pandemic lockdown and stay-home orders; this surge manifested across all demographics.[112] Alcohol sales saw a spike during this time, increasing more than 240 percent during the weeks correlated to shutdowns.[113] Support meetings for alcoholics were canceled, and alcoholism, along with drug use, saw a rise, as well. The number of drug overdoses marked an 18 percent increase during the pandemic.[114] The number of people suffering from depression nearly tripled during the pandemic,[115] those with mental illness experienced increased frequency and/or severity of symptoms, and the number of those having thoughts of suicide doubled over the statistics reported in 2018.[116] All this doesn't even *touch* on the long-term, economic wreckage caused by 2020's devastating series of events, which could be the subject of another book altogether.

Turning back to May of 2020, people who had spent the past two to four months (depending their region) on lockdown were finally being allowed to return to work, using appropriate social distancing and mask precautions. A tense, frustrated, fearful society emerged warily from their homes to see whether it was safe to enter and participate in "the world" again yet. When George Floyd died by the hands of injustice, the pent-up anxiety and negative energy that had been troubling the entire country could no longer be subdued. *And*, under the heading of a righteous cause, many people were uninclined to attempt restraint.

Among those who responded to Floyd's death with an unsurpassed level of fury were members of the Black Lives Matter (BLM) organization. That group formed in 2013, when the "neighborhood watch" volunteer who shot and killed seventeen-year-old Trayvon Martin was found not guilty on all counts of homicide.[117] The organization's mission is "to eradicate white supremacy and build a local power to intervene in violence inflicted on Black communities by the state and vigilantes."[118] This objective is noble in its approach to shielding victims of racial injustice from threat of discrimination or harm, and stated in this context, aligns with the principles America stands for.

And, as Christians, we *should* advocate for victims of injustice of all types.

Yet, many will agree that the fruit of 2020's riots somehow misaligns with BLM's honorable motives. What happened?

Initial protests were labeled "peaceful," but a passionate momentum began to propel the organization to the forefront of media reports, and soon, other movements were joining forces. A nation that had been stifling mounting tensions for months during COVID lockdowns seemed to collectively erupt in aggression. "'If you aren't moved by the George Floyd video, you have nothing in you,'…[stated University of Pennsylvania's professor D. Q. Gillion]. 'And that catalyst can now be amplified

by the fact that individuals probably have more time to engage in protest activity.'"[119] The racial injustice against Floyd was made worse by
the extreme toll COVID-19 had taken on his community: "The pandemic has disproportionately affected African American communities
both in loss of life and economic effect," stated one report. "As learned
in the Arab Springs and Tunisia, sometimes a simple spark will prove
to be the critical one."[120] The number of demonstrations soared, total-
ing nearly 5,000, averaging nearly 150 per day, and spanning approximately 2,500 towns and cities in the following months.[121] Those who
had never before participated in political demonstrations began joining in, and organizations such as Antifa (short for "anti-fascist") began
to hijack the press' attention. Protests became riots. City authorities
were overwhelmed with meeting the needs for crowd control, yet were
plagued by challenges that come with the obligation to allow peaceful gatherings, manage emerging COVID-19 social distancing policies,
and maintain order. Intervention by authorities fueled the public's rage
regarding governmental overreach and police brutality, placing them
in increasingly heated situations. Curfews were instigated and enforced
in major cities across the nation, and crowds were tear-gassed and pep-
per sprayed; many protesters were even arrested.[122] Federal forces were
dispatched as reinforcement in some cities, and temporary fences and
barricades were erected to protect official buildings and many private
businesses. Demonstrators responded by learning—via blogs, YouTube
videos, and other means—how to participate in rioting and looting
without being arrested or leaving fingerprints and how to use household items (such as baseball bats, tennis rackets, lasers, and frozen water
bottles[123]) as weapons. One video circulating on social media for a time
showed viewers how to use a window-punch tool to break into locked
vehicles during riots and encouraged viewers to become violent to those
who sought safety inside a locked car. The video was later blocked. Over
the course of the demonstrations, many cities saw property destroyed,
fireworks thrown at civilians and officials, buildings set ablaze, stores

looted, historical statues overturned, vehicles burned, and much more. In many places, shootings occurred.[124]

President Donald Trump promptly responded to the state of affairs by insisting that he would designate Antifa as a terrorist affiliation, stating that its far-left agenda was causing a state of anarchy to which the government must respond.[125] However, such swift and decisive recourse is much easier said than done. In order to designate *any* organization as a domestic terrorist or hate group, the accusation must be quantified with specific criteria.

For example, to be considered a terrorist organization, a group must state or demonstrate hatred toward a specific party, race, orientation, or other classification of people. But, since members of Antifa "do not promote hatred based on race, religion, ethnicity, sexual orientation, or gender identity," they don't fall within the legal "terrorism" parameters.[126]

Further, Antifa might have been guilty of creating havoc on the streets, but the group's actual objectives are vague, making it difficult to decisively categorize it as a terrorist group, which the FBI technically defines as one unlawfully using "force and violence against persons or property to intimidate or coerce a government, the civilian population, or any segment thereof, in furtherance of political or social objectives."[127] Additionally, according to the FBI, "there is no single, universally accepted, definition of terrorism,"—this vagueness leaves the positions of such groups as being legally subjective.[128]

Further convoluting the issue regarding whether Antifa falls within the FBI's definition of domestic terrorism is the obscurity of the organization's mission; many wonder precisely *who* or *what* is the real driving force behind it. After all, it's not organized in any official way (although in some regions, it *does* organize on a community level) and has no recognizable structure of leadership. It's merely considered "a loose affiliation of local activists scattered across the United States and a few other countries."[129] Additionally, Antifa, unlike many other causes, isn't as much defined by what it *does* stand for, but rather, what it *does not*:

"Fascism, nationalism, far-right ideologies, white supremacy, authoritarianism, racism, homophobia and xenophobia...[and sometimes] capitalism and the government overall."[130] Since many other, "non-terrorist" groups have this same position, the organization behind the riots is able to innocently deny instigating extremist or illegal actions. It merely puts the blame back on individual citizens who simply "got out of hand" or allowed their personal passions to escalate to an unhealthy level.

In Seattle in August, tensions heated up as residents remained locked in their homes, while protestors in the streets yelled at them, demanding that they surrender their house keys. Claiming the neighborhood had once been primarily owned by African American families, but had since been sold to white residents for less than market value, demonstrators shouted such demands as "Open your wallet!" "Check your privilege!" and "How do you plan to fix it...as a gentrifier [stating that these individuals were] part of that problem."[131] At the other end of the spectrum, defensive homeowners stood by, ready to protect their domiciles. For example, Mark and Patricia McCloskey soon became known as the "gun-wielding couple." The McCloskeys claim they were inside their residence in St. Louis when protestors busted through their gate and began "hurling threats." The couple felt compelled to respond by "protecting their property"[132] via brandishing weapons at the trespassers. Despite asserting that their actions were legal, the couple has now been indicted for "exhibiting guns...[and] tampering with evidence."[133] They say that more than political activism is at stake here; they believe this incident demonstrates the transition from the "government's job as protecting honest citizens from criminals...[to] protecting criminals from honest citizens."[134]

Further embodying the convolution on all sides of this issue are the actual activists themselves. Some engage in a "cause" because it gives them an outlet for spending their ambitious and passionate energy—even though the motives behind that "cause" might escape them. A vaguely stated goal such as "bucking the system" can be appealing, but without clear objectives and defined goals, it's an empty pursuit and yields no good, humanitarian results other than perhaps emotional rewards. These include such "feelings" as a boosted level of confidence, a sense of belonging, or even a channel for negative, pent-up energy). For example, activist Alycia Moaton became impassioned at a press conference where she stated that police officers were beating people up and laughing at/mocking innocent civilians "every single day."[135] Then, she said, "People are worried about looting and there are literal lives being taken away…people…are dying and y'all are mad about people looting…Get over it! These buildings are insured!"[136]

This young woman's perspective is revealing about the culture in which we live. First of all, buildings are not insured out of the generosity of society: Property owners pay premiums and accept liability for deductibles and policy requirements. *Then*, they're "covered" in the event of an emergency or unforeseen disaster. However, anyone who has ever made an insurance claim understands that even after all monies are paid out, there is always *some* measure of uncompensated loss to the policyholder. The very notion that being covered by insurance would grant permission for someone to destroy another's property—not to mention deal out damage that will result in longer periods of commercial closure for these victims—shows a gap in logic that prompts the notion of the "cause" to contradict itself. Under what heading is justice brought about for one person who's been wronged by destroying cities and attacking the property of *others*? This is an example of hijacked passion that lacks being grounded in the *spirit* of the cause one claims to support. If someone is so moved by compassion that he or she wants to propel humanity's well-being or stand up for the underdog, that person doesn't hurt *innocent bystanders'* property. The very idea is counterintuitive. The owners of destroyed businesses in no way deserved to have their possessions looted and demolished in the name of fairness toward a third party who was wronged. The irony of Moaton's rant is that she claimed to be acting in outrage about one injustice while propagating another. Every day during 2020 in which riots occurred under the heading of "justice and equality," people were injured and killed, suffered loss via damage and theft of assets, or simply remained in their homes, watching vigilantly in the hopes that nothing bad would befall them. Additionally, while damaged and looting businesses underwent repair and reopening, *more* people continued to see extended unemployment and loss of business.[137] Ironically, when all is said and done, it's likely that their insurance premiums will also spike.

Most revealing of all when considering Moaton's stance is the contradictory nature of many people's involvement in activism. As mentioned before, such vague headings as "buck the system" often become the label under which they operate. Yet, when society is torn down and someone must be held accountable, their default response is to call upon the safety net of a higher structure to rescue and restore them; they essentially expect a benevolent "they" to clean up the mess and facilitate/fund the rebuilding. Yet, America suffered a grotesque measure of damage beginning in 2020. Historical monuments were destroyed or defaced; economic damage occurred; businesses were closed, destroyed, and/or looted; conflict festered between citizens and authority figures; morale plummeted; and lives were lost in the fighting. Yet, for many, the motivation behind all of this fallout appeared to be more the sake of the fight than actually restoring justice. Did the tens of thousands of people destroying our cities learn anything through the warring? Was their mission accomplished? Who will step up and oversee the restructuring? Is there a benevolent "they" who will foster the reuniting of our country's society and actually work to bring people back together? The damage on a cultural level runs even deeper than what we see in the rubble of our buildings, historical monuments, and even our economy. No "insurance policy" can undo the wreckage our own people have wrought upon one another.

While racial injustice is indeed cause for outrage, Antifa's ambiguous objectives nurtured a setting wherein civil unrest could be instated and anarchy promoted. Soon, laws were broken, citizens were terrorized, and authorities were outnumbered. All the while, the true motivations of chaos and anarchy were able to fly under the radar, categorizing this brand of pandemonium as a "protest against racial discrimination." These destructive riots coat-tailed on the justified cause of racial equality and corrupted the initial mission statement with elements that seemed to contradict earlier objectives. In fact, many of the consequences of these demonstrations *injured* the goal they were supposed to serve.

For example, many people of color were killed during the riots. Among them were seventy-seven-year-old retired police officer David Dorn, who was investigating an activated security alarm when he was killed by looters.[138] Federal officer Patrick Underwood became another casualty when shots were fired at a courthouse from a passing automobile at a protest in California.[139] The life of twenty-two-year-old Italia Kelly was claimed instantly by a stray bullet as she was leaving a protest that had "turned unruly."[140] David McAtee, a fifty-three-year-old restaurateur, was killed in a volley of gunfire. The fifty-year-old father of four, Marvin Francois, was shot by three younger men presumably attempting to steal his car outside a protest.[141] Thirty-eight-year-old Chris Beaty was killed while he tried to save two women from being robbed near one of the demonstrations.[142] The list of casualties continues, and each name on it leaves the upsetting story of violent, untimely, and *unnecessary* demise, along with heartbroken families and loved ones. Ultimately, while peaceful protesting would have been an ideal way for those seeking racial equality to make their voices heard, the escalation of these events into riots and intense outbursts led to further atrocities against the very ones they stated they wanted to advocate for.

Some who observe the sociopolitical climate in America perceive the country as being in the embryonic stages of armed insurgency. "The official definition of an *insurgency* is the 'organized use of subversion and violence to seize, nullify, or challenge political control' of an arena."[143] It is certainly true that, as the heat rises between citizens and the populace becomes more polarized, this definition could apply to what we see happening today. Certainly, some of the violence in the streets this year has come out of counterdemonstrations, nineteen of which escalated to violence.[144] As the divide between political parties seems to broaden, tensions rise and the number of citizens taking up arms increases as well: Firearm sales hit a record high in June, when gun-purchase-related background checks spiked to 3.9 million in that month alone.[145]

A report released by the Armed Conflict Location and Event Data Project in September of 2020 stated that the country faces a mounting vulnerability to "political violence and instability" as a result of the increased need for governmental response to civic unrest and the recent spike in extremist activity, citing "violent political polarization" as a risk factor.[146] Further, the report stated that, should the 2020 election results be "delayed, inconclusive, or rejected as fraudulent," things could "boil over," resulting in the need for governmental intervention.[147]

Many believe that to label this recent rioting as domestic terrorism would be a rational statement. It's possible that domestic terrorism has become so commonplace in our environment that we're both desensitized to it and hypervigilant about it all at once. "Instead of the vertical escalation anticipated after 9/11, we have seen a 'horizontal escalation'—the proliferation of low-level attacks," points out the writer of one article written in the summer of 2020. "Indeed, terrorism has become so widespread, repetitious, and familiar in the 21st century that we are almost inured to its effects."[148]

For many, saying that America is experiencing domestic terrorism may seem extreme. They may regard the recent turmoil as simply part of the ebb and flow of history's cycles. Others readily accept this assertion, pointing to our cities' current condition as proof. Some who desire diminished governmental control believe the *true* recent harassment stems from overreaching authorities who regulate masks, shutdowns, quarantines, and so on.

Other groups state that there has been rampant domestic terrorism throughout the year, and that it's been dealt from multiple directions. As mentioned, the FBI's definition of "terrorism" is classified as "the unlawful use of force and violence against persons or property to intimidate or coerce a government, the civilian population, or any segment thereof, in furtherance of political or social objectives."[149] For those who remained locked in their houses while protestors outside filled their streets, shouting demands that they would relinquish their homes to another family based on race, this definition could apply. Those on the other side of the issue, who are aware of one killed or injured during an act of police brutality, would embrace the same vague definition for their position against authorities who have acted out of line and caused death or injury. For some, being intimidated into wearing a mask or mandated to stay home from work during the COVID-19 epidemic was a form of unlawful force and coercion to further both political *and* social objectives. Another crowd sees the definition as holding even to the way they're bullied into keeping their religious views quiet—coercion for the propagation of political and social objectives via methods of unlawful censorship and hate speech.

Still others point to a double standard regarding who would receive what labels in the roster of players, should the tables turn. For example, these authors have heard many Christians say that if religious organizations were to gather in large cities and make demands of any kind by using such tactics as those adopted by Antifa during the riots of 2020, we most certainly would have been declared terrorists and arrested. But, does this mean that we're living in a state of domestic terrorism? The picture of modern society is hardly a portrait of a peaceful, unified nation under God. Yet, perhaps domestic terrorism isn't what this nation is experiencing. Maybe we're merely suffering from adjustments that occur alongside normal societal shifts—"growing pains," if you will— that wreak temporary havoc, but that will mellow out on its own over time. Or, worse, could it be the case that our societal structure is about to undergo the most seismic shift to date?

The Perils of Designating Groups "Terrorist"

The many issues culminating in the ignition of the 2020 riots and the various interpretations of modern culture make the question of domestic terrorism a cloudy one, especially while events are still playing out. With such unclear parameters outlining the objectives, leadership, and strategy of groups that propagated extremist activities during the riots, officials' hands are tied where labeling groups as terrorist is concerned. After all, illegal acts carried out during these demonstrations can be pinned on individuals, allowing organizations to distance themselves from responsibility for such tactics.

Along that vein, it's difficult for authorities to lay the responsibility for one person's actions on an entire agency. For example, if three men associated with Antifa burn down a church building during a demonstration, *everyone* associated with Antifa can't be arrested for planning to burn down their local churches. *Nor* can we even confirm who is or is not acting on behalf of the agency. Thus, the three men in question can be arrested for committing arson, but Antifa can't be charged without the government risking being guilty of severe authoritative overreach. Antifa maintains no official roster of members and gives its supporters no specific orders. In this way, it stays in the background, where it's able to fuel the fire while evading culpability.

Groups like this—when they protest legally—are able to bring their malleable and sweeping ideologies into nearly any promotable or trending cause, and thrive beneath the surface of the initial objectives: gaining followers and repute, but lingering in the background seemingly supporting a "host cause" or target goal. Likely, the primary cause would be operating under the legal rights to conduct peaceful protest and free speech. Then, as troublemakers arrive and escalate the violence of the demonstrations, the organization can remain completely detached from individuals' actions.

This is where threats of classifying a group as "domestic terrorist" becomes easier said than done. When an organization's mission statement is ambiguous or even nonexistent, it's nearly impossible for officials to call the entire body of members "terrorists" just because some who claim affiliation with that organization have acted illegally. To attempt to classify all members in a certain way based on the actions of a few may instigate legislation that could backfire. For example, to say that a certain group, because of any one stated belief, should be viewed as a national threat could lead to responsive legislation. But the cost would be huge, and would likely result in reducing our freedom of speech.

If this were to begin to happen, Christians will be among the first to have their freedom of speech limited. In fact, one might wonder if some of the agenda that is currently dividing the populace might be provocative at its core. Perhaps a bigger enemy is at work, one whose entire objective is to foster such a string of events via distraction. For example, take Antifa's stance against "far-right ideologies." Because the group's name has been associated with so much of the rioting this year, some people would have no problem whatsoever seeing it classified as a domestic terrorist group—but that could cause their statements to be branded as "hate speech," and their stance, including their "anti-far-right-ideologies agenda," would likewise fall into a category of potential threat. Then, others who make similar statements could be arrested as potential terrorists for expressing similar values. (This is the cleverness of Antifa's stance; it isn't officially "for" anything as much as being "against" certain other things. This ambiguity will perpetually allow it to dodge having its statements labeled as "hate speech." But follow the scenario with us for a bit.) At this point, some may say they have no issue with this; the destruction our country has undergone demands that people take a stand and call terrorism what it is. But, this has the potential to backfire grotesquely.

If our government were to begin assigning terms like "domestic terrorism" in this way, all it would take would be a few strategically placed "radicals" or a manipulated "trigger event" to begin to illegalize Chris-

tianity. Think it's not possible? Many organizations that embrace traditional values are already being labeled as "hate groups," and many biblical
statements have already been pointed to as "hate speech." Further, terrible things have been done by people who proclaim to be Christian.
If we allow the government extensive freedom to interchange groups,
statements, and actions, the Church could find itself in the bull's eye.
Even more concerning is the ambiguity we've discussed in the definition
of domestic terrorism. Once activated against an organization, anti-ter-
rorist laws provide a heightened allowance for surveillance, censorship,
and prohibition of assembly.[150] These are dangerous lines for the government to be tampering with.

Are these authors saying we should ignore terrorism because
there's no clear legal way to define it? Not at all. Demonstrations that
result in the destruction of property and personal death or injury
should be dispersed—or even better, prevented; protests should be
required to be carried out peacefully and legally. Those who break the
law should be arrested, and when organizations that promote destruction or violence can be identified, sanctions should be applied.

However, if citizens frustrated with organizations such as Antifa
want—in order to obtain immediate relief from the consequences of the
group's actions—to slap a "terrorist" label on any who may be associated
with it, they run the risk of their *own* affiliations being illegalized next.

But maybe that is precisely what is happening. Perhaps that's where
some entities are currently going with all of the chaos of 2020. It seems
possible that much of these turbulent circumstances could have been
deliberate—with tragedies such as the death of Floyd seized to incite calculated chaos—to inspire a moment of desperation on the part of citizens. This, perhaps, to pave the way for an America that will allow entire
organizations to be labeled as hate groups or terrorists without extremely
careful filtering the wording of the legislation. Could this be the entire
subplot of the pivotal year's drama? If that's the case, and if such maneuvers were to begin occurring, we are very concerned about the future of

the Church's ability to operate legally in America. Soon, Christian beliefs about marriage, family, the unborn, the Second-Amendment rights, and oh so much more could be enough to brand believers as terrorists.

As mentioned, many Christian-affiliated organizations that assert patriotic and traditional values are already listed on certain "hate group" rosters. A simple Google search of the term produces surprising and dismaying truth of this reality.

War on Churches

Branding Christian Views as Hate Speech/Burning Bibles

When headlines announced the burning of Bibles and American flags on our own cities' streets during the riots, many Christians saw these events as a sign of the times. A day they thought they would never see in their lifetimes had arrived. Reminiscent of Adolf Hitler's mandated burning of the Hebrew Bible,[151] passages of prophetic Scripture came to believers' minds, and a whole new level of apocalyptic reality hit home. For many, figuring out how to respond was the focal question.[152]

As Antifa burned Bibles in the same streets where their demonstrations wreaked havoc over much of the summer of 2020, their anti-fascist proclamations became increasingly anti-Christian. We may wonder how the torching copies of Scripture relates to the professed issue behind the riots, and it's vital to follow this trail of thought lest our freedom of speech becomes jeopardized. Here's the sequence: Antifa and similar organizations claim an anti-fascist stance. As mentioned, they aren't as much "for" anything as they are "against" other things. Working "against" specific things is a limited effort, in that their cause focuses only on that issue. When they operate "against" a *list* of things instead, they can to add "similar" matters to the list, so they become anti- whatever that is as well. Whether the issues these groups oppose are really related is subjective, and to disagree with them is to merely disassociate from the organization. To be sure, many cases of racial injustice fueled the anger that was simmering before the death of George Floyd. But the trigger event that touched off the movement leading to the riots of 2020 was the death. As Antifa and similar organizations joined the movement against racism, they began to fold all forms of perceived hate together into one metaphorical envelope of issues protested during these demonstrations. It's no secret that modern culture has the desire to interpret truth subjectively. Throughout the Bible, however, the Lord sets some boundaries that are concrete—thus they're interpreted by some to be hate speech. The Scripture passages stating those hard-and-fast truths are then bundled with protests against racism. Soon, the content of *entire* Bible is labeled as hate speech, even at a rally fostering racial equality—a principle that God clearly deems as worthy (see Galatians 3:28–29). Yet, because of this chain of thinking, radicals burn copies of the Bible in the streets, calling it a source of hate. And, in the minds of some who witness this destruction, the Word even becomes implicated as guilty by association with the police brutality that sparked the series of events in the first place. Worse, since not many people understand what the Bible says on matters such as racial equality, few who see it burned in conjunction with the issue know how to objectively defend it—not that many would, even if they could, because it might deem them "racist." So the flames consume the holy pages while those nearby don't intervene—because they don't understand what the Bible says about racial equality, they're afraid of being perceived as racist, or they can't articulate *why* the blazing copies aren't related to the reason for the riots.

Do you see how quickly the baby is thrown out with the bathwater, with circumstances escalating until an angry crowd tosses Bibles on to the fire—when the Holy Scripture isn't even related to the reason for the protests? And, as hatred becomes more outlawed (which is happening rapidly), Scripture could, again, be heaped onto the pile of things that must be—mandatorily, next time—disposed of.

For those watching the flames, the book-burning certainly included elements of rebellion against all the protestors perceived to be hateful. However, it is readily observed as more an act of extremism than one that followed logic. Some witnesses described the Bible-burning as an effort to petition that "the police…be defunded or abolished," while others said it was the way the demonstrators strove "for racial justice."[153] One observer noted that the burning of the Bible and the US flag "relates to racial injustice wasn't immediately clear."[154] Yet, the same person stated that one thing *did* seem clear: "Their [the protestors'] intentions are not to increase personal freedom."[155] This is the order of destruction and lack of logic that occurs when radical extremism manifests in destructive hype that gets out of control. Soon, people lose sight of the initial issue and protest anything that comes to mind that they can loosely—even if not rationally—clump together. The damage can be great, as we see in this example. What starts as a plea for racial equality can result in groups of impressionable individuals associating God's Word with a racially motivated murder, thus it all burns together in the demonstration. Meanwhile, skeptics of the Word—who aren't personally familiar with its contents in proper context—arrive on the scene of the demonstrations and misinterpret Scripture to "prove" that God endorses slavery. (The "slavery" referred to in the Bible is actually not "slavery" as we understand the term today; more accurately, it is an early form of indentured servitude involving a *voluntary* term of service and a *guaranteed* release from it on the Jubilee year. Nothing in Scripture indicates that the Lord endorses the vicious kind of racial inequality and murder we've seen in recent American history.)

Mandated Church Closures

The Christian faith suffered an additional attack during the shutdowns of COVID-19 during 2020; the circumstances reveal a certain measure of where our rights to gather as the Body of Christ may be headed. Across the nation, the only exceptions to mandated closures were businesses and facilities deemed "essential." The list of exemptions did not include churches, but it did include grocery and convenience stores, liquor stores, marijuana dispensaries, gas stations, and restaurants (for delivery, takeout, and curbside service only, at least for a certain length of time). A variety of other types of businesses, such as medical facilities, construction companies, pharmaceutical corporations, and manufacturing plants were allowed to remain in operation, and public charities such as homeless shelters and food pantries were also listed as permissible.[156]

California saw some of the most heated friction between churches and government after stay-home orders were issued on March 19, 2020.[157] In May, twelve hundred members of clergy came together and presented a letter to Gov. Gavin Newsom stating that they intended to allow their congregations to meet on May 31, whether or not they had permission to do so. That day, the Day of Pentecost, was considered approximately the 1990th "birthday of the Christian Church," and the council of clergy would no longer be restrained from their right to lead worship.[158] Their stance wasn't an act of rebellion, but was a plea for the state's government to recognize the Church as an "essential" ingredient in humanity's well-being. Furthermore, they stated that by singling out religious institutions as nonessential, they were being limited in a way that violated the rights protected by the Constitution's First Amendment.[159] While the government *does* have the authority to limit certain activities of American life during a crisis, it does *not* have the right to adversely target religious institutions. Since many other, secular, aspects of lifestyle in our country were allowed to operate uninterrupted, the clergy believed they belonged to the segment being treated unfavorably.

The group of men and women in the coalition asking for places of worship to be deemed "essential" understood that the pandemic was a time of crisis, and they knew that during such times, anxiety and depression spike, making faith more necessary than ever.[160] (The letter noted that during one week, one county in Tennessee had seen more deaths related to suicide than to COVID, leading to statements such as the following: "Coronavirus anxiety threatens more health damage than the lockdowns can possibly hope to save.")[161] As we've discussed, suicide rates, domestic abuse, drug and alcohol use, and other personal struggles have increased during the pandemic. The alliance of clergy believed that if such coping mechanisms as drinking alcohol were made available to the public at this time, then certainly their access to faith facilities should be allowed. The group requested that Governor Newsom give permission to gather; otherwise, they would not comply with his mandate, stating however that "all services…[would] be held in compliance with CDC and state guidelines for social distancing as is required of 'essential businesses.'"[162]

The letter launched a series of attacks and legal battles that are still, as of this writing, being played out. While Newsom discussed a plan for reopening churches, much of his statement was mere lip service. Federal courts reinforced Newsom's stay-home orders pertaining to churches, despite President Trump's nationwide order that officials allow religious gatherings, stating that without "[tempering US Supreme Court legislation] with a little practical wisdom, it…[would] convert the constitutional Bill of Rights into a suicide pact."[163] However, Judge Daniel Collins, Circuit Judge of the United States Court of Appeals, disagreed with the enforced closures, stating that the limitation "illogically assumes that the very same people who cannot be trusted to follow the rules at their place of worship can be trusted to do so at their workplace."[164]

This assumption, however, seems to have caught on, since clergy have been taken to court, issued fines, and even spied on in their services since the dispute erupted.[165] Rumors even circulate that one county nailed a document of protest to the front door of a church—Martin-Luther style—although in actuality the document was *taped* to the building's entrance.[166] Temporary legislation has placed limitations on corporate meetings for Bible study, prayer, communion, and other sacraments, and has additionally prohibited "singing and chanting, even in...private homes."[167] Pastor Rob McCoy in Ventura County, California, was fined three thousand dollars for holding services at his church, Godspeak Calvary Chapel, in August after receiving orders to halt gatherings.[168] Religious espionage emerged as a unique tactic against Christianity when Santa Clara, California, plainclothes officers attended North Valley Baptist Church there and subsequently filed court documents that resulted in a cease-and-desist order, along with ten thousand dollars' worth of fines (five thousand per service) for singing during the two sessions.[169]

Churches continue to fight this legal battle, citing that it is inconsistent to allow an organization to feed people or house them overnight while prohibiting that same entity from allowing folks to pray or take communion while standing six feet apart. Additionally, these organizations are permitted to provide "counseling to find work but cannot... [counsel people] on finding eternal life."[170] With such backward logic limiting *only* the activities that would directly involve worship, praise, Bible study, faith coaching, and communal prayer within the same institutions, it's easy to perceive intentional discrimination against Christianity itself. Liberty Counsel, acting as legal representation for some of the attacked clergy, urged in a statement that "this unconstitutional hostility against religious worship must end."[171]

Battles like this are taking place across the entire nation at this very moment. While the "pandemic," "emergency" labels allow the government to enact legislation limiting activities, we must look to the future and wonder what restrictions will remain when the urgency subsides. Additionally, as much of the population increasingly begins to view religion as archaic, outdated, and even hateful, will there be a place for the Christian lifestyle to reemerge in society once—*if*—it becomes legal again to do so?

Will America Embrace Socialism?

As governmental crackdowns on freedoms of all types escalate, an alarming trend is occurring amidst the general population. This is the increasing interest of many in seeing America embrace the notion of socialism. In fact, nearly "40 percent of millennials and others are prepared to surrender their liberties to the absolute authority of the state."[172] This is likely because many people see the government as a potentially limitless entity that could, given enough power, solve the problems that its citizens face. For many, surrendering personal freedoms is a small price to pay for what might ultimately yield such dividends as better healthcare, improved education, increased protection, and material provision for all. The folks who see things this way view capitalism as the vehicle by which a select few have been made elaborately wealthy; they see that as keeping others from obtaining a share in that success. They believe that there are a few select billionaires who, once defunded, would see their wealth redistributed throughout the working class and used to improve society as a whole. It's easy, at first glance, to recognize the allure of these notions. What if, just by changing the overindulgent lives of a few people, the condition of all of humanity could improve? This is the rhetoric currently being propagated among our impressionable populace. Since it seems to be promoting the betterment of humanity, more and more are jumping aboard this worldview.

However, certain flaws in this ideology surface once the rubber meets the road. Economists warn that socialism has always failed the *citizens* it's supposed to serve. There are many reasons for this; we'll explain a few here.

Socialism operates on the premise that communities will work together and share responsibility, accountability, and accrued wealth. Thus, it promises equality and joint prosperity for all. This benefit is rewarded in trade for surrendering personal liberties to the governing powers, which run things much like a business. However, "any accomplishments quickly fade as the fundamental deficiencies of central planning emerge."[173] In contrast, capitalism's strengths are found in the fact that incentives exist: those that come from service, competitive pricing, the benefits of entrepreneurship and property ownership, opportunities for promotion, and other motivations for people to be the best that they can be.[174] This lends to a society of people who find work that fulfills them, who understand *why* they do what they do, and who challenge one another to perform competitively. When roles are dictated, property is owned by the governing powers, and people are without motivation to perform well, economic output fails as a result of lack of ambition and capped potential.[175]

One of the biggest pitfalls of a socialist society is that, when people feel as though they're part of a large machine that doesn't see them as unique individuals, they become unhappy. In America, we have a highly individualized culture, one in which folks want to feel that they're seen and heard. We see a great example of this in social media, which allows people to independently have and proclaim their opinions; their personal styles, which vary greatly; and the freedom to identify with a certain religion, gender, orientation, or other classification. In America, people are free to be anything or anyone they want to be! At this time, many are desperate to see socioeconomic divides narrowed, to see relief for the impoverished. These are wonderful goals. But socialism isn't the answer, because it contradicts human nature—especially how that nature has evolved in today's America.[176]

Essentially, socialism—even if it works perfectly, which it likely won't—offers to provide for physical and material needs, but reduces people to automatons in order to do so. We may not realize it, but similar ideologies fail or are rejected every day in society. For example, someone gives us a budget that's supposed to help us save money, but we don't follow it because it either doesn't work or we don't want to follow the spending constraints. As another example, foundations or clubs are started with a group of people stating that the cause is worthy, but members get tired and their support wanes. And nutritionists write rigid diet plans that diet-ers don't follow because they want to eat what they want.

Consider this: A group of people decide they want to make a better life. They purchase land together, designate communal areas for growing their own food, coordinate home-schooling their children, and manu-facture as many of their goods and meet as many of their own needs as possible. Along the way, they discover that, in the best interest of the community, many policies must be enacted.

Eventually, others join this community, making the shared load become heavier. Ideally, the newcomers would give as much dedicated effort and financial investment to the conglomerate as the original visionaries, but, as we all know, it is likely that they won't. Before long, the original dreamers will likely be those working the hardest and car-rying the heaviest financial burden, while others do the minimum to keep from being asked to leave. In addition, the more recent joiners may complain about all the rules that were put into place before they arrived, when they didn't have a say in the decision-making. Why will the scenario play out like this? Because the founders will have sacrificed much personal freedom in trade for a way of life that fostered secu-rity for themselves, but it was their ambition—their *dreams*—that will carry them through the effort and discipline. On the other hand, most newcomers won't have been personally invested in the success of the community, and likely will have joined in hopes that their needs would be met. In light of this, they will want to hang onto as much personal freedom as possible—while making minimal personal sacrifice. If they were somehow forced to contribute more effort or financial support, they would consider the trade unfair or demand more freedoms; any-thing less than the meeting of such demands would result in accusations of overreach on the part of the community's ruling body.

Yet, this is precisely the frustration that results from a switch to socialism, which requires that people trade 100 percent effort *and per-sonal freedoms* for security. Those living in an extremely individualistic society such as America may be drawn to this notion for a while—as many Americans currently are—but they won't be for very long. Unfortunately, by the time the citizens recognize socialism's shortcomings, it could be too late to get their power back. Worst of all, when it's discovered that the governing powers do not have—nor can they get—enough wealth to keep all the promises they've made, a disillusioned populace will realize that they face the same level of poverty and other socioeconomic issues they did previously. But once all ways of building wealth have been placed under governmental control, individuals will no longer have the power to try to restore the situation without attempting to overthrow the ruling body. At the end of the day, the type of life socialism promises would be difficult for anyone living in a collectivist society, but Americans will face a terrible and adverse culture shock if they actually get this trade, *despite* the fact that many currently believe it's the answer to their problems. And, once America becomes a socialist nation, it's very unlikely that the situation will be reversed.

Some readers may take this look at socialism to mean that we authors have no sympathy for those who are in need of resources that it *attempts* to provide, such as healthcare, education, equality, and necessities. That's not the case. In fact, we would *love* to see the Church come up with more answers to these problems, and we would celebrate interpersonal networking that would foster settings wherein people could help each other. By pointing out the flaws in socialism, we merely hope to call attention to the fact that it will not solve the problems it *represents* itself as being able to, and that ultimately the selling points are circulated to con citizens into undervaluing their liberties in trade for provision.

No Place to Hide

George Orwell's *1984* depicted a world wherein citizens were surveilled at all times, even on the level of their thoughts. As governmental control ramps up—and as citizens increasingly surrender their freedoms—its increasing intrusion can be seen in the way we're continually watched. Placidly adopting a level of invasion was once viewed as fantastical and dystopian, we are now almost completely desensitized to it and perceive it as being "for our own protection." Many Americans are aware that the National Security Agency screens billions of phone calls, text messages, and other communicative metadata for terminology or other activity that may flag suspicion of terrorist activity.[177] Additionally, pictures taken on smartphones are encrypted with data that can be traced, location devices track our whereabouts, and web browsers keep lists of our searches, purchases, preferences, and needs in order to suggest ads. On top of all that, facial recognition software has become commonplace. It would seem that no one can hide.[178]

Security expert Bruce Schneier relays that this level of surveillance is problematic on several levels. One pertains to the notion that people who have "nothing to hide" don't mind being watched. However, Schneier points out that this is untrue; the same people who claim passivity about this intrusion will not reveal or discuss information such as their finances or sexual fantasies.[179] So how is it that they don't mind being spied on? Likely, because they don't see watchmen and cameras, they lack a certain level of belief that it is *really* happening or can *actually* impact their lives. After all, people face "real, tangible" problems each day, so this falls low on the priority list. Yet, we're impacted daily in ways we're not aware of. Social media posts can cause us to be flagged for extra security checks at the airport; spyware causes media data uses to spike that we cannot otherwise account for; and even webcams are capable of being hacked and revealing private moments when we think we are alone.[180] Digital "cookies" send pertinent info in one of two directions: 1) to governmental sources to signal potential terrorist activity or 2) to advertising venues for use in marketing. Despite these and many other ways of digital invasion, culture seems disinterested in putting a stop to these practices.[181] Ultimately, the apathy likely stems from a trust most of us have in our government: We don't really believe it will misuse the information it collects or use it against us.

However, this logic is flawed. First of all, there is the possibility that, as the government gains more control, this data *could* and even *would* become ammunition against some people. There is also the potential that the information could be compromised and obtained by a third party with malicious intent. Additionally, consider CIA whistleblower Edward Snowden's own words: "Every border you cross…purchase you make…call you dial…cell phone tower you pass, friend you keep… site you visit, subject line you type…packet you route, is in the hands of a system whose reach is unlimited but whose safeguards are not."[182] (This means that, even for those who aren't worried about the government abusing the info, they're trusting that the database holding all the private information will never be breached.) With smartphones, smart TVs, laptops, tablets, and even reading devices (which even track the speed of our reading) on or near us at all times, our every move can be monitored.[183] Each financial transaction, from paying bills to making purchases of all types, is traceable, as is all activity we conduct via apps, such as catching a ride with companies like Uber, having meals delivered, searching for recipes and DIY (do-it-yourself) projects, designing nutrition plans, sending private emails and texts, engaging in social media through "likes," and so, *so* much more. Because our locations are also trackable, everywhere we go can be made public knowledge. *And*, thanks to new apps such as CarSafe, which auto insurance companies are using to identify high-risk drivers, even our method of driving along the way will be uploaded to a computer bank for future reference.[184]

Perhaps you've heard of a series of apps released early in 2020 to track COVID-19 exposures. Some were released by digital manufacturers, while others were distributed by state-level sources. They operated by tracking one's location as he or she went about the day, logging every stop. Those testing positive would update the app to send a notification to the smartphones or other devices of anyone they had been in proximity with during the previous days. Many of these tracking apps are accurate enough, via wi-fi connections, to triangulate a location down to "which aisle you're in at the supermarket."[185] This may sound to many like a great tool—and, we suppose, in the right context, it *could* be. But what about other uses for such an app? In the hands of someone with deviant intentions, this technology would leave citizens with literally nowhere to hide.

How might the government use this power if it was ever turned completely loose with it? Surely, as citizens placidly relinquish more control, the risks of abuse become greater. And, as Christians, we're forced to point out that as our brand becomes more hated, we can't ignore what we read in the book of Revelation, where we see that the Remnant Church will be forced to go underground. (Call us over reactive and apocalyptic; tell us we're wrong. We will *pray* that you're right). But one who sees this writing on the wall must wonder what type of agenda might be behind the drive to persuade citizens to download tracking devices that monitor not only their every move, but who they're near and the size of any group they might meet. Additionally, if we embrace the notion that it's for our own good that we're digitally followed, we wonder if the day is coming when such measures won't just be on a *device* that we carry, but *inside* our bodies in some sort of chip. Is this some sort of priming for taking the Mark of the Beast?

Schneier seems to be under the impression that, should the government ever mandate such tracking, "for certain you will rebel. But… [they don't] have to…[inject a chip] because you do it willingly [via your smartphone] and they just…copy the data."[186] But would we rebel against being continually watched? George Orwell painted a picture of a society wherein "Big Brother" watched everyone constantly and inescapably; even thoughts themselves were monitored by their own brand of police. In that world, citizens were so overwrought by the daily circumstances of their lives and so preoccupied with the constant state of war that they allowed themselves to be perpetually subdued.[187] Perhaps that contributes to the apathetic gaze toward such overt monitoring.

One thing is certain, though. As the masses look to the government to fix their problems, viewing socialism as the vehicle by which we all will obtain a more hopeful future, increased spying capability is certainly one way increased control could one day be enforced.

Social Distancing = Social Damaging

The COVID-19 epidemic spanning nearly the entire planet, as we know, has reduced the need for contact with other human beings. Social-distancing policies in all facets of life have required us to avoid large gatherings, remain at least six feet apart, and wear a mask or shield over the nose and mouth. While part of the population has followed these policies, believing mask-wearing to be beneficial, others have shirked them wholeheartedly, regarding the requirement as an infringement on their personal rights. The opposing views have created a vast rift in humanity's regard of one another.

The psychological consequences of social distancing are hardly debatable, even for those who see the practice as prudent while a virus sweeps across the nation. After all, people are social creatures, and we bond through contact: dancing, hugging/kissing, team sports, sharing food/meals, shaking/holding hands, and much more. Just as it can feel socially awkward when someone stands too close, it can also be off-putting when someone stands too far away during a conversation. It's also especially true that, during times of uncertainty, people turn to one another for emotional, social, and other forms of support. As such, the damage caused by the need to "social distance" during the pandemic has contributed to the struggle many have mental illness; it has even caused many who don't usually suffer such ailments to report trouble.[188] We've already mentioned that suicide rates have spiked since the start of the COVID-19 epidemic. Additionally, some professionals state that even after the world "returns to normal, the following year will not be a good one for mental health."[189] In fact, these say that the spike in substance abuse during the COVID lockdowns should illustrate that employees in "work-from-home situations" need to be made aware of the support available to them, and that managers should be aware that this type of working arrangement may not always operate as ideally as planned.[190]

Exacerbating the issue of social distancing is the way that increased screen time—via television, video games, social media, and such—has interfered with interpersonal relationships. Researchers have, for years, been concerned about the splintering of personal interaction and the desensitization caused by such use. In a world where engaging in community is one of the most vital ways people are meant to thrive, repeatedly witnessing killings and other violence dehumanizes our view of those around us. This point has been discussed elsewhere in this book (and in many other scholarly works), so we won't elaborate here. Suffice it to say, the devaluing of human life and depersonifying of our neighbors occurs every day in our world, thanks—in large part—to media and technology. Before "social distancing" even came into the picture, it was an issue threatening to diminish our love and compassion for one another.

However, the situation emerging along with COVID-19 has managed to escalate the issue. Social media had already made many feel as though they were in competition—who has the biggest house, the most successful career, the happiest marriage. The COVID distancing that drove folks to Facebook, Instagram, and other venues even more often further served to transition people from being peers to being competitors, stripping others of their humanity and strengthening their image as an icon of rivalry. Additionally, a new level of such contention was introduced, one that suggested that a person could *even* be a source of threat. No longer was the "boogey man" a frightening specter in a spooky movie. The "villain" had now become the woman next door who refused to wear a mask or the guy from church who grabbed the last five four-packs of toilet paper at the local supercenter. During the

COVID lockdowns, friends sometimes became enemies, posing dangers both viral and material. Our fellow man became those we were increasingly desensitized about, but they also became competitors for supplies...*and* they had the potential to contaminate us as well! In a world filled with digital ways to objectify and dehumanize the *people* around us, social distancing has severed our personal contact, which was among the last ways we still reveled in co-humanity. If our ability to have personal connections to and interactions with one another isn't restored, many could cross into psychological territory that it's extremely difficult to return from. The stay-home orders caused people to juggle the mental and emotional fallout of isolation and hopelessness without being able to access the emotional support of others; even when those orders ease and folks are allowed to venture out into society, they're forced to refrain from physical contact—no hugging, no hand-shaking...nothing. If social distancing becomes the "new normal," we face the bleak reality of learning to live without a vital coping mechanism—the human touch—during unprecedentedly difficult times. Consider this excerpt from *Unscrambling the Millennials Paradox* that elaborates on the damage dealt by isolation:

> Isolation is a form of loneliness that runs much deeper than rejection and leads to hopelessness that makes people feel that they are alone in the world. When people are exposed to short seasons of such conditions and have enough life experience to understand that the pain is situational or temporary, and supportive relationships are present, they can maneuver through these troubled times. But when...[people] are positioned within a society that carries a continual undertone of adversity [and] have few or no relationships they can call upon for help, their hope is diminished... Isolated long enough, people become particularly vulnerable to suicidal thoughts. The deadly problem with isolation is that when people begin to...[succumb to

such hopeless thinking as thoughts that prelude suicide], there is often no one around to tell them otherwise—or at least nobody they are capable of hearing in their moment of acute pain.[191]

Culture, at this time, is attempting to learn to carry on without physical contact. Yet, touch—whether it's the thrill of a first kiss, the brush of a finger on a newborn baby's cheek, a comforting embrace after the loss of a loved one, the silent communication with one who cannot speak, the hand-holding and ring-around-the-rosy playing of childhood, the sweeping away of another's tears, the laying on of hands in devout intercessory prayer—is vital to our psychological health. Touch is the first communication of love that we receive as infants, and it speaks to us long before we have learned language. It is the most basic of human needs, and it needs to be restored in our society.

Isolation Skews Reality

As social media, reality TV, and even lifelike online video games connect people, but through a digital means, the time-honored way that the mind interacts with others has the potential to become skewed. Consider the way social media distances and dehumanizes our neighbors, while shooting victims in video games, for example, become more real to us. As interfacing with computerized images gives those avatars a more intimate, tangible identity in the minds of those who are isolated than real people do, it's feasible to believe that harming a real-life acquaintance could eventually become even easier than it would be to victimize characters in a video game. This may seem far-fetched, but studies have shown that the media-aggression connection is real (as has been discussed in another part of this book), and many of our young people have spent *several months* alone with their video games during the pandemic lockdowns and school closures. Their impressionable minds are malleable, they face a world that currently offers little hope, and they're now struggling with the loss of human contact.

With online sites offering what many passively acknowledge as "fake news," these young people are also potentially struggling with their grasp of reality. It would seem that each time we engage in social media, there's a new report of something fearful, leaving users to decide what—and what not—to believe. For example, a meme circulating on Facebook during midsummer 2020 stated that the upcoming November election would be canceled due to the virus. The image was immediately removed by network admins each time it was posted, but there were people who saw it and panicked. Other memes making similar claims have been distributed without being removed. How can a young person, afraid and alone but for his digital friends, separate reality from fiction in this frightening world? Ordinarily, he might ask a teacher at school, but that's not much of an option when schools are closed. He might ask a friend, but mandated stay-home orders have diminished communication. He might even ask a parent or guardian, but the adults in his life likely seem so preoccupied with the financial (and other) stressors that accompany sudden unemployment or other virus-related fears that he may not bother. Further, if he's in an abusive situation, he merely stays hidden as much as possible during such times; drawing attention to himself by asking questions isn't something he's likely to do. Sure, he could call, text, or email someone his questions, but he may simply lack the boldness. The bottom line is that *much* of our younger generation spent the bulk of 2020 afraid, alone, interacting more with media than with people, lacking physical contact with caring people, and wondering if life would ever "be okay" again.

Interestingly, this period has the potential to alter one's perception of reality for the rest of his or her life not just emotionally but on a literal and cognitive level as well. The brain—literally speaking—is under heightened attack in our current circumstances. It isn't fully formed at birth, but continues physically developing via our memories and experiences throughout childhood and well into young adulthood, and sometimes even later.[192]

Consider one neuroscientist's comments on how our *experiences*—not only our genetics—hold vast authority over the way the brain can be permanently altered:

> At a microcellular level, the infinitely complex network of nerve cells that make up the constituent parts of the brain actually change in response to certain experiences and stimuli. The brain, in other words, is malleable—[capable of changing throughout the lifespan].[193]

Consider the recent isolation of our youth and the malleability of the brain in conjunction with what has become known as the TikTok suicide (although it may have originated on Facebook, not TikTok). In September 2020, a brutal video began to meander through social media that allegedly showed a man shooting himself with a gun. While sites scrambled to remove the graphic video, user re-uploads thwarted efforts to stop it completely. Warnings appeared stating that accounts reposting the media would be banned; others cautioned users "to look out for an image—a man sitting in front of his desk with a grey beard—and swipe away from the video."[194] Worse, new advisories surfaced, stating that clips of the suicide were being spliced *into* unrelated videos, meaning that a person could be watching something completely unrelated and suddenly see the awful act.[195] Some people were even twisted enough to cut the scene into videos geared *toward* young people, such as images containing kittens or puppies.[196] This isn't the only time such a clip has circulated, and once viral, it's difficult to completely, permanently remove. Copycat posts have also been dispersed wherein people pretend to commit suicide, but then later are revealed to have performed a sick joke. It is both sad and deplorable that our youth live in a world where they can be unwittingly accosted and made to witness an actual murder, suicide, or other violence while scrolling through social media on their phone or computer in search of connection to other human beings.

Again, in the long-term isolation of their bedrooms during COVID shutdowns, it's possible for a young person to lose touch with reality. (If you doubt this, consider how their days become nights and vice versa, and how even their wakeful moments can be spent in a dreamlike state.) While digital "people" become more humanized and the real people nearby become more distant, they're bound to experience increased confusion about reality in the upcoming months. The best remedy for this is to allow their human contact to resume. Some may think that can be accomplished with the reopening of schools. While school offers the opportunity for some socialization with teacher and peers, provides structure and routine to the day, and promotes accountability and responsibility, it's not a perfect setting. Our families, loved ones, friends, and churches need to be allowed to reach out to young people to remind them that they have a support network, should they need it.

{6}

CHECK THE CHILDREN

"There can be no keener revelation of a society's soul
than the way in which it treats its children."
~Nelson Mandela[197]

For many who study America's current direction, speculation about crossing a point of no return doesn't seem out of the question. After all, many of the ways culture presses against the outer limits of propriety are certainly bolder than in previous generations. But, what have we embraced as a society that signals we have, indeed, gone too far?

The answer to this question could come in many forms, but one key response is to consider the Mandela quote above stating that our children are the most accurate summation of society's condition. As culture plods forward, there is talk of compromising these cherished assets via a variety of elements, ranging from the decline of education to even the normalization of pedophilia. Surely such atrocities will never be embraced! Yet, we're closer than one may think to such extremities.

Education Indoctrination

"Not on my watch!"

That's usually the response to an immoral or distasteful proposition.

This is an admirable position, and one we should take when keeping an eye out for aversive agenda. However, it's often met with a subversive and even malevolent counterposition that says, "Not on your watch. Sure, no problem. We'll just condition the *children*, and let it happen on *their* watch instead." Unfortunately, this has taken place repeatedly in American (and *world*) history. And while these authors advocate for the post-COVID-19 reopening of schools and the resumption of structure for our children, there are flaws in the institutions they attend full-time. Similarly, we wish to acknowledge that there are many wonderful adults in our public education system who give sacrificially on a daily basis, and whose contributions should be applauded. But, unfortunately, this same system has—in many ways—been hijacked by a faction who wants to see our youth brainwashed to embrace destructive propaganda at the cost of their *actual* education, and perhaps even of their souls.

It's much easier to point out the flaws in the system than it is to outline the necessary overhaul it would take to right the wrongs. By and large, the right for *all* to obtain an education is a privilege our citizens enjoy because previous generations who went without public schools sacrificed to build such a system for future generations. Thus, we're thankful that it's available.

However, what was established as a tool for preparing students for a successful future in all facets of life (gainful employment, contribution to society, preparation for family and individual responsibilities, higher levels of thinking, and so on) has, in several areas, gone off course. Unfortunately, these areas now short-change academics while exposing impressionable students to subject matter and propaganda that their minds not only aren't often ready for, but that are issues that *should* be left to the parents.

A place to begin when looking at the evolution of education over the previous decades is at what is *no longer* taught. The list of subjects that have been dropped by many public schools may surprise you. It includes, but isn't limited to, the following: civics, US history, cursive writing, spelling, geography, home economics, public speaking, choir, drama, band, typing, and many foreign languages. Some of these have been assimilated into other subjects. For example, typing has been absorbed into computer classes, but the actual art of "keyboarding"—typing without looking at one's fingers—is no longer taught in many regions. Spelling is no longer its own subject, but words are checked and corrected in the courses of "parent subjects" such as creative writing. However, some question the value of these changes. Further, in many districts, the length of time kids spend in "recess" has been reduced—nearly cut completely in some places.

Decades ago, students said the "Pledge of Allegiance" each morning, and few balked. Although they've had the right to decline this recitation since the early 1940s under the First Amendment's right of free speech, it was still the majority's practice to participate.[198] However, as an increasingly pluralistic culture has permeated our schools, with each student bringing in his or her own religious views, the phrase "under God" became such a point of contention that most schools set aside the daily recital of the Pledge in hopes of keeping multicultural peace. Two decades later, school-led prayer was forbidden under the same constitutional parameters, allowing individual and small groups of pupils to pray only when it is student-led and noncoercive.[199] Via these and many other changes, God has been nearly removed from our school settings.

As parents have spent more time at work in recent years and less at home, schools have increasingly assumed more responsibility in child-rearing. In some ways, this intervention has provided a welcome relief. Summer-school programs help parents who work full-time by providing daytime childcare; school-bus operations help save on transportation costs and allow parents of older children some work-time flexibility.

And food-service programs are another sign of the escalation of schools' involvement in caring for kids. But note the shift in the school's role: It has gone from providing no lunch (in earlier years, students always brown-bagged it) to offering hot lunch and even breakfast in more recent decades. During the coronavirus shutdowns, many schools continued to provide lunches, delivered to private homes via school busses, because of the awareness that, for many children, school meals are the only hot meals they can count on. (This service isn't unique to the pandemic; backpack programs across America have for years sent nutritious food home with children to sustain them over weekends and holiday breaks.)[200]

Of course, extended hours, transportation, and meals are wonderful programs that make a huge difference in the lives of families, but the fact that they're even needed at all highlights another issue: Parents have become spread so thin that they increasingly rely on schools for help. Unfortunately, the tradeoff for such reliance is sometimes made in allowing—whether explicitly stated or not—the school to reach into parental authority. In other words, the assistance parents receive is often accompanied by relinquishment of their power and influence over their own children. Many feel that schools in recent decades have gone too far where education is concerned, violating the rights of parents—all while even becoming less effective academically.

Mild versions of this transgression can again be seen most obviously through meal programs. Due to laws regarding nutritional requirements, many schools have overstepped their boundaries by disallowing students to eat lunches that parents send from home. In one instance, a preschooler in North Carolina was given chicken nuggets since an inspecting agent said the child's packed lunch of a "turkey and cheese sandwich, banana, potato chips and apple juice…didn't meet U.S. Department of Agriculture guidelines."[201] A simple Google search gives links to dozens of reports of schools interfering daily in matters that should be left to parents and their children.

More severe examples of this type of parental usurpation can be found in the teen years. Since the 1990s, public school administrations have teetered back and forth on the issue of distributing condoms and related items through CAPs (condom availability programs), a tandem effort of the Centers for Disease Control (CDC) and the school districts.[202] Teenagers often see the school as an alternate source of authority and resources when their desires don't align with their parents' or guardians' principles or when parents or guardians are unavailable to help them get such supplies. Many people are surprised to learn that most states designate medical autonomy to individuals when they are in their mid-teens—usually between fifteen and sixteen years old. This means that (depending on the state) students as young as fifteen can seek medical treatment, make decisions regarding gender reassignment or hormone therapy, obtain birth control, have an abortion, get vaccinations, or do nearly anything else that falls into the "medical" category without so much as consulting a parent. And in some cases, schools help them achieve these goals.

Vaccinations are currently available *at* schools, via "school-based programs" that only require students under a certain age to provide a signed parent's consent. However, even with a parent's consent, schools won't enforce a non-mandatory vaccine on a child who doesn't want one.[203] On the other hand, the school-based clinics *will* allow a teenager who has reached the state's legal age for medical consent to accept the vaccinations without a guardian's consent or notification. So, a parent who has requested a vaccine for a minor could find that the child has declined, while another parent whose teenager is fifteen or sixteen may find that his or her child has received a treatment that he or she did not approve of.

Worse than the notion that a child could be vaccinated/not vaccinated against a parent's wishes are stories such as that of a Seattle mother, whose fifteen-year-old daughter obtained an abortion arranged by the girl's high school without the mother's knowledge.[204] The woman had signed a consent allowing her daughter to be treated by the school nurse for what she perceived would be limited to assessing minor health issues. Later, however, she found that the young girl had gone in for treatment and had been given a pregnancy test. She was then provided with a taxi that took her to an abortion clinic. She was told that if she kept the matter secret, there would be no financial repercussions.[205] The form the parent signed also apparently permitted her daughter to receive birth control. Most shockingly, no laws were broken in this whole scenario. The law allowed for minors to obtain "an abortion and abortion-related services at any age without the consent of a parent, guardian, or father of the child…[along with] testing for sexually transmitted diseases… mental health care, and prenatal care…under the law."[206]

Aside from the issue of the school's overreach, parents who have experienced this type of atrocity face another devastating problem: the fact that their child made a life-altering decision and underwent a traumatic clinical procedure without parental counsel—and *alone*. Although this practice is widespread in American schools, it happens in other countries as well, with much the same devastating impact on families. For example, a New Zealand mother found out four days after it happened that her sixteen-year-old daughter had received an abortion. "I was horrified," the mom said, "horrified that she'd had to go through that on her own, and horrified her friends and counsellors had felt that she shouldn't talk to us."[207] The woman pointed out the irony of school administrators who phone parents to discuss academic slumps or behavioral issues, but keep a pregnancy and terminations secret. She was further outraged that the "follow-up counselling for her daughter was 'nonexistent.'"[208]

Some will quickly defend schools, stating that secret abortions and other medical treatments arranged behind parents' backs aren't every-day occurrences. Others may point out, however, that these happenings are, by their very nature, *not reported on*. So, in truth, we don't know how often things like this happen. What we *do* know is that they *have taken place*—and it could again. Also, as culture changes, the types of medical decisions a student can make without a parent's involvement become more varied. With the uptick in the number of children and teens showing interest in gender reassignment and/or hormone therapy, these subversive and usurping acts made by schools can cause deeper harm to families by intruding into conversations that *desperately need to* take place between children and parents and should *never* happen without a parent's knowledge.

Sexual-Education Revolution

Public-school health teacher Deborah Tackmann has been in her line of work since 1976.[209] She notes that, in her early years of teaching health classes, there wasn't a national directive or common curriculum for her students; rather, the class was designed to simply take a look at an individual's overall health and explain how physical systems within the body work together. "It was a systems approach," she said. "Here's the respiratory system, the circulatory system." Then later, she said, as statistics began to highlight the issue of teen suicide, the school's response was, "Oh! We have an issue with suicide. Maybe we should talk about it."[210] As a teacher who calls her middle-school students "hormones with legs," she says that one challenge of teaching sex education in modern culture is instilling within students "skills to access…information…and say no to certain behaviors but yes to relationships."[211] To be certain, the topic of sex ed in public schools has become convoluted over her teaching years. Whereas health and physical education classes started with studying nutrition and running laps, significant changes—such as the intrusion of media in recent years that has impacted children's health, emergent diseases such as HIV making sexual education a frontrunner among health-related topics, and the commonplace status of same-sex relationships—have caused educators to talk more openly than ever about many aspects of sexuality.[212]

In a nutshell, culture changes outside the school heavily influence what goes on behind classroom doors. And, unfortunately, school is no longer the innocent place a youngster goes to learn the ABCs and memorize multiplication tables. As the world drifts further into confusion, kids carry their questions into the academic setting and often ask faculty for answers, with the responses not always reflecting parents' standards.

Did Google Hijack the Public Education System?

A large rift formed between many parents and their children's schools when Google Chromebooks became commonplace in the classroom. This may seem like quite a leap, but it has actually created more issues than one might realize at first glance. Chicago's public schools were among the first to transition from written work to an online interface using Google-sponsored helps such as Google Classroom, Gmail, Google Calendar, and Google Docs. The changeover was initiated in 2012 by nearly four hundred thousand students in Chicago; and now more than thirty million students are using these tools.[213] Google has outperformed many of its scholastic-supply competitors (such as Apple and Microsoft) by not only making its Chromebooks extremely affordable, but by creating software that provides teaching helps that permit students and educators to interface completely via the small laptops. The devices graduated from being "very useful" to "invaluable" during the COVID-19 school closures, allowing academics to carry on despite the pandemic. In the face of such drastic shutdowns, you'd think the technology would be embraced, yet there is resistance. Why?

Natasha Singer of the *New York Times* says, "Unlike Apple or Microsoft, which make money primarily by selling devices or software services, Google derives most of its revenue from online advertising—much of it targeted through sophisticated use of people's data."[214] This single point leads many to wonder whether Google is *really* striving to benefit educational institutions by making creative online helping tools and affordable laptops, or whether there's more to this scheme. Is Google providing such a wide swath of the population—students—with the technology so it can gather data that will help it make money from the same segment of the population later, when they're grown? Many argue that we can't be sure whether information collected from children will ultimately serve to help or harm them.[215] It's hard at this point to get any answers; Google has declined to outline precisely what data it collects from its students and how such information is used.[216]

Additionally, can we assume that this information won't fall into the wrong hands? This concern isn't unfounded. These authors personally know someone whose daughter was lured into online chatrooms by a predator; the matter required police intervention before it could be resolved. New Mexico Attorney General Hector Balderas seems to believe that the low retail prices Google offers schools don't stem from benevolence, but from the promise of some kind of gain.[217] Banderas' accusation involves Google's violation of the Children's Online Privacy Protection Act, which mandates parental consent for information to be collected on children under thirteen years old. According to the attorney general, this technology has "stripped children and parents of autonomy...forcing children to acquiesce to constant monitoring, in perpetuity, in exchange for their education."[218] Google has been accused of using Chromebooks to surveil children "across the internet, across devices, in their homes, and well outside the educational sphere."[219]

All this concern, yet many parents who wish to find a work-around for their children are stonewalled: "No [G]oogle, no access. No access, no education."[220] To many for whom home-schooling or private education aren't options, compliance with the Google-based schooling is an only choice. This is upsetting when we know that predators target technology used by children and teenagers, so Chromebooks and other educational materials and devices will be at the top of the list of those under fire. Further, many schools that assure parents that they have installed cyber-security apps on devices issued to students fail to mention that these safeguards are usually only effective when logged in to the school's wi-fi. This means that the student may be most vulnerable when he or she is at home—perhaps alone.[221] The FBI has issued multiple warnings that using educational-tech hardware and software can make minors susceptible to a variety of risks, sometimes offering "unique exploitation opportunities for criminals," including but not limited to "social engineering, tracking, identity theft, or other means for targeting children."[222] Note that tracking is one of the potential hazards listed and acknowledged by the FBI. For many of these devices, locations are easily obtained by hackers, meaning that if a predator does target a child, the hacker likely knows where to find him or her.

Are We Being "Dumbed Down"?

The accusation that Americans are being intentionally dumbed down is nothing new. The phrase is scattered throughout the early years of Hollywood filmmaking, when scripts had to be adjusted to meet the educational level of a targeted audience. In 1991, John Taylor Gatto released the book *Dumbing Us Down*, wherein he stated that the education system stifles children's ability to thrive creatively and victimizes them, teaching them to be mere "cog[s] in the machine" of a standardized and broken system.[223] Since that book and others similar to it have been released, the phrase "dumbing down" has usually been in reference to an agenda that has infiltrated the public education system in an effort to render a more malleable, controllable, impressionable society that's deprived of personal empowerment, ingenuity, and self-sustainability.

It is no secret that, over preceding decades, academic scores have fallen. A study conducted in 2018 by the US Department of Education found that nearly 20 percent of high school graduates are illiterate, and an equal number reads only at an elementary level.[224] For some, this is the dismal result of having a school system that has become increasingly responsible for tasks that parents should be carrying out at home, while others point to budget cuts and understaffing as the culprit.

Some, however, believe this to be the outcome of an intentional and subversive eugenics project by which the population is being groomed to become "a population of mindless, robotic citizenry that simply does what it's told...[and by which] the brainwashing commences early in America's schools."[225] Those who believe this readily connect the premeditated academic decline of today's generations with the preselection process of a labor force for the New World Order.[226] If there's truth to these speculations, then the school's willingness to overextend into parental authority takes on a new dimension, while the alarm associated with the passivity in which many parents allow this intrusion elevates as well.

Either way, one thing that must not escape note is an undeniable correlation between socioeconomic status and academic performance.[227] This becomes a recurrent familial trap that subsequent generations have difficulty breaking out of. Early on, statistics show that families struggling financially often have children who also face challenges in school, and the connection is a complex one that many have studied at length. Some perceived contributing factors are that these youths have fewer experiences that encourage academic development; less access to helpful resources such as computers, books, and tutors; and even diminished opportunities for continuing their education beyond high school.[228] However, the lower socioeconomic status, linked to a lower likelihood that a student will extend his or her education post-graduation, is also a predictor of one's *future* socioeconomic status.[229] Thus, educational performance and future financial well-being become cyclical in families, a wheel many young people feel they're unable to jump off of, thus they're not motivated to even try. As academic ideals drop, entire family trees see a continued decline in the standard of living—unless their youngest generations change the momentum. With schools focusing less on many scholarly topics of yesteryear and spending more time taking over parents' roles and discussing political propaganda in the classroom, it would seem that many of these youngsters are at a disadvantage from every direction.

National Security Breach

Regardless of the reason *behind* the decrease in academic success in recent generations, we can hardly debate that the issue is problematic. Upon graduation of high school, students primarily choose one of three pathways: continued education, employment, or military service.[230] One problem stemming from the modern educational system, which "places scores from standardized testing at a higher value than the actual curriculum taught in the classroom...means that students are only learning how to take tests, but are lacking in other learning opportunities to develop their potential skills and knowledge."[231] The problem for national security comes in when those who graduate intending to enroll in armed services find that they cannot pass entrance exams. Military recruiters face the challenge of filling openings with an upcoming generation from which "30 percent of possible recruits...[failed] the Armed Forces Qualification Tests" as a result of "inadequate education."[232] When this is added to the 27 percent who are disqualified due to obesity; the 10 percent who have legal infractions that prevent their involvement; and the others who are denied because of "vision, conditions like asthma and diabetes, and mental illness," officials are left with slim pickings from which to staff an entire military.[233] This, paired with the direct correlation between academic success and economic security, makes our nation seem as though it could be headed for serious trouble. After all, America has a formidable military power, but it will do us no good if there aren't individuals rising up to fill it.[234]

The Normalization of Pedophilia

Sexuality has become one of the most convoluted and debated aspects of our culture, and as the topic becomes more heated, all sides have become increasingly volatile. As diversity allows for increasing polarity where sexuality is concerned, many show concern for fostering both their own rights and those of subsequent generations. As such, children slowly become entangled in the web that is self-expression, both by those who defend *and* exploit them. In this postmodern society where people view and defend truth from different angles, the innocents are quickly caught up in the crossfire, resulting in what could be damaging, long-term consequences.

In a previous chapter, we discussed that one method of manipulation is the skewing of the concept of love. Few will disagree that, over time, the definition of "love" has radically changed. With physicality having replaced the importance of a heartfelt connection with others, it easy to see that sex has become confused with affection. In turn, as increased availability of physical titillation encumbers our culture, many are left progressively unsatisfied, leading to elevated levels of sexual deviance, increased use of pornography, and higher demands for sex workers (human trafficking). With the intensifying appetite for nefarious sexual exploits comes tactics that are increasingly convoluted and defended by large-scale society. These defenses are often presented as being "current" or "in the interest of everyone's civil rights." And, it is the exploitation of the innocent that drives such movements forward. The expanding room for diversity paves the way for certain factions to move to center stage, demanding to be recognized as having an orientation with equal rights. Emerging now to that point on center stage is the pedophile's opportunity to frame his or her illness as an "orientation."

According to the American Psychiatric Association, pedophilia has been considered a psychiatric disorder since 1968.[235] Thus, the "normalization" of it seems contradictory, yet it is beginning to occur. However, the technicality making this sickness defensible in today's society is its label. That a person would have the compulsion to become sexually involved with a child but would choose not to act on it, for many who defend this position, creates a point of safety, and even of sympathy, for the pedophile. Many are working to rename the condition in a more politically correct, nonthreatening way. Several terms have recently surfaced, one of which is MAP ("minor-attracted person"),[236] and under the new headings, the attraction to children is being increasingly asserted as an "orientation." This is a vital distinction, because if pedophilia is a psychiatric disorder, the pedophile becomes obligated to obtain treatment or attempt to overcome the desire. However, as an orientation, pedophilia stands to become fostered via the same sympathy and equality promoted by the LGBTQ community. The difference is crucial: Until now, the LGBTQ community has fought for impartiality as it pertains to consenting adults. If pedophilia is embraced as an orientation (and it's rapidly moving in this direction) our children will be targeted by pressure to engage in relationships that their minds and emotions aren't ready to encounter. The damage dealt to these innocents will be irreversible and lifelong.

De-villainizing the MAP's image is already being sown into the public's worldview. Statements are being made citing the loneliness and disparagement of those who are attracted to people who are off-limits. This is a dangerous propaganda: It enables the disease aspect to become accepted, while freeing those who suffer it from the responsibility of finding another way to deal with these urges—likely by seeking professional help. If pedophilia (or the same condition presented under a different label) were to become an orientation, then it could be used as a premise to claim that the pedophiles are free to pursue their happiness as long as there are no victims. (The problem is that, in pedophilia, there *are always* victims, as statistics indicate. We'll come back to this in a bit.) On a more immediate note, once children are conditioned and coerced into showing curiosity about sex, then to involve them in the pursuits of a pedophile *could* become viewed as reciprocation of predatory advances, to which some will likely try to put forward a "victimless" argument for the activity. If the movement catches on, pedophilia could become legalized, sympathized with, and even justified as a new orientation. Allow us to elaborate.

In order to present this orientation as an interaction that exists without victims, then the issue must become one of making a case that a child would actually want to have sex. If it's consensual, there's no problem, right? However, this thinking produces some obstacles, since a child's curiosity is, left to develop on its own, a slow process that's incremental to what is age-appropriate. As such, children won't reciprocate an adult's desire to have sex with them unless conditioning is involved. Developmental stages occur over a period of years and render people—in an ideal society that isn't sexually charged—ready to follow such urges in their early adulthood. This leaves those who move toward pedophilia with one major problem: Their intended victims aren't interested. In order to foster a sexual connection with the young and still-developing population, the interest has to be carefully seeded and cultivated. And, since the way to legalize pedophilia will be done from the position of defending the rights of the child, the conditioning of such thought has to hide in plain sight so that it will *appear* that this interest and desire is instigated *by the children themselves*.

Like taking candy from a baby…

These authors wish we had time to elaborate on the type of public gaslighting taking place here on a large-scale, cultural level. However, for the sake of time, let's use an example of the type of exchange we're explaining. Since, when discussing our children, we're speaking of the most trusting and vulnerable members of our society, the example below is reasonable using the example of an elderly woman:

~

Let's say an elderly woman lives down the street from me (Allie Henson). She has a hundred dollars in her bank account, and I am aware that she is in the early phases of dementia, so she is cognitively interactive but malleable (just like a child). Now, let's say that I want her to give me that hundred dollars. However, she doesn't want to give it to me, because she can't afford it and has no interest in sharing her money with me. I continue to press her, placing messages in her mailbox and at her door about how fun it is to give away money. I even walk up and down the street singing songs about it (this might seem ridiculous, but it's a fair comparison to how a child's life is inundated with sexual content via media, ads, music, movies, and so on). I even promise to use the money to take her on trips, shopping sprees, and fine dinners at beautiful restaurants (thus attaching the notion of "relationship" to my agenda). She is allured by the camaraderie that she believes I am promising, and her desire for friendship and people-pleasing is piqued (just as that of a child would be under the right conditioning).

During this process, onlookers begin to stand up for her rights, telling me that she doesn't have to give me the hundred dollars. They can see that I will never make good on the promises that I've made, because it's impractical to imagine that a hundred dollars will do all the things I say it will. (This is just as "romantic" love with a child can never do what the perpetrator promises. Such love requires an intellectual connection that one can never have with a brain still traveling through the developmental stages of childhood/teenage years. This very point reinforces why children aren't ready for sexual connection.)

Then, I subtly change my approach. I continue to tell the woman how much it will enrich her life to give me the money, but this time I explain to her that it's in her own best interest that I'm asking for it. I tell her it's because I care about her and want her to enjoy all the rewards that she'll get by sharing her money with me. When onlookers oppose my agenda, I state that they're attempting to control her (the same way society tells children whose innocence is being protected by parents or guardians that the custodians are being repressive or overprotective). I even go so far as to claim that those who would barricade my plans for the woman are only trying to control her, to deprive her of all the joy it will bring her to give me her money. I become more assertive, telling her that it's her right to give me the hundred dollars if she wants. If she feels so inclined, nobody should try to stop her. I begin to implant indignation against her protectors in her thoughts. I say, "How dare these others try to stop her from pursuing happiness?" I remind her that she should be allowed to make her own decisions regarding her money, and state flat-out that anyone who tries to change her mind needs to back off and respect her decision. (Does any of this sound like the narrative children are being fed regarding their sexuality right now?)

After all, why are these third parties barging in on our conversation? This has nothing to do with them! How dare they not let her decide what she wants to do with her money?! Why, these others are infringing on her civil rights! As I begin to stir up enmity against those who stand up for her, I continue the slow, extensive conditioning that occurs via the conversation being continually repeated. Eventually, the woman becomes so accustomed to hearing this dialogue about the hundred dollars that the lines of the conversation begin to blur in her easily influenced, elderly mind. She doesn't remember her original reasons for wanting to keep her money, and I've filled her mental and physical space with so many messages of all the good things that will happen to her if she gives me her money that she becomes curious about what it would be like to give her money to someone else. (Again, if you don't think this type of conditioning is happening with our children, then look around at the music, toys, television sitcoms, commercials, and even cartoons that are being thrust into our children's psyches at perpetually younger ages.)

I begin to rally for her "right" to give me the money, and eventually that gains momentum. When she finally surrenders her hundred dollars to me, those who acted on her behalf in the first place because they saw her as mentally vulnerable and me as predatory have been painted as the enemies. The one who wanted to exploit her finances (me) has done so and drained her bank account, with the woman's consent. Those who make it legally easier for con artists like myself celebrate the victory, and the woman returns home penniless. My promises of vacations and fancy dinners are, of course, never kept, because they were never possible in the first place with a budget of a hundred dollars (just as authentic, mature love cannot happen between a child and an adult). The camaraderie the woman hoped for never occurs, because I wasn't after her companionship in the first place (just as an intellectual connection is not what a pedophile is looking for with a child). The woman lives out her years penniless, deprived of medications she can no longer afford (just as exploited children grow up unable to reclaim and restore the damaged stages of their development), and I have now paved the way for others with malevolent intentions to more easily prey on other vulnerable and weak members of society.

Long-term Consequences of Early Sexual Encounters

Because children aren't ready for sexual interaction until their bodies and minds have fully formed, earlier encounters have the potential to impact them in the same way that abuse does, even if it is the child's coerced perception that he or she is consenting. Researchers have found direct connections between child sexual abuse and later risky and maladaptive behavior. Most often cited among women—but certainly not the only ones—are post-traumatic stress disorder, eating disorders, anxiety, low self-esteem, relationship issues (such as conflict and toleration of violence), risky sexual behavior (such as that which can lead to unplanned pregnancy, transmission of disease, or lack of discrimination regarding a number of sexual partners), and depression with or without suicidal thoughts.[237] Studies have shown that child sexual abuse is linked to increased subsequent risky activity such as prostitution and engagement in activities that place them at elevated risk for transmission of HIV.[238] CSA (child sexual abuse) has been, in males especially, connected to risky sexual decision-making and behavior and increased alcohol consumption, a cyclical issue that self-perpetuates as each of these factors then fuels the other.[239] Among adult men, it is found that surviving CSA "[influences] risk-taking in an early and ongoing fashion...[contributing to] elevated...number of sexual partners...inconsistent condom use... exchanging sex for drugs or money...using alcohol prior to or during sex...[and] elevated rates of sexually transmitted infections."[240] CSA is associated with younger alcohol use (as early as preteen years) and higher rates of "binge drinking," with victims often indulging in "3 times the amount of alcohol consumed by their non-abused counterparts."[241] Likewise, many report consuming multiple drinks in one setting and at times drinking alcohol before or during school hours.[242] By mid-life, "men who experienced unwanted sexual activity during childhood were significantly more likely to report alcohol-related problems" than those who don't have such childhood experiences.[243] Studies have revealed that 59 percent of incarcerated males report CSA occurring before their thirteenth birthday, and 64 percent experienced unwelcome advances (such as kissing or fondling).[244] CSA is conclusively linked to later-life difficulties such as nightmares, flashbacks, denial, repression, abusive relationships, domestic violence, difficulty with sexual function,[245] and even violence and sexual aggression.[246]

Unfortunately, there are well-meaning people who believe that children are sexually repressed unless encouraged to explore this area of their identity. Sadly, the efforts of adults are being exploited by a larger hand that wishes to destroy our children and instill irreversible damage upon their lives. Introducing an idea to a child doesn't mean he or she is ready to explore such realms. Children show curiosity about crossing the road long before they are rationally developed enough to understand how to go about it safely. Children indicate interest in jobs—wondering what they'll be when they grow up—long before they're cognitively ready to juggle the responsibilities that come with employment. I (Allie Henson) remember a time when I was about nine when I had done the math and decided that it would be just as cheap for our family to eat McDonald's Happy Meals for breakfast, lunch, and dinner rather than to fuss with buying groceries and cooking. Thank God my mom didn't indulge that silliness; a diet like that leads to obesity, diabetes, autoimmune conditions, heart conditions, hypertension, skin problems, and myriad other health problems. Young people often *think* they know what's in their best interest, but it is adults' jobs to guide them. It is vital to understand that being capable of expressing curiosity about an area of life doesn't mean they're ready to explore it.

Conditioning through Toys

At this very moment, children are being groomed to embrace sexuality, whether we recognize it or not. One of the most obvious ways this conditioning is occurring—besides media, television shows, movies, and music—is through the toys marketed to them. One example is the Trolls World Tour Giggle 'n Sing Poppy Troll Doll, which features a button placed between the legs that, when pushed, causes the doll to make surprised sounds such as gasps and shocked giggles.[247] After outrage incited the circulation of a petition signed by nearly 325,000 parents, Hasbro pulled this doll from shelves.[248] The company's explanations for the button's placement ranged from it being a complete accident (yeah, right…) to it being intended to trigger the doll making funny noises when seated.

Other toys that have yet to be called out include LOL Surprise dolls, which come with androgynous clothing but are available in both genders. Several layers of packaging wrapping the boy dolls are suspiciously riddled with drawings of pizza—a sign many link to pedophilia and even human trafficking—and these male dolls come equipped with testes. The girls, when dipped in cold water, manifest lingerie of various styles and colors (some of which are mature, sexy, or appear in adult themes such as black, strappy fishnet). Since they're sold in opaque packaging, shoppers can't see what the doll is until the purchase has been made, hence the "surprise." For parents expecting toys as innocent as those of yesteryear, these dolls are aptly named.

Drag Queen Story Hour

Other ways children are being taught too early about sexuality can be seen through recent events appropriately titled "Drag Queen Story Hour" wherein drag queens host story times at local libraries. Some appear, in demonic dress, reading children "gender-fluid novels,"[249] while others strip in front of the children[250] or teach them to twerk (a dance wherein the rump gyrates quickly).[251] Some readers have even been seen lying on the floor, with children sprawling on top of them.[252] In one instance, a drag queen wearing only sheer tights under a miniskirt sat, legs wide open, frontal-flashed children at eye-level when bending over to pick up a book.[253] Worse, in at least one case, the hosting library neglected to run a background check on the drag queens, and "a man charged for sexually assaulting…[an eight-year-old boy[254]] was allowed to entertain children at drag queen storytime" (confirming the *very* point we're attempting to make here).[255]

Allowing this type of activity introduces sexual confusion to children at an age when they're not ready to process what they're seeing. Since children aim to please, they're easily swayed into playing roles that aren't healthy for a developing mind. The organizations behind activities such as the drag-queen story time readily admit that their goal is to "groom" the next generation to accept greater sexual diversity, and they state that they're actively recruiting younger members to join their way of life.[256]

The agenda *sounds* good to many citizens: "A lot of core values of being a drag queen—love, acceptance, joy, laughter, self-expression—are values that we want to instill in our kids, so it is very important that we bring this program...[to share] the joy of reading, and the joy of just spreading love." However, the images of these interactions posted online—children sprawled across semi-clad drag queens laying on the floor and adults nearly nude/dressed in S&M-style clothing while posing with children—make it seem that a far darker agenda clouds their motives.[257]

And, this agenda could be escalating as younger children take an interest in joining these efforts. Recent drag sensation Desmond Napoles, known as "Desmond is Amazing," was born in 2007 and is the youngest drag queen at this time in America. An icon in the LGBTQ culture, he is celebrated, featured in magazines, and marches in pride parades.[258] As he gains popularity, it's likely that other children will want to follow this movement, but they'll do so at the peril of being exploited by those who would abuse their impressionability.

Who Is Behind These Agendas?

One must wonder, if all involved in both sides of this issue are truly seeking the betterment of society, why things progress as they do in spite of the opposition. One church in California was vandalized after its pastor openly protested the story hour led by drag queens. The church building was marred with pentagrams scrawled in spray paint alongside "vulgar [and satanic] phrases."[259] These authors believe that there is a link between movements such as these and those that sexually exploit and traffic children behind the scenes. In a nutshell, the violation of our youths' innocence is being moved from the privacy of the back room and into the public sphere. Where such atrocities have been met with outrage and increased awareness/crackdowns, the powers that be have maneuvered to make it appear that children actually want to be involved in their sick fantasies. Conditioning kids to want to participate isn't very hard. But what about the adults who promote this activity? These authors also believe that many of the grown-ups active in these circles are actually being played as well. After all, as we've stated, one of the manipulation methods used by the enemy is to skew the comprehension of what it means to love. And, some of those who speak out for such advancements of humanity are well-respected, educated people who have advocated for other aspects of human equality or emancipation, with the "sexual liberation" of children being only one aspect of their agenda. Consider the words of Kate Millet, American feminist writer, author of the book, *Sexual Politics*, and activist, who stated of children in 1980: "Certainly, one of children's essential rights is to express themselves sexually, probably primarily with each other but with adults as well… the sexual freedom of children is an important part of a sexual revolution…What is really at issue is children's rights and not, as it has been formulated up to now, merely the right of sexual access to children."[260]

We must understand that the public is filled with well-meaning—albeit often misled—individuals who will stand for what they believe is right. In fact, much like the scenario regarding the elderly woman and her money, many believe they are taking a stand for the interests and liberation of children when they advocate for this premature and intimate self-expression. They're unaware that as the final phases of the sexual revolution occur—ringing in the era of children's erotic liberation—deviancy previously hidden will be embraced publicly at our children's expense.

Many of those advocating for this movement are doing what they believe is right.

Therein lies that key element that can be spun against humanity by the craftiest of them all. How is it that entire populations will allow children to be exploited in such a way? It is by conditioning the children to show curiosity and even express interest in being involved in these activities. When this occurs, those who stand "for the children's rights" make it a cause for which they perceive efforts to be righteous. In that way, a few key people can trick an entire population into selling the innocence of their young without even realizing the prize that they've traded away.

Yet, we must be logical. It doesn't occur to children on their own that their bodies may interact sexually with an adult's—or any other person's, for that matter. These ideas come from outside the spectrum of a child's thought processes. And in response, many well-meaning adult influences give kids an overly cultivated environment wherein they can follow the curiosity that accompanies implanted ideas. Society teaches our parents that this is how you create a safe, nonjudgmental way for youngsters to develop a healthy view of themselves. Often, in an effort to be helpful (and with key coaching), adults offer too much information in response to introductory inquiries, which stirs further questions in the mind of a child. One can see how this cycle creates a perpetual line of curiosity that appears to be originating from children, but that is actually prompted by conditioning. Soon, a child's innocence is abandoned or compromised under the heading of self-discovery, while loving, well-meaning caregivers facilitate this robbery. Children are malleable. If they believe what they're doing is normal and pleasing to the adult influences in their lives, they'll become conditioned to see nearly any activity as acceptable. Meanwhile, goodhearted guardians are told that this is the way to be a supportive parent.

All the while, pedophiles are increasingly relabeled with such euphemisms as "minor-attracted persons," and sympathy is fostered for their lack of legal ability to make connections that coincide with their attractions. (Understand that these people *should be offered help* and they desperately need intervention. This is not a hate statement. However, their attraction is problematic in that it renders a lifetime of pain and should thus be treated.) The currently emerging narrative around pedophilia must change. The presently propagated notion that one can't help whom one loves and that he or she is powerless to redirect his or her thoughts is the theme by which MAPs are slowly shifting from being recognized as a public threat to being instated as an orientation. Further, those who would redirect this attraction to age-appropriate peers and overcome the compulsion might be able to find a fulfilling, *appropriate* relationship, thus avoiding a lonely lifetime of isolation.

In the meantime, via outspoken activists allied with the pedophile's cause like Mirjam Heine, the attempt at putting salve on such a societal wound as accepting pedophilia is worded by placing the onus on non-pedophiles who are responsible for accepting them into society, understanding that their urges are not their fault. She states:

> We are not responsible for our feelings; we do not choose them. But, we are responsible for our actions. It is our responsibility to reflect and to overcome our negative feelings about pedophiles and to treat them with the same respect we treat other people with. We should accept that pedophiles are people who have not chosen their sexuality and who, unlike most of us, will never be able to live it out freely if they want to lead an upright life. We should accept that pedophilia is a sexual preference; a thought, a feeling, and not an act. We should differentiate between child sexual abuse and pedophilia.[261]

One problem with this logic is that, when a desire is maladaptive or even dangerous, people have two options. One is to seek counseling and intervention for the destructive desire, attempting to trade it for a healthier one. The other is to accept the desire as permissible while attempting to stifle it, which likely won't work for long. When the individual's mind and the general population have accepted the desire as appropriate and well founded, they can work together to enact the legalities that justify the action. When the action has the potential to cause physical, emotional, psychological, or developmental harm—and without a doubt, pedophilia does *all* of these to our children—a case and system for making it appear safe for potential victims will become the championed cause for the most deviant, malicious, and self-serving minds so that the exploitation will be viewed as acceptable.

Legislative Efforts That Protect Perps and Increase Victim Vulnerability

Some recent legislation regarding sexual predators serves perpetrators over victims. As increasing sympathy for the wrongdoer is nurtured and a victim's best interests are decreasingly prioritized, a disturbing trend emerges. For example, a bizarre law passed in Victoria, Australia, in 2020, essentially placed a gag order on victims of rape and sexual abuse, stating that those who name their abusers could face up to roughly 120 days of jail time or fines exceeding three thousand dollars for violating their attackers' privacy.[262]

Yes, you read that right. We'll give you a minute to digest it.

In fact, we'll repeat it: Victims of sexual abuse in that region of Australia are now legally prohibited from speaking their perpetrators' names; they are being censored in favor of privacy for the guilty, even during litigation. This amendment to the existing Judicial Proceeding Reports Act has been noted as a triumph for those who have abused or exploited others, and it would appear that the only way for targets to retrieve their right to tell their story is via court order, "which is a lengthy process and could cost them more than $10,000."[263] Victims have launched a campaign asking legislators to modify the law to give them back their voice—as they have now been silenced, thus victimized *twice* over: once by the abuse, and again by the prohibition against telling their story.[264] Likewise, the measure stops family members of deceased victims from being able to name perpetrators.

This may seem alarming—these authors certainly find it so! One would hope that it's some calamitous legislative error that will be corrected in the upcoming months. Even as we write this, the amendment is being revisited and debated, with the goal of "[fixing] botched laws enacted…that gagged assault survivors from publicly talking about their experiences without a court order."[265] Certainly, the hope is to see this reversed. If not, this is a blatant account of laws designed to protect the guilty and destroy victims' rights.

We understand that much of our narrative speaks of modern American culture, and that Australia, where this happened, to some, might be too far away to deem relevant here. But, if it can occur in other progressive countries, then it is certain that people in pluralistic America will eventually advocate for similar measures as well. A little closer to home, another bill currently being considered is one in California that would alter the definition of statutory rape as it pertains to certain types of sexual intercourse to protect perpetrators from being classified as sex offenders. The legislation would allow for a ten-year age difference regarding various types of intercourse, citing LGBTQ equality rights as the motivation for this redefinition. The premise is that, currently, "there is…[an] exemption from mandatory registration [as a sex offender] for [heterosexual] intercourse between partners of a similar age difference."[266] In other words, the current law is more lenient on statutory lines regarding heterosexual couples than it is on homosexual couples, because their physical method of intercourse is legally categorized differently. As it stands, consensual, heterosexual intercourse between two people on either side of eighteen years of age can result in misdemeanor or felony charges being filed, depending on the situation. Thus, leniency will be added to other types of intercourse within current legislation under the notion of nondiscrimination.

This concession could leave our teenagers and younger children wide open to ambiguity where sexual assault is concerned. California State Senator Shannon Grove tweeted: "If signed into law, a 24-year-old could have sexual relations with a 15-year-old child without being required to register as a sex offender."[267] Causing even more concern for these authors is that, at this time, we have read the bill itself and can find no specification of minimum age. Someone might be all right with legalizing sex between a twenty-seven-year-old and a seventeen-year-old, but what if that same seventeen-year-old becomes attracted to a seven-year-old child? Because the bill is still being debated, this could mean that—should there be a legal bungle such as the one in Australia regarding victims' rights—an oversight could render it legal for a thirteen-year-old to be seduced by a twenty-three-year-old, and in turn, coerce an elementary-aged youth into sexual acts. The key, in such circumstances, would be determining whether the interaction is consensual. However, studying previous cases of claimed rape, we can quickly see how hard it often is to *prove* rape when one of the parties asserts that it was consensual. Then we have a case of one person's word against another, and often it's not until repeated complaints from multiple victims are filed that charges are brought against an offender. This loophole regarding the sexual safety of minors could open doors that subject our most innocent to a whole new level of depravity—and legally! Furthermore, these would, like the Victoria bill, protect the perpetrator while forgetting the vulnerable. This graying of the waters could quickly become too murky to clean up. And with victims too young to articulate their stance on consent—or even to understand what's happening to their bodies—this has the potential to negatively impact all of society in ways that we'll be unable to measure. Additionally, consider this: The legal drinking age in California (and all states) is twenty-one. The minimum age for purchasing tobacco products is eighteen. In many states, minors are prohibited from purchasing products such as spray paint, glues, and other items as well. How is there any logic to creating legislation that permits a minor to have sex with an adult up to ten years older, when that same minor isn't allowed to purchase spray paint or superglue? The consequences of intercourse are vast, including emotional and psychological repercussions, the sense of loss over virginity, risk of becoming pregnant, threat of contracting sexually transmitted diseases, painful emotional and physical aftermath of abortion or miscarriage, social and romantic fallout, and confusion regarding orientation or sexual identity. Also, even though these authors applaud those willing to carry an unexpected pregnancy to full term, there is also the particularly difficult struggle single parents often face after their physical actions yield consequences their minds aren't prepared for.

Meanwhile, in the Classroom...

A group of parents in Madison, Wisconsin, came together in February of 2020 to file a lawsuit stating that their children's school acted unconstitutionally via its transgender policy, which required the school to conceal from parents any sexual-reassignment actions taken by students.[268] The policy allows children to self-designate their own identity based on "male, female, a blend of both or neither," and vows to "'disrupt the gender binary' with books and lessons stating that everyone has the right to choose their gender."[269] It also permits students to make off-record changes to their names and pronouns unbeknownst to their guardians, an offense that these parents state undermines their rights to maintain an advisory role in their children's lives and usurps familial religious values.[270] The subversive element of this particular instance is that it was instituted in a way that intentionally kept parents out of the loop. While they were to fill out paperwork reassigning names, pronouns, or genders for students, the students were given liberty to do so on an unofficial level—without the parents' signatures. Then, teachers were instructed to comply with children's requests when unsupervised, but to revert to the formerly used names or pronouns when parents were present—an overtly deceitful role.[271] In some cases, students even dressed in the opposite gender's clothing or used a different locker room at school, and parents did not learn about it until after the fact.[272]

Think back to the situations mentioned earlier in this chapter regarding school-arranged abortions, vaccinations, birth control, etc. Now, imagine if schools' overreach ever maneuvered into the realm of chemical gender transition (if they haven't secretly done so already). The situation in Madison, in conjunction with the other scenarios we've mentioned, shows that it's not out of the question. Additionally, some puberty-blocking drugs (used to stave off puberty, sometimes for medically necessary reasons such as halting premature puberty, but recently used in conjunction with gender assignment), have been found to have very serious side effects. For example, between 2012–2019, the Food and Drug Administration (FDA)-approved drug leuprolide acetate, also known as Lupron, manifested more than forty thousand cases of documented side effects. Amongst these, more than twenty-five thousand "were considered 'serious,'" with that number "including 6,370 deaths."[273] The pharmaceutical, formerly used in rare cases of premature puberty to stave off the transition until the appropriate age, has recently been prescribed to children as young as eight in conjunction with "cross-sex hormones" to help young people with gender dysphoria and transition.[274]

California endocrinologist Dr. Michael Laidlaw, however, asserts that there are long-term consequences associated with using this drug in such a way, some of which include inhibited genital development and/or loss of all sensation in the genital areas. Laidlaw adamantly points out the flaws in allowing children to utilize their "core internal sense" in choosing a gender, rather than their biology.[275] He holds that the practice compromises the long-term safety and well-being of these children; furthermore, he states: "This whole thing is an experiment on children. We are ignoring the voices of desisters and people who have come out of this and recognized their sex…the NIH [National Institutes of Health] is allowing unethical research to be conducted on adolescents."[276]

With the alarming possibility that these drugs could be administered to children without their parents' knowledge due to a minor being at the age of medical autonomy—and considered in conjunction with the potentially devastating, lifelong side effects—it stands to reason that parents would want to be part of the decision of whether a child should be placed on these drugs. The entire process of transition/gender reassignment is new and still largely untested. Studies and outspoken medical personnel asserting the dangers of these drugs are only now stepping forward. Unfortunately, their statements are often silenced as hate speech, despite any scientific data that supports their position.

Children want to be accepted, and throughout childhood they often "try on" several identities that they later abandon for the identities they choose permanently. Allowing them to take chemical substances that could make one of their "trial" identities permanent could have lifelong consequences. At this moment, such actions are applauded in the public sphere, meaning that a child who doesn't fit in with peers may choose such an avenue as a means of finding belonging and affirmation. Questioning one's gender is trending heavily right now, and it's vital that parents *are not* left outside the conversation when their children have such questions.

Schools such as those in Madison, Wisconsin, aren't the only places where sexuality is being conditioned. Pedophilia is being floated as an orientation in classes at a University in California, according to student Alex Mazzara.[277] He notes particularly that those with this orientation call themselves "self-identified pedophiles" and comments on how openly they report their troubles.[278] In his opinion, this idea is headed into the mainstream arena of orientations in the upcoming years, and these authors fear that this is a well-founded concern.[279] Others have come forward with names that euphemize the position, such as "non-offending pedophiles," while still other groups have broken the label into age groups of attraction: "pedophile" for pre-pubescent attraction, "hebephile" for those who seek eleven- to fourteen-year olds, and "ephebophile" for those whose desires are for youths between ages fifteen and nineteen.[280]

Ultimately, what's behind this agenda is the enemy's desire to destroy the lives of the innocent. If he can do that—with the permission of society, cultural counterparts, guardians, and even the children themselves—then he's even more pleased. In a land that has already allowed the blood of innocents to be shed under the label of convenience via abortion, the trusting, vulnerable children who are our nation's next generation are now at risk of being further compromised for the fulfillment of twisted pleasures of the depraved. It is time to stand, *now*, and defend the defenseless.

The world we live in has been set to ensnare our children with a million traps that will destroy their lives and jeopardize their souls. They've been placed in schools where—for whatever reason—their education often becomes second to an ulterior agenda that costs them academic success, peace of mind, and compromised innocence, and they're separated from parental influences and familial religious values. The world is waiting at every turn to make them doubt what God created them to be, to instill qualms about their sexuality, and to isolate them so that the nefarious movements will hold allure for their young minds. The world that surrounds our children—*your* children—is being groomed to passively allow pedophilia to creep in via the guise we call "orientation." Well-meaning individuals will fight for this atrocity to occur under the heading of personal, civil rights. If we remain silent, *this* is the world that will come to be in a shorter span of years than most people realize.

{7}

MARK OF THE BEAST

Over the centuries, many have speculated regarding what the manifestation of Antichrist might look like. Such imaginings bring about a variety of notions regarding the Mark of the Beast: how it will look, what format it will be, how it will be enforced, etc. Modern technology has invited new theories about how it will be implemented, with some of the concern focusing on the movement toward a cashless society, mandatory vaccines for COVID-19, universal basic income, and the geopolitics shaping a One-World Government. While these issues may not indicate the ultimate manifestation of the Mark of the Beast, they certainly might be paving the way for it, so they deserve our attention.

Cashless Society

The Mark of the Beast is commonly understood to involve a global economy that operates on a mutually shared currency. Many in previous generations believed it would involve a new dollar bill featuring an image of Antichrist that would replace and nullify currency featuring the photos of forefathers such as Washington or Lincoln. Such imaginings, of course, sprang from a world where tangible cash was the means by which business was transacted.

However, since the advent of the Internet, worldwide banking has been revolutionized. Monies are now transmitted—even internationally—with the click of a button. No longer is there a need for writing a check, heading to the bank to withdraw the funds, or making international currency exchanges. Considering these economic advancements, the "one-world" monetary system our forefathers dreaded has likely already arrived. As the exchange of funds for goods and services increasingly moves online, people carry less cash and fewer (or no) checks, with credit and debit cards the preferred way to pay for nearly any purchase. Further, all transactions—both online and in person—are recorded digitally.

While COVID-19 shutdowns were occurring, many businesses changed how they operated. For example, we saw more and more restaurants offering their menus, accepting orders, and receiving payment via online apps. Patrons taking advantage of this convenience simply log on to an app to place their order and submit payment, then they drive to the establishment's designated pickup area, where an employee delivers the food to the car using "no contact" delivery. This is also how lots of consumers purchased groceries and other supplies. Turnpikes that utilized cash tolls in some places quickly switched to an invoice-mailing system to remove the need for workers and travelers to handle unclean currency; even casinos, via permission from the Nevada Gaming Commission and the American Gaming Commission, broadened payment methods to include the use of electronic currency.[281] A number of companies stated these measures were precautionary in the wake of the pandemic, suggesting that the new practices might be temporary. However, many completely discontinued their acceptance of cash, shifting to totally cashless commerce. In some cities (Philadelphia, for example), this conversion was blocked, with government officials stating that the most impoverished households make up a greater percentage of cash-paying customers, and refusing cash, then, means excluding the demographic that may be in the greatest need.[282] (This distinction is important, and we'll return to it in a bit.)

The CDC encouraged cashless commerce for safety reasons, but many have asserted that this redirection toward electronic interface is a strategic move in favor of Big Finance. These sources point to a few factors behind their reasoning. A great majority of banks, credit unions, and other financial institutions have closed their lobbies, encouraging customers and members to conduct business online.[283] This cuts costs related to the facilities and staffing, while generating, on average, a 3.4 percent fee per transaction for digital users, equating to higher profits and lower overhead expense.[284] This increase in profits became especially lucrative for financial institutions during the COVID shutdowns, when digital transactions saw a 285 percent increase for food and beverages alone, and that's aside from purchases made for other necessities and supplies.[285] To further highlight the dramatic shift toward a cashless society, banks have seen a decrease in ATM activity—amounting to approximately one-fourth the usual usage in the US—and a 90 percent decrease in locations with high revenues from the tourism industry.[286]

Are We Headed for UBI?

We mentioned that lower-income consumers tend to pay for goods and services with cash. This is often because they struggle to find banking options that work with their budgetary challenges or history. (As one example, those who tend to have too many overdrafts might prefer to use cash, or they might, because of their track record, have difficulty opening a checking account.) Imagine, however, if there was a way they could receive the funds digitally. That might happen if a new stipend—wrought from very old ideas—were to be instituted. Many call this idea a UBI, for "Universal Basic Income." Some may recognize the concept because it nearly succeeded once. It actually "passed in the US

House when Nixon was president," says journalist John Miller an article in *American Magazine*. "The bill failed in the Senate when Democrats did not think the payments were high enough." But the innovation far predates Richard Nixon or any of his comrades. In fact, philosopher Thomas Paine made a plea for such an action in his 1796 work, *Agrarian Justice*. He proposed that everyone should be given a stipend of fifteen pounds at age twenty-one, then ten pounds a year once an individual turned 50.[287] If something like this were to be implemented, any argument enforcing the need for cash would be quashed, and society would be free to go cashless—all while the powers that be maintain the appearance of benevolence for even the neediest of citizens.[288]

This is precisely the type of situation that may be created through the Automatic BOOST to Communities Act proposed by Congress during the COVID-19 economic upheaval. This was only one of many proposed stimulus/economic relief efforts discussed for helping families survive the financial tumult of the coronavirus wreckage. This plan appears at first glance to solve many of the economic challenges faced by citizens, but it *could* come with a higher long-term price attached. This particular plan proposed to send, in the form of prepaid debit cards, two thousand dollars to every person—including each dependent—in America. Then, each month, the card would be reloaded with a thousand dollars until "one year after the end of the Coronavirus crisis."[289] So let's do the math: For a family of four, this is equivalent to an initial payout of eight thousand dollars, with an additional forty-eight thousand over the first year.[290] This benefit would likewise be paid out to "non-citizens, including undocumented people, permanent residents, and temporary visitors whose stay exceeds three months."[291] Users of the debit cards have the option of merging their own funds with those backing the card, consolidating outside banking to one source they could use indefinitely.[292] Anyone can easily see two things: 1) This is enough money to dramatically improve the quality of living across the board; and 2) It is difficult to imagine where all this money is going to come *from*.

Another issue a person may quickly recognize is that such an irresistible payout will likely prompt citizens to be very proactive about keeping the relief program going. It's unlikely that the government would stop paying out these sums in the future, once aware that consumers rely on the income to maintain their standard of living. It's also likely that these individuals would soon take advantage of the ability to blend their other finances into the account affiliated with this card, centralizing the location from which all their funds are managed.

This amount of money is more than subsidiary. Many families don't make that much working one or even multiple jobs full-time at entry-level wages. Thus, once the dole-out begins, shutting off the stream will be *much* easier said than done. So, here's a question to ponder: What if these installments continued under subsequent "crises" once the COVID-19 train has run its course? Certainly, we're not saying that this pandemic hasn't been a crisis. However, if keeping society in a perpetual state of turbulence becomes the means by which these payments are extended, everyone will surely see the benefit of laying claim to troublesome conditions that serve the purpose.

Here's another question: What if the "card" were ever mandatorily replaced with a microchip implanted in our bodies? If this happened, we would face a terrible decision: either part with much-needed funds and return to impoverished conditions or allow the invasive technology into our bodies. For those who believe the implanted device is the Mark of the Beast, this proposition would be, literally, asking them to trade their soul for the right to conduct business, as foretold in Revelation 13:17: "That no man might buy or sell, save he had the mark, or the name of the beast, or the number of his name."

Some may think that by speaking against such a citizen-payment plan, these authors aren't sensitive to the financial woes of those who have struggled throughout the pandemic. This couldn't be farther from the truth. However, we do wish to point out that the orchestrations seem to "conveniently" place the public in a position of having the powers that be exert a firmer grip of control than they would otherwise have. Recall the manipulation method we discussed called "learned helplessness," then revisit the notion of a UBI. The government mandates the closure of businesses and that all workers—except a few who are "essential"—are to stay home. This brings all income to a standstill for most families. In the meantime, companies modify to operate without as many employees, thus they don't need them as badly once the world becomes safe again. Likewise, many businesses that have had to adapt will have found ways of permanently replacing workers with technological and robotic means.[293] *Then*, those same authorities speak of future shutdowns and subsequent rounds of stimulus packages. Eventually, the public is beaten into submission—brought to their knees by the desperation of financial pressures. Do you see where this could be headed? The same powers who told the public to stay home and then lifted their financial load then became the cash cow keeping each family afloat. By the time such powers decide to make changes to their program (like adding eligibility requirements or altering its format of delivery), the citizens will feel they have no choice but to comply. Further, if society has embraced socialism by that point (and, as we've discussed, we're quickly headed there), we may have no problem allowing such demands to be placed upon us, because we already will have relinquished control to the government we look to for protection and provision.

There are a few problems with attempting to keep the populace on a regulated, automatic, government-issued salary. We can see some of them by looking at smaller but similar economic examples. Consider past efforts to equalize the quality of living by raising the minimum wage. The idea sounds wonderful on the surface, but never seems to pan out the way it's anticipated. Historically, those who suffer the most from minimum-wage hikes are the small-business owners, who often end up making labor cuts to save on costs, but then are forced to work more hours themselves to compensate for the loss of manpower. (We realize that the reader may not yet see how this connects to the concept of UBI, but hear us out; this diversion won't take long.)

Businesses that don't reduce their workforce often find they need to raise their prices to recoup the increased salaries. This sabotages the economy on a few levels. Those with higher levels of education and thus have higher-paying jobs see their own salaries diminish proportionately to starting wages. This means that those who have worked to obtain an advantage in the workplace see their salaries reduced to being barely higher than those who have no post-high school education. This is a problem, because it means that putting out great monetary investment and effort no longer carries the payout known to previous generations in the same situation. Further, those with higher education often have student debt, and the inflation that drove up other positions' wages and prices of goods and services offsets the economy in such a way that, despite slightly elevated salaries, they struggle to make their student loan payments. Eventually, the economy adjusts and the new minimum wage is as poverty-inducing as the previous. No matter how optimistic individuals are when there is talk of raising the minimum wage, the idea always holds more promise than actual benefits. Some say that it isn't the wage that drives the spike in the economy; rather, it's inflation that demands wage increases. This is also possible. However, the truth remains that anytime the cost of labor is elevated, so are the costs of goods and services.

Some, naturally, argue that a UBI won't change the cost of labor. They say this approach will be unique in its strategy and financial impact, particularly since it will be offered to *all*, whereas the wage hikes we've discussed target a small demographic in localized areas. Contrariwise, everyone would receive this funding regardless of age, ethnicity, education, or skillset. This argument may certainly be well-founded. Moreover, at this time, such a measure would only be enacted in the hopes of subsidizing the economy, as it already stands, until the crisis is over, whereas wage increases are motivated by an entirely different set of criteria. However, with the sums being discussed as part of BOOST, anyone who opts out or no longer qualifies would immediately fall far below the income level of the rest of mainstream society. If inflation rates were to adapt to this kind of boost (pun intended), those living on only the amount of money they could earn would face hyperinflation, which matches what's foretold in Revelation 6:6—an entire day's wage is said to be enough to buy food for that evening alone.

Even those who aren't deterred by the prophetic implications of the UBI must agree that the money to initiate the program has to come from somewhere. The bottom line is that America doesn't have the wealth to disburse these amounts. If the funds already existed in our country, we wouldn't be facing such great national debt. "If you gave $1,000 a month to every American," John Miller said in *American Magazine*, "that would cost almost $4 trillion, 60 percent more than the current level of social welfare spending."[294] An argument can hardly be made that this monthly allocation would replace existing welfare programs. Consider a family who receives food-stamp benefits and health/dental insurance assistance alone. If other assistance programs were cut and they were expected to purchase these amenities through their BOOST funds, the monies would suffer quite a dent. In fact, it's likely their money would *still* be very tight, while others who still have other source of incomes would simply be receiving the funds as extra (until hyperinflation occurs). This would mean that by distributing money ostensibly to help the needy, the very plan designed to equalize the rich and poor could actually widen the rift! There are even economists who, like us, state that this hyper-infusion of extra cash into circulation could "flood the economy with too much cash, triggering inflation."[295] So, while the theoretical approach of the UBI *does* seem like a unique strategy, there is no way to calculate its long-term ramifications. What begins as a great effort at humanitarianism could—just like the hiked-minimum-wage efforts on smaller, local scales—result in a similar, but worse, version of the scenario that already existed, but it would be exacerbated by a deeper deficit. Then, how will we undo the financial wreckage?

Ultimately, however philanthropic a UBI sounds, it's likely that what we can expect to materialize from such a thing is inflation, which causes people to depend on *both* the UBI funds and earned income to make ends meet.

But, with increased automation taking over jobs—a phenomenon happening even more quickly because of COVID-19—employment will be hard to find. As it stands, "half the world's jobs could be automated using 'currently demonstrated technologies,' amounting to 'almost $15 trillion in wages.'"[296] All the more convenient that the government is ready to step in and save us…

Like most good economic Band-Aid plans, it will probably work for a few years, then backfire. But, if a UBI or variation of it is the Mark of the Beast, then isn't that precisely what we are to expect? We understand that Antichrist will appear with solutions that seem to *finally* offer answers to all the complex challenges that have harrowed human existence from day one. And, the solutions don't actually *have* to work, since the entire time of Antichrist's administration is brief. They only need to *appear* to work for a period of three and a half to seven years.

The Pope Is Pushing for UBI

In his 2020 Easter address, Pope Francis mentioned his hopes that, in response to the coronavirus pandemic, a UBI would be implemented. Many quickly responded to this statement with the usual suspicion that he might, again, be indicating a desire for the establishment of a One-World Order. When the reports that the pope was pushing for a UBI started to circulate, media sources then began to cite Cardinal Michael Czerny's clarification of the term. Quickly backpedaling, Czerny explained that the Spanish phrase is *salario universal,*[297] which *can* be translated to mean "UBI." However, Czerny explained, *in this case*, it was meant to refer to a "universal basic wage."

He continued, "This is not to be understood as…universal basic income, but to a different notion, coming from the pope's Argentinian background and his involvement with cartoneros [residents who collect and recycle trash for compensation] in Buenos Aires."[298] In other words, it's not a base *income* that he wants to allocate to the entire population, but rather a minimum wage he'd like to see implemented across continents. (*That*, considering the various economic conditions across the world alongside the aforementioned scenario outlining only a few consequences in regards to the wage-inflation ratio, has the potential to be an economic train wreck. Regardless, the pope, who seems to repeatedly promote an agenda for a single world order, has made yet another statement about his desire to see global regulation implemented.)

The Appeal of Singularity

When I (Allie Henson) was with a team of researchers at Burning Man in 2018 collecting data for an upcoming book, the theme that year was "I, Robot." Understandably, the trending discussion at every turn was that of singularity. (For those not clear on the meaning of this term, "singularity" here doesn't mean the point when AI surpasses human intelligence. Nor does it mean "uniqueness"; in fact, it indicates quite the opposite, in that it refers to the time when people lose their individuality and upload their consciousness into a computer in which everyone dwells in a type of online database, a digital community.) I found myself wondering how one would market such an idea to a group of people who were so passionate about their own individuality that they even rejected all branding, down to their clothing. I was aware that the idea of singularity had been met with great interest in this crowd, and was even embraced.

Curious (and *needing* an answer regarding this matter for the work I was assembling at that time), I attended workshop after workshop and learned that not only did the gathering's attendees welcome the arrival of a digital age wherein people would be uploaded into singularity with one another, but they also saw it as the solution to many of the age-old problems of humanity.

They believe the answers to world hunger, the global financial crisis, inequality, and much more come via a utopian world wherein we're relieved of the need for employment at all. In such an existence, our "digital twin" is created by making a copy of our consciousness, which operates inside a computer. This duplicate earns our income so that we are free to live an existence of relaxation and self-expression. Should we ever manage to legislate the convoluted moral and ethical issues of this type of life, we could find ourselves in a stage of humanity wherein our digital clones actually become our virtual slaves—not too much unlike the scenario on the movie *The Island*, mentioned in a previous chapter. The salary earned by our computerized selves could easily be used to make purchases through the same digital, communal monetary system as the potential UBI.

In this proposed society, as mentioned, a "digital twin" would work and perform the jobs we currently do. (With so many of us working at computers full-time, the idea isn't too far-fetched.) Since our current income would be supplemented to reach the same level that we ourselves could obtain (being that, virtually, we *are* the ones working), the "real" individuals would be free to live without being employed. This is where the idea of a perfect, harmonious world comes in. Many believe that it's the constraints of human need that keep the world plagued with trouble. Eliminating that, they think humans would then transcend to a higher level of enlightenment, becoming more perfect beings who leave behind the previous ills of mankind's existence. Similarly, we would live in a society where people share with one another on a new level, expressing themselves artistically and indulging in self-discovery without fear of their material needs going unmet.

Unfortunately, humans have historically persecuted and made war with one another, pursuing selfish ambitions at the expense of others' happiness and well-being. Despite the staunch belief that removing our material problems will somehow instill within our souls the necessary growth it would take to render a more enlightened and kind creature, it's more likely that such conditions will yield a more evolved and depraved person who believes himself or herself to be godlike (masters of convincingly real but completely powerless digital copies of men, women, and children). Thus, current problems will be elevated while additionally, deeply disturbing ethical lines would likely be crossed regarding the treatment of our digital twins. To shed further light, studies on the nature of mankind (such as the Stanford Prison Experiment, which we'll look at later) have revealed that, when left to their own devices and with too much time on their hands (*especially* when some have been given an allotment of power), mankind has a greater capacity for evil than good.

In addition to concerns regarding the direction mankind may take when—literally—left to his own devices, there is the issue that singularity would offer more than just an upload into an individual's brain. After all, it's no secret that digital doors often allow pathways in both directions, allowing for intrusive spyware, malware, adware, or even viruses to creep into computers and other devices. For this reason, most people use extreme caution when installing any new programs or apps onto computers, phone, or other electronics. If the day were to come when an individual had the opportunity to upload his or her consciousness into a digital sphere, what might it look like? To make one's mind as vulnerable as any laptop connected to the Internet for intrusive digital interference could have vast potential spiritual risks. People could receive "downloads" of nearly any imaginable (or unimaginable!) content—some that could even reprogram aspects of their thinking, implementing new and twisted forms of temptation, and dulling sympathetic or philanthropic veins of thought. Worse, some have made a case that, should malevolent spiritual forces infest the machine, one could even become possessed or overtaken by evil forces via this method of digital community.

If artificial intelligence (AI) technology were ever to become self-aware or even evil, this is certainly within the realm of possibility. Further, if a person is given completely over to evil at the moment of upload, would malicious influences not follow him or her into the machine? These are questions that would need to be addressed before agreeing to allow one's consciousness to be digitally fused.

How Might This Be Implemented?

With COVID-19 (and those who seized the opportunity it provided) creating so much chaos across the globe, many have wondered if vaccinations will be mandatory. Similarly, many Christians have been afraid that they will somehow be tricked or forced into taking this or a similar vaccine, only to later learn that they have taken the Mark of the Beast.

The truth about such a quandary can be a bit convoluted, because it is two-fold. First of all, allow us to say that we don't believe that the vaccine developed to protect recipients from the coronavirus is that. The COVID-19 inoculation is still emergent and under trial status as we write this, and for that reason we are personally wary of it. However, setting that aside for a moment, let's explore the theological angle of this situation.

If the Mark indeed involves an injection, those who receive it, unlike those who get the COVID-19 vaccination, will be required to make some sort of denouncement of prior loyalties (especially for those who state their allegiance is to God). We know that Antichrist will demand to be worshiped as god (2 Thessalonians 2:4), so we understand that accepting his Mark requires an alignment with his power. However, we're repeatedly warned of how very compelling—charismatic—his manner will be. Thus, many will be deceived into taking his Mark. In this way, on one hand, people cannot take the Mark without making the deliberate decision to do so, yet, the deception will mean that they're not aware of precisely *who* or *what* they're dealing with. Clear as mud?

The issue is that we must be wary of anything that forces us to pledge our loyalty to human, political, or religious leaders and requires that we mark that allegiance in a permanent physical way. Thus, the danger is in aligning with the Man of Sin (another name for Antichrist) and accepting his brand. The way to act preemptively against this danger is by drawing close to God and *listening* closely for discernment. Doing this regularly will produce what we authors call a "gut-check"—a sense of direction that comes from somewhere deep in the spirit that doesn't go away after persistent research and prayer.

As for those who worry that the Mark will manifest as a mandatory a chip implant that will be hiding inside a syringe labeled as a vaccine, think about this: Accepting the Mark of the Beast will be an intentional act. If it is received unknowingly (as through an injection intended for another purpose, such as COVID prevention), then it's not likely the Mark. Antichrist wants each person's stated loyalty to accompany the sign of affiliation with his administration. (However, there are those who assert that the "stated loyalty" is presumed via the acceptance of his brand, which is a noteworthy argument. Again, discernment is key.) As for the idea that a vaccination would sneak an implantable chip into people unbeknownst to them, for now this concept is alleviated. At this time, identification chips are still about the size of a small grain of rice, so it's unlikely such a thing could be "snuck" into a vaccine—for now. In fact, many sources report that microchips are still large enough to be considered intrusive to their host, and couldn't go undetected by the recipient.[299] As technology improves (and it is doing so quickly, as we all know), this possibility may soon reach new levels.

So, let's review some of the facts we've discussed about the Mark: 1) It's a gesture of loyalty to a political figure or faction; 2) Its benefits will be so appealing that many will be deceived; 3) It will be identifiable to those who are watching for it, as different from routine vaccinations and such. So why would anyone receive the Mark in the first place? If it's not subversive enough to be implemented without our knowledge, yet is so evil that it has the power to condemn one's soul to hell, it doesn't seem that anyone would take it. This is where a manipulation method will likely be used to condition the crowd to ignore any warning signs and accept it. Some may, as we mentioned, have to intentionally work around a gut-check signaling them to stop, while others will be whole-heartedly deceived and welcome it.

We don't know the specific circumstances regarding how the Mark will be implemented. That would make things much easier, wouldn't it? However, we *do know* it will be extremely appealing—even essential, since no one will be able to buy or sell anything without it. We are aware only that a political figure who seems to have the answers to human-ity's problems will arise. Out of this benevolent ingenuity will spring solutions that will draw the loyalty of much of mankind. This is why so many will line up to take his Mark.

In this way, a chip-implanted means for disbursement of UBI or similar element could be considered a candidate for the coercing the masses to receive the Mark. With all the talk of mandated vaccines, with-out which purchases or travel could be denied, one *does* wonder if they could be a trial run to test the populace's willingness to line up for the injection. Many believe that if a form of UBI isn't the way the Mark will be ushered in, then it could be via some type of crisis, such as another pandemic. In that case, the body count could mount so quickly that people would disregard any gut-checks signaling caution, opting instead to choose the Mark because it assures survival. However it happens, as we've suggested, it seems reasonable to believe that a swift and fear-some crisis event could occur that prompts people to accept the Mark while ignoring any of their hesitations, because "desperate times call for desperate measures."[300] The idea that some type of a crisis will trigger the implementation of the Mark is reinforced by the timeline provided in prophetic Scripture, where we read that circumstances escalate just before those who refuse the Mark are martyred. This measure will be ushered in swiftly, as the entire world appears to change rapidly over a three-and-a-half-year period, giving people very little time to reflect on the long-term consequences of their decisions.

This is where our proposition of "trial runs" comes in. Consider the manipulation tactics used by Jim Jones at his Peoples Temple (Jonestown) compound in Guyana in 1977. (Now, before the reader protests that this is an *entirely* different type of situation, hear us out.) The phrase "drink the Kool-Aid" became a popular term following the Jonestown tragedy wherein nearly one thousand cult members lined up and willingly drank the cyanide-laced beverage.[301] However, there was much more to the story than this. For example, a few cult members did not consume the drink, and they were killed by gunshot; also, about thirty people escaped.[302] However, the remaining nine hundred or so had been conditioned over time to drink the beverage (which, as mentioned earlier, was Flavor Aid, not Kool-Aid[303]) without question. Over a period of time before the massacre, Jones continually presented suicide as a necessary and impending end—and completely inevitable. By fostering a herd mentality about this, he began to run "suicide drills," wherein his followers were forced to drink the beverage suspecting it was poisoned, only to find that it was not. These exercises were tests of loyalty Jones called "white nights."[304] "Increasingly paranoid...Jones went to greater lengths to assert his control," stated one article. "In staged suicide rehearsals...members were told to drink red liquid which may have contained poison [to ensure that] his followers would follow his orders unhesitatingly."[305] He would then tell those people: "In forty minutes, you will all be dead."[306]

However, only during one of the "white nights" was there, indeed, cyanide in the drink. After having endured the "fake suicides" repeatedly, cult members had become desensitized to the act of drinking the beverage. In an affidavit signed by former Jim Jones follower Deborah Blakey regarding the "white night" drills, "We all went through it without a protest," Blakey recalls. "We were exhausted. We couldn't react to anything."[307]

This same behavioral response can be related to society today, despite the fact that the circumstances are entirely different. Upon repeatedly drinking the liquid—thus "facing death"—yet subsequently surviving, the perception of threat is reduced as a result of the continual internal determination to silence the gut-check that would accompany drinking poison. In this example, we see how a society that has endured repeated crises accompanying the need for "drastic measures" (think economic shutdowns, emergency vaccines, etc.) would opt for the path of least resistance, following a herd mentality in hopes that the white night drills will only be a temporary situation.

This may seem like a strange comparison, but if society is currently undergoing "trial runs" for the implementation of the Mark, then we could be undergoing conditioning for the real event. Consider this: If a politician came out of left field with talk of a mandated injection of *anything*, the public would likely refuse it wholeheartedly. However, if many crises necessitate cooperation from the public—and if these measures actually *provide* the solution they promise—then it will be much easier to rally the masses in future circumstances. This is further reinforced by the fact that, in previous times of fear, everything turned out okay, just as it was during all but the one "white night."

The chip-implanting technology is also already in use. We see it applied in varied ways, including identification, integration with smart buildings (for opening and closing doors, etc.), and storing medical records and other information. In Sweden in 2018, "4,000 citizens… [used] microchips implanted in their hands to store emergency contacts and enable easy access to homes, offices, and gyms."[308] While some companies in the US offer (and likely even encourage) chipping to their employees, pushback has been successful. Many states have legislation in place that forbids requiring of chip-implanting at this time.[309] However, during the pandemic lockdowns, many people began to fear that not only would a vaccine be mandated, but that such measures could be a precursor to chip implantation.

Many other theorists—some within SkyWatch TV and Defender Publishing circles—have presented various concepts of Mark of the Beast requirements which, like ours, involve the vulnerability/fragility-of-human-life conundrum. Some such as Thomas Horn have even speculated that the Mark *could* be a chimeric, DNA-altering machination that literally and physiologically changes a human into something else, while simultaneously saving the person's life—a price most people will pay. If a plague of apocalyptic proportions were to fall upon the human race, accompanied by news coverage of it being highly fatal and swift in contagion, the impulsive reaction of the masses—in the interest of survival—would be to get in line to "take the vaccine." If such an inoculation did harbor the Mark, many may *still* blatantly ignore any implications suggesting such a notion, simply because the fear-mongering of the day (and the observation of mounting global casualties) will drive them to make a rash decision.

(Note: It bears repeating that these authors do not believe that a potential COVID-19 vaccine will "be the Mark." It doesn't line up with the order of events—or the cataclysmic proportions—of the scenario we're given in the book of Revelation. However, we see the possibility that some of the motives behind this pandemic mitigation might render this a "practice round" or a grooming of the masses toward a Mark agenda, much as the "white nights" were for those in Guyana.)

Will This *Really* Be Enforceable by Execution?

One thing that may make people doubt that the Mark of the Beast would actually come to pass is the idea that it is foretold to be enforced by threat of execution. Most find it difficult to imagine an advanced society that would embrace such a drastic measure.

First, the Bible describes Antichrist as a great deceiver of many (Revelation 13:13). This deceit explains why the Mark will strangely make sense to a great percentage of the masses. Second, since Antichrist's agendas will appear to solve mankind's problems, he'll probably have some way of presenting execution of the noncompliant as an "unavoidable evil." Third, despite what many believe, mankind *does* have a sinful nature (Mark 7:21; Romans 5:12) and migrates toward evil when the forces of righteousness aren't present. This is where the removal of what theologians call the "restraining force" comes into play.

The Restrainer

Take a look at the main passage describing this "restraining force"—referred to as "what withholdeth" in 2 Thessalonians 2:3–8:

> Let no man deceive you by any means: for that day shall not come, except there come a falling away first, and that man of sin be revealed, the son of perdition; Who opposeth and exalteth himself above all that is called God, or that is worshipped; so that he as God sitteth in the temple of God, shewing himself that he is God. Remember ye not, that, when I was yet with you, I told you these things? And now ye know what withholdeth that he might be revealed in his time. For the mystery of iniquity doth already work: only he who now letteth will let, until he be taken out of the way. And then shall that Wicked be revealed, whom the Lord shall consume with the spirit of his mouth, and shall destroy with the brightness of his coming.

While the wording of this passage may sound a little confusing, it describes an evil that currently awaits its moment to strike mankind, but is being held back by God's holy forces. Note this excerpt from *The Messenger*:

According to this passage, many people interpret the phrase "he who now letteth will let" to indicate a force which restrains the one who "might be revealed in his time," and whose "mystery of iniquity doth already work." Thus, the elucidation holds that the source of evil, iniquity, and the...[spiritual evil behind] end-times manifestations already occupies this earth, awaiting his opportunity to act, while the restraining force holds this malevolence at bay "until he be taken out of the way." This, in modern theology, becomes referred to as the "Restraining Force" which we sometimes hear spoken of regarding prophecy.[310]

According to this theology, once the restraining force has been removed, the powers of evil that have been present the earth but without free rein since the beginning will be unleashed in their full fury upon mankind. Even now, while the righteous element is at work (most people believe this is the Holy Spirit), mankind still wrestles with a sinful nature, and malevolent powers already thwart our existence. Imagine, then, a day when there is nothing present to hold back the potential impact of our already corrupt nature in conjunction with the uninhibited influence of satanic forces. Truly, on *that day*, nothing will seem impossible where the potential of evil is concerned.

Thus, the answer to the question in the subheading of this section is, in a word, *yes*. Yes, man will be depraved enough to stand by as Antichrist executes those who refuse the Mark of the Beast. For anyone who still needs convincing, however, we can see the early priming for such potentialities occurring in society today.

Euthanasia

Some may wonder how the practice of euthanasia would prime society to accept the Mark. (An additional argument lies in the issue of the legalization of abortion, which we won't get into here. Besides falling outside the scope of this work, these authors presume that the reader is already familiar with the pro-life argument.) The connection between execution for refusing to take the Mark and euthanasia, however, is that the death of an innocent person is sometimes considered acceptable when that death is for a greater good or diminishes suffering. So, euthanasia, while seeming by many to be justifiable under the right circumstances, prepares society to accept a mounting body count of innocents—those we may not suspect: *not* convicted serial killers or demented minds who were sentenced to die for heinous deeds against humanity, but rather of innocents.

In 2017, headlines surfaced alleging that the state of Oregon had passed a law allowing mentally ill patients to be starved to death. Understandably, much of the public responded with outrage to what would legally "allow for the starving and dehydrating to death of patients with dementia or mental illness."[311] Official response was that the bill only added new language to existing laws outlining how a committee of medical professionals could handle a scenario wherein an individual being kept alive with interventions such as life support or feeding tubes had no advocates present. The officials acknowledged that the bill needed clarification, since it allowed custodial appointees too much sovereignty over the lives of those who don't have relatives or other guardians to make decisions for them.[312] However, the legislation continued to move forward, and was presented to the Oregon Senate Rules Committee as a "'simple update' to Oregon's current advance directive."[313] For many, the leap from legalized abortion to assisted suicide, followed by the inevitability of euthanasia, was an easily perceivable sequence: "When Oregon became the first state in the nation to legalize the practice of assisted suicide, pro-life advocates argued this would be a slippery slope that would lead to euthanasia."[314]

While many only recognize the concept of euthanasia from such sci-fi movies as the aforementioned *Logan's Run*, it's actually already happening in countries such as Australia and Canada. Furthermore, prominent American politicians are becoming more outspoken regarding the possibility of it taking place here. Considering the type of people who may be candidates for euthanasia, we often picture extremely sick elderly men and women, such as those who would meet the criteria described in the Oregonian legislation: those who are on life support, who can't speak for themselves, and who have no family guardians or advocates. There are many who would consider it a kindness to end the struggle for people in this condition.

In addition, if the bill in question is used as lawmakers state it's intended, it applies more readily to removal of life-support than actively ending life. We believe protestors were right when they called this legislation a "slippery slope."[315]

The circumstances surrounding euthanasia, as it is currently being practiced in other parts of the world, are taking place in a much different context. One would be surprised to learn of the ages and condition of many who have opted for euthanasia with their families' support. These authors find this state of affairs devastating. Between June of 2016 and July of 2019, more than 3,300 people—ranging in age from 106 to 22 years old—were euthanized in Ontario, Canada, alone.[316] Many of the deaths were related to cancer, respiratory illness, or neurodegenerative diseases, while others were unspecified.[317] The Australian state of Victoria has also legalized the practice, two decades after repealing what they called a "mercy killing law for the terminally ill."[318] In Quebec, Canada, prior legislation requiring patients to prove they had a medical condition that would render death inevitable was overturned in 2019, qualifying those who suffer a disability that negates their autonomy for assisted suicide: "Having a disability is a fate worse than death."[319] Thus, patients who wish to die must either prove that they are terminally ill or that their suffering is "intolerable."[320] Sadly, this subjective term is already being brought into question regarding cases of mental illness and depressive disorders. Many young people who might be treatable could (and have been trying to) channel their suicidal tendencies toward the mission of broadening the qualifications for assisted suicide or euthanasia. Since, for many, the argument becomes that once someone is resolved to self-terminate, he or she will do so anyway, the approach fosters the notion of allowing the person to die with loved ones present, rather than alone. Similarly, the same stance is supported via the statement that a planned death relieves friends and family of the aftershock of a suicide of the terminally ill, or a drawn-out, traumatic demise riddled with suffering, and allows them the opportunity to say goodbye. There are such cases of activism on behalf of euthanasia, but these authors chose not to include them here out of respect for the brokenhearted families involved.

As for the legal parameters of euthanasia, the more it becomes what many perceive to be a viable option, we could eventually arrive at the place where the only boundaries are regarding the best interest of the individual. "As not all homicides are illegal judicially, it appears that not all euthanasia are," stated an *Annals of Neurosciences* article on the topic. "The question remains who can decide in favor or against any form of euthanasia and what safety net has to be there to protect patient's best interest."[321]

Many become highly impassioned about this topic, and it's easy for some folks to see both sides of the issue as defensible. The problem arises in the ambiguity of the bill that surfaced in Oregon regarding those who cannot advocate for themselves. In such cases, who has the final authority? And here's another question: What if similar circumstances were to emerge after some swiftly moving epidemic of a disease with only one cure (administered via the Mark and required immediately to reduce the risk to public health)? What type of legal authority might be released to officially—even temporarily, under emergency conditions—make such judgment calls?

Desperate times do call for desperate measures, don't they?

If the public becomes complacent about the unnecessary or premature deaths of innocent people, our mindset shifts into a more casual (conditioned, desensitized) approach to seeing others die. Then, in times of crisis, we may be willing to embrace measures that previously would have seemed inconceivable. Just as abortion allows us to kill hundreds of thousands of innocents each year in the name of convenience, increased acceptance of euthanasia could cause society to remain silent while growing numbers of lives are claimed under the labels of "preserving dignity" and "showing kindness." After this conditioning has had its season (similar to the ninth or tenth "white night"), a new crisis could enable the masses to more easily adopt another point of view of killing those who have done nothing wrong other than to refuse the mandated "treatment."

Experiments Revealing Human Nature

Studies abound that reveal surprising results regarding the behavioral patterns of various groups. However, they seem to render deviant patterns a great percentage of the time, especially when individuals are clustered into groups or given authority. We will discuss two of the most relevant and revealing findings here.

First, in the 1960s, Yale University's Stanley Milgram conducted a study of unconditional obedience to authority. The following from *Unlocking Eden: Revolutionize Your Health, Maximize Your Immunity, Restore Your Vitality* explains how it worked:

> The experiment worked like this: Volunteers were assigned the role of "teachers," and believed the "students" were participants in the study as well. The represented premise for this research (not the real one) was to test memory retention when it's reinforced by punishment. This was (supposedly) assured by an electric shock applied when volunteers asked to recall information gave incorrect answers. However, these "students" were actors pretending to convulse in pain when they were "shocked" for giving a wrong answer. The unsuspecting "teachers" were instructed to relay two words to their counterparts, who suppos-

edly would attempt to remember the words in order to avoid the punishment. When the time came for recall, if the "students" didn't remember the elements of the memory test, the "teachers" were to administer the penalty, a consequence technique said to increase learning, thus (supposedly) making this step a vital part of the process.... This discipline was administered by requiring participants to press a series of buttons they were told delivered voltage. The severity of surges was labeled on the mechanism in these increments: "Slight Shock," "Very Strong Shock," "Danger: Severe Shock," and even "XXX." As the number of incorrect answers given by the "students" (recall that the volunteers were unaware that they were dealing with actors) increased, the volunteers were instructed to administer shocks in mounting levels of intensity. As the power of the shocks escalated, those receiving the punishment would complain that the pain was becoming more intense. Eventually, the actors would be screaming, even stating the desire for the experiment to end and saying that they no longer wanted to participate. At times, some would refuse to answer the questions, supposedly afraid they would give the wrong response and be shocked again. However, the conductors (individuals in charge) instructed volunteers to treat nonresponses as wrong answers; this caused volunteers to have to administer severe shocks to people who did not respond.... Usually, those asked to predict what they would do in such a situation would assert their refusal to initiate or continue administering shocks as the intensity escalated, yet surprisingly, two-thirds of Milgram's participants remained obedient all the way through the experiment: Two out of three continued to send electrical surges past the time when the "student" asked for the procedure to stop, beyond the point of becoming completely unresponsive and even to the place that he or she was directed to administer the maximum voltage, which was said to equal 450 volts.… Milgram noted visual signs of inner conflict among participants, such as "sweating, trembling, stuttering, biting their lips, and so on," but despite this, they still yielded authority to those they perceived to be the "experts" or "in charge." The experimenter found similar results when conducting the same study but with one variation: At the beginning of the procedure, the individual receiving the voltage mentioned having a heart condition. Even with this, the percentage of people who followed the order to deal out shocks was 62.5 percent.[322]

Through this study, Milgram learned that people often obey authority without question, even when that obedience requires harming another person. Milgram's goal via this experiment was to explain how people with free will remained obedient during such heinous circumstances as the My Lai Massacre or the Holocaust.[323] His findings relayed that subjects often show the desire for approval from those in authority, and that when a seemingly professional or benevolent faction is at work, they perceive a safety net of permissibility over the instructions. In other words, they assume the person or organization in charge operates with ethical and moral integrity, thus, their instructions are vetted via such standards and, despite these, are still deemed necessary.[324]

In a second study, the Stanford Prison Experiment, which was conducted during the summer of 1971, results showed that, given a little power, some people become extremely sadistic and dominate others just for a sick type of entertainment. The evil seen in this study—originally slated to span two weeks—escalated so quickly, in fact, that it was called off after only six days.[325]

Here's what was involved: A wing of Stanford University was transformed into a makeshift prison, wherein twenty-four carefully chosen applicants were split into groups of prisoners and guards, decided by a coin flip.[326] Those selected to be prisoners underwent a mock arrest at their homes before they were taken to the "police station," fingerprinted, and placed in a holding cell. They were then strip-searched, sprayed with lice treatment, assigned a uniform, and given a number that replaced their name.[327] These received a nylon stocking to place over their hair to remove the individuality of their appearance, and a chain was placed around each young man's ankle.[328]

Guards weren't given specific parameters of behavior. Instead, they were told they could use their judgment to maintain order and secure prisoners' respect.[329] They were issued uniforms, night sticks, and mirrored sunglasses to create the impression of having a universal, omnipresent power over the prisoners. Prisoners performed "counts," wherein they were lined up and told to rattle off their numbers while standing at attention. Those who failed to comply with this practice were punished by being made to do jumping jacks or push-ups.[330] As guards became more comfortable with their authority, some began to step on prisoners' backs or have others sit on their backs while they were performing the exercises.[331] By the second day, prisoners rebelled, barricading the cell doors with their cots and tearing at the numbers that had replaced their names. In response, the morning guard shift assumed that the night supervisors had been too passive with the prisoners, so they responded with overcorrection.[332] Other guards were called in to help bring the prisoners under control; they used spray from a fire extinguisher to force the captives back from the doors of the cell. Those who were least antagonistic in the uprising were removed from the group and rewarded. Later, the inmates were replaced with others who were also given special treatment. This caused others to presume they had somehow betrayed an unspoken allegiance among convicts.[333] Tensions between factions escalated, and prisoners were denied basic rights, such as using the restroom or brushing teeth. One prisoner became so distraught that he manifested signs of emotional trauma—"acute emotional disturbance, disorganized thinking, uncontrollable crying, and rage"—while another "began to act 'crazy,' to scream, to curse, to go into a rage that seemed out of control." Both of these men were released.[334] Myriad subsequent events involved a potential prison break whereupon the convicts were relocated to another part of the prison; a visitation day wherein parents expressed concerns for their sons' well-being; and an inmate sobbing uncontrollably, unable to believe that he was free to stand up and walk out of the experiment until an authority figure reminded him of his *name*, and not his number.

The short duration of this experiment is surprising, considering each person's response. Instead of bonding together under duress, the prisoners' interactions were suspicious and fragmented; each regarded the other as a potential enemy. This seemed to actually *worsen* when one was standing up for prisoners' rights.[335]

As for the guards, they seemed to fall into three categories: those who were "tough but fair"; the "good guys," who didn't punish captives and even at times showed kindness; and those who became "hostile, arbitrary, and inventive in their forms of prisoner humiliation."[336] Surely, it was this third category from which the night-time torment sessions occurred. At these moments, prisoners were sexually abused, forced to mimic sexually humiliating acts with one another, and degraded in ways so psychologically damaging that authorities ended the study early.[337]

Interesting to note regarding this experiment is how those who were persecuted separated from others rather than joining forces. They didn't support one another, but merely tried to survive. Some forgot their names, lost awareness that they had personal rights, and even attempted to decline offers to walk away from the whole process. On the other hand, men whose personality assessments gave no indication that they may have had a sadistic streak became vile and power-driven tormentors who had no qualms about intensifying their torturous activities—including sexual abuse. *All* of these changes took place within a six-day period.

Lucifer Effect

As a result of the findings obtained during the Stanford Prison Experiment, director Phillip Zimbardo coined the term the "Lucifer Effect," which explains the transformation of ordinary people from good to evil. He has also offered expert opinion regarding the aftermath of such situations as Abu Ghraib (an Iraqi-war prison at which otherwise ordinary American soldiers and CIA personnel became capable of extreme abuse of their captives). In Zimbardo's view, while people have varying dispositions, anyone has to the potential to become evil. In fact, recall that those who were delegated prisoners or guards in his Stanford experiment were divided by a mere coin flip. No personality profiling was used in determining who would play what roles, yet many guards—over the six days—became so sadistic that Zimbardo was forced to stop the procedure. In other settings, people have performed atrocities against one another, and Zimbardo claims that distinguishing "good people" from "bad people" simply isn't a clean-cut line. In fact, the researcher describes that line as "permeable."[338] When people are exposed to situations in which they're subjected to a seemingly unified power and when the criteria or cause for compliance to that authority appears justified, victims are often depersonified and powerless. When officials hold extreme power over those who are de-individualized, the changeover from ordinary to evil can happen quickly—even in people who showed no prior tendency toward such actions.[339]

When we consider Phillip Zimbardo's findings alongside those of Stanley Milgram's experiment, we can see how a society ruled by evil people would quickly organize into a hierarchy operated by the most vicious and cruel personalities, while those who are subordinate obey without question and those who resist scramble to survive.

When *True* Christianity Becomes the Enemy

When the populace is without the restraining force and a crisis or event presents citizens with the choice of whether or not to accept the Mark, we Christians will be the first group to be fingered as a public enemy. When we refuse the mandate, we will be prioritized as a type of resistance force: a public enemy. Then, Christians—who, for a period of time will have been increasingly framed for propagating "hate speech"—will be targeted as ones to eliminate. At this point, if it hasn't already happened, the Church will split. One side will say anything necessary to appease the powers that be—denouncing scriptural integrity, Jesus as Lord, and anything else that ruffles the feathers of its cozy existence. The others will refuse to do this and will likely be forced to go underground (more on this in an upcoming chapter).

When the visible, legal, topside "Church" goes apostate, there will be far fewer voices warning of the dangers that Antichrist's agenda poses for society. Then, the Mark mandate will further polarize factions, dividing the "good citizens" of the newly united world (who will be allowed to live) from those who will be designated terrorists and/or public enemies. At this point, Antichrist will have those with a stronger propensity toward homicide right where he wants them.

The One-World Order will probably introduce the Mark gently, with singsong lip service about how people will "*never* be coerced into accepting it." Then, after a short time, it's likely that the situation will shift suddenly—possible via some contrived, "unforeseen" event—with seemingly justifiable reasons for why the Mark is politically and socially necessary. The Mark doctrine will be accompanied by verbiage that makes every "defiant nonconformist" look like a dangerous threat to the population, and the subsequent deadly persecution will begin involving the murder of anyone who doesn't step in line with the Mark mandate. (As mentioned previously, for any who may exhibit lingering doubt regarding the executions, this will likely be portrayed as a necessary evil for the betterment of all mankind.) Free will, at that moment, will be a faded memory of principles held by a society long gone, and folks who show resistance will be eliminated. Everyone on earth in that day will see people they know (and possibly loved) put to death, and the pressure upon them to submit to Antichrist's laws will introduce unparalleled feelings of defenselessness. Meanwhile, since the True Church will be underground and the restraining force will be gone, there won't be many voices in the public arena to speak truth, to comfort the bereaved who may watch loved ones perish, or encourage these frightened people to fight the good fight.

Further, when Antichrist deceives many, causing them to believe him to be god, allegiance to him and worship of him, as we've made abundantly clear, will be legally required. The topside church will embrace him, believing in his divinity. At this, the apostate church will rejoice. After all, the church has always wanted to make converts of all of society. Once their leader has been granted the worship of every citizen by threat of fatal legal recourse, it will be a paramount victory; the conquerors will dance in the streets at the blood-spilling of true Christians, while the idolaters wear the same label in profane blasphemy.

{8}

FROM BRIDE TO HARLOT

If any man defile the temple of God, him shall God destroy;
for the temple of God is holy, which temple ye are.

1 CORINTHIANS 3:17

Syncretism Dressed as Pluralism: A Cult Gateway

A syncretistic agenda is boiling up behind the scenes like a witch's brew—only this time, the witch isn't a green-skinned, wart-covered, cackling old lady from an animated Disney cartoon. It's that old liar, that Satan, the Red Dragon of Revelation who was alive and well the day he first inspired the Fall of Man in the Garden of Eden. The Accuser who will still be alive and well the day his puppet, Antichrist, introduces the Mark that renders those who take it permanently irredeemable. The Deceiver who lives to confuse pluralism as a cultural ideology and identity, with syncretism that is unconditionally and eternally spiritual infidelity.

The term "pluralism," in context of society and culture, refers to religious, ethnic, racial, and social diversity. When left in its proper, unadulterated context, it describes people of all backgrounds and convictions coming together and occupying the same space on our planet peacefully. As pluralism pertains to religion, it paints a society wherein Muslims, Christians, Jews, Hindus, Buddhists, atheists, Gnostics, agnostics, etc., are all free to worship however they wish, and are never coerced to worship in a way they do not wish. When pluralism *works* in a society, Muslims don't prevent Christians from following Jesus, Christians don't prevent Buddhists from concentrating on their philosophies, and on the circle goes, while idyllically, *all* peoples are at liberty to practice and express their beliefs without fear of persecution. One person might share his or her beliefs to another, but it will happen because of individual motivation, not because of the pressures of a geographical religious identity.

However, it's important to remember that pluralism *is not the same thing* as syncretism.

The term "syncretism" refers to blending two (or more) religions to form a new belief system. Whereas some might feel that such a goal might work for *other* world religions that don't see the new hybrid faith to be a complete abandonment of their roots, by default of the commands from the God of the Bible, neither Christianity nor Judaism is compatible with being doctrinally syncretized with any other religion. Doing so breaks every rule in both Testaments of the Word (not the least of which are *the first two* of the Ten Commandments; also see the following references, which don't even scratch the surface: Exodus 20:3–6; Leviticus 26:1; Daniel 9:27; 12:11; Ezekiel 6:5, 9, 13; 14:4; 16:36–37; Matthew 24:15; Mark 13:14; Revelation 9:20; 13:14–15; 19:20).

These authors fear that, although most can/do comprehend the difference between pluralism and syncretism, many are not seeing that the pagan reality of syncretism is currently crouched behind the shining, exterior glory of pluralism. In other words, while we have been dancing wildly to the tune of religious freedom, a sinister song has been playing quietly underneath, subliminally blurring the clear and definite lines of Christianity that the apostles and disciples died for together with paganism. The subtlety of this has been such that many conservative Christians would balk at the very thought, claiming that *their* Christianity has done no such thing…that *their* Christianity is pure, holy, and righteous. However, for many, tragically, *their* Christianity is going to mesh seamlessly into Antichrist's Superchurch of the End Days.

A person could *easily* claim to support healthy, societal pluralism in which all religions "play nice" in the same "playground" on the outside, while secretly aiming for syncretism and the contamination of Christianity underneath. These authors believe this is exactly what many world powers are up to when they aim for a One-World Religion, and it's *certainly* what Antichrist will be all about when he claims the throne of the cult stage we've built for him. All that's left in order for this apocalyptic scenario to play out on a grand scale is for Christians to see the signs of their belief system getting hacked by another in a syncretistic/pagan agenda and then choose not to react.

Then again, as the following chapters will show, we already don't seem to react to anything anymore.

Defining "Cult"

At the beginning of this book, we said we would define the word "cult" as the Word of God would define it. That is still our goal, though a brief discussion is due here because of how the word has morphed through the years. To remind the readers: Today, the *Merriam-Webster's Collegiate Dictionary* defines a "cult" as "a system of religious beliefs and ritual…a religion regarded as unorthodox or spurious; also: its body of adherents."[340]

Etymologically, "cult" has roots from primarily Latin (*colere, cultus,* and later *cultivare*) and French (*culte*), and further from Indo-European prefixes (*quel-, quol-*). Although it's a longer story than most readers want to know, suffice it to say that the word was used in various earlier forms to refer to what we now recognize in English as "wheel" and "cycle," which slowly, metaphorically changed to mean "inhabit a place," and later to "making a wild place suitable for crops."[341] But, because of the historical-religious link between a section of land and the deity that makes that land fruitful, the Latin *cultus* and the French *culte* directly translate to "worship" in both cultures as "originally denoting homage paid to a divinity." So, the order goes like this: "[first] inhabited, [then] cultivated, [then] worshipped."[342]

Thus far, collectively, we have a group of people heading out to new territories and finding land to settle upon and farm; this is where we get the English derivatives "cultivate" and "colony." As they harvest the lands they've nurtured, they worship the deity from whom they believe the harvest comes. The blend of a regional people nurturing a plot of land together and then together worshiping the deity who provides crops on that land becomes "culture," since these are the elements that build civilization.

As cultures came about with established religions, any cluster of people who depart from their native religion—*any groups attempting to syncretize their religion with one that has settled in or around their land later*—could be seen as controversially divorcing themselves from the spiritual heartbeat of their homeland. This "unorthodox" or "spurious" move (as *Merriam-Webster's Collegiate* defines) rendered them guilty of spiritual infidelity.

This, throughout history, would eventually warp the word "cult" from meaning simply "worship" to meaning "deviant worship," though scholars, academics, and social scientists have a hard time agreeing on exactly when and how that shift first occurred.

Unfortunately, because the line is so blurry and complicated regarding the shaping of the word that defines these groups and/or movements, it's also fuzzy when it comes to outlining the differences between a "cult" and genuine "faith." Its use as an *ad hominem* slap to groups that are different in their beliefs and adds a layer of mud that is hard to scrub off (for example, a Baptist calling all Pentecostal churches "cults" and vice versa; they are technically denominations of the same religion, so the term should not be used in that way). And as a *tragic* result of all this confusion, terminology is already being threaded into our society to normalize and even applaud what might be heretical or deviant religion, as one enormously popular book, *Misunderstanding Cults*, celebrates: "Cults are a genuine expression of religious freedom deserving tolera-tion."[343] (That's all fine and dandy until such "genuine expressions [of] religious freedom" lead to such atrocities as the Manson murders, the mass suicide in Jonestown, or the pedophilia within the Children of God cult. At *some* point, we need to stop tolerating when a "religion" poses a threat to people...and remember that the Antichrist Superchurch will be a global slaughter.) This is a word game at its finest. At least where the contemporary, North American society is concerned, the word "cult" is heavily associated with the dangerous religious sects that have ended in murder, terrorism, human trafficking, and severe member abuse (to say the least), so presenting it as everyday "religious freedom" sounds to most of us like postmodernist waffling. Granted, this same source does imme-diately go on to clarify that these groups, when left unchecked, could result in "exploitation of followers by leaders deserving civic scrutiny,"[344] but it's treated as if that is the exception and not the rule; it is presented as if a "cult" is only dangerous *after* an identified leader has begun to cause damage, not earlier, when the fledgling seeds of insanity are first planted.

If discussed to the exhaustive end, this trail of thought could lead to a whole book *just* attempting to define a word in a way that it will massage the intellectual cramps of scholars, academics, and social scientists, many of whom believe so strongly in their own definition that their approach to the subject has led to strong language and vehement slander of those who should otherwise be seen as philosophical peers. These authors wish to proceed with a definition supported by the Bible—God's Holy Word and Revelation about Himself, His thoughts, and His character—to allow God to weigh in on the conversation.

The Bible Warned Us

Jesus, in Matthew 7:14–18, warns about false religions that will spring from heretical teachings of those who look like beautiful sheep: "Beware of false prophets, which come to you in sheep's clothing, but inwardly they are ravening wolves." It's interesting that He uses *sheep* to describe how these cult leaders will present themselves, because later, Jesus reveals that the False Prophet who leads the world to join the Superchurch and worship Antichrist *looks like* a lamb but speaks words inspired by Satan (Revelation 13:11). This connection is more than just interesting coincidence. We here get a peek at the False Prophet, who will play a key role in building the biggest, deadliest, "looks-like-Christ" cult in the world, and the description via the same Witness (Christ) is almost word for word the description of the many false teachers who will build smaller cults around the globe throughout history, as Jesus mentioned in Matthew. It's not hard to see that our Lord, in Matthew 7:14–18, is portraying all "Christian" cults as practice rounds for the End-Times Superchurch. One commentator, while reflecting on Christ's "you will know them by their fruits" test, recognizes: "Here Jesus sets out not a doctrinal but an ethical test…[because] even Christian behaviour may be counterfeited."[345]

Turning to 1 John 4:1–4, we land at a more precise instruction for how to apply the test and expose the "fruits" for what they are. Both the legitimate Christian response and the cultic response by pretenders are discussed in this section of Scripture: "Beloved, believe not every spirit, but try the spirits whether they are of God: because many false prophets are gone out into the world. Hereby know ye the Spirit of God: Every spirit that confesseth that Jesus Christ is come in the flesh is of God: And every spirit that confesseth not that Jesus Christ is come in the flesh is not of God: and this is that spirit of antichrist." A rudimentary reading of these verses makes it appear as if anyone who states that Jesus was the Incarnation of God would pass the test. Scholars clarify that correct teaching about Christ and His nature amounts to more than this, because: "An eloquent teacher of God's Word might agree to the divinity and humanity of Jesus, but have other things so out of bounds in his theology that he still might qualify as a false prophet. Jesus himself said that not everyone who called him 'Lord' would enter the kingdom."[346] Another commentator states: "It is important to observe that the command to believe in the name of God's Son Jesus Christ (3:23) is followed by the prohibition *do not believe every spirit*…[because] Christian faith is not to be mistaken for credulity. True faith examines its object before reposing confidence in it."[347]

Elsewhere, in Romans 16:17–20, we're told that we should never follow anyone who teaches us anything "contrary to the doctrine" of the Word of God. The context of "doctrine" here, as written by Paul—who wrote most of the New Testament and confirmed the teachings of the other New Testament writings, all of which validate the Old Testament with its many Messianic prophecies *also* describing Christ—refers to the Word as a whole teaching.

So far, the New Testament has taught us that a cult is a pseudo-Christianity that "looks like" Christ but attempts to mislead believers into apostasy by just shifting a few gears away from the true description of Christ as identified through the teachings of the *whole* Bible. We are charged with the responsibility to examine all teachings against the entire Word of God, or else we will find ourselves following "ravening wolves."

In his epistle to the Galatians, we find the Apostle Paul at just about the angriest he becomes anywhere in his writing. As commentators and scholars note, Paul follows a formula in his writing: He begins with a greeting, moves on to a prayer or commendation of praise for what the congregation is doing correctly, and then slowly, gently moves into telling the church he planted what areas they need to adjust or reform. This time, however, Paul throws that formula out the window and jumps straight into a powerful rebuke. The blast of passionate words written by the Lord's great Damascus-road convert luckily "saved the early church from a cultic division."[348]

What is he responding to? What has him so stirred up?

According to a string of verses near the beginning of the letter (1:6–10), the congregation in Galatia was becoming a cult by syncretizing Christianity with Judaism. This hybrid religion, Paul says, *looked like* Christianity, but was, in fact, a twisting of the truth where Christ was concerned. Anyone who preached this false gospel would be cursed, Paul warned.

The fastest, most cunning way to turn Christianity into a cult is through syncretism. Take the Gospel essentials and blend them with heresy *just enough* that they still look like Christianity, and nobody will notice when the hybrid faith fails to be legitimate. On the other hand, every cult needs a *leader*, and the most effective way of ushering in Antichrist when he comes is to bring in many pretenders who will bungle their own opportunities to resemble Christ. The more foolish they look, the better, if we're going to follow Antichrist.

In addition to pseudo-Christianity, Christ warned that there would be many deceivers claiming to be the Messiah (Matthew 24:3–5, 23–26). These cult leaders are deceivers their followers believe to be either a) the direct mouthpiece and chief servant of God, whose words and teachings are therefore infallible, *or* b) God, Himself, appearing in the flesh (most often as Jesus Christ [known as a "Messiah claimant"], and frequently understood to be the form He has taken in the Second Coming). In some cases, this line can pass back and forth between these two concepts, producing a leader who is at times God in the flesh and at other times simply His mouthpiece. A few familiar names in recent history who had notable success convincing others they were *both* are:

- **Father Divine** (real name unknown and highly debated, but most likely George Baker)—Leader of the "International Peace Mission" movement who claimed to be God from 1907 until his death in 1965 (although he has followers to this day that, somehow, still believe he is God)

- **Krishna Venta** (Francis Herman Pencovic)—Founder of the "Fountain of the World" cult who claimed to be Jesus from 1948 until his assassination ten years later in 1958
- **Sun Myung Moon**—Leader of the Unification Church who presented himself repeatedly as Jesus and the restored/sinless "True Parent" Adam from circa 1980 to Moon's death in 2012
- **Charles Manson**—Leader of the Manson Family cult who claimed he was the reincarnate Jesus Christ circa 1967 to his arrest for the famously violent Manson murders in 1969
- **Jim Jones**—Leader of the People's Temple who taught that he was the reincarnation of Jesus, Buddha, and even the ancient pharaoh Akhenaten/Amenhotep IV, who controversially forsook the traditional Egyptian polytheism for the monotheistic Atenism (a divergent form of sun-god worship) from the 1970s to the Guyana Jonestown Massacre in November 1978 (though his mainstream Protestant ministry began decades before he introduced the insanity)
- **Yahweh ben Yahweh** ("God, son of God"; his real name was Hulon Mitchell)—Leader of the "Nation of Yahweh" (or "Black Hebrew Israelite") movement who called himself "son of God" from the founding of the organization in 1979 (it's not completely clear that he initially intended to be a Messiah claimant as opposed to a sort of "child of God," but when the deification took hold, he didn't openly fight it) and the concept held steadfast among his disciples through his murder trials in the 1990s and to his death in 2007
- **David Koresh**—Leader of the Branch Davidian cult who shared his "Son of God, the Lamb" prophecy in 1983 (debate rages whether he meant to position himself as Jesus incarnate or just the last prophet), ten years before his compound was set fire,

with himself and his followers inside, during the famous Waco siege tragedy

- **Hogen Fukunaga**—Leader of the "Ho No Hana Sanpogyo" foot-reading cult who claimed he was Jesus Christ and Buddha in 1987, from which point he then gained a reported thirty thousand followers, though the cult is now defunct due to the recent international attention of his religious-training fraud conviction and potential manslaughter charges for deaths that occurred as a result of his practicing medicine without a license

- **Shoko Asahara** (Chizuo Matsumoto)—Leader of the "Aum Shinrikyo" cult who officially and publicly asserted himself as Christ in his 1992 book, *Declaring Myself the Christ*, and the deity claim withstood among his closest doomsday disciples through both his sarin-gas, Tokyo subway terrorist attack trials as well as his subsequent execution in 2018 (offshoots of his cult, Aleph and Hikari no Wa, still exist today)

- **Vissarion** (Russian: "He who gives new life") or "Jesus of Siberia" (Sergey Torop)—Leader of the "Church of the Last Testament" (alternatively "Community of Unified Faith") cult who continues to claim that in 1990 he was "reborn" as "a" Christ, a clever word game that maintains he is not actually "God," but the "word of God," a position he still holds over his four-thousand-follower commune in the Russian boreal forest (he was arrested in September 2020 for extortion and abuse charges)

- **Marshall Applewhite**—Leader of the Heaven's Gate cult who officially announced that he was Jesus on September 25, 1995, about a year and a half before his group's mass suicide in 1997 as an attempt to board the spaceship behind the Comet Hale-Bopp, though some testimonies assert that he had been positioning himself as God as early as the mid-1970s

- **José Luis de Jesús Miranda**—Founder of the Creciendo en Gracia (Spanish: "Growing in Grace") movement who officially announced that he was Jesus in 2005, as well as the Antichrist in 2006; thereafter, the most devoted of Miranda's two million worldwide followers proceeded to get a "666" tattoo to commemorate Jesus' "true" teachings (that He, Himself, would come back *as* the Antichrist) until Miranda's death in 2013

Of course, the full list is certainly much longer and involves Messiah claimants worldwide who are currently leading dangerous and heretical cults, though they aren't as well-known in the media because the world is getting bored of having another "Jesus Christ" announced in the headlines every fifteen minutes. Social media has assisted in making any Messianic claimant the master of his or her own universe for a day—until it fizzles. Self-proclaimed reincarnates of Christ happen by so regularly today that even when details of their stories are blatantly blasphemous, we're so culturally desensitized that it simply doesn't surprise anyone or draw media attention anymore. The "Jesus" appearances are commonplace now, and they keep coming.

One based in Australia today is led by a certain "Jesus Christ" reincarnate (Alan John Miller) whose romantic partner (Mary Suzanne Luck) claims to be the reincarnated Mary Magdalene. Another, narcissistic seventy-one-year-old Álvaro Thais, known by his followers as Inri Cristo, likes to make guest-celebrity appearances on Brazilian comedy shows when he's not being arrested in, or expelled from, other countries as a result of acts such as cathedral vandalism. Jesus of Kitwe makes his meager living as a tennis-shoe-wearing taxi-cab driver in Zambia, whereas Moses Hlongwane (Jesus of South Africa), when his marriage to disciple Angel launched the end of the world in 2016, prefers dressing in gold and silver bling and sunglasses reminiscent of Vanilla Ice and other rap artists of the '90s. Messiah David Shayler, on the other hand, delivers some of his sermons in drag as the "transvestite Jesus," Delores, who is able to bring a woman's perspective to mind as he teaches his gospel.

Again, the Bible warns about these End-Times blasphemies:

- "And as [Christ] sat upon the mount of Olives, the disciples came unto him privately, saying, 'Tell us, when shall these things be? and what shall be the sign of thy coming, and of the end of the world?' And Jesus answered and said unto them, 'Take heed that no man deceive you. For many shall come in my name, saying, I am Christ'" (Matthew 24:3–5).
- "Now the Spirit speaketh expressly, that in the latter times some shall depart from the faith, giving heed to seducing spirits, and doctrines of devils" (1 Timothy 4:1).
- "But there were false prophets also among the people, even as there shall be false teachers among you, who privily shall bring in damnable heresies, even denying the Lord that bought them" (2 Peter 2:1).
- "For many deceivers are entered into the world, who confess not that [the true] Jesus Christ is come in the flesh. This is a deceiver and an antichrist" (2 John 1:7).
- "For the time will come when they will not endure sound doctrine; but after their own lusts shall they heap to themselves teachers, having itching ears; And they shall turn away their ears from the truth, and shall be turned unto fables" (2 Timothy 4:3–4).

And before it's assumed otherwise, yes, these authors know how this looks. These false messiahs we just reflected upon are extreme examples who aren't captivating the attention of the mainstream. It would be a weak argument to use them as proof that, in the end, a vast majority of believers will fall away. However, these men are serving Antichrist's cause from two other, more effective angles: 1) The continual onslaught of false christs is gradually breaking down our culture's respect of the True Messiah; 2) The obvious failure of these men to resemble Christ will make the impressive Antichrist look legitimate by comparison.

The Bride of Spot and Wrinkle Blushes for Her Leader

Of all the classifications of cults that academics have compiled, by far the most dangerous and concerning is referred to as simply a "destructive cult." This is the category into which Antichrist fits, based on the actions Revelation prophecies say he will take in the End Times. There are also three main recognizable characteristics of what history has shown to be a typical cult: 1) a leader, 2) indoctrination, and 3) exploitation.[349] We've already shown how Western society, in general, is being trained to accept all sorts of evils, and this in turn results in the manipulation of society's people. As such, the latter of these subjects (indoctrination and exploitation) have been covered to a great extent in the context of Western society. However, we want to address these elements again, specifically as they relate to the Church. Between the secular and religious world, we're building a One-World Cult. At the time of this writing, however, the Man of Sin who will run this cult hasn't yet assumed the throne. This renders us a "leaderless cult," and we will, for a moment, turn our attention to the first characteristic of a cult: who our leader will be.

In the majority of cults, a leader doesn't rise overnight. He waits until he has identified a group of people who share vulnerabilities and lack direction. He tests them with small instructions or teachings over time to see who is prone to listening to the loudest voice in the room. In this way, almost every cult is "leaderless" until its official formation.

As noted earlier, Antichrist will be the son of Satan, "one with" his father in every way Jesus was "one with" His Father. As such, he will operate in satanic power to its fullest extent. The brainwashing we relate to the cult leaders of recent history is, in every sense of the term, child's play compared to the kind of conditioning Antichrist will have in his arsenal to confuse his followers. He will exercise sovereign undue influence (or "mind control," which is quickly becoming an outdated term in the field of "cult" study) over a vulnerable and directionless people he's had the benefit of watching develop since Adam and Eve.

He's not in a hurry. He doesn't have a pressing music-career dream (like Charles Manson did) that drives him to manipulate as many people as possible around him so that he can achieve his goals before his thirtieth birthday.

He doesn't need to be obvious or desperate. He doesn't need to spend his woman and child sex-abuse coupon on a following the size of David Berg's "Children of God" group when his global sex-trafficking agents are at work. Nor does he feel the pressure to convince anyone that a comet will open heaven's gate like Marshall Applewhite when, to his grim satisfaction, worldwide suicide statistics show that every forty seconds another person takes his or her own life.[350] (And, based on the increasing trend of assisted suicide discussed earlier, we can expect this alarming number to escalate exponentially in the coming years.)

And he won't get caught by authorities like David Koresh did during the FBI siege at Waco—because he will *be* the authority.

A typical, regular-human cult leader will spend months, years, or even decades testing which manipulation tactics work and upon whom, but their experience and power over other humans will always be limited in ways that Antichrist will soar past in the first five seconds of his rule.

Undue influence and mind control in the context of fanatical religious faiths and movements could be defined as "any *system* of influence that disrupts an individual's authentic identity and replaces it with a false, new one," further described as "practices [that] violate personal boundaries and human integrity, as well as ethics and, often, the law."[351] At times, this is apparent in extreme ways from almost the beginning. Part of what Keith Raniere and "Smallville" actress Allison Mack were up to in the NXIVM cult involved the literal branding of women like cattle. And other obvious, but less graphic, identity-replacement ploys are as old as dirt, such as the practice of giving disciples new names.

Sometimes, however, the undue influence is a slower burn, one that's not recognizable in the beginning, but that leads to an ensuing brainwashing effect.

The key consideration here: When it comes to labeling a new religion as a "cult," it's not always about a body count, and certainly not at first. Obviously, if the group or its leader successfully implements undue influence in the interest of murder, suicide, torture, rape, or other acts of physical violence, it would be demonstrably destructive. But even before such an act has occurred, if the undue influence is such that it makes the group *liable to* carry out violence eventually, it still falls into the classification of a destructive cult. Though some scholarly personalities differentiate physical harm from psychological, many others, like psychologist Michael Langone of International Cultic Studies Association, would openly define a destructive cult as "a highly manipulative group which exploits and sometimes physically and/or *psychologically* damages members and recruits."[352]

So, you see, *well before* Antichrist's Superchurch begins to kill, it will use a counterfeit love to groom and condition its adherents into embracing the unthinkable down the road. Before the first head rolls (whether the beheading is literal or symbolic of some other form of execution), members of Antichrist's Superchurch cult will believe they're "doing the Lord's work" and contributing to a healthier society.

So, it doesn't make the Western Church "less of a cult," because we are currently leaderless. It makes us *more of a cult* than if Antichrist had shown up too desperate or too hurried, if he appeared at the wrong time, during an era when Christians read their Bibles enough to recognize him as the supreme con artist he is and will be. We, the "Bride of Spot and Wrinkle" (cf. Ephesians 5:27), are now developing the One-World Cult, waiting for our leader to rescue us just like Manson rescued *his* girls.

With this in mind, let's glance over the known process and endgame of cultic indoctrination and exploitation.

Indoctrination and Exploitation of the Wrinkled Bride

This form of intense group manipulation has been referred to with a few mainstream terms such as "thought reform," "mind control," "brainwashing," etc. But, in the context of a cult, experts of psychology and psychiatry essentially point to the eventual process of "forced indoctrination." Consider the following in light of what we know Antichrist to be.

According to *Merriam-Webster's Collegiate Dictionary*, "indoctrination" can be defined as follows: "1: to instruct esp. [especially] in fundamentals or rudiments...; 2: to imbue with a usu. [usually] partisan or sectarian opinion, point of view, or principle."[353] But "indoctrination," when further defined by the well-recognized term "brainwashing," produces a slightly more direct (and justifiably more aggressive) description: "1: a forcible indoctrination to induce someone to give up basic political, social, or religious beliefs and attitudes and to accept contrasting regimented ideas; 2: persuasion by propaganda or salesmanship."[354] In other words, a central characteristic of a cult involves the gradual process of reshaping followers' religious beliefs and worldviews to match that of the group, which is truly only an extension of the cult leader's hidden agenda.

Cult leaders' approaches to this goal vary, but one immensely popular method is to: 1) establish the Holy Bible or a culture's "Sacred Texts" as the final word on every situation; 2) twist writings from that source to fit the programming and agenda of the cult leader, with the ultimate objective of gaining further control/power; 3) introduce some level of shame upon any follower who doesn't accept the interpretation, insinuating that, in rejecting the leader's interpretation, the follower is rejecting the Bible itself and therefore is forsaking God.

More simply put: A cult leader twists Scripture whenever it suits him to further his sway, and whenever challenged, he then uses the Bible as a dictatorial weapon with which to discipline and publicly shame any potential doubters.

As far as cultic exploitation goes, there are likely as many examples as there are stars in the sky, but the most notorious cult leaders of history have carried out tactics similar to the following pattern:

First, the leader warmly invites outsiders into the fold, introducing them to what appears from the outside looking in to be a strong community. For obvious reasons, the more vulnerable and lonely new members appear to be, the more enthusiastically the leader will present his group as the family they never had, with answers to whatever ails them in life. This group, this *family* (made up of members who are as yet unaware that they're in a cult), wants nothing more than for new followers to shed their griefs and sorrows in the embrace of their newly acquired brothers and sisters.

Second, once they've joined the group, members will be given new identities and/or names and made to believe they have "cast off" their painful past and are now reborn. Separation from "the old life" is emphasized, and the leader's control deepens as the rest of the "family" encourages widening the gap between the new members' present and past identities. Although it is presented in glorious, poetic, revolutionary verbiage so the shedding of the past life is seen as a positive and liberating event, the leader knows he has just gained more people as his emotional and mental property.

Third, through the passing of time, the leader increasingly positions himself to be the answer to members' problems, drawing them farther into his psychological game.

Without a doubt, Antichrist and his False Prophet will establish the One-World Order and the Apostate Superchurch under the guise of family, and it will appear to be the healing people from every walk of life need (except for those devoted to truly following Christ). Antichrist will solve so many problems politically and socially that he'll appear to be the godlike answer to all problems. The psychological harvest for Antichrist will be a no-brainer (no pun intended).

Often, when news about a destructive cult involving mass casualties is covered, the public responds with such questions as: "How could anyone be so naïve as to fall for that guy's tricks?" "Why didn't those people just leave?" or "Those beliefs were simply crazy! How were they so tragically misled? Did they *really* believe they were doing the right thing?"

Sometime later, the books, documentaries, scholarly journal articles, etc., all come forward with the explanation: It was a gradual indoctrination by a brilliant mastermind who found ways of exploiting his victims' weaknesses and vulnerabilities, promising to have all the answers of love (or success, etc.) in the precise areas his victims needed it. In so doing, he proved calculating enough to deceive regular people, just like us.

Now, considering how commanding Antichrist will be—both as a saint in the beginning as well as a devil later on—with all of his abuses of Scripture, knowing the Word well enough to twist it to confuse even the greatest of scholars, and having established himself as world leader, can you even imagine the scope at which he will utilize methods of cultic indoctrination and exploitation? He will mislead the "Bride of Spot and Wrinkle," that Superchurch, into the One-World Cult who, while hand in hand with other world religions, will call herself "Christian," never believing (or caring) she's in fact the Harlot who simultaneously rides the Beast. If our world's most influential Antichrist to date, Adolf Hitler, could accomplish the murder of seventeen million people (six million Jews, approximately nine million Soviets, and two million others), then there's no doubt *the* Antichrist is capable of surpassing these efforts by multiple billions of deaths when he decides to part ways with the Harlot whom he devours.

A Harlot to the World Already

Now that we know what it is we're comparing ourselves to, the next step is to acknowledge that the outside world is already viewing Christianity as a cult, and an agenda is at work to exacerbate this on a global scale. The faster we collectively are made to look like kooks—never mind that the Remnant Church is a different, living and breathing entity than the apathetic Bride of Spot and Wrinkle—the faster Antichrist can split us up and identify the Remnant's firm stance on correct interpretation of the Word as "hate speech."

And don't misunderstand: This reflection isn't necessary "because we care what the world thinks." We don't, and we shouldn't…at least not in the context in which these words are casually and commonly used today, like when someone wears pajama pants to the grocery store. Scripture is clear that Christians will be tragically misunderstood, rejected, and even persecuted for our belief in and work for Him (2 Timothy 3:12; Luke 6:22); that we don't have to feel alone in this because Jesus faced it first (John 15:18); and that these experiences can actually bless us by making our faith stronger (Matthew 5:10–11; 2 Corinthians 12:10). To deny this is to deny Scripture, so there's no point in wasting time trying to "make the Church popular."

On the other hand, we must momentarily consider what the increasingly secularized West thinks when it hears "Christianity," so that we may know the impression the Bride of Spot and Wrinkle (who doesn't read her own Book) is making on those whose souls may hang in the balance. It is in the interest of the final great harvest of souls that the Remnant Church—the image-bearers of the Creator and the ambassadors of Christ's Great Commission message, the Church who will still care and be spiritually alive in the end, can commit ourselves all the more to glorifying God by presenting Him accurately to the lost.

Consider *The Handmaid's Tale* television series as one obvious example. For those who aren't familiar with it, this program, based on the book by Margaret Atwood, paints a dystopian future wherein natural human reproduction is threatened by plummeting fertility rates that are a result of sexually transmitted diseases and environmental contaminants. The American government, now known as Gilead, is run by totalitarian, theonomic dictators who have established a new hierarchy of social classes involving extreme subjugation of women, including their being prohibited to read or write. Inhumane cruelty is commonplace for anyone who steps outside the favor of tyrannical authority, and the worst of all evils is committed by the most fanatically religious devotees. Democracy is dead, and there is only one permissible religion to which everyone in society must submit: a fundamentalist Christian belief system called the "Sons of Jacob."

At the lowest social rung are the "Handmaids"—ritual fertility/sex slaves modeled after a warped interpretation of Laban's handmaid, Bilhah, from Genesis 29:29—who are forced to bear surrogate children for the "Commanders" in order to contribute to a streamlined human population. This sexual act, known as "the Ceremony," takes place with the Commander's wife's participation as she sits behind the Handmaid's head and holds her arms down, symbolically insinuating that the forced act of copulation is consensual between man and wife.

What explanation might there be for this show's immense popularity? Is it merely a gripping plot? Does our society tune in more than it would have because of a huge advertising budget? Was there a greater buzz about this particular Hulu title than so many other programs due to the awkward, twisted scenes between the male masters and their birth-slave women?

Or, is there perhaps another, more sinister reason that a story based on one of the most banned books in the country for twenty years[355] has become such a regular, contemporary living room companion?

Today's average Hulu junkies aren't likely to stop and consider these questions; they simply return to their screens at the release of every new episode, seemingly heedless of the diametric shift our American culture has made in the last few decades from the *Brady Bunch* entertainment standards of yesteryear. Now, our most crowd-pleasing programming shamelessly involves a man raping his slave in the presence of his accomplice-wife to the reading of God's Word.

That's one small step for television, one giant leap for Western culture…

Please understand that we're not passing judgment on anyone who watches this show, or any other like it. (In fact, some, like Jessica Crooke of the conservative *Christian Post*, believe an argument could be made for why this particular show might be useful in exposing the extreme societal dangers of widespread acceptance and implementation of misinterpreted Scripture.[356]) Rather, we are hoping to point out the not-so-gradual desensitization of our responsiveness to perversion as it plays out on screen, *especially* regarding the distortion of Christianity into a cultic installation of sadistic abusers driven by the hunger for sex and domination. There is no way the Church would have been painted in this light, fictional or otherwise, on the big *or* the small screen, just a few decades ago. Oh, how fast our culture is changing!

How have we come to a point where we can watch a plot about something so alarming and depraved yet call it a regular Tuesday night? What developments have taken place in our country in recent years that would render us so psychologically anesthetized that we see such evil portrayed as the mainstream Christianity of the future?

You've already read about psychological manipulation tactics earlier in this book that answer all of these questions and more regarding how Christianity's teachings can be labeled "hate speech," our sacraments called "rape," and our contribution to society considered "establishing a dictatorial theocracy and reconstructing slavery."

These are the kind of statements that *The Handmaid's Tale—while supplemented with the rising number of negative reports in the news and media about conservatives and conservativism that have already begun!*—has the propensity to contribute. It's eventually a firm, negative psychological imprinting and resolve about Christians in the minds of unbelievers: Christians can't be trusted; they're dangerous and unpredictable; their God, lifestyle, creeds, fanatical adherence to the Word above even science (and so on) are a blight on the community; and it would be better if they took their beliefs and went on to the next town.

We know what at least some readers are thinking right now: *It's just a show! Our society knows that this is fiction. This isn't really what the world thinks of Christians. Why are you making such a big deal out of this?*

Here's the thing…it's only one show.

Countless others portray us Christians in an awful light—as crazed cult leaders, pedophiles, hypocrites, and at the very least, bumbling dimwits useful only for comedic relief. Consider *Watchmen, The Big Bang Theory, Rise, The Unbreakable Kimmy Schmidt, Crazy Ex-Girlfriend, Major Crimes, Orange Is the New Black, Scandal, Awkward, The Simpsons, Daytime Divas, South Park, Young Sheldon, and Will & Grace*—and don't get us started on the character Joe Hart, aka "Teen Jesus," from *Glee*, whose appearance in the show launched several character-dialogue scenes questioning the integrity and/or sexual orientation of key Bible characters.

This is, of course, in addition to the overnight, bold progression of outright blasphemy across the board that depicts Christianity as largely undeserving of any respect whatsoever. In television *alone*, we're being daily mocked, taunted, parodied, and heckled. If our beliefs are at this moment that easily converted into the subject of an entire culture's amusement, how can we expect to be taken seriously when we're called to reach the lost…you know, those who are currently sharing a laugh at our expense?

Perhaps you don't yet realize how out of hand this has become. We'll give you just a chip from tip of the TV-iceberg here:[357]

Warning and disclaimer: The following list is shocking. These

authors are shaken, appalled, and more outraged than we can describe at the time of this writing to see how our precious Lord's message is being presented on screen. Far too many Christian books "sanitize" what they have to say to avoid offending their readers, and in the end, the reader is less informed of reality. In the interest of raising awareness, we will simply describe what we have to about what is happening in television right now and move on. However, if you choose to take our word for it that this is extremely disturbing for those who love Jesus, and you don't feel the need to satisfy your curiosity, feel free to skip past these bullets and onto the sentence starting with "Friends."

- Main characters of *Will & Grace* intermittently make fun of Scripture and Bible characters, they have suggested that the apostles were all gay, and their gay-conversion-camp episode suggested that the entire Christian agenda at this time is to undo homosexuality by sending our youth to getaways where lyrics to well-known Sunday school songs (in this case, "He's Got the Whole World in His Hands") are divorced from their original meaning and rewritten to severely indoctrinate homophobia.
- Rosie O'Donnell's *SMILF* ("Single Mother I'd Like to [have adult relations with]") character, Bridget, laughs about how the Virgin Mary conceived Jesus as a result of rape by one of the apostles.
- Cameron Monaghan's *Shameless* character protests outside a church by yelling crude and obscene urban slang terms for homosexual acts and calling them "Jesus' love," and is subsequently heralded as the viral hero "Gay Jesus" as a result of his demonstrations.
- Fiona Gubelmann's "hateful, hypocritical," but Christian *Daytime Divas* character, Heather, who is mother to a transgender child she declares was made transgender by God, engages in abusive S&M sex with her husband while reading from the Word and

getting spanked and bruised with a cross-shaped paddle—an act described later in the episode as a "kinky three-way with God."

- IFC's *Brockmire* included an episode wherein the lead character, Jim, during an Alcoholics Anonymous meeting, calls Jesus the "Mayer of Auschwitz" and went on to say something so blasphemous that we can't bring ourselves to write it verbatim here, but a synonymous—and *far* less profane—way to state what he said was that "God needs to man up."

- Second place for the "most blasphemous" award is the episode of Netflix's *Insatiable* involving the enthusiastic "Miss Magic Jesus Pageant," wherein young teenagers compete to win the "Crown of Thorns" in a choir number, citing the lyrics, "Sweet, sweet Jesus inside me…. Yeah! Oh, Spirit, please ride me."

- At the absolute top of the list of offenses we've found is an episode of *Preacher* that begins with a "graphic and gratuitous sex scene portraying Jesus losing his virginity with a married woman the night he was arrested in the Garden of Gethsemane."[358]

Friends, as sickening as it is to read all that, there are certainly other examples worthy of mention (some, believe it or not, are actually worse than these); however, they, too, are so shocking that we will refrain—because, by now, we know you get the idea.

In the past, Christians were simply a part of one populace; in the present, we're being represented as our own pitiable, misguided clique as we gradually migrate away from secularistic culture and legislation that cannot agree with Scripture; in the future, if things continue to go the current direction, we will be a completely polarized faction, considered hostile to the world around us, because there are people in high places—*and in all places* (influential media personalities, university professors, politicians, etc.)—who have successfully combined foot-in-the-door, door-in-the-face, and other methods of manipulation to paint us as dangerous, cultic, radical fanatics whose beliefs are only worthy of satire.

Okay, *now*, take every concern that you just read about television alone and apply it to trends we can expect to see (and are already seeing) in movies. That exponentially increases the grooming of society to view Christianity as a cult. (Some report that a new independent film, *Habit*, casting popstar idol Michael Jackson's daughter Paris Jackson as the lead, depicts Jesus Christ as a beautiful lesbian who intervenes on behalf of a young girl pretending to be a nun. As of mid-pandemic, 2020, information about the film is scarce since COVID-19 has slowed down much production in Hollywood. These authors, however, won't be surprised if this "lesbian Jesus" film hits the screen at a later time.)

And then, to TV shows and movies, add music…

Don't forget books, magazines, and newspapers…

Gotta get the radio, video games, podcasts, and Internet sites in there, too…

Cultural identity is positively driven by the machinations of its media. It's happening outside the Church already.

But it's not just media. It's a worldview being perpetuated and embraced by the secularization agenda of Western society…and it's feeding right into the eschatological scenario described in Revelation.

Think that's sensational? Perhaps it isn't…

Preparing Our Land—and Churches— for Satan's Arrival

This book isn't solely focused on the subject of occult influences in the public sphere; therefore, to give attention to all trends from every country in the West would be beyond our scope. It would take multiple encyclopedic volumes to discuss how symbols of the occult are edging their way into all societies throughout France, for example, and though that land may be a part of the "Western problem" of the Body of Christ, it is easier to show our widest, English-speaking audience some examples they can see closer to home. In America—a nation birthed in Christian values and goals (at least by the arriving Puritans, if not by the forefathers, whose religion was often anything but Christian, despite popular beliefs to the contrary)—demonic imagery on public grounds should be an outrage, a scandal…a *crime*. Nevertheless, we have reached the day when blatant occultism isn't at all uncommon.

One demoralizing example of this is when a state capitol building either displays a demonic sculpture *or* takes down its time-honored Christian artwork in the interest of religious impartiality just to avoid having to include a demonic sculpture.

Both of these circumstances have happened recently several times nationwide. We'll look at Arkansas/Oklahoma and Illinois as merely two examples of this large-scale mess.

In 2015, the Satanic Temple requisitioned a large statue of Satan, appearing in the classic "Sabbatic Goat" Baphomet likeness created by mystic Éliphas Lévi. Unlike the traditional Baphomet, however, the hermaphroditic breasts would be traded out for the inclusion of two young and assumedly innocent children, one boy and one girl, gazing up in awe, wonder, and clear admiration at Satan upon his throne. This adjustment would be carried out in order to "make the statue more publicly palatable."[359] Yet, the sight of these two virtuous adolescents forever worshipfully taking in the "majesty" of Satan in this sculpture is, to be honest, more disturbing than the breasts would have been, in the opinion of many believers, as it represents potential eternal damnation for two pure souls as opposed to the same kind of public breast indecency we're all exposed to at any feminist march these days.

Upon its completion, the Satanic Temple planned, the statue would be installed on the lawn of the Oklahoma state capitol building, right next to the Ten Commandments monument that had been privately funded and previously raised without objection. The Oklahoma Supreme Court's hands were tied in regards to refusing the Baphomet while retaining the Ten Commandments, as such a decision would violate the state's Constitution.[360] This was decided to be the case despite those who rose to remind the Court that the Ten Commandments isn't just a "religious document," but a set of rules that greatly influenced the "formation of American law," and was, therefore, justifiable as an exhibit on capitol grounds based on its national "historical context" alone.[361] In the end, the Court not only had the Satanic Temple threats to consider, but also those of Universal Society of Hinduism's president Rajan Zed, demanding that if the Ten Commandments were allowed to remain, their prized "Lord Hanuman" (the "protector" monkey-god of the *Ramayana* Hindu epic) must have a place on the property as well.[362] (What a circus!) So, when put to a vote, the majority ruled in favor of prohibiting *all* "religious" structures, and the biblical Commandments were ordered to be removed. Four months later, they were transported to another location in the middle of the night, "in the dark," under the supervision of "at least two dozen troopers"[363] to avoid civil unrest, which would most likely have come in the form of protests by Christians or taunts/provocations from Satanists.

Far from considering the Court's decision a loss, the Satanic Temple celebrated. Its spokesperson stated that the entire purpose of the Baphomet from the beginning had been to reaffirm "that we live in a nation that respects plurality, a nation that refuses to allow a single viewpoint to co-opt the power and authority of government institutions."[364] Feeling they had accomplished their goal, and with the Ten Commandments out of the picture, the Satanic Temple discontinued the pursuit of installing the satanic statue on Oklahoma Capitol grounds.

From there, the Satanic Temple shifted their attention to the Little Rock, Arkansas, state capitol building, another property with a Ten Commandments monument on display. The group's attempts to have Baphomet installed as the lawn neighbor of the depiction of God's laws were initially unsuccessful, due to Arkansas laws requiring that state monuments must have legislative sponsorship. The Satanic Temple responded by starting, and quickly reaching, a twenty-thousand-dollar

"Bring Baphomet to Arkansas!"[365] fundraising campaign to fight the ruling and organize a protest to take place in the summer of 2018. That August, the rally became a showdown between vociferous Satanists, atheists, and Christians alike on the steps of the Arkansas capitol, but overall, the results were inconclusive. The Satanic Temple and the state of Arkansas are currently awaiting court hearings since the Temple filed a lawsuit against the state for infraction of constitutional religious equality.[366]

While the Satanic Temple continues to pester government buildings for the rights to display the Baphomet Satan as an equivalent to God, their other endeavors toward the goal of extreme blasphemy have already proven successful.

In the October following the Arkansas rally, the Satanic Temple of Chicago started a GoFundMe fundraiser for fifteen hundred dollars toward the installation of their "Snaketivity" (a blatant demonization of the word "Nativity") display inside the Illinois state capitol building. The artwork depicted a black hand gripping an apple with a snake coiling around it (an *obvious* visual reference to the forbidden fruit and the serpent from the biblical account of the Garden of Eden). The campaign—which began with the plea, "Please consider what you may do to help us bring Satan to Springfield!"[367]—was a success, and ultimately raised more than twelve hundred dollars above their goal.[368]

This sculpture, bursting from a red-lit, four-foot base that reads with a Gnostic "Knowledge is the Greatest Gift" mantra, was settled in warmly next to a Christmas tree and Nativity scene with the intent that passersby would be enraptured with "Satanic holiday cheer!" from December 2–29, 2018.[369]

Of course, someone had to up the ante from the old-news Freedom from Religion Foundation Christmas display, as its statement that "religion is but myth and superstition that hardens hearts and enslaves minds"[370] was evidently no longer liberating enough by itself...

Speaking of old news, in case you're assuming that this is the beginning (and hopeful end) of the Satanic Temple's "religious equality" demonstrations, it's actually not a surprise anymore when maneuvers like this make headlines. In 2014, the Satanic Temple shared space with the Christian Nativity scene at the Michigan state capitol building to show off a red snake curling around a black cross topped with a Baphomet pentagram. Officials on site—*some of whom were professing Christians, themselves*—were obligated to increase security measures in the interest of protecting the blasphemy from local protestors. One article covering the story captured well the tragically crooked and uncomfortable position this placed the capitol facility director, Dan Brocklehurst, in. It wouldn't be surprising if the final sentence in an article about the event made history as the documentation of that bleak moment in time when America began to realize the corner of irony we've painted ourselves into: "On Sunday, Brocklehurst will visit the state Capitol to [check on] the Satanic Temple display—before continuing on to attend worship services at his church."[371]

The same year, stationed in Florida's capitol building next to a sepia-toned, scroll-style paper with Isaiah 14:12 showing biased capitalization—"How you are fallen from heaven, O Day Star, son of Dawn!"—stood a classic, Punch-and-Judy-type exhibition depicting an effeminate angel falling from clouds to flames. At the top, a crudely hand-painted sign said, "Happy Holidays from the Satanic Temple."[372] This same work of "art" had been rejected by state officials the year prior, but in 2014, the Temple's spokesperson "arrived with lawyers" and the piece was, as a precursor to the more elaborate "Snaketivity" of later years, placed directly next to the Christian Nativity.[373]

Then, of course, there was the Boca Raton, Florida, "In Satan We Trust" lighted lawn structure of 2016 featuring Freedom from Religion Foundation's large, red pentagram wedged between a Christmas tree and a Nativity scene. Locals weren't happy that the sign next to it said both

"'Celebrate Winter Solstice,' as well as, 'Hail Satan, Not Gods,'"[374] but because it had been erected within a government "free speech zone," they were all politely informed that nothing could be done.

We shouldn't naively assume that all satanic demonstrators will be so quiet. Their boldness is increasing as we type this. *Two minutes before* the time of this writing, a story was released covering the "Let Us Worship" event at the National Mall in Washington, DC, at which a Kenyan-American pastor Dr. Charles Karuku, from the International Outreach Church, was accosted by a Satanist who drenched him in blood. Pictures of the incident show that the blood splashed its way past the pastor's poncho and COVID-19 mask, reaching his eyes and covering his nose and chin. Details as to where the blood came from were not disclosed in the story. This attack followed one from a previous "Let Us Worship" gathering in Seattle, where Satanists marched and chanted "Hail Satan" before "sabotaging the generators being used to power the sound system."[375]

Understandably, many conservatives in our country will find it appalling that all these pagan/satanic events are happening in a "Christian nation." Or, maybe these folks aren't aware that most, *including our former United States president*, don't believe that's what we are any longer, and aren't afraid to say as much, even when the audience is, eventually, all of North America. Barack Obama, in his pre-election "Faith and Politics" speech in 2006 at the "Call to Renewal's Building a Covenant for a New America" conference in Washington, DC, quite openly stated that, "Whatever we once were, we are no longer a Christian nation."[376]

And the disheartening reality that America—the most powerful country in the West—has hogtied itself into tolerating all "religions," including satanic ones, is absolutely less than ideal, but at the very least, these events are only happening on government property, for the most part, right? Of course, there was that time when the Holy Trinity Church in Westminster stopped using its building as a place of worship and later allowed Paul Fryer's grotesque, terrifying, offensive, completely nude (and anatomically correct) Lucifer sculpture called "Morning Star" to dominate the entrance to a once-holy gathering place, sure.[377] But that was after Fryer's other blasphemous displays—a gorilla being crucified on the cross[378] and a Jesus with charred, blackened skin being shocked to death by an electric chair[379]—had already heralded that one particular retired church as a place of sacrilege. You can't base what's happening in other Christian churches that are currently, actively engaged in worship meetings on the events taking place in a single London building. Of course, there were all those other times that a bunch of actively worshiping Christian churches took down their crosses so they wouldn't offend the non-Christians in their area.[380] Yeah, there was that.

Maybe we're not doing so well, huh, now that we've processed this trail of thought? That remove-the-cross trend was certainly concerning, considering that the cross upon which Christ died is the universally recognized symbol of redemption and all that believers are given freely because of His voluntary act. If we're willing to denounce our central symbol for the sake of the world, we're guilty of worse than mere syncretism. When we see our land, our capitol buildings, and important landmarks falling under the dominion of the prince of the power of the air, the ruler of this earthly kingdom (Satan; see Ephesians 2:2, John 12:31, John 14:30, and John 16:11), and our response is to further surrender our land and take down our crosses, syncretism is small potatoes.

The Body is already splitting. Don't you *feel* that? One group is on the surface, seemingly unfazed by the cultural shift from "one nation under God" to "one nation under Satan." The other group, who refuses to syncretize and "play nice" with paganism, is becoming fed up with Western Christianity's gimmicks and is moving underground in a mass exodus from the spirit of religion.

Someone needs to alert the Christian leadership in the West and tell them all this is happening! Maybe we should call the pope!

Oh, fiddlesticks. That's right, we forgot for a second. He's too busy trying to launch the One-World Order and get child-sacrifice idols placed in the Catholic Church. Crud. There went that idea.

But wait…we're getting ahead of ourselves.

Postmodernism's Contribution to a Collective Vulnerability

After taking in that revolting list of blasphemous moments on the small screen, as well as the efforts of satanic groups to boot Christianity out of the West for good, some of what will be talked about in this section will seem tame. We assure you, however, this discussion here outlines by far the greater worry for all who identify with the title of "Christian" and who weep on the inside for the lost.

When the Body is ridiculed from the outside, we can boil with righteous anger about how that reflects on us as well as on God, *and* we can blame ourselves for allowing it to happen (which is partly true). But, no matter what, we can't say we didn't see it coming (2 Timothy 3:12; Luke 6:22; John 15:18; Matthew 5:10–11; 2 Corinthians 12:10).

When the Body deteriorates from the *inside*, spawning generations of a weaker Bride, we stand far less a chance of being able to successfully respond to what's happening with the reputation of Christ and His Church on the outside, and more importantly, we pollute our Great Commission endeavors. Put another way: When a *physical* body is sick, it can't be counted on to run the fastest race or stand the test of endurance; when the corporate Body of Christ is sick, it promises a similar collapse in its own race for the lost that Paul talked about in 1 Corinthians 9:23–27.

Consider a quote by Professor Douglas Groothuis, a well-known doctor of philosophy who specializes in postmodernism and the failure of our culture to recognize and report genuine truth. In his book, *Truth Decay: Defending Christianity Against the Challenges of Postmodernism*, Groothuis first states that the media does, in fact, "affect how people view truth, what questions they ask, what they take for granted and about what ideas they are skeptical,"[381] which relates to the role of the social science influences we addressed earlier. Then he spends a good chunk of his book explaining how the gouging detriments of fake news, media manipulation, and popular dissolution of an "absolute, objective, and universal"[382] truth in our society (among other things) not only lead to the development of cultural hostility against Christianity, but feed the disease of postmodernist reasoning, which ultimately states that everyone can believe whatever they feel good about regardless of reality. (The *Handmaid's* depiction of cultic Christianity, under the influence of postmodernist reasoning, joined by biased subjectivity in news related to Christianity on a global scale, almost guarantees that the twisted, dystopian religion of television will be how we are eventually viewed on a large scale. It's simply what happens when logic and deep thinking are traded for partisanship.) Later, Groothuis delivers this gem regarding the Church's role, specifically:

> When the people in the pews are soaked in postmodernist assumptions and sensibilities that erode the biblical view of truth, they are in no position to program the life of God's church—for teaching, evangelism or anything else.[383]

What a humbling thought. Whether or not the "people in the pews" are to blame for our culture's "truth decay" and constant barrage of miscommunications about God and His people, so long as we're a *part* of that nonsense (and we are, whether individually or corporately, as we will soon address), we don't have the right, or the capability, to lead Christ's Church the way it should be led. We are incompetent to teach and evangelize, whether our purpose is for edifying the Body of already-saved saints or ministering to the lost.

While we're on the subject of postmodernist philosophy, its relationship to religion, and its effects on the Body of Christ, let's visit a few *absolutes* that some forces at work in today's secularizing culture are attempting to dissolve. Regardless of what you decide to believe, and no matter how you feel about Christianity, certain fundamental facts apply in order for the title of "Christian" to mean anything. Howell wrote at great length about this in her previous book, *Radicals*—a line-by-line study of the entire book of James and the power it holds to reform the current pop-culture, social-club Church into the wise, self-controlled, familial structure it's meant to be—so we won't go into it at length now. Suffice it to say that there are countless current misapplications of Martin Luther's *sola fide* ("faith alone"; see Galatians 2:16) doctrine in an increasing number of mainstream Protestant ministries today (lies that state we can live however we want to and get by on "just believing," which is *not* what Luther meant, although it's a clever postmodernist approach to avoiding divine accountability). But it goes beyond only "Donna Howell's opinion" that "just believing God exists" (like a child does in the bogeyman or fairies) doesn't inscribe the "Christian" moniker on our spiritual nametags. Not only does James—the half-brother of Christ, Himself—state that "faith without works is dead" (James 2:14–26), he also dispels the liberalistic application of the *sola fide* doctrine by stating that the very demons of hell have *also* achieved "just believing" (2:19), and they're scared out of their scaly skins at the mere thought of God, because they know they're doomed and salvation is eternally out of their grasp. Choosing to generically "believe God exists," then sharpening that faith with the wet noodle of postmodernist philosophy that builds hear-then-disobey foundations on sand (Matthew 7:24–27) doesn't secure even salvation, let alone a successful approach to the Great Commission. And, when the Great Commission isn't top priority for a Christian, then that person cannot be a Christian, regardless of what culture or society says, simply because the Commission is the purpose of the Church.

If we don't care about these principles, we may as well be a cult…

Because of the apathetic stance the Western Church has taken on the tenets and spiritual disciplines of our faith, the Church has morphed into something appalling. We may not always be able to stop the outside world from being what it will be, simply because, when left to mere human moral conviction (as opposed to an absolutely governing moral law, like that found in the Bible), fallen man will produce fallen worlds. But when we "do as the pagans do" and embrace their evil ways, we *become* pagan while we are "dressed like" Christians…and this is precisely what will happen in the End Days, when the visible, legal Church—under the influence of the Man of Sin—persecutes and murders the *true* disciples of Christ.

As demoralizing as it may feel to some to read the following words, they are nonetheless true: In the End Times, the Church of Rome can't save you, because she, too, is a Bride of Spot and Wrinkle. Every effort by the powers that be are in place to make her the mother of all Harlots.

{9}

VATICAN BABYLON

These authors don't want to talk about the pope all day long. Assuming you weren't born yesterday, you've already heard multiple theories regarding how this Roman Catholic uber-shepherd is either Antichrist or the False Prophet, and by now it's simply old news that the Church of that "city on seven hills" (Revelation 17:9) is at the center of most dispensationalist theologians' apocalyptic forecasts. *However*, because of this glaring fact, we believe it's necessary to look at two top headlines regarding what Pope Francis has been up to lately: his letter and that idol-worshiping incident last year that people keep pretending never happened.

Pope Unabashedly Calls for Antichrist System

Just days before the time of this writing, Pope Francis' most recent encyclical, "Brothers All" (*Fratelli Tutti*), used "love" as a repetitious theme to call for a One-World Order. Due to his position, whatever goals he has must be motivated by the Gospel of Christ…or at least it must *appear* to be, if he is to save face. Yet, by using love and Jesus as the motivation behind establishing the One-World Order, Francis is unequivocally positioning Christianity at the forefront of launching the Antichrist system.

The pope's letter begins with a reference to "a way of life marked by the flavour of the Gospel…that transcends the barriers of geography and distance." From this syrupy beginning, Francis spends several long paragraphs developing his call for a "fraternal society," before clarifying that he doesn't intend to teach on the subject of fraternal love; rather, his purpose is to emphasize its "universal scope." Then, in a manner predicted by just about every prophecy-watcher on the planet, he mentions that COVID-19 has exposed vulnerabilities in the working relationships each country has with its neighboring nations. He states that simply improving existing communication strategies is equivalent to "denying reality." Something *far* more drastic must be done to correct this malady…like a united world (*so* predictable). Therefore, Francis poetically writes before continuing on to discuss his propositions in more detail, "Let us dream, then, as a single human family, as fellow travelers sharing the same flesh, as children of the same earth which is our common home."[384]

Next, Francis, most certainly banking on the idea that his readers can be fear-mongered and made to feel defenseless without radical intervention in lieu of future COVID-19-like outbreaks, goes on to talk at length about certain evils within humanity's current social condition: world hunger, war, poverty, terrorism, racism, slavery, trafficking, religious persecution, and generally all other affronts to human dignity. For pages and pages, he continues this thread, listing every negative reality of the Fall of Man. By this point in his letter, any reader is a bleeding heart. The sheer barrage of depravity that readers are blasted with would stir even the coldest person to mourn the wanton state we all share as people of earth. The pope's One-World Order undertones as a cure for all these ills is already almost irresistibly persuasive.

Striking while the iron is hot, Francis returns to the subject of the pandemic, capitalizing on the recent loss of lives as a result of the lack of respirators to further his religio-political agenda, this time suggesting that all would be fixed by a global healthcare system. His choice of words is once again poetic and desperate, calling for cooperation with his forthcoming ideas so that "our human family can experience a rebirth, with all its faces, all its hands and all its voices, beyond the walls that we have erected…[lest we] collapse and leave many in the grip of anguish and emptiness."[385] In a vein similar to his reflections on the pandemic, the pope calls attention to the drug and arms cartels, migration and border issues, fake news, the woes of digital communication, public safety, and myriad other categories of contemporary maladies that are provoking a greater tension between international human communities. Again, he conditions his reader to accept that only a truly united world can apply salve to the rash of troubles plaguing the human race.

From this point, Francis weaves an extensive exhortation on the idea of embracing those who are foreigners to us using many Scriptures. He leads with our Savior's Parable of the Good Samaritan, who aided a stranger on the road who was not of his own people; notes the offense of Cain in his famous retort, "Am I my brother's keeper?" (Genesis 4:9); provides a long list of Scripture passages remembering the Israelites' days as foreigners; shows the mounting commands of the New Testament to love all people; and then comes round about, landing back at the Good Samaritan before challenging his readers to consider whom *they* identify to be their own beaten and bloodied strangers on the roadside, left to die without their assistance. Francis continues to form a sermon using the characters in Jesus' narrative to represent different people groups today, even going as far as to state that, like the priest and Levite in the story, all the piousness and religious authority in the world are meaningless if we neglect the needs of our fellow man. By this, the underlying statement is heavily implied: Anyone who resists uniting the world for a Christ-like cause, even those whose resistance stems from religious conviction, are guilty of going against Jesus' example as laid out in the parable He, Himself, gave us to follow. Pope Francis reiterates:

May we not sink to such depths! Let us look to the example of the Good Samaritan. Jesus' parable summons us to rediscover our vocation as citizens of our respective nations and of the entire world, builders of a new social bond. This summons is ever new, yet it is grounded in a fundamental law of our being: we are called to direct society to the pursuit of the common good and, with this purpose in mind, to persevere in *consolidating its political and social order* [!!!].[386]

Did you catch that? *Jesus* is calling us to a One-World Order…? If Francis didn't convince his readers to agree to a One-World Order by pulling on the heartstrings during the "human depravity and global issues" presentation, his manipulation of scriptural context swung around for a "gotcha" that his God-fearing audience would feel compelled to obey. (In case some are wondering how the pope could be wrong in his application—and these authors will admit that, without a good foundation of biblical understanding, the pope's challenge *does* sound feasible—the proper context of Jesus' parable of the Good Samaritan was a call for universal love for one another, and it was the extension of Christ's salvation work to the Gentiles during a time when the Jews believed themselves to be the elect. By wrapping the "One-World Order" blanket around the parable, the pope has expanded [translation: *twisted*] the Word to imply that Jesus wanted a social and political unification of earthly territories…even though His kingdom is "not of this world" [John 18:36]. Don't forget, too, that the *entire book of Revelation*—including all those bits about Antichrist and his One-World System that solves all the problems within humanity for the first half of his rule—is "The Revelation of Jesus Christ" [1:1]. It's *His* warning to begin with! Either Jesus warns against Antichrist, or He endorses One-World Order ideologies like the one the pope is vying for here. He can't be behind *both*, and the Bible is clear about one of these possibilities.) After using Jesus' parable to back his united world plan, Francis then quotes the words of wise men like Thomas Aquinas along with another grand (and drawn-out) entreaty of flowery words about brotherly love and a chastisement of radical individualism to perpetuate his aims of a universal society.

Gaining momentum, Francis moves on to boldly address the opening of international borders, because all people are born equal, so all people have the equal right of enjoying the land God created and all that is upon it. Likewise, there is much to learn from those coming in from other cultures, and the human race can only benefit from trading information and intelligence with those from other perspectives (just like Francis has personally observed in his relationships with other world leaders he has met, and so on). Noting the existence of impoverished people groups who otherwise cannot participate in this kind of beautiful cultural sharing and expansion, Francis says we need to "attain a global juridical, political and economic order" to reach them. Anything less, the pope eventually coins as "local narcissism." This evil is juxtaposed by Christ's loving ideal, which was earlier in the letter referred to as "universal communion."

After a discussion about the misapplication of certain political and religious terms, the pope finally arrives at the point where his (now obvious) aims toward a One-World Order are put in clear terms:

> The twenty-first century is witnessing a weakening of the power of nation states, chiefly because the economic and financial sectors, being transnational, tend to prevail over the political. Given this situation, it is essential to devise stronger and more efficiently organized international institutions, with functionaries who are appointed fairly by agreement among national governments, and empowered to impose sanctions. When we talk about the possibility of some form of world authority regulated by law, we need not necessarily think of a personal authority.[387]

This last sentence about a "personal authority" suggests it wouldn't have to be a single person in charge, like Antichrist, though the words "not necessarily" leave that possibility *wide* open. The pope immediately goes on to describe the circumstances of the global system in place at the time of Antichrist's rule:

> Still, such an authority ought at least to promote more effective world organizations, equipped with the power to provide for the global common good, the elimination of hunger and poverty and the sure defence of fundamental human rights.
>
> In this regard, we would also note the need for a reform of "the United Nations Organization, and likewise of economic institutions and international finance, so that the concept of the family of nations can acquire real teeth." [This is a quote by former Pope Benedict XVI.] Needless to say, this calls for clear legal limits to avoid power being co-opted only by a few countries and to prevent cultural impositions or a restriction of the basic freedoms of weaker nations on the basis of ideological differences.... [T]he work of the United Nations...can be seen as the development and promotion of the rule of law, based on the realization that justice is an essential condition for achieving the ideal of universal fraternity... There is a need to ensure the uncontested rule of law and tireless recourse to negotiation, mediation and arbitration, as proposed by the Charter of the United Nations, which constitutes truly a fundamental juridical norm. There is need to prevent this Organization from being delegitimized, since its problems and shortcomings are capable of being jointly addressed and resolved.[388]

In other words, he is pointing to a world superpower over all nations in compliance with one law or "juridical norm," born under the ideal of justice and universal brotherly love, that cannot be contested or delegitimized, because any weaknesses this superpower has will obviously be worked out through global negotiations. It would be risky for the pope to come right out and say that a single world leader, like the one who will oversee the Superchurch, is in mind here, lest he provoke worldwide panic about Antichrist. What is astounding, however, is that he portrays the possibility of a reformed United Nations and all of its potentially benevolent achievements, after having technically allowed for the prospects of an *eventual* single leader, as well as the firm establishment of global mandatory compliance with the system by that time. Later in the letter, Pope Francis writes:

> The seventy-five years since the establishment of the United Nations and the experience of the first twenty years of this millennium have shown that the full application of international norms proves truly effective, and that failure to comply with them is detrimental.... Here there can be no room for disguising false intentions or placing the partisan interests of one country or group above the global common good.

"Failure to comply." Those words are always so reassuring...

Anyway, you get the idea. Pope Francis' letter is 42,990 words (just under the length of the average nonfiction book in today's industry), so we won't continue to pour over it. We just want to make the point: If you think this "final pope" is going to save us from Antichrist—this last pope listed in the chillingly accurate "Prophecy of the Popes" that ends with the destruction of Rome—he's not. Everything he says appears to be in support of the whole idea. His letter is remarkably persuasive regarding the benefits of bringing the world together. He weaves so much Christ-resembling love and beauty into his end goal that it's nearly impossible for the untrained Christian eye to see how *anti*-Christ it really is.

Have you ever handled counterfeit money? If so, then you know it looks *identical* to the real thing. It's only when the fake copy is examined by *a trained eye* that it's exposed as fraudulent. Not just any Jane Doe at a grocery checkout is going to know when a counterfeit bill comes her way. It has to be scrutinized and pass or fail certain tests in order to be identified as phony money. The same principle applies here: The pope's plan for world unity, *to the untrained eye, looks identical* to Gospel-Kingdom work. In order for it to be recognized as a counterfeit, it would have to be examined and pass or fail certain tests of Scripture. When that is done, Francis' goal fails every time, exposed as a fraudulent kingdom work...and, just like Jane Doe who doesn't realize until later on at the bank that she has been scammed, when the One-World Order of the End Times is officially inaugurated, people won't know until afterward that what looked like a beautiful and legitimate thing was a counterfeit. Unlike Jane Doe, we'll be out more than twenty bucks...

The problem is, Christians would have to know the Lord and His Word well enough to examine the pope's plan to expose it as fraudulent. That is the testing mechanism in this case.

Jesus would love nothing more than for His followers to wake up and *spiritually* unite all across the planet in His name, but if it was a sincere, *spiritual* endeavor, world peace and every kind of philanthropic/humanitarian objective the pope listed in his letter would naturally stem from that movement anyway, because that is the truer sense of "universal fraternal society" that naturally bubbles up from loving our Savior. The only reason we're in such need of the benevolent intervention Francis identified is that the most powerful and prosperous Christian Church in the known universe is currently using her own pile of resources as the mattress upon which she sleeps. No kingdom work can be done for Christ when His Bride won't get out of bed. So, when a Christian leader as prominent as Pope Francis shows up and points to a political, earthly kingdom work that counterfeits the true Gospel, the sleepy Bride yawns and says, "Thank goodness someone has figured it out. Looks good to me!" A Bride this lazy, who can hardly lift her lethargic hand in the air to give a thumbs-up to a plan she hasn't analyzed against the warnings of

Scripture, has set herself up to cheat on her Betrothed for another man from another kingdom. She has set herself up to be the Harlot.

The worst part is this: If we're anywhere as close to this reality as Francis wants us to be, the end is *very* close…yet, tragically, when the world's most influential Christian takes the pulpit to usher in Antichrist's system, Christians everywhere shrug and say, "Oh…he did? I musta missed that. Oh well, back to Netflix."

We are *so* dead inside. So asleep. We are *so* the church at Sardis…

[Sardis,] I know your deeds; you have a reputation of being alive, but you are dead. Wake up! Strengthen what remains and is about to die, for I have found your deeds unfinished… But if you do not wake up, I will come like a thief, and you will not know at what time I will come to you. (Revelation 3:1–3; NIV)

But why should it be a surprise anyway, to think that the pope would use the Gospel of Christ as his platform to promote evil? He did that very thing last year, and what should have been the biggest news in history wasn't even a blip on anyone's radar.

Praising the Pachamama: A Motion for a One-World Religion

In October of 2019, in the Vatican Gardens during the Feast of St. Francis, the Pope—*himself* one of the most prominent world leaders and role models of the Christian Church (albeit Roman Catholic)—sat front and center at an idol-worshiping ceremony dedicated to the Mother-Nature-esque Incan goddess of fertility, earth, and the harvest, known as Pachamama. Photos and videos[389] taken at the site commemorate the entire tree-planting ritual, from the women lying prostrate on the ground in worship of the naked, pregnant goddess made of wood and surrounded by offerings of fruit and candles, to Pope Francis standing and offering his official benediction blessing upon the idol.

Though the general public was largely unaware of the earth goddess and her past prior to all of this, after the pope's irreversibly reckless deed, there was an initial surge in online research linking to Pachamama's consistent, historical lust for the blood of children. The Incan child-sacrifice ceremony was known as the ritual of Capacocha, and its relation to Pachamama is commonly known. A growing number of mummified adolescent remains, along with ancient cultural documentation, has helped fill in the blanks about these young victims. Three of these children—a seven-year-old boy, a six-year-old girl, and a fifteen-year-old girl known as "the Maiden" (La Doncella)—are so well preserved after five hundred years that they appear to have passed away yesterday. (Warning: Related photos online may be graphic to some viewers.) Another two mummies, "Sarita" and "Juanita," are the attraction of Arequipa, Peru. One peer-reviewed scientific journal article notes that, in Pachamama's ritual of Capacocha, the "victims were selected, elevated in social status, prepared for a high-altitude pilgrimage, and killed."[390] The details regarding how the youth were put to death are disturbing enough that we will not delve into the subject further, but suffice it to say that it was *not* a quick or painless process to offer a child to the goddess. In fact, studies have shown that these progenies were prepared for months or years prior to their death, or, as is the case with "the Maiden," they might be "raised in status [from birth], presumably for the express purpose of making her an appropriate sacrifice,"[391] so they had ample time to fear their own end. This is, of course, emotional torture *on top* of the slow, ritualistic, human sacrifice.

When Pope Francis was asked why he would facilitate a worship ritual of this blood-hungry, pagan idol, then participate in his own authoritative and example-setting act of worship at its close by enacting the benediction blessing upon her, some rose to his defense by saying that the wooden sculpture wasn't Pachamama, but "Our Lady of the

Amazon." Anthropologists, like Steven Mosher of *LifeSite News*, took a close look at the event at the Vatican Gardens and responded otherwise, explaining that the effigy and other idols like it "were worshiped in the fertility cults of many primitive cultures around the world and still are in the recesses of the Amazon." In his article titled "Not Even Pope Francis Can Deny the Pachamama Is a Pagan Idol," Mosher goes on to explain that the nature of these cults *does* involve human sacrifice as a means to satisfy the deities' demands, and that, particular to the "South American Pachamama cult, child sacrifice was practiced."[392]

Awareness of this connection was raised in the days following the event at the Vatican, and, not unreasonably, some questioned whether the pope *knew* at the time of the ritual that the goddess they were worshiping was such an image of evil, as opposed to a more ethnic depiction of Mother Mary. And, of course, one might argue in kind that it is extremely unlikely that, out of *all* the pope's advisors and officials, not one would have known who or what they were really worshiping. (Even if that *were* the case, that level of ignorance regarding pagan influence is alarming, considering how many top-level leaders of the Roman Catholic Church must have approved this idol ceremony "innocently." Surely at least *someone* in that circle has enough education in theology and its sister study, anthropology, to ensure that their beloved pope doesn't "accidentally worship a pagan idol"?—or, if not, at least enough discernment to check the background of each statue brought to their group before the ceremony is scheduled to take place? Even if their motivation is simply to avoid a scandal? No? Nobody? Does the pope just go around blessing any ol' idol that comes into his presence without accountability?)

Regardless, it didn't take long before the pope, *by his own admission in a public statement*, just after this statue and several others like it were stolen out of the Santa Maria church just outside the Vatican and thrown into the Tiber River, acknowledged that the figurine involved in the ritual was *not Mary at all*, but "Pachamama."[393] He proceeded to criticize and condemn those who had removed the idols from the church, even though their presence inside the house of God is overtly prohibited by Scripture.

Thus far, the whole ordeal may otherwise have been chalked up as a giant misunderstanding. But after the highest Christian leader on the globe acknowledged his role in and subsequent endorsement of this apostasy, you would think the media blast would be enormous.

…And it should have been.

Was everyone asleep? Why were so few people reacting to this story? Something is very wrong here…

Quite unbelievably, in practicing some of the weakest (and most profane) exegesis, hermeneutics, and homiletics these authors have heard to date, Pope Francis used the Bible, itself, as justification for his worship of the idol and the defense of idols being displayed in the church. In a lackluster, lazy sermon, he unambiguously wove together a response to the few folks in public who cared enough to demand answers—delivered to the "general audience" at St. Peter's Square on Wednesday, November 6, 2019. Francis zigzagged around a few verses in Acts 17:15–23 and even twisted a verse to relate the opposite of what its meaning in proper context. Acts 17:16 states: "Now while Paul waited for them at Athens, his spirit was stirred in him [i.e., he was upset], when he saw the city wholly given to idolatry." Pope Francis' warping of this verse, in a reading from some translation of the Bible that was left ambiguous (at least in the sermon transcript from the official Vatican website), stated that Paul "thrills within himself [i.e., he couldn't be happier] to see the city full of idols."

We don't need to launch into a formal word-study diatribe about whether Paul felt angry versus overjoyed at the sight of the God-offending idols all over town. But just in case "common sense" isn't enough of a resource platform to dismiss what the pope just said, we'll hit this one quick: The word behind the KJV's "stirred" and the PFT's (Pope Francis Translation; excuse our sarcasm) "thrills" is the Greek *paroxuno*. Here are the concordance, lexicon, and biblical dictionary verdicts from just a *few* of the world's leading scholarly word-study resources:

- "to *exasperate*:—easily provoke, stir"[394]—*Strong's Concordance*
- "to irritate, provoke, rouse to anger...[as is the context in] Acts 17:16; 1 Co. 13:5"[395]—*Thayer's Lexicon*
- "be upset, be angered, irritated, distressed"[396]—James Swanson's *Dictionary of Biblical Languages with Semantic Domains*

Of course, we could throw in another twenty-five sources identifying the same context slaughter that Francis committed here, but you get the idea. An argument *could* be made for *paroxuno* meaning to "make sharp," "sharpen," "stimulate," "spur on," or "urge" (all related to the roots *para* and *oxys*, which describe something unexpected and sharp),[397] but only as it pertains to something adverse or undesirable, like a sharp pang of hurt or agitation over something. With this in mind, Francis' application of this verse makes as much sense as saying that Paul was "absolutely thrilled to be swiftly and sharply stabbed at the sight of idols." Under no circumstances, the ancient language experts unanimously agree, would Acts 17:16 *ever* suggest that Paul was pleased to see so many idols in Athens. (This is, again, assuming a "word study" on such a thing would be necessary, since the more obvious "character study" in *any* language would be enough to show that our Lord's great apostle would be devastated to see a cluster of idols in a city of lost souls.)

> For the time will come when they will not endure sound doctrine; but after their own lusts shall they heap to themselves teachers, having itching ears; And they shall turn away their ears from the truth, and shall be turned unto fables. (2 Timothy 4:3–4)

In any case, after this Scripture defacement, whereupon Pope Francis established Paul's boyish glee, he proceeded to explain how the apostle chose to "open a gap between the Gospel and the pagan world" as an intercultural "pontiff, builder of bridges."[398] Though he avoids explaining how this behavior could be consistent with Paul's message to the church at Corinth that merging the Gospel with the pagan world is a literal, spiritual impossibility—"the things which the Gentiles sacrifice, they sacrifice to devils.... Ye cannot drink the cup of the Lord, and the cup of devils" (1 Corinthians 10:20–21)—Francis heavily implies that Paul would have been incapable of witnessing to the Athenians without their "idol to the unknown god" as a conversational genesis. Aside from the fact that this application is totally debatable and grasping (by no means did Paul *need* a pagan idol to complete God's work), the emphasis of the sermon is not just a statement of relief that Paul conveniently had a tool to reach the lost. Francis is playing an ingenious, and very *dangerous*, word game. Note his closing statement:

> Today we too ask the Holy Spirit to teach us to build bridges with culture.... Always build bridges, always an outstretched hand, no aggression. Let us ask him for the ability to delicately *inculturate* the message of faith, placing a contemplative gaze on those who are ignorant of Christ, moved by a love that warms even the most hardened hearts.[399]

Simply put: "Inculturation" is the emphasizing of Christian teachings in a pagan culture; "acculturation" is when one culture changes (religiously and otherwise) as a result of exposure to, or a merger with, another. By endorsing "inculturation," Pope Francis was technically only guilty of suggesting that we need to witness to the lost. However, in context of—

a) the child-sacrifice goddess "Pachamama" idol service he facilitated on "Christian" grounds;

b) the decision to house these idols in a church that is (supposedly) consecrated to the God of the Bible;

c) the statement of condemnation against the personalities who *removed* said idols from the house of God; and

d) his subsequent maiming of Scripture that belied Apostle Paul as one who finds idols to be resourceful and opportunistic

—he is actually pushing the agenda of *acculturation* and the syncretizing of the Gospel with culture and its little-*g* gods. Though some superficial elements of acculturation are quite innocent (for example, residents of an American city move to Beijing, learn Chinese, and adjust to standing a lot closer to strangers than we do in the States), the Bible is clear on the following: God's people have been set apart (Genesis 12:1–3; Isaiah 43:21); we have nonnegotiable boundaries that say we're *never* to live the way the pagans do or entertain the worship of their gods, lest we be found detestable and completely cut off from God (Leviticus 18:3; Deuteronomy 12:29–31); God's supreme and all-encompassing judgment is a direct response of knowing this kind of idolatrous behavior is forbidden, and then doing it anyway (Jeremiah 44:23; 1 Kings 9:9).

Pope Francis' sermon, in lieu of both his actions and words, has a clear scheme, and it's *not* just to show the love of Christ to "hardened hearts" and "build a bridge" to the pagans, but to *merge* the Gospel with the pagans, which, as any one of the verses just referenced will show, leads only to having the blessing of God over a nation entirely removed. Using the Bible to excuse and endorse actions that the Bible forbids will do that… Meanwhile, the pope positions himself as an intercultural bridge-builder who peacefully and innocently champions inculturation and healthy societal pluralism.

Hey, remember when we said that syncretism is the evil crouching behind the glossy veneer called pluralism?

Woe unto them that call evil good, and good evil; that put darkness for light, and light for darkness. (Isaiah 5:20)

Woe unto them that use their position as the most powerful religious figure in the (current) world to justify and make holy a pagan goddess with a known history of child sacrifice.

Then again, this is coming from the same "Holy Father" who, in 2018—when members of the Vatican hierarchy were confronted with numerous allegations of concealing child sexual abuse within the Catholic Church—backwardly identified Satan as the one who "uncover[ed] the sin" of the accused leaders. It *should be* more of a shock to all of us that he didn't use his platform to defend the kids whose innocence was defiled. But even the Vatican's own news website quotes from that public statement, when Pope Francis said, "The 'Great Accuser' has been unchained and is attacking bishops."[400] Perhaps we shouldn't assume that kiddos are at the top of the Holy Father's priority list, eh?

Of course, we really shouldn't be surprised. Technically, the papacy has been promoting worship of Pachamama since 1985. Pope John Paul II, in a public homily to citizens of Cuzco, Peru, on Sunday, February 3, of that year, spoke directly to the Incan people, saying:

The Church, in effect, welcomes the cultures of all peoples. In them there are always the traces and seeds of the Word of God. Thus your ancestors, when paying tribute to the land (Mama Pacha), did nothing but acknowledge the goodness of God and his benefactor presence, which gave them food through the land they cultivated.[401]

It appears that the agenda to drink the cup of the Lord and the cup of Pachamama has been brewing for quite some time.

Ye cannot drink the cup of the Lord, and the cup of devils: ye cannot be partakers of the Lord's table, and of the table of devils. (1 Corinthians 10:21)

Due to the nature of Pachamama's adolescent bloodthirst, after Pope Francis' pagan-worship story hit a few "nobody cares" corners of the Internet, locals linked this religious leader's questionable decision to the influence of the child-sacrifice god Moloch of the Old Testament. His idol, too, had been given a place of honor stationed at the entrance of the Roman Colosseum just outside the Vatican days earlier. The Roman Colosseum, as many know, is a key location of interest to those who study the spread of early Christianity; it was in this very spot that many Christian martyrs were executed in unnecessarily violent and bloody ways, primarily as entertainment for the Romans who watched them die. This enormous statue of Moloch, according to tourists, appeared to sit as the gatekeeper to the site, leering down at passersby "to mock the sacred place where the holy martyrs spilled their blood for the True Faith."[402] The irony of the timing between the appearance of the Moloch idol at the Colosseum and the pope's benediction of Pachamama wasn't lost on everyone...

Ya know, it's *really* no wonder that many dispensationalists believe that the pope will either be Antichrist or his False Prophet. If a *central* event of the End Times involves placing the Abomination of Desolation idol in the Temple (see Daniel 8:11–14; 9:27; 11:30–31; 12:11; Revelation 13:15; Matthew 24:15; Luke 21:20–21), then Pachamama is a clever public grooming tool.

Recall that lightning struck the Vatican on the night the last pope, Benedict XVI, resigned—February 28, 2013. Might that have been the God of the Bible marking the very day His enemy entered into covenant with the Roman Catholic Church? Could Francis actually *be* one of these eschatological figures from the book of Revelation, as so many voices are claiming?

Catholic Leadership Says Pope Is "False Prophet"

Even some leading Catholic sources believe this to be obvious. As noted earlier, discussions related to the pope being either Antichrist or the False Prophet aren't hard to find, especially in literature provided through Defender Publishing and SkyWatch TV. However, in case you haven't yet had a chance to check out some of the astonishing trails and links Thomas Horn recently blew the whistle on in his "Stand 2020 Defender Conference" presentation, "Visions, Chaos, and the Coming of Antichrist," here's a short excerpt that, by now in this chapter, may not surprise you:

> Both Catholics and Protestant evangelicals see the current pope, Francis, echoing a prophesied role in pushing…the system that Antichrist will employ. And, in fact, several Catholic Defenders of the faith—including the largest Catholic news agencies in the world, CAN and EWTN News, as well as several of Rome's leading theologians like Archbishop Carlo Vigano—have recently stated publicly that Francis *is* this man from the book of Revelation and Daniel, even writing letters to President Trump to warn him….
>
> But for mystic Catholics, it's much more than that. Many of them believe in the Prophecy of the Popes, which predicted nine hundred years ago that one hundred and twelve pontiffs, from the day that Saint Malachy had his divine vision in Rome and forward. One hundred and twelve popes would arrive, with the last one ruling over the Vatican when the Church and the world enter the Great Tribulation period, according to that prophecy. Well, Pope Francis, as you may know, is, or appears to be, pope number one hundred and twelve…. [Pope Francis'] namesake, the man that he chose to name himself after, Francis of Assisi, actually predicted that the final pope would be a deceiver….

Now, think about that for a minute, folks. Given that both current popes and their closest advisors at the Vatican have considered whether Pope Francis is the last pope, Petrus Romanus, and that the reality "gives them the shivers" and is perceived by them as a "wake-up call," is it any wonder that conservative scholars within the Catholic Church have taken this increasingly careful view of Pope Francis and the subsequent question of whether Pope Francis is the False Prophet from the book of Revelation? Is it the reason canon lawyers and theologians for the Vatican hosted a conference in Paris a while back to discuss how to depose a heretical pope?…

A respected Italian monsignor and a former consultor to the Vatican's congregation for the doctrine of the faith—a man by the name of Monsignor Monsignor Nicola Bux has even gone on record as saying, Pope Francis needs to stop the "confusion and apostasy" he is sowing among priests and bishops, and he needs to do this by "correcting" his "ambiguous and erroneous words and acts." Perhaps even more so than any others, influential Catholic Television Network director Jose Galat. He publicly claimed not long ago that Pope Francis is, *in fact*, the "False Prophet," who, he says, is "paving the way for Antichrist."…

There was an inquiry not long ago in which the Vatican launched an investigation into a Catholic group of exorcists known as the Herald, who, [the investigation] said, after "having discussions with Satan, have determined that Pope Francis is 'the devil's man.'"[403]

When the secular world looks for a religious leader to rise up and solve all the problems of humanity, many will look to the pope, since his position has been historically associated with theocratic authority since the formation of the Roman Church hierarchy. Meanwhile, Western Protestants—who are right now scoffing at Rome for her current *and* future immorality and loose positions on idolatry—will be sitting there, patting themselves on the back for being theologically enlightened, ready to rise, willing to stand for something and make a change…except that it won't, because it's a cult.

{10}

PROTESTANT BABYLON

The pope isn't the only leader currently preparing our land and churches for a satanic covenant of End-Times proportions, and Catholics aren't the only Christians who need to open their eyes to the present-day apostasy. Protestants often stand proudly puffed up, slinging their own version of anathema condemnations at the "Catholic Church's spiritual failings," citing such reasons as the worship of Mary, indulgences, sin-booth confession sessions using priests as mediators, discouragement of individual Bible study, dictatorialism in the history of the hierarchy/papacy, and so on. These authors are not insensitive to any of these complaints, and we agree that these topics are extremely concerning. But before Protestants can congratulate themselves on being masters of the universe, we, also, are contributing to the formation of a currently leaderless cult that will be too vulnerable to recognize Antichrist for what he is when he shows up to lead. There are so many examples of how we're getting it wrong that it's difficult to know where to start. But, because readers may assume that some of what's about to be discussed is "heresy in some other denomination and therefore someone else's problem," it's crucial to remember:

1. The most convincing and deceptive cult of all is one with members who "look like" and "act like" regular, everyday people who follow Christ.
2. Following Christ requires believing what the Bible says of Him, as well as strictly adhering to a list of tenets.
3. The members of the Western Church "look like"/"act like" regular, everyday people who follow Christ (with certain exceptions we will soon discuss), *but*…
4. The Western Church has forsaken both the key doctrines of Christ and central Christian tenets. *Therefore*:
5. The Western Church is the most convincing and deceptive cult of all.

As we've said, central tenets apply across the board. Both the Catholic Church with all its sects and the Protestant Church with all its denominations are bound to them, and this numbered list applies to both. However, due to the fragmented denominations in Protestantism that tend to represent seemingly countless variations of doctrine, assigning "cult" as a label for the whole of the Protestant Body is a more enigmatic and complicated process.

Deeds vs. Creeds

When ruminating about the disease of the Protestant Church, truly "being" followers of Christ and not just "looking like" followers of Christ is by far the most important consideration, since any other position is a cultic counterfeit.

The *creed* of the Church says, "I follow Christ."

The *deeds* of the Church say, "I don't follow His tenets or believe what the Word says about Him."

For instance: The Christian statistics research group, Barna Group, in its definition of the term "biblical worldview," identifies six universal nonnegotiables within Christianity as a belief system, based on interdenominational tracking of central Christian tenets compiled since 1995. These essentials, which apply to *all* Protestant denominations, are:

1. "[A]bsolute moral truth exists."
2. The Bible is wholly reliable and accurate.
3. Satan is a real being, not merely a symbol of sin.
4. Simply being a good person does not send one to heaven.
5. Jesus came to earth and was sinless.
6. "God is the all-knowing, all-powerful creator of the world who still rules the universe today."[404]

These authors (and everyone in the SkyWatch TV and Defender Publishing circle) concur with every item on this list. Though we would likely add several things, we certainly wouldn't take anything away from these rudimentary, fundamental components of Christian belief. However, Barna reports, *only a staggering 17 percent of practicing Christians in the US have a "biblical worldview" based upon belief in these six things.*[405]

That may come as a shock (it certainly did to us!), but it's a plausible statistic when we really dig to see what today's Western Christians actually believe: One study reports that 45 percent of American *Christians* admit that "certainty about [Christ] is impossible," and only 34 percent believe He is "involved in their life,"[406] whereas another study states that 46 percent of born-again Christians believe that Jesus sinned while He was on earth.[407] One report shows that only 41 percent of self-identified US Christian adults in the Baby Boomer generation consider Scripture to be "totally accurate in all of its teachings," and this staggeringly low number only jumps to 43 percent for the same category of believers in the Millennials, Gen-X, and "Elders" generations.[408] Between 1993 and 2018, Christians declined from 89 percent to 64 percent in their belief that witnessing to the lost is a duty of their faith,[409] whereas 47 percent of

Millennial-aged, practicing Christians actually think evangelism is morally *wrong*, as it may pressure someone to change faiths![410] These authors don't know what's worse: the fact that so many Christians don't think the Great Commission is their responsibility—*or* the fact that, out of 1,004 *regular Christian church attenders* in the US who were asked about the Great Commission in 2017, 25 percent couldn't remember what it was and 51 percent had never even heard the term in their lives![411] This means at least 76 percent of Christians are ineffective in spreading the Gospel. Maybe the numbers would be more impressive if we knew how to pray with people, but as it currently stands, only 2 percent of praying Americans do so with another person present.[412]

As of October 2020, the latest large-scale research and statistics report reflects that 58 percent of evangelicals have "demoted the Holy Spirit to symbolic status," denying His role as a true Person of the Trinity. A lie is no longer a sin, according to 40 percent, so long as "it advances personal interests or protects one's reputation," and premarital sex is agreeable to *half* of all evangelicals. Salvation can be earned by doing good, 48 percent say. Abortion is morally acceptable to 34 percent, which makes sense when 44 percent don't think the Bible's teaching on the subject is clear and 40 percent don't believe human life is even sacred. This is probably why 39 percent don't respect anyone who holds to a different faith (which is ironic, since the entire faith system being described here isn't orthodoxically *any* religion). Pentecostals/charismatics aren't any more impressive, however: 69 percent reject absolute moral truth; 54 percent disagree that human life is sacred; 50 percent claim the Bible is ambiguous about abortion; and *45 percent are not born again*! But of all groups, mainline Protestants take the lead for syncretizing their Christianity with the secularized culture of the West: 63 percent say God is *not* the provider of truth and the Bible *cannot* be trusted to fully represent God-given principles; a shocking 81 percent believe that people can be their own moral compass because humans are essentially good; only 33 percent make it a habit to confess sins and seek forgiveness from God, and a meager 13 percent read their Bibles regularly. The summary provided by the study states: "Sixty percent (60%) of mainline Protestants' beliefs directly conflict with biblical teaching."[413]

When our creeds don't match our deeds, that's called "hypocrisy." Keep that in mind.

It's not all about what data the veteran research group Barna collects, though.

Ligonier Ministries conducts up-to-date surveys about the state of the Church, and researchers there have dedicated themselves to reporting every two years about how Protestant churchgoers in the West feel regarding the central doctrines of Christianity. The most recent survey, conducted in partnership with LifeWay Research, was released in September of 2020. The findings were appalling. Thousands of people of all faiths, as well as atheists and those with undisclosed or undecided positions, weighed in. In total, 48 percent agreed that the Bible was merely one of our world's historic "sacred writings" that record "ancient myths," but that it does not contain any truth, and 52 percent denied the divinity of Christ. This is sad for the public, surely, but far, *far* worse were the numbers reported specifically about the belief of evangelical Christians in the West, which start off bad and only get worse:

- 26 percent think that church ministries cannot be effective to the world unless their worship services are "entertaining."
- 39 percent agree that "material blessings" are a *guaranteed* reward of faith (that evil prosperity gospel of recent decades is still clinging on...).
- 46 percent take a relaxed position on sin, agreeing that people are generally "good by nature."
- 65 percent believe that Jesus is a being whom God created (as opposed to belief in the Incarnation of God, the Word made flesh, aka the way through which salvation is even possible—cf. John 1:1, 8:58; Romans 9:5; Hebrews 1:1–4).

- 30 percent agree with the statement that "Jesus was a great teacher, but was not God" (an outright denial of Christ's divinity).

- 18 percent answered that the Holy Spirit *can* tell a Christian to do something that the Bible expressly forbids (folks, 18 percent may look like a small and encouraging number, but remember that it represents almost one-fifth of all evangelicals, which is alarmingly high considering how blasphemous it is to suggest that the Spirit of God would lead us in the opposite direction of His own Word!).

And, finally, the most demoralizing statistic of all is that:

- 42 percent (almost half!) of all evangelicals embrace the blatantly syncretistic/idolatrous heresy that "God accepts the worship of all religions."[414]

President and CEO of Ligonier Ministries, Chris Larson, is correct in his rebuke when he writes, "People inside the church need clear Bible teaching just as much as those outside the church."[415] Elsewhere, the ministry's chief academic officer, Stephen Nichols, who also sits as president of Reformation Bible College, offered his opinion after seeing the crushing blow of the survey: "As the culture around us increasingly abandons its moral compass, professing evangelicals are sadly drifting away from God's absolute standard in Scripture.... This is a time for Christians to study Scripture diligently."[416]

No, Stephen, that time was yesterday. Today, we are late, and the injury our tardiness has caused the Body is a festering maggot pool.

Take a moment to look at what train-wreck statement this single study makes about what we believe as the people of God: Theologically speaking, the denial of Christ's divinity is a return to Arianism, the belief that Jesus was "created *by* God," which naturally denies that He "is" God. This heresy mostly died out in the fourth century after the Council of

Constantinople in 381 when the Cappadocian Fathers—Basil of Cae-
sarea, Gregory of Nazianus, and Gregory of Nyssa—brilliantly silenced
Arius' otherwise baseless "theology." According to this survey, Arianism
is now the position of *65 percent of all evangelicals!* Meanwhile, the number of people who accept within their heart that Christ's work on the
cross was for "entertaining" worship or "material blessings" makes these
authors gag. Even the age-old "they mean well" retort cannot be offered
here. There is simply no excuse to mix any part of our Savior's salvation
mission with pop culture. On the other hand, almost half of us believe
that people are generally good by nature—so, meh...who needs saving,
anyway? We can just save ourselves. Or maybe that Holy Spirit—who
apparently tells us to carry out acts that contradict His own Word—can
lead us to that other world religion He also accepts. Maybe *that* religion
will have a messiah in it that can help us out—since a third of us don't
even believe Jesus is God at all!

This is the summation of our "Christianity," guys. It's what one
journalist calls "self-constructed, Build-A-Bear, buffet-style belief...
[that] the Westernized, New-Agey offsprings of Eastern pantheisms" can
feel comfortable with.[417] And maybe this is why, when Christians experience doubt crises in their faith in God, a "pastor or spiritual leader" is
only the person they would think to seek help from a mere 18 percent
of the time.[418]

Without true fruit, the Church is just a social club. What were once
corporate goals of holiness, godliness, sanctification, and seeking the
presence of God have been replaced with greatly rehearsed entertainment and production spectacles. Some of these places of "worship" have
gone so far that (in our opinion), if Jesus were to appear in these buildings, He would overturn tables and clear them out: "And [He] said unto
them, It is written, My house shall be called the house of prayer; but ye
have made it a den of thieves" (Matthew 21:13). These authors wonder what Jesus would think of some of the churches that—after paying
inflated salaries to ministers and staff, covering administrative expenses,

installing flashy facility upgrades and amenities (such as espresso stands and gift shops), and establishing ostentatious "worship concert" services—delegate *less than 5 percent* of their massive, megachurch budget to the kind of charitable endeavors Jesus championed (feeding the poor, caring for widows and orphans, etc.).[419]

Astonishingly, the respected, check-before-you-donate organization, Charity Navigator, in their "Financial Efficiency Performance Metrics" analysis, states that seven of every ten charities they appraise (the majority of which are secular) give *three quarters* "*at least*" of all their accumulating monies on those they set out to benefit. In a slightly less impressive statistic, every nine out of ten will redirect "at least 65%" of all income to helping the needy in the area of their conviction.

You with us so far? This means that only *one* out of ten listed charities in this country *outside* the Church would perform abysmally enough to donate less than 65 percent of their budget on the programs they designed to provide others some form of relief.

Charity Navigator goes on to say: "We believe that those spending less than a third of their budget [that's 33.3 percent in total] on program expenses are simply *not living up to their missions*. Charities demonstrating *such gross inefficiency receive 0 points and a 0-star rating.*"[420]

Let's revisit this breakdown:

- The foundation of today's North American Church claims—by the nature of the commands of our Chief, Jesus Christ—that charity is at the center of all we do. We exist to "be more like Jesus," who advocated relief work and humanitarian goals more than *any other religious figure in world history*, and to do this very work He would want us to do in His name. Therefore, both verbally and because of our affiliation, we promise the world to prioritize charity over any other entity or organization.
- Only one out of every ten non-church-affiliated charities in our country would dare spend less than 65 percent of their

budget to achieve their relief, assistance, or humanitarian goals. Anything less than that would place them in the minority of embarrassingly unsuccessful organizations and would utterly *destroy* any chance they had at a reputation of reliably handling any donor's money. But the *real* dagger in this picture are the charities that have the audacity to give less than 33.3 percent of their budget to their beneficiaries. *Tsk-tsk*. They get a *zero-star* rating. Their promises to the world are basically worthless.

- North American churches are *frequently* guilty of giving around, even less than, 5 percent.

Do a little math. That's more than just mortifying. It's flat-out disgraceful that some of our *wealthiest* churches (what the world expects to be "Jesus Christ's Relief Organizations") can't be counted on for much, if anything, when it comes to helping the poor. We show how much we care about the destitute and the sick by rigging confetti cannons and fire-retardant curtains to our stages for the weekly worship-service productions. These authors honestly believe that the Lord will someday require an answer about who would have used that same money to put food on tables overseas.

Yet not only are churches failing miserably in their compassion for the needy, like Christ commissioned. Theologically, there also seems to be a lack of conviction, as ministers everywhere now preach self-help and self-improvement rather than the fundamental (yet world-changing) doctrines of the apostles. Churches are more concerned with branding and advertisement than teaching Scripture and making disciples. The corporate attitude rings: "As long as our attendance is up and our offerings are good, that must mean God approves of this ministry, our feel-good sermons, and our fog-machine worship productions. Teaching a profound, theologically sound message is *nice*, but it would go over the heads of our congregation, so let's leave that to the seminaries. Sin is complicated. Our job *here* is only to let the people know that Jesus came so that we can experience love and joy more fully and life more abundantly."

Initially, this approach to ministry doesn't sound too offensive, but when it becomes a nationwide pattern for all Western churches (and it's our opinion that it has), the study of salvation and of Christ is polluted with the underlying—yet far-reaching and culturally influential—concept that Jesus came to fluff our pillows and bolster our bank accounts when we behave ourselves. It's another era of the prosperity gospel all over again, just waiting to be given its own label when "Progressive Christianity" gets old.

And what happens when theologically sound biblical teaching evaporates from the Church?

We land at a day when only 17 percent of Christians have a "biblical worldview."

And what happens *then*?

Stuff like *this* happens: In September of 2019, the United Presbyterian Church of Binghamton in Binghamton, New York, moved its communion table aside and erected the idol of the Slavic god, Svetovid, in its place during the celebrated Luma Festival. Known for being the pagan god of the four cardinal directions—as well as the god of fertility, war, and, of all things, *divination* (a form of witchcraft directly prohibited multiple times in the Bible)—Svetovid had no business being allowed in a Christian church to begin with, but to boot Christ's "do this in remembrance of me" sacrament tools out of the way to make the god a focus in the house of the Lord Jesus is blasphemous beyond comprehension. The leadership of this congregation knew very well that some of the people drawn in from the streets merely to see the colorful light display wouldn't have sufficient education or background to know just how anti-Christian it is to bring a pagan idol into God's holy place. Many likely assumed that Svetovid was part of some "Christian pantheon," or that this spectacle was just "how Christians do church," which is an outrageously disgraceful misrepresentation of and assault against our core doctrines and creeds.

Later, when a bold journalist had the leadership of the church cornered with a theologically sound argument for why God would forbid such a thing to occur in His house,[421] their retort was profoundly progressive and laden with New Ageism. The response was lengthy, wordy, and wove unbiblical rhetoric around an argument based on (at best) human reasoning and logic; but, to boil it down, their conclusion was that either: a) Svetovid isn't sacred or related to God's grace in any way, which makes the idol only a secular and artistic (as opposed to spiritual) concern; or b) Svetovid *is* sacred, in which case he is so as under the grace of God, who bestows upon mankind the capability of creating such works of beauty in the first place.[422] At no point was the journalist's scriptural challenge countered by the church leadership's scriptural rebuttal. Much to the contrary, the people in charge of raising that idol in God's house didn't quote one verse—not one!—to justify the act. (The only verse they did quote was entirely unrelated to idolatry.)

Guess who all reacted to this? Other than the journalist, a few people posted on their social media. Within two or three days from the initial story outbreak, nobody cared. We are "used to" this kind of "Christianity."

So used to it, in fact, that nobody cared a few years back when that whole "pole-dancing for Jesus" trend gained ground for a spell. Because nobody explains *context* of Scripture in Church anymore, we have women using Psalm 149:3—"Let them praise his name in the dance...[and] with the timbrel and harp"—as "biblical approval" for "our temples [bodies]" to "spin without sin" using "moves once meant for strippers." When ABC News covered the story in an article called "Hallelujah! Christians Pole Dance for Jesus in Texas," it was reported that the strip-tease-for-Jesus routine is an "opportunity" for dancers "to worship God and practice their faith. The students dance to contemporary Christian music." A portion of the discussion introduced the idea that married couples within the Church could be brought closer together with this kind of excitement, though nobody pointed out the obvious side effect—that a group of people from the same church getting together to pole dance *could* lead to countless marital problems as well. Consulting a pastoral leader near a Christian pole-dancing studio as to whether he thought it was a good idea, he responded in the negative (thank the Lord, a church leader with brains!), saying that, regardless of whether clothes came off, the dance, itself, was associated with scandalous things. He suggested the women do yoga instead (ughhhh, *so* close, then he blew it...). On the other hand, this pastor saw a positive: If people could be drawn into Christianity by seeing these women dance on poles, *that* would be good. (Because, ya know, "pole-dance-ianity" is *kinda* what Jesus wants us to pull the lost into, right? [By the way, the answer to that is a hearty *no*, just so we're clear, though it's pathetic that has to be clarified.]) This particular article listed other mainstream churches throughout the US where Christ's followers could experience similar praise and worship through "sexy workout classes," including belly dancing at a Presbyterian church in Virginia.[423]

Weirdly, once the craze (translation: "crazy") took root with women, as one story reports, men began to trickle in: "What was once seen as sleazy practice is now gaining steam as a way for some women—and men, too—to get closer to God." Videos of both men and women being sexy for their Savior were uploaded online where anyone can access them. One proud male dancer, who later became an instructor of the art, boasts: "I am a very deeply spiritual follower of Christ."[424]

When gathering a bunch of women to simulate a stripping event as a form of praise and worship isn't enough, bringing in the men to join them is the natural next step. These authors hope some Christian marriage out there was inadvertently and fortuitously blessed, because this foolhardy drivel is more a recipe for a scourge of overnight infidelities to sweep through congregations. (As a byproduct of this activity, newly single, financially strapped women are then equipped with vocational training for a career in exotic dance, courtesy of their local church!) That is, of course, apart from how blasphemous this "exercise" is to begin with.

These authors wonder: How many of these men and women know about the associations between today's stripper pole and the ancient rituals to the Canaanite goddess of fertility and erotic love? Asherah—mother of Baal, wife and sister of El—was worshiped by pagans in the Old Testament; her presence in a community was marked with tree groves. In and around the trees were idols of Baal as well as tall, wooden "Asherah pole" idols, which God declared throughout the Old Testament must be burned or torn down (see Deuteronomy 12:3; 16:21; Judges 6:25, 28, 30; 2 Kings 18:4). Scholars acknowledge that these idols represented the female body at some point upon its engraving, but they were often also phallic in nature and shape, rendering an idol that celebrated all forms of deviant consummation. Do Christians who "spin without sin" know that today's "dance" takes Asherah worship to the next level with a living, breathing body upon the pole of a pagan goddess of sex? Are they aware that this "exercise" was the prostitutes' launching pad for demonic, orgiastic ecstasy-worship in the groves of God's sworn enemies?

These Christians are just lost…and how can the lost lead souls to salvation?

Is it any wonder that the lost see us the way they do? Are we seriously still confused about why the media depicts us as a bunch of hypocritical, bungling clowns? When research organizations like the Barna Group report that one out of three young adults reject Christianity because of hypocrisy they see in the Church, and about 50 percent of them "still feel the Church cannot answer their questions…[because of] flaws or gaps in [our] teachings,"[425] do we feel *any* responsibility at all to react? Are we surprised when we hear about the mass exodus the Church of the West is facing today, or the literal doubling of the number of people identifying as atheists in the last decade (as the Pew Research Center reports[426])? Is there any shock value to the fact that 32 percent of American Christians left their churches and didn't return when the pandemic forced religious gatherings to close the doors for a month?[427]

It's shocking from every angle, and it only mounts. Earlier we looked at statistics that showed how far away from core Christian doctrines that Western Christians have wandered, but by further reflecting on "deeds vs. creeds," the scandalous behavior we're engaging in, the idolatry we're tolerating, we have been building to a climax. It's not just about whether every Christian believes in total biblical inerrancy or whether some allow abortion to be morally acceptable under some circumstances. Even as recently as September 22, 2020, according to the American Worldview Inventory conducted through the Culture Research Center at Arizona Christian University, only 6 percent of all adults and 2 percent of all Millennials hold a truly biblical worldview accountable to the most *basic* essentials of Christian doctrine—such as the inerrancy of Scripture, the necessity of prayer and worship, the belief that Satan is real, or the acknowledgment that sin exists and it is bad. Nevertheless, this study indicates that 61 percent of Millennials identify as Christians.[428]

This automatically introduces the logical question (and we ask with genuine respect): What *are* you, if you identify as Christian but don't believe in anything Christianity teaches about the reality of sin and the need to be cleansed of it through a Savior described in a Bible you also don't trust to be true in the first place?

Technically, this has been answered before, over a century ago, by world-renowned New Testament scholar and Princeton Theological Seminary professor, J. Gresham Machen. All of the "Christianity" we see in the West today is nothing more than veiled liberalism—and by using "liberalism" here, we are referring not to the similar-sounding label in politics, but to school of thought under the same name within theological study. The application of liberal conviction, as defined under the umbrella of liberalism as a theology, found its roots in the rationalism of the Enlightenment era, which recognized humanity's ability to reason as the new empirical authority over the words of the Bible. If something defied *reason*, as it was defined by each individual, it simply "wasn't true." Liberalists (though they were not called that at the time) approached Scripture with a postmodernist, "What's true to *me*?" application and either disregarded everything else or chalked the rest of the Word of God up to allegorical suggestion, rendering Christianity into a mere subjective experience. More simply put, liberalism is what happens when people call themselves "Christian" but "interpret away" the bits of the Bible they're uncomfortable with. Today, we hear it called "progressive Christianity," but before it got cute, it was acknowledged as a slap in the face of God and strengthened such false teachings as antinomianism (the idea that God's grace outweighs our responsibility to live righteously; the opposite of legalism).

Machen's writing, which was a shameless throat punch to liberalism, demanded that those who championed human reasoning use their own capabilities of logic to question the senselessness of their Christianity. By introducing new liberties to theology that contradicted basic essentials of Scripture, they repackaged their religion into an illogical, irrational box with more limitations on its own claims to reason than Christianity had prior. He wasn't shy in his attack against the logic (or lack thereof) of only accepting what parts of a religion gives a person happy feelings. In his *Christianity and Liberalism*, after devoting several pages to exposing the inconsistency and absurdity of the logic liberalists so championed, Machen summarized how this approach to Jesus always leads back to the black hole of unfulfillment: "Religion cannot be made joyful simply by looking on the bright side of God. For a one-sided God is not a real God, and it is the real God alone who can satisfy the longing of the soul.... Seek joy alone, then, seek joy at any cost, and you will not find it."[429]

Though he wasn't the only theologian who has skillfully and convincingly criticized the ludicrousness of liberalism (which he occasionally referred to as the alternative "modernism"), there is a reason these authors chose to highlight Machen's work at this point in this book. He called the kettle black in a way his contemporaries hadn't: While other scholars were attempting to entertain the massively popular liberalism shift long enough to sort out which new "theologies" were reliable and which weren't, Machen recognized the whole of liberalism as a *completely different religion* altogether: "[L]iberalism not only is a different religion from Christianity but belongs in a totally different class of religions."[430]

If Machen were around to lend his thoughts to the mess we're in now, his golden response to the kind of postmodern evangelicals reporting their beliefs to the Ligonier Ministries survey just discussed would likely be disregarded as an overly conservative voice from the minority. Nevertheless, for the Remnant Church who cares, his historical genius lingers on the page forever…*or* until it's outlawed by the global system we're helping to form and ends up in the "propaganda burn piles" the chaos in the West is currently reserving for our Bibles. For now, we still have gems like this:

> In trying to remove from Christianity everything that could possibly be objected to…in trying to bribe off the enemy by those concessions which the enemy most desires, the apologist has really abandoned what he started out to defend. Here as in many other departments of life it appears that the things that are sometimes thought to be hardest to defend are also the things that are most worth defending.[431]

Bottom line: A "picked apart" and "partially true" Christianity is *not* Christianity. It is a completely "different religion" from Christianity. It is—*once again*—a cult, regardless of how "normal" it looks on the outside.

Sometimes it becomes a bigger concern than whether one church removes Jesus to hail Svetovid for a weekend, or whether a group of tragically misled Christians worship provocatively. And sometimes it's not "normal looking" from any angle at all. More often than we would like to admit, colossal movements spread over regions of the world that affect all Christians in a negative way.

When Progressivism Meets Emotionalism

Perhaps the most glaring example is some of the witchcraft and occultism that had global attention during a well-known revival that drew multiple millions of people all over the world in the 1990s and dramatically and permanently changed the landscape of Sunday morning worship practices in the West. Because there was actually some calculable good that came from this revival—and because several of those who perpetuated the more negative aspects of it have since repented of their involvement—we will sensitively refer to this period in time as the "Charisma Revival." (As a quick disclaimer: These authors have studied the Charisma Revival throughout the years, and we want to be clear that the Lord certainly met many seekers at those altars. The movement was popular enough that readers *may* recognize which revival we're writing about. If readers of this book were among those who attended and had a real encounter with God, *we are not questioning the authenticity of your experience*; we merely want to look at some of the questionable origins and goings-on of the movements that began in the area at that time.)

Some may wonder why, when so much of the discussion about Protestantism has taken place across all denominations, we're about to look back at a movement that was primarily Pentecostal/Charismatic. There are three reasons:

1. Demographically, if we don't count Catholicism, with approximately 584 million members, Pentecostals and Charismatics make up the largest population of Christianity not just in the

West, but around the globe, accounting for 26.7 percent of the world's Christian population (8.5 percent of the human population).[432] Since the Catholic Church represents 50.1 percent of the Christian population of the world, that makes the remaining 26.7 percent of Pentecostals and Charismatics an *enormous* part of the Body. As a result, though not all readers are Pentecostal or Charismatic, many likely are, which makes the warnings from this movement invaluable.

2. The Charisma Revival, regardless of denominations, stands as a *great* example of what can happen when the Church forsakes her True Love (Jesus) and goes in her own direction to feed emotional phenomena. The correct teachings from the Word end, worship gets *insane*, the lost remain lost, God's heart breaks, and Christians lose patience waiting for their religious identity to iron itself out, so they eventually give up and leave the Church. Everyone loses.

3. Long-term damage inflicted upon the reputation of and theological trends within the Church can take *eons* to sort out. In this way, the Charisma Revival affected *all* Protestant denominations. It was such a grand-scale Western movement that egg was thrown on the faces of other traditional Christian faiths that were not involved, putting believers from all over the West in the uncomfortable position of answering for why *their* religion appeared absurd.

Lessons from the era of hype… Lessons learned the hard way.

This moment was marked by a resurgence of the "hellfire and brimstone"-style sermons similar to those of Jonathan Edwards' "Sinners in the Hands of an Angry God" in the mid 1700s, but this time, the messages were reprimands for not being "fired up like the folks at those Charisma Revival churches." These charges were often followed by the obligatory "get fired up" exhortation to which the congregants dutifully responded by demonstrating their (imitated) excitement…all for the sake of appearance. There was a lot of religious propagandizing to support the idea that this was the one, the only, and the last golden age of revival—that "God wouldn't wait on the lazy ones," and He would "work miracles" through those willing to "punch Satan in the face" and "reclaim our territory." But because the Holy Spirit wasn't truly behind all this "pulpiteering," no real fruit was produced. True followers of God were worshiping one day, then they blinked and found themselves in a cult the next; the lost had little reason to think that cult had any legitimate answers about how to be saved.

Right from the beginning, despite some very real demonstrations of God, something just "felt off" about the Charisma Revival. Stories from that congregation involved deeply unsettling "manifestations of God," even though there was almost never any scriptural foundation for those goings-on. This didn't seem to bother most Church leadership, though. Many people traveled to the churches that were right in the thick of it, having been instructed by their pastors to go see what's going on and "bring the revival back with them," as if they had been sent to pick up a loaf of bread. (One of these authors heard that very "bring it back" command in two different churches and by two different leaders. It was like they were suggesting that their ministry staff could just fling a revival in their backpack and feed it crackers on the plane.) In our opinions, these were pastors' efforts to try to "fix" the apathy of their home congregations because they weren't willing to do the work it would take to see a true revival of interest in following Christ.

In the following excerpt, award-winning journalist of religion, spirituality, culture, and history, Steve Rabey, describes the reputation that several churches earned during this movement:

> As [churchgoers] walk down the wide carpeted aisles—aisles that in a few hours' time will be filled with the lifeless bodies of stricken worshipers—some tread lightly, as if they are walking

on holy ground.... All told, more than 2.5 million people have visited [one of] the church's Wednesday-through-Saturday evening revival services, where they sang rousing worship music and heard old-fashioned sermons on sin and salvation. After the sermons were over, hundreds of thousands accepted the invitation to leave their seats and rush forward to a large area in front of the stage-like altar. Here, they "get right with God.".... Untold thousands have hit the carpet, where they either writhe in ecstasy or lie stone-still in a state resembling a coma, sometimes remaining flat on the floor for hours at a time. Some participants call the experience being "slain in the Spirit." Others simply refer to receiving the touch of God. Regardless of what they call it, these people are putting the "roll" back in "holy roller."[433]

Another outside-perspective report we found particularly eye-opening is by *World Magazine* reporter Edward E. Plowman, who documented his own observations on the spot during one of the 1997 Charisma Revival services. Bob Jones of the same magazine assisted in writing the article that would appear in the December 20 issue of that year. The article begins with an account of the opening of the service, when two ministers on stage begin to jog in place and dance excitedly, while families all over the enormous room jump about wildly. One woman in the front row of the balcony seating caught the reporter's eye, and he took note: "Looking like a geriatric cheerleader, she crisscrosses her arms in front of her and chops wildly at the air above her head. When she finally falls to the floor and thrashes about for five minutes, her fellow worshippers burst into applause."[434]

The story goes on to state that this same woman, likely tired from all the physical activity, fell asleep as soon as the sermon began, staying asleep until the altar call, when she revived and resumed her frenzy...

Assigning the personnel to work specific roles in such a gathering was no small feat. For example, at one church that was centrally involved in the Charisma Revival, "catchers," designated by the red armbands they wore, were responsible for doing just that: catching people who had been touched on the forehead and proceeded to fall. These men would lower the fallers gently to the floor, ensuring there were no injuries. There was also a "modesty patrol": These folks draped cloths over the women who fell in dresses or skirts to prevent possible flashing of too much skin or undergarments to those nearby. An employee or volunteer served as a scorekeeper, responsible for seeing to the constant updates on the sign out front displaying the number of souls saved to date. *World Magazine* reporters remember the sign as a way that church could claim its bragging rights—in much the same way that 1990s McDonald's signs flaunted how many cheeseburgers they had sold.

But, for all the trouble that these congregations went through to ensure God's movement had organization and boundaries, the teaching—which is the part true Christians consider the most crucial detail—lacked substance. The *World Magazine* article includes several quotes from the ministers the evening they compiled their report; their words sounded akin to the "punch the devil in the face"-style messages we mentioned earlier. What these authors find far more concerning than the record of bizarre behavior, however—and Plowman and Jones agree—is the concentrated focus on having an experience instead of edifying the Body with correct teaching and dividing (interpretation) of the Word (2 Timothy 2:15).

In the article, the writers raised the question of whether some of the dramatic falling episodes had actually been choreographed and staged. But that isn't even what bothers these authors the most, because that's an issue between them and God. What we find most troublesome is that, according to Plowman and Jones, *not one word* of the sermon they sat through addressed any theological concepts that could be soundly traced to Scripture, the doctrine of salvation, creeds of the faith, or anything else of that nature.[435]

Joe Horn, in his autobiographical and theologically rich book that addresses healthy use of the gifts of the Spirit, *Everyday Champions: Unleash the Gifts God Gave You, Step into Your Purpose, and Fulfill Your Destiny*, shares a telling testimony. This grand display of 1 Corinthians 14-style, chaotic occultism is only one of many examples of how, in many pop-culture, contemporary church congregations, discernment has left the building. The church Horn tells of was located near Portland, Oregon, at the height of the Charisma Revival; the leadership there had sent an agent to "bring the revival" back with them, as many were apt to do. His tale is similar to what everyone else was hearing at the time:

> People were "getting drunk in the Spirit," which [in this Oregonian congregation] meant that they would sway, stagger, and laugh out loud at everything they saw during service. A few times, married folks interacted with other people's spouses in a way that could be described as flirtatious, raising an eyebrow or two, but because their actions were the result of "something the Spirit was doing in them," the behavior wasn't questioned. On several occasions, this phenomenon engulfed twenty or more people at once, and the only thing distinguishing the altar atmosphere from a small-town bar atmosphere was the absence of liquor.…
>
> I'll never forget the "birthing in the bathroom" incident. A guest speaker came to town and spoke about end-time "birthing pains of the Church Body." I can't remember his message, so I have no idea whether his conclusion was theologically sound. I also can't assume that what occurred next was or wasn't via his influence, but I didn't need a seminary degree to immediately recognize it as bizarre heresy.
>
> A grown man was found on the floor of the bathroom "giving birth in the Spirit." He was moaning in agony from "birth-

ing pains," he said. That's what the story was by the time it reached me…

I was as curious as anyone to hear what the pastor would say about the bathroom incident that morning.… Surely the shepherd of the flock [read "pastor"] would either denounce the whole matter as heresy that he planned to deal with or he would justify the news with a verse.

When service began, the incident was the first thing the associate pastor addressed (the pastor never said a word that I can recall), but to my surprise, he didn't make a calculated conclusion one way or the other. He gave a quick, nervous comment… about how God works in mysterious ways, and then moved on to the announcements listed in the bulletin. I don't know if the pastoral team was simply trying to keep the peace or what, but their tolerance made the situation worse. A few weeks later, as I was still marinating on how to react, the same thing happened again—but this time, the second man "giving birth" in the bathroom went as far as to say that he was spiritually becoming Mary in labor, and that the baby "inside" him was the Son of God.

…I was disgusted that the only person questioning these odd "movements of the Spirit" was a fifteen-year-old who earned the title "Doubting Thomas" the first time she introduced logic to the discussion. The situation was already way out of hand, and just about everyone in the congregation could do anything they wanted, as long as they described what they were doing as "in the Spirit"—and it was not only allowed, it was celebrated! This church easily fit into the category of chaos Paul referred to in 1 Corinthians 14.[436]

If those experiences were faked, they were a sacrilegious mockery of the Holy Spirit's gifts and manifestations—nothing less than a circus in the house of God—because nowhere in the Word does Scripture suggest the Spirit would move upon His people in such a way. If those experiences were *real*, then, since it couldn't have been anything "of God," they must have been "of" something else…which is far more terrifying.

Part of what led to all of this was a war the Church was engaged in against an enemy that didn't really exist. Let us explain.

The Church was still wrestling through the "Satanic Panic" era of the 1980s—a time when its enthusiastic rebuke of underground satanic ritual activity launched little more than moral panic and witch hunts in our country. Multiple best-selling books (such as *Michelle Remembers*) flew off the printing presses and into immediate fame; their authors claimed they were involved with or victims of secret, demonic cults that participated in all kinds of evils, including human sacrifice, rape, torture, blood-drinking, and every other dark thing the imagination could come up with. Of course, such claims as ritual murder and crimes of a similar nature won't bob around society for long before being investigated. As it turned out, most of the claims *did* materialize in the imagination, and nothing more. This was an instance of one scam after another being perpetrated by brilliant actors who found a way of exploiting the Church for attention and royalties on a few million books.

But Christians fell into a panic. They believed they were a part of a war, but while they were preaching about pushing against the devil, the real enemy used all the hype about evil to his advantage. The Church had given *so much* attention to Satan that a societal/cultural platform was built upon which Satan could introduce his symbols, music, and satanic gospel to the public. Everyone was talking about him, so everyone was learning his ways. The Church, by putting aside its focus on the Great Commission to reach the lost and instead throwing its resources into waging war against the enemy, ironically helped facilitate the enemy's publicity coverage to those who would be enticed.

This development in the Church is, *surprisingly*, only rarely discussed amidst Christians, as if believers either didn't see it for what it was, or they don't want to talk about it. The secular world, on the other hand, continues to have a good laugh at our expense. The takeaway for our purposes here is how it affected Western Protestants for many years.

Jesus never told His disciples, "Go ye, into the world, find those who oppose me and take them down." As His followers, we should remember that, lest we maim the Commission we were given by turning it into another gospel that has no power to save. At the very least, we were distracted. Consider this excerpt from *Redeemed Unredeemable*:

The "Satanic Panic." It was an era throughout the '80s and '90s when interest in the occult, especially amid teen circles, was a nationwide phenomenon. Gone were the flower children of the '60s. The twinkling disco ball of the '70s had dulled with the dawning of the new gothic age. Kids traded in their afros and bell-bottoms for mohawks and black fishnet stockings. Dark Baphomet pentagrams shamelessly appeared on necklaces and earrings in respectful jewelry shops. Drug use landed on a much younger generation and included more powerful intoxicants than the world had ever seen. Inverted crosses and "666" became typical graffiti symbols spray painted next to gang tags on buildings. Newspaper headlines heralded a new trend in murder: ritualistic human sacrifice in the name of Satan....

Satan loves a good distraction. While the Christian Church was pulling its focus together to wage war against a decoy called "the satanic underground," the enemy brought a real spiritual warfare against the people in the Church, attacking them from any vulnerable angle. So many pastors put their disapproving stares against those in their congregation for the way their flock members dressed or pierced their ears or tattooed their biceps or listened to music with "that devil's beat" that people became estranged from the Gospel, and a rebellion arose even higher and with more zeal. And what happened when people were estranged from the Gospel and feeling spiritually suffocated, losing interest in the church as a result of religious abuse, and feeling too exhausted to fight? They left their rear exposed to the dragon. When real attacks did come, sometimes now with authentic ties to the very satanic underground that the panic had assisted in establishing by this point, resulting in murder and crimes unthinkable, every fraudulent personality's "I told you this was happening; I told you so!" diatribe caught a second wind, which begat more panic and, sadly, more adherence to misdirection....

The more the flags of warning were enthusiastically waved by the Church, whether or not the flags were legitimate, the more children and teens felt it was exciting to shock the conservative world and concerned parents around them by living on the gothic edge.[437]

Then, while we were vulnerable, distracted, and too consumed by the fear-mongering control of the witch hunt to bother reading more than just the "rebuke the devil" verses of our Bibles, up sprouted the popular but theologically paper-thin prosperity gospel. So, to anyone who might have otherwise been reached by the saving Gospel message, "Give us all your money and God will bless you" was likely, and tragically, the takeaway.

What a disastrous day for the Church that was. What an appalling ball-drop. How lethargic and inadequate we were in our true purpose of reaching the lost!

And what's the result?

Well, turn back a few pages to all those inexcusable statistics we listed at the beginning of this section if you'd like to be reminded.

The "punch the devil out" services/sermons of the Charisma Revival age can be thrilling, and they do at times inspire Christians to wake up, stand against evil, and work for the Lord. But when the effort turns into a holiness competition among believers, the motivating sermon becomes a doggedly wet thing that dies under the weight of the exhausting, rote obligation of once again spending an entire Sunday afternoon swaying at the altar (on an empty stomach). And that's not to mention all the totally weird "theologies" and "Holy Spirit manifestations" that swept through the Pentecostal Church (and then clung on for some time) as a result of the Charisma Revival. Every other Sunday, it seemed, we would hear yet another story about feathers falling from rafters and gold dust producing itself miraculously on people's scalps. Once, a man we knew even joyfully testified that his silver tooth fillings had all turned to gold at the altar. The pastor at that church was usually a very sensible man, so we were surprised when, instead of finding a gentle way of redirecting the focus of the service, he led the congregation into several minutes of praising the Lord for the aesthetic work He had done in our brother's now-blingy mouth. (These authors are convinced that Rumpelstiltskin had more to do with that manifestation than God.)

When the world hears this kind of crazy talk, they wonder why Jesus' miracles went from mercy to nonsense—from raising the dead and making the blind see to transforming a gentleman's dental work into another color. To the lost, Church becomes a godless cabaret, and even the small-town shows are able to invest in their glitter cannons because God is their declared producer. It turns into a "Spirit-led" extravaganza. A contract with the high-kicking Rockettes is the only missing element from the pageant called "church." A whole world of the lost is dying out here, and the Church is a college of the performing arts, training its people to sing, dance, and act.

The greatest offense of excitable movements like these within the Body is when the purpose of the Church (the Great Commission) is corporately set aside in trade for experience, because that leads to emotionalism…which leads to religious ecstasy and counterfeit revival.

What does counterfeit revival produce?

Men giving birth in bathrooms, pole-dance worship, and other such occult nonsense that defiles the temple of God as much or more than any Svetovid light display. As a further assault to God's kingdom, the victims are *both* believers and nonbelievers.

Regardless of the level of heartfelt sincerity anyone may have about the Lord, if a "movement of God" isn't truly in line with Scripture, it introduces confusion, associates that chaos with the name of Christ, collapses into the history books as an embarrassing and short-lived behavioral phenomenon, and ends up leaving a bitter "religious" taste in everyone's mouths for decades.

Meanwhile, mock revival truly *does* lead to spiritual death.

To illustrate this point, consider the opinion of Frederick William Robertson, the famous Brighton, England, Holy Trinity Church preacher who graduated from Oxford and went on to memorize the entire New Testament in both English and Greek while producing some of the most celebrated evangelical Anglican Bible commentaries on the planet. While relating the early-1800s "camp meetings" revivals of his own time to the religious ecstasy habits the Apostle Paul repudiated in 1 Corinthians 14:24–25, Robertson writes of not only the unfruitful ministry of those caught up in the show church, but also of the spiritual death that imperceptibly creeps into their routine. (Note that Robertson isn't attacking the gift of speaking in tongues, but specifically the religious ecstasy that was a problem first in Corinth, and again in the 1990s.)

Robertson says:

Respecting [the act of speaking in] tongues, note the following directions. 1. Repression of feeling in public. This state of ecstasy was so pleasurable [to the Corinthians], and the admiration awarded to it so easy to be procured, that numbers, instead of steady well-doing, spent life in "showing off." The American camp meetings, &c., show how uncontrolled religious feeling may overpower reason—mere animal feeling mingling with the movements of Divine life. There is great danger in this, and just in proportion as feelings are strong do they require discipline. When religious life degenerates into mere indulgence of feeling, life wastes away, and the man or woman becomes weak, instead of strong. [Sounds similar to what Machen said about Liberalism…] What a lesson! These Divine high feelings in Corinth—to what had they degenerated! A stranger coming in would pronounce the speakers mad![438]

When the Syncretized Saints Go Marching In?

Sadly, we could go on and on, giving more true "occult inside the Christian Church" news stories that have swept the Christian West of late, because the list just grows and grows. Within just the last couple of years, Steven Bancarz, Josh Peck, Dr. Thomas Horn, and countless other well-known and celebrated Christian authors just from within our own circle have released several titles raising awareness in this area.[439] Each has shown how today's pop-culture, contemporary Church is beginning to incorporate such evil, occult practices as cartomancy (fortune-telling with cards), under the guise of Holy Spirit-directed "destiny cards" or "prophecy cards" (other names for tarot cards); "angel boards," identical in every way to the Ouija board; yoga, which, if you didn't know, incorporates physical stretch-poses that are, in and of themselves, postures of worship to specific pagan gods of old (note that there are *many* other alarming details the average Christian has never heard of regarding yoga); teachings about karma, which is strictly a New Age philosophy; Mother Earth-style training programs on the "God is all, and all is God" philosophy of pantheism; "walking prayer labyrinths," which participants largely don't know draws its origins from sexually deviant Greek mythologies resulting in the birth of the half-man, half-beast Minotaur; "contemplative prayer" and/or "soaking sessions," which involve some variation of "Christ consciousness" or prayer-to-angels (or spirit guides) meditation originating straight from the New Age or Wicca; new and false "Jesus" gospels, based on pop-culture scriptural interpretations that paint Jesus to be anything *but* what and who He was described as in the New Testament; and other disturbing, anti-Christian, religious beliefs and practices, such as the following list taken from Bancarz' and Peck's *The Second Coming of the New Age*:

- Opening up portals with your minds for angels and energies of Heaven to come through
- "Spirit-traveling" out of body [called "astral projection" or "astral travel" in pagan circles today]
- Practicing "spiritual smell," "spiritual taste," and such
- Engaging in guided meditations
- Going through guided visualizations into one of the "Heavens"
- Using tuning forks and "sacred sounds" for energetic alignment
- Manifesting one's own destiny through visualization
- Believing that thoughts emit metaphysical vibrations and frequencies that create reality
- Practicing telepathic communication to put thoughts and images into another's mind[440]

These authors can bet many readers just went through this list and thought to themselves, *Yes, this is a shame, but it's not surprising.* That, in itself, is a shame. We're "used to" Western Christianity ebbing more and more toward this misdirected reality every day, so much so that we're desensitized by the level at which the Precious Yeshua's house has been tarnished.

{11}

WE *DARE* YOU!

A lot of terms and euphemisms are being tossed around in today's political and social climate that sound intimidating to Christ's followers, "post-Christian" certainly being one of them. Particularly throughout the West, we're hearing it said so often that our culture is "becoming post-Christian." Even Barna, in one of the studies referenced earlier regarding the secularization of our faith, maintains that the West is engaged in a "post-Christian Reformation."[441] Some may feel that it's no longer a future reality, but that we're already there…and these authors agree.

Apostate vs. Remnant: A Battle for Domination

But before we all bid Christianity adieu, drive in the final nail of the coffin, and whisper a melancholy "rest in peace" over faith's grave, it's crucial to understand and accept *which* Christianity we're saying goodbye to. Until recently, the tares (fake Christians) and the wheat (true believers) have been occupying the same space in the Church, but they cannot remain in the same soil forever. We believe one of these is about to be gathered in bundles where they wait to be burned, while the other is taken into the protection of the barn (see Matthew 13:24–41).

Technically, the term "post-Christian" is a misnomer anyway, even an oxymoron, because a) the currently forming Apostate Superchurch is already spiritually dead, but will only increase on Western soil as it syncretizes with paganism, and b) the Remnant Church of true believers *cannot* die—it's a literal, theological impossibility. Therefore, neither the genuine nor the counterfeit Church is going away anytime soon.

The Remnant, on the other hand, is currently feeling the separation pains that are a side effect of watching authentic Christian doctrine be replaced with the flimflam theology of the Church as an institution. So, when we hear or say "post-Christian," the reality that it actually represents is a cultural departure from pure doctrine, not the death of a religion.

First of all, Christ *is and always will be* the King, seated on the throne over the whole world and all its nations and inhabitants at all times, regardless of shifting religious trends and survey cards and without threat from mankind's constant inclination to champion human reasoning above reliance on God's provision or being held accountable to His authority. *Nothing* happens on our earthly soil that God doesn't see coming from His nonlinear, eternal, immutable, omniscient, omnipotent, and omnipresent perspective that existed before even the formation of our planet. And, as any real Christian would agree, He is always in control!

The Church that *Christ* built, the True Church or "Remnant Church," as we've been referring to it, isn't going anywhere. It never will. It *can't* "go anywhere." The Power behind it is impenetrable. The Man who assembled it with His blood is a Force that no entity in the universe can come against. The Word of God is clear on our Church's victory. Even in every fathomable eschatological scenario, where the world is meeting its apocalyptic end and the enemy holds global power, the Church that Christ built wins. For all the fears churchgoers have today that the Western world is becoming less and less a "Christian" territory, the promises of Scripture show that even if that happens on a political and social scale, it's impossible for the secularization of our culture to be victorious in the dissolution of Jesus' true followers. And that power, that *heartbeat* of God, as realized through the dramatic actions of His people, beats throughout all time—regardless of what "local churches" as *buildings* (or human institutions) do.

As so many preachers quipped throughout the '80s and '90s: Read the back of the Book and take it to the bank. We win. End of story. This "Satan wins" scenario everyone is panicking about when they drop terms like "post-Christian" is a theological incongruity, and it only serves as an enemy-pleasing distraction that says everyone should drop their Great Commission duties in a demoralized surrender because "fake news" says Christianity is dead.

But this "social club" we've built—the organized institution we *call* "Christianity"—wherein we gather every Sunday to hobnob with the "pretty people" who "have their lives together" but who are too busy working out their politics, their opinions on social affairs, and their favorite Starbucks coffee drink…this "Occultianity" that will be key to Antichrist's system? This pop-culture, lazy Bride of Spot and Wrinkle, who currently only gets out of bed long enough to give the Beast a jaunt around the riding trail? The lethargic, apathetic Woman whose contaminated robes are about to be traded for the scarlet draperies of the Harlot, whose true name is False Religion?

Yeah, she can go anytime. If "post-Christian" means the split between the Remnant and the Superchurch, these authors are at peace with that reformation, allowing the Remnant to become "post-whatever-that-is." We shouldn't fear the split! We should embrace the idea that we will no longer be joined with that Woman, but that we will be severed from her, purified of her contamination, *even if* it means she takes over the buildings.

Bring on the cleansing of the temple!

At this point, it appears certain that the war between the tares and the wheat—that battle for dominance between the forming Apostate Superchurch and the Remnant—will end with the Remnant going underground very soon. Antichrist will not allow real Christians to be out and about in public once he rises to power, and a great many signs are pointing to the idea that his rise is just around the corner.

On the other hand, if these authors are wrong and the Church as an institution does have *some* breath of true life left in her—if there is any remaining life in the Western Church that was built upon the backs of those men and women whose blood, sweat, and tears stood for an unadulterated message of the cross—then we might just buy ourselves another season of grace before the inevitable concealment of the saints underground.

If this were to occur, it would likely result in another Great Awakening—what could be the final harvest of souls before the end of days. A Holy-Spirit-directed "house-cleaning." It could even bring in a Church reformation bigger than the one of Luther's day, whereupon those tares who treat Christianity as a sort of "GolfClubanity" will be weeded out and exposed. A time when that Western religion, that cold, dead, useless thing that is *surprisingly* devoid of scriptural truth, moves out of the way so the New Testament Church can take ground in a resurgence. And a third of churchgoers who are still on the fence about which group they belong to will receive a strong message delivered in no uncertain terms: "God is in control of His own house. It's time to get serious or get out of the way for the next generation of on-fire believers to blast their way onto the Great Commission scene."

Readers, we beseech you… If *this* is the scenario you crave to come to pass, take heed and understand that it requires a return to some ancient roots.

And we mean this both theologically *and* methodologically.

Delaying the Wrath of God

While we're on the thread of personal responsibility within the Body of Christ, we need to address one crucial aspect of theology. So often, Christians "date-set," see signs where there aren't any, or get a little too trigger-happy in recognizing the Mark at every turn. This tends to make us all look silly, for certain, and it makes the Word appear less reliable. On the other hand, identifying the signs of the times, calling for worldwide prayer from Christ's disciples, and watching as a crisis is diverted *is* a biblically sound reality.

These authors have lately received phone calls, emails, texts, and other interactions from concerned believers regarding how much the year 2020 feels like the beginning of the end. Some have tossed around the idea that a certain politician might be Antichrist, and that a COVID-19 vaccine might be the Mark of the Beast (or a practice round for it), and so on. Whether all or none of this is true, we are called to pray for the grace and provision of God. Doing so in all sincerity can cause an alteration in God's plan of an otherwise certain, catastrophic scenario.

It is an oft-misunderstood biblical subject: Though God is immutable and His will, character, and holiness standards never change (Malachi 3:6; James 1:17; Hebrews 6:17; 13:8; Job 23:13; 1 Samuel 15:29), it's not theologically accurate to say that "His wrath will come at a fixed hour regardless of what we do." Under this belief, the terrifying episodes of Revelation already have an immovable future date as divined by God, and nothing the True Church does can delay it; therefore, repentance is futile since "there isn't anything we can do about it anyway." Such spiritual lethargy, when corporately applied, is ironically part of what ushers in the End-Times scenario in the first place.

On the other hand, it would also be inaccurate to say that we mere humans can do anything to change the Lord's divine and perfect will for His earth and its inhabitants.

So where is the answer between defeatism ("we can't do anything; we should just give up") and hubris ("we can change God's mind if we just do [fill in the blank]")?

Using the story of Jonah as an example, we find that when humans repent, turn to God, and align with His ways, the Lord's wrath can be postponed. This is *not* because God is unstable and goes back on His word. It's because the *reason for His wrath* is removed when people bring themselves into harmony and accord with His will. Jonah was sent to Nineveh with a specific message: Everything was going to be destroyed in forty days. This was because the Ninevites had been living in a way that blasphemed and opposed God. Their evil presence was a scourge upon the earth. But when the Ninevites repented and petitioned for God's mercy, He spared them (Jonah 3:3–10). (This isn't the only story with this outcome in the Word. Another example is when the prophet Isaiah delivered the message of God to King Hezekiah that his death was imminent and he needed to get his house in order, because he would *not* recover. Hezekiah prayed and cried out to God, and the Lord responded by sending Isaiah back to the king with the message that he would live another fifteen years, and the city was delivered from the hands of King Ahab [2 Kings 20:1–7]. We could give even more examples, but you get the idea.)

Some English translations unfortunately bungle the concept of the "delay of the wrath of God" when they state (like they sometimes do regarding verse 10) that God "repented" or "changed His mind." It isn't that these translations are *wrong*, it's that they are *incomplete*. When we hear those terms/phrases, we imagine He is feeling guilty for something He's done wrong. Because some of these translations are mainstream, but dated (such as the KJV), we continue to trip up on the idea that God would a) announce an upcoming event through a prophet like Jonah or John at Patmos (Revelation), and then b) switch gears and either flip-pantly move on with His linear, forward-moving rule over the world like some capricious king of impulse, *or* cry over His own shame in having set out to announce the event in the first place.

We won't go into the deep-trench "nerd avenues" of this complex word-study topic because of time and space restraints. The bottom line on this language conundrum is that these "repent"/"changed His mind" moments are ultimately anthropomorphic (descriptions of God in human terms; giving God human attributes). We have a hard time relating how God—who is completely outside of time, eternal in nature, and never restrained to a linear (forward-moving), four-dimensional, three-spatial-coordinates-and-one-temporal-coordinate, space-time continuum reality—could promise to destroy Nineveh *and* restore it in the same story without thinking of it as an inconsistency. This is because mere humans cannot "step out of" the space-time continuum, so for us, it *would* represent an inconsistency. Therefore, Hebraic concepts of unlimited cosmos control and will by the Creator of the universe find their place in English as "God flip-flopped His stance" or "then He was sorry."

Think of it like this:

1. When God's eternal, unlimited-by-time holiness standards are immutable and unchanging, then He is *only* consistent. No matter what happens, God's judgment will start to "kick in" on Nineveh whenever Nineveh becomes the evil thing that God's standards of holiness cannot allow to exist.

2. However, because God is eternal, immutable, and unchanging, then His "mercy that endures forever" (Psalm 107:1) as another part of His nature and character is *also only* consistent. If a nation or a people strive to meet His expectations and be what He asks, then mercy will "kick in" when Nineveh becomes repentant and they will be spared, in uniformity with God's nature.

3. Therefore, the inconsistency is with us finite, linear, ever-changing, and inconsistent humans. We are blessed when we

seek God's heart, and we are punished when we turn away from Him.

Again, to drive it home: It's not about God changing and conforming His immutable will to accommodate imperfect humanity, it's about us changing and conforming our human will into alignment with God's expectations to the best of our ability.

4. Then, *when it is sincere*, there *has been* an invisible, spiritual, supernatural, transcendent, "unseen realm" exchange that breaks the barriers of *our* natural laws and understanding (not His), and our redemption is no longer bound to the reality that it had been before.

With language problems out of the way, it's easier to see what the Bible directly states about a delay. Prophetic declarations of future judgments of God are *conditional*, not absolute. They challenge us with action. From the Lord, Himself, on the subject, we read:

> If at any time I declare concerning a nation or a kingdom, that I will pluck up and break down and destroy it, and if that nation, concerning which I have spoken, turns from its evil, I will relent of the disaster that I intended to do to it. And if at any time I declare concerning a nation or a kingdom that I will build and plant it, and if it does evil in my sight, not listening to my voice, then I will relent of the good that I had intended to do to it. (Jeremiah 18:7–10; ESV)

It's like when your mother saw you break a rule repeatedly and said something like, "I am going to take that toy away from you." She didn't have to state the condition ("if you don't stop disobeying my rule") in order for you to understand that the condition was there. You knew that if you immediately stopped breaking the rule and apologized for your disrespect (conforming to her expectations of you), she would let you keep the toy. That is the logic here.

But please understand that the "delay of wrath theology" we've looked at here is not a "cancellation theology"! What God says He will do, He *will* do (Numbers 23:19; Deuteronomy 7:9; Joshua 21:45; 1 Corinthians 1:9)! The events of Revelation *will* happen in the end. Therefore, there *is* coming a separation of the true Christians (who refuse to worship the Man of Sin) from the false Christians (who are deceived into embracing Antichrist), and God's judgment will be upon the Apostate Superchurch that "looks like" the Christian Church (and other world religions). When God said Nineveh would be destroyed, then "relented" and spared them, it wasn't a permanent arrangement or "once spared, always spared" pact. As history tells, when the Ninevites' sin grew out of alignment with God's holiness standards again, about a 150 years later, after the warnings of Habakkuk (and others) were ignored, they *were* destroyed in 612 BC, just as God said (cf. Nahum 1).

From this, we learn: Though Revelation will eventually play out just as it describes, the "delay" of God's wrath is *our responsibility*. If we don't want the End Days to be soon, or even within our lifetimes, then we Christians, the ambassadors of God's only Son, have no choice but to align with His holiness standards.

This means refusing to participate in perpetuating the heresy that has contributed to building the Cult of Western Christianity. We demonstrate this refusal, in addition to repenting, by getting into our Bibles like never before, praying to God with an earnestness we've not yet shown, aggressively applying true Christian spiritual disciplines to our daily lives, inwardly and outwardly upholding the essential tenets of the Christian faith, and striving by every effort humanly possible to be the Bride *Without* Spot or Wrinkle.

Do these things, and you will be a part of the True Remnant Church: the one out of two End-Time Churches that holds the greater power.

The Jericho Project—
A "New Testament" Homecoming

Have you readers ever heard of the ichthys? Maybe not, but you've no doubt seen it.

This Greek word for a symbol that looks like a simple drawing of a fish frequently appears on Christian merchandise such as jewelry and bumper stickers. But its background is deeper than most of us realize. Its name is an acronym for "*Iesous Christos Theou Yios Soter* ('Jesus Christ, God's Son, [is] Savior')."[442] As the *Lexham Geographic Commentary on the Gospels* explains:

> The first letter, *iota*, is the initial letter in the Greek word for "Jesus".... The second letter, *chi*, is the first letter in the word for "Christ".... The third letter, *theta*, is the first letter in the Greek word for "God".... The fourth letter, *upsilon*, represents the Greek word for "son".... And the last letter, *sigma*, is the first letter in the Greek word for "Savior".... As it does today, the early symbol of the fish could be used to identify a believer in Jesus without the need for verbal communication.[443]

Interesting... Why would early believers need to be identified "without the need for verbal communication"? Because, the early Church was, just as we will be in the End Times, facing persecution that drove them into secrecy. The Roman Empire saw to the death (or severe beatings) of anyone openly claiming to be a Christian for about three hundred years after the Resurrection, so the first Christians couldn't simply stroll down to the local church building on the corner to connect with their spiritual family and strategize about how they would reach the lost with the Gospel. They needed a way for disciples to recognize one another or mark the location of a Christian gathering without blowing their cover. If a disciple wanted to find out whether he was in the presence of another

Christian, he would casually draw an arc shape on the ground—representing half of the fish symbol we so quickly recognize in our iconography. If the other person completed the drawing, he or she could silently alert the disciple that he was in the presence of a fellow believer. If the second person *did not* complete the drawing, the first man's nonchalant "doodling" would escape notice, and the second man would be revealed as a nonbeliever.

When the Remnant Church is forced into secrecy, whether that will be sooner or later, we will find ways of communicating that are similar to the way the ichthys was used in the early Church. We, just like the early Christians, won't be able to meet at local churches. Yet, "taking church outside the building" shouldn't be a new or frightening concept. It's *precisely* how the early Christians "did church": "They broke bread in their homes and ate together with glad and sincere hearts" (Acts 2:46; NIV).

Somehow—because the Remnant is always spiritually alive on the inside—we will continue to prioritize the Great Commission until the very end. (This is true regardless of what one believes regarding the Rapture. Even if it occurs before the Tribulation, the Remnant will awaken and arise from the population of those who were left behind.) In addition, at some point during the Tribulation, survival will require that the Remnant develops some form of community that can trade and function under the radar. Exactly what this will look like and how it will be carried out is obviously unknown at this time.

However, sometime between now and then, the Remnant will have to learn a new way to "do church" outside of the institution. We'll need "practice rounds," so to speak, of the style of worship we read about in the New Testament. It will mark a return to the old ways.

On the other hand, while true Christians are already exhausted from trying to remain alive in the institution that brings death anyway, there are already *ample* benefits to worshiping together outside the building in the "usual" way, *not the least of which is the fact that the government cannot shut down these nontraditional church gatherings like it did the mainstream churches during the pandemic!*

And, before anyone thinks this sounds too complicated or mysterious to invest much mental or emotional energy into, please note: It's easy to lazily rest in the comforts of "God is in control" theology. He certainly *is* in control, and most definitely He is at all times, but we must remember that the control He holds has established an eternal plan for mankind, and it involves our participation, whether we like it or not. Creating a permanent buttocks-imprint in the sofas of our spiritual living room with the attitude that God "has it handled" is vile negligence in the Lord's eyes that could result His command: "Depart from me…I never knew you!" (Matthew 7:21–23). There are serious chores to do, and if we ever wish to hear the beautiful words, "Well done, my good and faithful servant" (25:21–23), then we need to dust off our timecards and clock in for work. Far, *far* too many Christians are late in reporting for duty, and the evidence of that has made the Cult of Western Christianity thrive…and stink.

On the other hand, it may not be the intimidating prospect many Christians fear. These authors have started a personal ministry movement beyond the walls of the Church that:

1. Follows the New Testament model;
2. Has a proven track record of immense ministerial success;
3. Doesn't cost a dime;
4. Takes place on an organic, customized schedule (and therefore naturally prevents "ministry burnout");
5. By its very nature accomplishes the *true* meaning of communion (as well as many other benefits briefly covered in the next few pages).

Just as the Battle of Jericho was fought with peace, we believe our present-day battles should be fought with peace, because, in our current culture and political state, the Body's refusal to compromise on certain secular trends is more and more being recognized as "hate speech." Just as the warriors in the Battle of Jericho reclaimed territory for Jehovah's purposes and will, we believe our grounds (churches, houses, ministry properties of all kinds across the West) need to be reclaimed for the Lord's purposes and will. Thus, this new kingdom initiative has been coined the "Jericho Project."

Though, alternatively, in the interest of the discretion that will brand the communication habits of the future underground Remnant Church, we *could* simply call it "dinner with a friend."

We will let you in on what *we* are doing. It's been some of the most important Gospel work we've ever done. (Within just the first month of its inception, one person accepted Christ as Savior.)

As a study in the revivals and Great Awakenings of history will show: In the past, most recognizably during the day of the "Jesus People Movement" following the Vietnam War, some of the most passionate churches began outside church facilities on "grass roots" soil, such as wheat fields, abandoned coffee shops, barns, and most often, peoples' living rooms. "Church" feels a bit stuffy these days, but believers and nonbelievers alike can benefit from a well-cooked meal and some hearty conversation. If a gathering is presented as a "meal," it accomplishes what the New Testament communion sacrament *really* looked like (not the Dixie-cups-of-grape-juice-and-one-bite-oyster-cracker communion frequently shared in Western churches). When we serve dinner ("break bread") and talk about the Lord ("in remembrance of Him" [Luke 22:19–20]) with fellow members of the Body (the *ekklesia*, the "church"; gathering of the saints together), we are technically fulfilling "church" and "communion" as the early Church experienced in the New Testament.

In this way of "doing church," dinner can be by a host or hostess who wants to bless the others, or it could be a potluck meal. For true believers, a box of cereal is enough of a dinner if it means joining in badly needed spiritual connection with the Body. (An unleavened meal might also be a fun way to gather together and reflect on the *first* communion, which was a Passover meal, though these authors don't think it's mandatory.)

As the conversation allows, *at whatever speed fits the mood,* those present can begin to discuss the Gospel. The Bible should be kept handy so it can be opened and read from during these gatherings. (But note: Proselytizing is *not* the goal here! Remember that bringing lost souls into our homes to browbeat them or pressure them into repeating "sinner's prayer" words that only lead to an obligatory, imitation conversion experience does *nothing* for the kingdom. It actually has the potential of placing unsaved people on a more direct path to damnation, Jesus says [Matthew 23:15].)

With the ensuing teaching, Bible study, conversation, worship (again, when appropriate), communion, and fellowship, we are, *literally and theologically,* a New-Testament-style church with far more flexibility on the schedule than the building on the corner could ever have.

Some may be unable to have people visit their homes for a number of reasons, including safety concerns. Certainly, caution should always be a priority. But if that's you, somehow, *somewhere,* you need to interact with people for the purpose of bringing the Gospel outside the four tired walls of a church building. Perhaps it's at the fitness gym, the salon, a waiting room, a school, the grocery store, at work...

You get the picture: "For where two or three are gathered together in my name, there am I in the midst of them" (Matthew 18:20).

Every time you interact with others and carry the name of Jesus on your lips, you're having the type of Church fostered by those New Testament radicals who flipped the world on its head and forever changed the notion of organized religion.

And *you* can do it, too!

No more ministry burnout. No more getting someone to cover the class you teach on a Sunday morning when you'll be out. No more preparing three-point sermons in the middle of a busy schedule. No more feeling overwhelmed with the responsibilities of active church member-ship. No more obligations to stay to the end of a service, and, on the other hand, no more wishing that great service had gone on longer.

We can't say it enough: Simplicity is key in this type of worship and ministry, whether it's just having a friend over for dinner, taking some-one to the library and talking about God in the car on the way, or giving someone a discount on a haircut or an oil change while reminding that person that the Creator has a plan for his or her life.

This makes ministry organic, unstrained, and welcome to the hear-ers, because the intensity can be adjusted to the individual's needs. *And*, if the Church were to come back to life by means such as these, it wouldn't be such a shock when, in fulfillment of prophecy, the institution goes apostate and true believers are forced underground. We'll simply keep doing what we already do!

Aside from taking Christian practice outside of the building on the corner so as not to rely on the institution as our only future lifeline—which is a valid reason on its own—the need for a fresh kind of fellow-ship connection within today's Body has been surfacing for a long time. The Church, as an institution, has been continuously deteriorating. True believers are tired of "spirituality competitions" between believers and interdenominational squabbles, pressures to keep up with the Jone-ses, "feel-good" (but theologically deficit) worship songs and sermons, and focus on feelings and/or prosperity over the Great Commission as well as the "take up the cross daily" message of Christ.

Meanwhile, in recent years, the Gospel has not been "taken to the streets" as it should. We are missing a massive opportunity while the West is still free enough to reach as many people as possible. This is especially true the longer the lost feel that the church on the corner will be unwelcoming to them, which is a perception that increases each day as our Body is further polarized by the unscriptural trends of the cul-ture. Yet, for the reasons we just mentioned, many sincere Christians feel that "inviting nonbelievers to church" just isn't the answer anymore.

Additionally, certain evangelistic methods of the past—such as standing on the corner preaching, handing out tracts, or offering to pray for the needs of strangers on the roadside—will be more and more unwelcome in some cities, even when they're *not* engulfed in flames or rioting.

But if the church on the corner is out of the question, how can true Christians witness to nonbelievers if the tired, ritualistic "sinner's prayer in the middle of a coffee shop" makes them feel awkward, as we know it does?

Reaching the lost appears to be increasingly insurmountable in today's social and political climate...and Christians are starving to meet like-minded folks whose walk with Christ is genuine.

The motto these authors have tagged to the Jericho Project is: "To reach the lost and sharpen the sheep." It's for *both* believers and non-believers. We wish to reach the lost with the message of the Gospel of Christ in the way they may not have ever heard it before and in an unintimidating, relaxed atmosphere that doesn't feel like "church." Yet, by sharing what we know with fellow believers—as well as being challenged and sharpened by what *they* know—"Iron sharpens iron, and one man sharpens another" (Proverbs 27:17). There is no "one minister" whose full-time responsibility it is to be the sole teaching leader of the flock. Much to the contrary, in this model, everyone is equally ministered *to*. An added benefit of this sharing of perspectives is that it forces believers to accept that we don't know everything; another viewpoint can be a soul-saver (maybe even literally).

Another benefit: In a one-on-one setting, our attention is wholly given to only one guest or family rather than divided among a crowd. This gives our guests the opportunity to: 1) share freely without the (sometimes intimidating or inhibiting) pressure of others' presence, 2) ask questions that might traditionally never be answered in church, 3) tackle their own personal issues instead of hoping that the sermon Sunday morning will cover what they need to hear, 4) take as much time as they need to discuss the topic, 5) make them feel like they have a place of honor at our table, 6) allow them to focus on the Lord without the drama that occasionally comes with going to church, and 7) let them know we care enough to plan a gathering around them specifically.

In doing all of this, we "reclaim our territory and land," just like the ancient warriors did for Jericho. We consecrate our own homes for the Lord's purposes, while showing others how to do the same. This brings families closer together, teaches us how to address through our issues via a Bible-centered strategy, and brings Jesus back into the *family*, not just the church building (that He's likely standing outside of anyway, knocking, and hoping to be let back into [Revelation 3:20]).

Of course, nothing about an initiative like this is designed to "replace" or "take over" the Church as an institution; rather, it is a supplement. Nobody on this end is telling anyone else to quit the Church. With that in mind, we want to challenge *readers* to pray about doing something similar, something that may or may not look like what we've described here. By sharing with readers what *we* have been up to, we don't intend to inspire a fresh ministry idea and then hold folks to a structure we've outlined. One of our ministry associates, whom we recently met with about the Jericho Project, said, "Structure *kills* a movement." Another colleague, over a Jericho Project dinner, said, "I hate it when I see Christians get tired of something they see in the Church, decide to start something of their own outside the Church like these home-churches you see, and then gradually bring what they learned from the structured Western services into it so they're back where they started." But whatever it looks like, if the Lord has prompted you to do something outside the institution of the Church, be obedient! If He hasn't, pray about whether He has something like this in mind for you! Minister to someone in a way the Church has failed to do. Minister to someone in a way that the institutionalized Church was never created for! This is the *real Body of Christ!*

We also have a responsibility to reflect Christ in all that we do. If you *do* decide to take the Jericho Challenge and minister from your home (or something similar), every move you make *must* be in an effort to please the Lord. Planning to host a Saturday luncheon for a couple from church, then throwing in a pole-dance worship session after a couple shots of vodka, would *not* be pleasing to the Lord. As the Body of Christ, we are accountable to representing Jesus in *all* that we do, whether we're in a church building or not. No endeavor to "do church outside the building" frees us to behave in a way that contradicts the Word of God. If we wish to bless someone else, but we don't know Scripture well enough to teach it with authority or recognize when an activity would contradict the guidelines given us in Bible, then Scripture reading should be "the" activity of the event…no gossiping, no shaking feathers from the rafters, no spiritually giving birth, no dancing Salome's dance of the seven veils, no nonsense. Simply inviting friends over to read the Holy Bible with like-minded believers can be as refreshing as anything else. And, always remember, saying "I don't know" when asked a question about the Bible, *when it's the truth*, is never wrong. "Let's look it up and read it together" is a beautiful and humble suggestion that many people outside the Body of Christ only *wish* they heard more often, since the Church has a repu-tation of being filled with a bunch of judgmental know-it-alls.

We have one last suggestion for you if you're considering this type of ministry. In fact, absent this, no ministry approach can *ever* be suc-cessful: We *must* return to preaching that Jesus is both *Savior and Lord*. Many churches, in response to modern culture, express Jesus' love and ability to save—and this is good—but they stop short of teaching that those who accept Him as Savior must also give Him lordship over their lives. When we forget this, we advertise "another Jesus," as we're warned against doing in 2 Corinthians 11:4. Jesus becomes reduced to little more than a "get out of jail free" comrade handing out free candy on street corners, but who is never given transformative power in an individual's life. Often, those who neglect to submit to Jesus as Lord backslide, and Christianity becomes another checkmark on a list of things they've tried, but that didn't work. Why? Because there are two ways of inviting Jesus into our lives: 1) We ask Him to "save us," and allow Him to fill the space we have created in our lives as long as He doesn't bump the furniture; or 2) We surrender our *entire* lives to Him, and understand that by asking Him to "save us" from our sins, we're asking for Him to deliver us from that which causes us to sin. When we do this, we're not merely giving Him permission to come into our space; we invite Him to rearrange *whatever* it takes to truly transform us into the new creation, as we're promised in 2 Corinthians 5:17. For decades, God has been increasingly reduced to two things in the Western Church: 1) a name-it-and-claim it Santa dispersing whatever humans ask for as long as they ask for it in "His name"; and 2) the get-out-of-jail-free Savior who requires no lordship in trade for salvation. Each designation strips Him of His dignity and authority. It's time to restore Him to the throne He deserves to be on in our Churches *and* our personal lives.[444]

It starts when we restore Him to Savior *and* Lord of all…

Imagine an active, vibrant and organic Church working each day on the streets to collect as many souls as we can while fostering *lasting conversions!* This is what we are encouraging you to be a part of through the Jericho Movement. What will happen when the government tells the Church it can't meet because of yet another pandemic lockdown? We'll just keep doing what we do on the streets! When the powers that be label the Church institution as hateful and try to shut it down? Mkay, *again*, let's hit the streets! And on that day when the top-side church goes apostate and the *real* church is forced underground? We will already be practiced and ready.

Just think: If every person touched by this ministry idea were to repeat it even once, passing along the challenge to another in a "pay-it-forward" gesture, it could start a very powerful, New-Testament style movement that has the potential of ministering to countless spiritually starving folks.

We could, if God blessed this endeavor, see the very beginnings of how the End-Times Remnant will remain active…and alive, no matter what.

The world around us has already been conditioned to embrace

Antichrist and the end-times agenda of the enemy. This can be easily seen when we look at what's already being implemented. We've shown, through our discussion of the manipulation methods being used on a large scale in our nation, that many practices and activities that would have been quickly rejected by previous generations—such as socialism, euthanasia, even pedophilia—are quickly being offered to society as appealing movements. In this way, the world is already primed for the unthinkable. There is only one voice that can offer hope and direction in times like these, and it is the Word of Jesus Christ. The Church has been called to be a beacon to the lost, yet, these authors have shown that much of the Church will lead the world into the end-times destruction foretold in Revelation. It is time to stop waiting for someone else to fix the religious institution. It is time for us to take the Word and start making a difference in the culture around us—and in our religious institutions—if indeed these can be saved.

The *real* Church, however, is that which dwells within the Body of Believers.

Those who have taken Jesus as both Savior *and* Lord.

If that's you, then we dare you. We double-dog dare you—

No, we *triple-dog-dare* you to join the Jericho Movement.

The Church That Blows Through the Stop Sign

While Jesus walked the earth with His disciples, He promised them, "upon this rock I will build my church; and the gates of hell shall not prevail against it" (Matthew 16:18). The "gates of hell," itself, folks. As far as the losers on the dark side go, that's a collective mass of *all* the greatest powers of hell rolled into one pathetic hand-slap attempt against Christ—a corporate body of demons and devils He can obliterate with less effort than it takes to fire an invisible, "pew-pew" fingertip gun.

From the very blessed moment Jesus began building "His Church," until today, and farther into eternity, His Church *will stand and accomplish His will and purpose*. There is no disputing that. Not long after His resurrection, but before He ascended to the Father, He gave His disciples the Great Commission, through which He would fulfill His promise to build His Church. Those who believed in Jesus were to be baptized: a spiritual symbol of the death of the old life, transformation into the new life through the cleansing power of the blood, and official adoption into the family of God. Then, they were to make true disciples by teaching these new believers everything that Christ had commanded and taught them. So the very simple and direct purpose of the Body is to proclaim and teach the Gospel of Jesus Christ, baptize the new believers, and continue to impart to them the ways of Christ. And there is *no prevailing against this*. If "the gates of hell" can't, then neither can any political or social movement, governmental leader, secularization trend, syncretistic agenda, or anything else.

Remember what the Word has promised you!

Some sermons today make us laugh. Preachers, in their (completely innocent and endearing) sarcasm, poke fun at the "twelve guys Jesus picked" or some equivalent. However, Christ clearly knew what He was doing.

After Matthias was chosen to replace Judas as the twelfth disciple following Judas' suicide upon learning that Jesus was to be crucified (see Acts 1:12–26), Jesus' closest followers—giants of the faith—faced the very real prospects of bitter persecution, imprisonment, and even execution. They felt *constant* distress, not knowing if the next moment would be lived in peace or despair. An immensely strong rejection of Jesus as the Messiah of God by the established religious hierarchy had paved the way for historically unparalleled tyranny. Many in the temple and synagogue leadership, as well as government authorities, used their lofty positions to try to squelch or snuff out the growing group of "Christ-followers" (or "Followers of the Way") during the first century, but every attempt would fail. The lively, passionate, unstoppable disciples of

Christ, whose numbers quickly involved countless more than "twelve," gave everything, including their lives, for the sake of their Savior's Great Commission. And the worse things became for the trailblazers of the Messianic Church, the louder their voice became. They died in bloody, brutal ways: some were stoned; others were sawn in two or thrown from buildings. Having lost everything, these heroes of the faith looked forward to the promised eternity in the presence of God. The Church, the *True Church* of Jesus Christ, was built upon the promise of Christ and the power of the Holy Spirit using the people who would stop at nothing to see the corrupt world irreversibly flipped on its head.

Worst-case scenario, Christianity goes underground for a while as it strengthens itself in preparation for an explosive resurfacing according to God's timing…but the Remnant *never* dies. Southern Gospel singer and songwriter, Bill Gaither, knew this truth as well as anyone, as he wrote in his "The Church Triumphant" interlude:

> God has always had a people. Many a foolish conqueror has made the mistake of thinking that because he had forced the church of Jesus Christ out of sight, he had stilled its voice and snuffed out its light, but God has always had a people. The powerful current of a rushing river is not diminished because it's forced to flow underground. The purest water is the stream that bursts crystal clear into the sunlight after it has forced its way through solid rock. There have been charlatans who, like Simon the magician, sought to barter on the open market that power which cannot be bought or sold, but God has always had a people: men who could not be bought and women who were beyond purchase. Yes, God has always had a people! There have been times of affluence and prosperity when the Church's message has been nearly diluted into oblivion by those who sought to make it socially attractive, neatly organized, and

financially profitable, but God has always had a people! Yes, it's
been gold-plated, draped in purple, and encrusted with jewels.
It has been misrepresented, ridiculed, lauded and scorned,
but God has always had a people. And these followers of Jesus
Christ have been, according to the whim of the times, elevated
as sacred leaders and martyred as heretics. Yet, through it all,
there marches on that powerful army of the meek—God's
chosen people—who cannot be bought, flattered, murdered or
stilled. On through the ages they march, the Church: God's
Church Triumphant is alive and well![445]

Ha! Are you as excited as we are to be a part of this people? Man,
we *never* die! We *never* quit! *We* are the "Church that Blows Through
the Stop Sign"! And when we're forced into silence or "post-Christian"
minority groups, we get on our knees and wait for that day when we'll
burst through the solid rock like that crystal-clear stream and shine
brighter than *anything* the world has on the surface!

Don't fear the coming Church split. Embrace its cleansing.

Don't mourn the Harlot. Keep your focus on reaching and loving
the people Jesus commanded us to.

Jesus' model works, because, during the Intertestamental Period and
through to the early New Testament age—when oral tradition, legalism, judgment, rules, and "holier than thou" elitists represented everything that "religion" had to offer—Jesus made it clear (John 13:35)
that the true mark of authentic disciples of Christ is their love for one
another. And so it was that multitudes became believers, and their constant expressions of love set them apart from the rest of the world. This
"Christian Church" was built on the teachings and doctrines of the same
Jesus Christ, who already proved—with His life, works, miracles, signs,
wonders, resurrection, ascension, and every demonstration of power carried out in His Name since—that He is Lord.

The True Church of Jesus Christ knows no bounds and stops for no force. The Church as an *institution* came about as a result of the Church as a *Body*, not the other way around. You cannot kill the Remnant, because it's made of Spirit-filled radicals like the Twelve all over the world, sold out for Jesus and ready to do whatever it takes to thrive in His calling, and it will always exist, even unto the end.

NOTES

1. "*Clogmia albipunctata*, filter fly, Size: 5.1 mm, ID Confidence: 88," uploaded by Robert Webster of Xpda on October 6, 2014, to *Wikimedia Commons: The Free Media Repository*, last accessed December 17, 2020, https://upload.wikimedia.org/wikipedia/commons/1/10/Clogmia_albipunctata_P1130225a.jpg.
2. Gilbert, Derek, in a text exchange November 24, 2020.
3. Favara, A., "Dagon," in J. D. Barry, D. Bomar, D. R. Brown, R. Klippenstein, D. Mangum, C. Sinclair Wolcott, … W. Widder (Eds.), *The Lexham Bible Dictionary* (Bellingham, WA: Lexham Press; 2016).
4. "Cult," *Merriam-Webster's Collegiate Dictionary, 11th Edition* (Springfield, MA: Merriam-Webster, Inc.; Kindle ed., 2014), locations 111635–111637.
5. Westlake, George W. and David D. Duncan, *Daniel and Revelation: An Independent-Study Textbook* (Springfield, MO: Global University; 2013; 4th Ed.), 227.
6. Barry, J. D., D. Bomar, D. R. Brown, R. Klippenstein, D. Mangum, C. Sinclair Wolcott, … W. Widder (Eds.), *The Lexham Bible Dictionary* (Bellingham, WA: Lexham Press; 2016), under the heading "Apostasy."
7. Jones, M. R., D. Mangum, D. R. Brown, R. Klippenstein, & R. Hurst (Eds.), *Lexham Theological Wordbook* (Bellingham, WA: Lexham Press; 2014), under the heading "Apostasy."
8. Whitaker, W., (2012). *Dictionary of Latin Forms*. (Bellingham, WA: Logos Bible Software; 2012), under the heading "Apostasia."
9. Larson, K., *I & II Thessalonians, I & II Timothy, Titus, Philemon: Vol. 9*

(Nashville, TN: Broadman & Holman Publishers; 2000), 105–106; bold in original; italics added.

10. "Cult," *Merriam-Webster's Collegiate*… locations 111635–111637.

11. Reagan, David R., "The One World Religion: How It Is Coming Together and How It Relates to the Coming of Jesus," *Lion & Lamb Ministries*, accessed October 6, 2020, https://christinprophecy.org/articles/the-one-world-religion/; excerpt quoted with permission from Nathan E. Jones, Internet Evangelist, Lamb & Lion Ministries on October 8, 2020.

12. Beale, G. K., *The Book of Revelation: A Commentary on the Greek Text* (Grand Rapids, MI; Carlisle, Cumbria: W. B. Eerdmans; Paternoster Press; 1999), 691; emphasis added.

13. Beale, G. K., *The Book of Revelation*, 304.

14. Ibid, 304; emphasis in original.

15. References to the syncretism within tribes of Israel frequently use the term "cult" to describe unfaithfulness. In this particular case, Ephraim is referred to as a "cult" in: Hubbard, D. A., *Hosea: An Introduction and Commentary: Vol. 24* (Downers Grove, IL: InterVarsity Press; 1989), 118.

16. Beale, G. K., *The Book of Revelation*, 305.

17. Parker, C., "The Social and Geographical World of Laodicea (Revelation 3:14–22)," B. J. Beitzel, J. Parks, & D. Mangum (Eds.), *Lexham Geographic Commentary on Acts through Revelation* (Bellingham, WA: Lexham Press; 2019), 686–690.

18. Carpenter, John, director, *They Live*. (United States: Alive Films, Larry Franco Productions, 1988), DVD, 94 min.

19. Orwell, George. *1984*. (New York, NY: Harcourt, Inc.; 1949), 2.

20. Ibid,. 156.

21. Sloane, Paul. "How Star Trek Inspired an Innovation." Destination Innovation. 2020. Accessed November 6, 2020. https://www.destination-innovation.com/how-startrek-inspired-an-innovation-your-cell-phone/.

22. Costello, Sam. "How the iPod Got its Name." Lifewire. December 10, 2019. Accessed November 6, 2020. https://www.lifewire.com/how-did-ipod-get-its-name-1999778.

23. Engber, Daniel. "Who Made That Earbud?" *New York Times*. May 16, 2014. Accessed November 6, 2020. https://www.nytimes.com/2014/05/18/magazine/who-made-that-earbud.html.

24. Westaway, Luke. "See the 2015 Tech That 'Back to the Future Part II'

Predicted, and What It Missed." CNET Online. October 17, 2015. Accessed November 6, 2020. https://www.cnet.com/news/heres-the-technology-back-to-the-future-part-ii-predicted-and-what-it-missed/.

25. Lang, Fritz, director, *Metropolis*. (Babelsberg Studios, Universal Film A.G.; 1927).

26. Prince, Alicia. "15 Awesome Things You Didn't Know Siri Can Do For You." Lifehack Online. 2020. Accessed November 6, 2020. https://www.lifehack.org/articles/technology/15-awesome-things-you-didnt-know-siri-can-for-you.html.

27. Profis, Sharon. "10 of the Best Things You Can Do with the Amazon Echo." CNET Online. February 13, 2017. Accessed November 6, 2020. https://www.cnet.com/how-to/the-best-things-you-can-do-with-amazon-echo/.

28. "9 Ways a Smart Home Can Improve Your Life." SmartThings Online. March 31, 2015. Accessed November 6, 2020. https://blog.smartthings.com/news/roundups/9-ways-a-smart-home-can-improve-your-life/.

29. Ibid.

30. Ibid.

31. "Meet Kodomoroid, Japan's Android Newsreader." *Sydney Morning Herald*. June 25, 2014. Accessed November 6, 2020. https://www.smh.com.au/technology/meet-kodomoroid-japans-android-newsreader-20140625-zskoq.html.

32. Caballar, Rina. "What Is the Uncanny Valley?" IEEE Spectrum. November 6, 2019. Accessed November 6, 2020. https://spectrum.ieee.org/automaton/robotics/humanoids/what-is-the-uncanny-valley.

33. Haselton, Todd. "Samsung's Neon 'Artificial Humans' Look Like Super-Realistic Video Chatbooks." CNBC Online. January 7, 2020. Accessed November 6, 2020. https://www.cnbc.com/2020/01/06/samsung-neon-artificial-human-announced-at-ces-2020.html.

34. LaFia, John, "Intersections in Real Time," Babylon 5: Season 4, Episode 18. (Burbank, CA: Warner Brothers, 1997). DVD.

35. Ibid.

36. Grush, Loren. "NASA Is Opening the Space Station to Commercial Business and More Private Astronauts." The Verge. June 7, 2019. Accessed November 6, 2020. https://www.theverge.com/2019/6/7/18656280/nasa-space-station-private-astronauts-commercial-business.

37. Ibid.

38. Mizokami, Kyle. "Russia to Demonstrate Active Camouflage for Soldiers, Tanks." *Popular Mechanics*. August 20, 2018. Accessed November 6, 2020. https://www.popularmechanics.com/military/research/a22777736/russia-to-demonstrate-active-camouflage-for-soldiers-tanks/.

39. Dar, Talha. "This Is How Invisibility Cloaks Work To Make You Disappear." Wonderful Engineering. May 13, 2015. November 6, 2020. https://wonderfulengineering.com/this-is-how-invisibility-cloaks-work-to-make-you-disappear/.

40. "Virtual Reality: Another World Within Sight." Iberdrola Online. 2020. Accessed November 6, 2020. https://www.iberdrola.com/innovation/virtual-reality.

41. Cammell, Donald, director, *Demon Seed*. (United States: Metro-Goldwyn-Mayer; 1977). Amazon Prime, 94 min.

42. Adams, Scott. "Can Humans and Computers Mate and Have Babies?" Scott Adams Says Online. February, 23, 2018. Accessed November 6, 2020. https://www.scottadamssays.com/2018/02/23/can-humans-computers-mate-babies/.

43. Ibid., Accessed November 20, 2020..

44. Chandler, Diana. "Teen Is Youngest Legal Euthanasia Victim in Belgium." *Baptist Press Online*. September 19, 2016. Accessed November 9, 2020. https://www.baptistpress.com/resource-library/news/teen-is-youngest-legal-euthanasia-victim-in-belgium/.

45. Carpenter, John, director, *They Live*. (United States: Alive Films, Larry Franco Productions; 1988). DVD, 94 min.

46. Ibid.

47. Prestigiacomo, Amanda. "Abortionist Testifies: 'No Question' Babies Being Born Alive to Harvest Organs." *The Daily Wire Online*. September 26, 2019. Accessed October 8, 2019. https://www.dailywire.com/news/abortionist-testifies-no-question-babies-being-born-alive-to-harvest-organs.

48. Fox, Maggie. "Planned Parenthood Video: Why Use Tissue from Aborted Fetuses?" *NBC News Online*. July 17, 2015. Accessed October 9, 2019. https://www.nbcnews.com/health/health-news/planned-parenthood-video-raises-question-why-use-tissue-fetuses-n393431.

49. Prestigiacomo, Amanda. "Abortionist Testifies: 'No Question' Babies Being Born Alive to Harvest Organs." *The Daily Wire Online*. September 26, 2019. Accessed October 8, 2019. https://www.dailywire.com/news/abortionist-testifies-no-question-babies-being-born-alive-to-harvest-organs.

50. "Use of Aborted Fetal Tissue: Questions and Answers." *Charlotte Lozier Institute*. June 5, 2019. Accessed October 9, 2019. https://lozierinstitute.org/use-of-aborted-fetal-tissue-questions-answers/.

51. Ibid.

52. "Induced Abortion in the United States." *Guttmacher Institute Online*. 2019. Accessed October 2, 2019. https://www.guttmacher.org/fact-sheet/induced-abortion-united-states.

53. Bay, Michael, director, *The Island*. (United States: Dreamworks, Warner Bros.; 2005). DVD, 2hrs 16min.

54. Greely, Henry. "Human Reproductive Cloning: The Curious Incident of the Dog in the Night-time." Stat News Online. February 21, 2020. Accessed November 6, 2020. https://www.statnews.com/2020/02/21/human-reproductive-cloning-curious-incident-of-the-dog-in-the-night-time/.

55. Burger, Jerry. *Personality, 10th edition*. (Boston, MA: Cengage Learning; 2018), 356.

56. Anderson, C. A. & Bushman, B. J. (2002). "The Effects of Media Violence on Society." *Science, 295*, 2377–2378.

57. Eron, L. D. (1987). "The Development of Aggressive Behavior from the Perspective of a Developing Behaviorism." *American Psychologist, 42*, 435–442.

58. Johnson, J. G., Cohen, P., Smailes, E. M., Kasen, S., & Brook, J. S. (2002). "Television Viewing and Aggressive Behavior During Adolescence and Adulthood." *Science, 295*, 2468–2471.

59. Burger, Jerry. *Personality, 10th edition*. (Boston, MA: Cengage Learning; 2018), 358.

60. Ibid., 359–360.

61. Ibid., 352.

62. Ibid., 357.

63. Actors Lowell Byers (boyfriend) and Ted Yudain (doctor), *Chilling Visions: 5 Senses of Fear*, horror anthology film, "See" segment, 27:07–36:37, written and directed by Miko Hughes, broadcast on Chiller Network May 31, 2013, released to Blu-ray October 22, 2013.

64. Aaron Dykes, producer, *Midsommar: Initiation into the Ancient Religion of the Future*. (Truth Stream Media, Cedar Park, TX; 2019).

65. Bitelabs: Eat Celebrity Meat. 2020. Accessed November 6, 2020. http://bitelabs.org/vision.

66. Knibbs, Kate. "No, This Website Won't Actually Make Salami Out

of Famous People." *Time*. February 28, 2014. https://newsfeed.time.
com/2014/02/28/celebrity-meat-bite-labs-fake/.

67. Merchant, Brian. "The Guy Who Wants to Sell Lab-Grown Salami Made of
Kanye West Is '100% Serious.'" Vice Online. February 26, 2014. Accessed
November 6, 2020. https://www.vice.com/en/article/kbz8ky/the-guy-who-
want-to-sell-you-salami-made-out-of-james-franco-are-100-serious.

68. Ibid.

69. Cuties: Trivia. IMDB Online. 2020. Accessed November 6, 2020. https://
www.imdb.com/title/tt9196192/trivia?ref_=tt_trv_trv.

70. Morton, Victor. "'Surprising' Backlash: Netflix Co-CEO Defends
'Cuties'." *Washington Times*. October 12, 2020. Acccessed November
20, 2020. https://www.washingtontimes.com/news/2020/oct/12/
ted-sarandos-netflix-co-ceo-defends-cuties-misunde/.

71. Ibid.

72. Hawley, Josh. Letter to Reed Hastings, Chief Executive Officer, Netflix,
Inc. United States Senate. September 11, 2020. Retrieved on November
20, 2020. https://twitter.com/HawleyMO/status/1304503913606000640/
photo/1.

73. Spangler, Todd. "Netflix Defends 'Cuties' as a 'Social Commentary'
Against Sexualization of Young Children." September 10, 2020.
Accessed November 20, 2020. https://variety.com/2020/digital/news/
netflix-defends-cuties-against-sexualization-young-girls-1234766347/.

74. Hawley, Josh. Letter to Reed Hastings.

75. Ibid.

76. Morton, Victor. "Netflix Indicted on Child Porn Charges over
'Cuties.'" *Washington Times*. October 6, 2020. Accessed November
20, 2020. https://www.washingtontimes.com/news/2020/oct/6/
netflix-indicted-child-porn-charges-over-cuties/.

77. Ibid.

78. Kripke, Eric, creator, "What I Know," The Boys: Second Season, Episode 8.
(Amazon Studios; 2019).

79. Chasmbers, Hannah. "Uh…Can We Talk about All the Weird Sex Stuff
Happening on 'The Boys'?" *Cosmopolitan*. August 29, 2019. Accessed
November 19, 2020. https://www.cosmopolitan.com/entertainment/tv/
a28858403/amazon-the-boys-chace-crawford-weird-sex-scenes/.

80. Griggs, Richard A., *Psychology: A Concise Introduction: Fifth Edition* (New
York: Worth Publishers, 2017), 152.

81. Ibid., 152.

82. Ibid., 319.

83. Ibid., 378.

84. Ibid., 378.

85. Robert Aldrich, director, *What Ever Happened to Baby Jane?* (The Associates & Aldrich Company; 1962).

86. Griggs, Richard A., *Psychology: A Concise Introduction: Fifth Edition* (New York: Worth Publishers, 2017), 379.

87. "FDA Approves Cloned Meat for Consumption," January 16, 2008. *ABC News Online.* Last accessed April 19, 2017, http://abcnews.go.com/GMA/OnCall/story?id=4142120&page=1.

88. Ibid.

89. Rodenhizer. Samuel. "Some People Create Their Own Storms and Then Get Mad When It Rains." Quotation Celebration. August, 24, 2018. Accessed November 6, 2020. https://quotationcelebration.wordpress.com/2018/08/24/some-people-create-their-own-storms-and-then-get-mad-when-it-rains-unknown/.

90. Sarkis, Stephanie. "11 Warning Signs of Gaslighting." **Psychology Today.** January 22, 2017. Accessed November 6, 2020. https://www.psychologytoday.com/us/blog/here-there-and-everywhere/201701/11-warning-signs-gaslighting.

91. Burger, Jerry. *Personality, 10*[th] *edition.* (Boston, MA: Cengage Learning; 2018), 363.

92. Anderson, Allie. *Unscrambling the Millennial Paradox: Why the "Unreachables" May Be Key to the Next Great Awakening.* (Crane, MO: Defender Publishing; 2019) 32.

93. "History.com Editors." *History.com.* Accessed December 5, 2018. https://www.history.com/topics/renaissance/renaissance.

94. Groothuis, Douglas. *Truth Decay: Defending Christianity Against the Challenges of Postmodernism.* (Downers Grove, IL: Green Press; 2000) 39–40.

95. "The History of Bricks and Brickmaking." Brickarchitecture. 2020. Accessed November 6, 2020. https://brickarchitecture.com/about-brick/why-brick/the-history-of-bricks-brickmaking.

96. Anderson, Allie. *Unscrambling the Millennial Paradox,* 35.

97. Kluger, Jeffrey. Is God in Our Genes?. vol. 164. (New York: Time Inc.:, 2004). 5.

98. Ibid., 2.

99. Ibid., 5.

100. "The Renaissance: Overview; History and Culture." *Norton Anthology*. 2020. Accessed November 6, 2020. https://wwnorton.com/college/english/nawest/content/overview/renaissance.htm.

101. May, Gerald. *Addiction & Grace*. (New York: HarperCollins Publishers; 1988) 2.

102. Ibid., 14.

103. Ibid., 29.

104. Hill, Evan; Tiefenthaler, Ainara; Triebert, Christiaan; Jordan, Drew; Willis, Haly & Stein, Robin. "How George Floyd Was Killed in Police Custody." *New York Times*. May 31, 2020. Accessed November 6, 2020. https://www.nytimes.com/2020/05/31/us/george-floyd-investigation.html.

105. Ibid.

106. Kane, Libby; CFEI; & Loudenback, Tanza. "The IRS Has Sent over 159 Million Stimulus Checks so Far. Here's What to Know if You're Still Waiting on Yours." *Business Insider*. June 23, 2020. Accessed November 6, 2020. https://www.businessinsider.com/personal-finance/coronavirus-stimulus-check-questions-answers-2020-4.

107. "Coronavirus: Devon and Cornwall Key Workers Assaulted 99 Times." BBC Online. April 24, 2020. Accessed November 6, 2020. https://www.bbc.com/news/uk-england-devon-52414290.

108. Brito, Christopher. "Retail Worker Creates Facebook Support Group for Essential Employees after She Was Allegedly Attacked by a Customer." WBTV Online. May 25, 2020. Accessed November 6, 2020. https://www.wbtv.com/2020/05/25/retail-worker-creates-facebook-support-group-essential-employees-after-she-was-allegedly-attacked-by-customer/.

109. White, Dawson. "Slashed Tires and Violence: Health Care Workers Face New Dangers Amid COVID-19 Battle." *Miami Herald*. April 23, 2020. Accessed November 6, 2020. https://www.miamiherald.com/news/coronavirus/article241967281.html.

110. Calaway, Jeff. "Spike in Severe Child Abuse Cases Likely Result of COVID-19." Checkup News Room. May 6, 2020. Accessed November 6, 2020. https://www.checkupnewsroom.com/spike-in-severe-child-abuse-cases-likely-result-of-covid-19/.

111. Inglesias, Veronica Balderas. "Over a Dozen US Cities See Domestic

Abuse Spike During Pandemic." VOA News Online. September 10, 2020. Accessed November 6, 2020. https://www.voanews.com/episode/over-dozen-us-cities-see-domestic-abuse-spike-during-pandemic-4415471.

112. Ibid.

113. "U.S. Online Alcohol Sales Jump 243% During Coronavirus Pandemic." Associated Press. MarketWatch Online. April 2, 2020. Accessed November 6, 2020. https://www.marketwatch.com/story/us-alcohol-sales-spike-during-coronavirus-outbreak-2020-04-01#:~:text=U.S.%20sales%20of%20alcoholic%20beverages,while%20beer%20sales%20rose%2042%25.

114. Mann, Brian. "U.S. Sees Deadly Drug Overdose Spike During Pandemic." NPR Online. August 13, 2020. Accessed November 6, 2020. https://www.npr.org/sections/coronavirus-live-updates/2020/08/13/901627189/u-s-sees-deadly-drug-overdose-spike-during-pandemic.

115. Boston University School of Medicine. "COVID-19 Has Likely Tripled Depression Rate, Study Finds." ScienceDaily. ScienceDaily, 2 September 2020. <www.sciencedaily.com/releases/2020/09/200902152202.htm>.

116. Stephenson, Joan. "CDC Report Reveals 'Consideraly Elevated' Mental Health Toll from COVID-19 Stresses." JAMA Health Forum. August 29, 2020. Accessed November 6, 2020. https://jamanetwork.com/channels/health-forum/fullarticle/2770050.

117. Alvarez, Liz & Buckley, Cara. "Zimmerman Is Aquitted in Trayvon Martin Killing." *New York Times*. July 13, 2013. Accessed November 6, 2020. https://www.nytimes.com/2013/07/14/us/george-zimmerman-verdict-trayvon-martin.html.

118. Black Lives Matter. 2020. Accessed November 6, 2020. https://blacklivesmatter.com/about/.

119. Buchanan, Larry. "Black Lives Matter May Be the Largest Movement in U.S. History." *New York Times*. July 3, 2020. Accessed November 6, 2020. https://www.nytimes.com/interactive/2020/07/03/us/george-floyd-protests-crowd-size.html.

120. Williams, Heather. "The Dangers of Designating Antifa as a Terrorist Organization Now." RAND Corporations. June 22, 2020. Accessed November 6, 2020. https://www.rand.org/blog/2020/06/the-dangers-of-designating-antifa-as-a-terrorist-organization.html.

121. Buchanan, Larry. "Black Lives Matter May Be the Largest Movement in U.S. History."

122. "Antifa: Trump Says Group Will Be Designated 'Terrorist Organization.'" BBC News Online. May 31, 2020. Accessed November 6, 2020. https://www.bbc.com/news/world-us-canada-52868295.

123. Holton, Chuck. "As Antifa Agitators Burn Bibles in Portland, What Role Should Christians Play?" CBN News Online. August 8, 2020. https://www1.cbn.com/cbnnews/us/2020/august/as-antifa-agitators-burn-bibles-in-portland-what-role-should-christians-play.

124. Davenport, Christian & Scruggs, Gregory. "Protests Explode across the Country; Police Declare Riots in Seattle, Portland." *Washington Post.* July 26, 2020. Accessed November 6, 2020. https://www.washingtonpost.com/nation/2020/07/25/seattle-police-declare-riot-renewed-black-lives-matter-protests/.

125. "Antifa: Trump Says Group Will Be Designated 'Terrorist Organization.'" BBC News. May 31, 2020. Accessed November 6, 2020. https://www.bbc.com/news/world-us-canada-52868295.

126. Farivar, Masood. "Four Extremist Groups Suspected of Involvement in Protest Violence." VOA News Online. June 1, 2020. Accessed November 6, 2020. https://www.voanews.com/usa/four-extremist-groups-suspected-involvement-protest-violence.

127. "Terrorism." States and Services: FBI. 2002–2005. Accessed November 6, 2020. https://www.fbi.gov/stats-services/publications/terrorism-2002-2005.

128. Ibid.

129. Gornstein, Leslie. "What Is Antifa? Is It a Group or an Idea, and What Do Supporters Want?" CBS News Online. October 16, 2020. Accessed November 6, 2020. https://www.cbsnews.com/news/what-is-antifa/.

130. Ibid.

131. Miller, Joshua. "Seattle BLM Protestors Demand White Pople 'Give Up' Their Homes." *New York Post.* August 14, 2020. Accesssed November 6, 2020. https://nypost.com/2020/08/14/seattle-blm-protesters-demand-white-people-give-up-their-homes/.

132. Trager, Lauren. "Indictments Allege McCloskeys Altered Pistol and 'Obstructed Prosecution.'" KMOV News. October 9, 2020. Accessed November 6, 2020. https://www.kmov.com/news/mccloskey-case-couple-indicted-by-grand-jury/article_892b9ba4-0807-11eb-8750-b3b2937f7e0b.html.

133. Ibid.

134. Henney, Megan. "McCloskeys, St. Louis Gun-Wielding Couple, Warn: 'Your Family Will Not Be Safe in the Radical Democrats' America.'" Fox News. August 24, 2020. Accessed November 6, 2020. https://www.foxnews.com/politics/mccloskeys-st-louis-gun-toting-couple-republican-national-convention-trump.

135. Kangadis, Nick. "'Get Over it!' These Buildings Are Insured! Chicago Activist Angry at Those Upset by Looting & Rioting." MRCTV. August 24, 2020. Accessed November 6, 2020. https://www.mrctv.org/blog/get-over-it-these-buildings-are-insured-chicago-activist-angry-those-upset-looting-rioting.

136. Ibid.

137. Ibid.

138. Fox News. "Deadly Unrest: Here Are the People Who Have Died Amid George Floyd Protests Across US." June 8, 2020. Accessed November 6, 2020. https://www.fox6now.com/news/deadly-unrest-here-are-the-people-who-have-died-amid-george-floyd-protests-across-us.

139. Ibid.

140. Foley, Ryan. "Woman, 22, Killed at Protests as Civil Unrest Roils Davenport." AP News. June 1, 2020. Accessed November 6, 2020. https://apnews.com/article/18e8ec5a9b8e7175a128254d55df41e3.

141. Spoerre, Anna. "Man Shot and Killed after Protest Sunday in Kansas City Was Family man, Photographer." *Kansas City Star*. June 8, 2020. Accessed November 6, 2020. https://www.kansascity.com/news/local/crime/article243230041.html.

142. Brew, Tom. "Chris Beaty's Final Moments: 'He Died Trying to Help Others.'" Hoosiers Now. June 2, 2020. Accessed November 6, 2020. https://www.si.com/college/indiana/football/chris-beaty-died-helping-others-final-moments.

143. Kaplan, Fred. "Is America in the Early Stages of Armed Insurgency?" Slate. September 8, 2020. Accessed November 6, 2020. https://slate.com/news-and-politics/2020/09/america-insurgency-chaos-trump-violence.html.

144. Ibid.

145. Ibid.

146. Craig, Tim. "'The United States Is in Crisis': Report Tracks Thousands of Summer Protests, Most Nonviolent." *Washington Post*. September 3, 2020.

Accessed November 6, 2020. https://www.washingtonpost.com/national/
the-united-states-is-in-crisis-report-tracks-thousands-of-summer-protests-
most-nonviolent/2020/09/03/b43c359a-edec-11ea-99a1-71343d03bc29_
story.html.

147. Ibid.

148. Jenkins, Brian. "Deadly Terrorist Threats Abound in U.S. and Abroad.
Here Are Danger Keys." RAND. July 20, 2020. Accessed November
6, 2020. https://www.rand.org/blog/2020/07/deadly-terrorist-threats-
abound-in-us-and-abroad-here.html.

149. "Terrorism." States and Services: FBI. 2002–2005. Accessed
November 6, 2020. https://www.fbi.gov/stats-services/publications/
terrorism-2002-2005.

150. Williams, Heather. "The Dangers of Designating Antifa as a Terrorist
Organization Now." RAND. June 22, 2020. Accessed November 6, 2020.
https://www.rand.org/blog/2020/06/the-dangers-of-designating-antifa-as-
a-terrorist-organization.html.

151. Confino, Alon. (2012). "Why Did the Nazis Burn the Hebrew Bible?
Nazi Germany, Representations of the Past, and the Holocaust," *Journal of
Modern History* - J MOD HIST. 56. 369–400. 10.1086/664662.

152. Holton, Chuck. "As Antifa Agitators Burn Bibles in Portland, What Role
Should Christians Play?" CBN News. August 8, 2020. https://www1.cbn.
com/cbnnews/us/2020/august/as-antifa-agitators-burn-bibles-in-portland-
what-role-should-christians-play.

153. Ibid.

154. Ibid.

155. Ibid.

156. Frank, Stephen. "REVOLT: 1,200 Calif. Clergy Tell Newsom They're
Meeting in Person, With or Without Permission." California Political
Review. May 21, 2020. Accessed November 6, 2020. http://www.
capoliticalreview.com/capoliticalnewsandviews/revolt-1200-calif-clergy-
tell-newsom-theyre-meeting-in-person-with-or-without-permission/.

157. Hutchinson, Bill. "Federal Court Backs California Gov. Gavin
Newsom's Orders Keeping Churches Closed." ABC News. May
24, 2020. Accessed November 6, 2020. https://abcnews.go.com/
US/federal-court-backs-california-gov-gavin-newsoms-orders/
story?id=70856597.

158. Frank, Stephen. "REVOLT: 1,200 Calif. Clergy Tell Newsom They're Meeting in Person, With or Without Permission."
159. Ibid.
160. Ibid.
161. Ibid.
162. Ibid.
163. Hutchinson, Bill. "Federal Court Backs California Gov. Gavin Newsom's Orders Keeping Churches Closed." ABC News. May 24, 2020. Accessed November 6, 2020. https://abcnews.go.com/US/federal-court-backs-california-gov-gavin-newsoms-orders/story?id=70856597.
164. Ibid.
165. Taft, Victoria. "California's All-Out War on Church Worship Intensifies with Bans, Fines, and Sending in Spies." PJ Media. August 24, 2020. Accessed November 6, 2020. https://pjmedia.com/news-and-politics/victoria-taft/2020/08/24/californias-all-out-war-on-church-worship-intensifies-with-bans-fines-and-sending-in-spies-n834623.
166. Ibid.
167. Ibid.
168. Ibid.
169. Ibid.
170. Ibid.
171. Ibid.
172. Dobson, James. "Critical Issue #6: Capitalism v. Socialism." FaithVotes Critical Issues: James Dobson. 2020 Accessed November 6, 2020. https://www.drjamesdobson.org/critical-issue-6-capitalism-v-socialism.
173. Eldeas, A. "Why Socialism always Fails." AEI News. March 22, 2016. Accessed November 6, 2020. https://www.aei.org/carpe-diem/why-socialism-always-fails/#:~:text=Socialism%20does%20not%20work%20because,are%20of%20the%20utmost%20importance.
174. Ibid.
175. Ibid.
176. Ibid.
177. Johnson, Andy. "Surveillance Society: 7 Ways You're Being Watched, and Didn't Know It." CTV News. June 22, 2013. Accessed November 6, 2020. https://www.ctvnews.ca/sci-tech/surveillance-society-7-ways-you-re-being-watched-and-didn-t-know-it-1.1337075.

178. Ibid.

179. Baraniuk, Chris. "Surveillance: The Hidden Ways You're Tracked." BBC News. October 26, 2014. Accessed November 6, 2020. https://www.bbc.com/future/article/20141027-the-hidden-ways-youre-tracked.

180. Weiler, Lauren. "15 Signs the Government Is Spying on You (and 5 Ways They're Already Watching You Every Day)." CheatSheet. December 18, 2018. Accessed November 6, 2020. https://www.cheatsheet.com/health-fitness/signs-the-government-is-spying-on-you-and-ways-theyre-already-watching-you-every-day.html/.

181. Ibid.

182. Snowden, Edward. "First Mails to Laura Poitras (Citizenfour)." Genius. 2020. Accessed November 6, 2020. https://genius.com/Edward-snowden-first-mails-to-laura-poitras-citizenfour-annotated.

183. Baraniuk, Chris. "Surveillance: The Hidden Ways You're Tracked."

184. Ibid.

185. Ibid.

186. Ibid.

187. Orwell, George. *1984*. (New York, NY: Harcourt; 1949).

188. Czeisler MÉ , Lane RI, Petrosky E, et al. "Mental Health, Substance Use, and Suicidal Ideation During the COVID-19 Pandemic — United States, June 24–30, 2020." MMWR Morb Mortal Wkly Rep 2020;69:1049–1057. DOI: http://dx.doi.org/10.15585/mmwr.mm6932a1external icon.

189. Blanchard, Dave. "The Unintended Consequences of Social Distancing." EHS Today. September 1, 2020. Accessed November 6, 2020. https://www.ehstoday.com/covid19/article/21140779/the-unintended-consequences-of-social-distancing.

190. Ibid.

191. Anderson, Allie. *Unscrambling the Millennial Paradox,* 50.

192. Susan Greenfield, "Modern Technology Is Changing the Way Our Brains Work, Says Neuroscientist," *MailOnline.com*, http://www.dailymail.co.uk/sciencetech/article-565207/Modern-technology-changing-way-brains-work-says-neuroscientist.html.

193. Ibid.

194. Alexander, Julia. "TikTok Is Racing to Stop the Spread of a Gruesome Video." The Verge. September 7, 2020. Accessed November 6, 2020. https://www.theverge.com/2020/9/7/21426176/tiktok-suicide-video-remove-ban-community-warnings-creators.

195. Ibid.

196. WPTV News, FL Palm Beaches and Treasure Coast. "Parents Warned of 'Graphic' Suicide Video on TikTok." September 10, 2020. YouTube Video, 1:57. Accessed November 6, 2020. https://www.youtube.com/watch?v=sju74FfFaSs.

197. Mandela, Nelson. "Nelson Mandela Quotes about Children." Nelson Mandela Children's Fund Online. December 8, 2015. Accessed November 6, 2020. https://www.nelsonmandelachildrensfund.com/news/nelson-mandela-quotes-about-children.

198. Criss, Doug. "Here's Why Students Don't Have to Recite the Pledge of Allegiance." CNN Online. February 19, 2019. Accessed November 6, 2020. https://www.cnn.com/2019/02/19/us/pledge-of-allegiance-explainer-trnd/index.html.

199. Ordonex, Franco. "Trump Defends School Prayer. Critics Say He's Got It All Wrong." NPR Online. January 16, 2020. Accessed November 6, 2020. https://www.npr.org/2020/01/16/796864399/exclusive-trump-to-reinforce-protections-for-prayer-in-schools#:~:text=The%20U.S.%20Supreme%20Court%20banned,others%20to%20do%20the%20same.

200. "BackPack Program." Feeding America. 2020. Accessed November 6, 2020. https://www.feedingamerica.org/our-work/hunger-relief-programs/backpack-program.

201. "School Lunch Guidelines: Preschooler Told Homemade Turkey Sandwich Not Nutritious Enough, Given Nuggets Instead." Huffpost. February 15, 2012. https://www.huffpost.com/entry/school-lunch-guidelines-p_n_1278803?ref=food&ir=Food.

202. "Condom Availability Programs." CDC: Adolescent and School Health. 2020. Accessed November 6, 2020. https://www.cdc.gov/healthyyouth/healthservices/caps/index.htm.

203. "HPV Vaccine for Adolescents Aged 12 to 13 Years Old." NI Direct. 2020. Accessed November 6, 2020. https://www.nidirect.gov.uk/articles/hpv-vaccine-adolescents-aged-12-13-years-old#:~:text=Although%20it%20is%20very%20unlikely,given%20at%20an%20earlier%20age.

204. Friedman, Emily. "Teen Gets Abortion with Help of Her Seattle High School." ABC News. March 24, 2010. Accessed November 6, 2020. https://abcnews.go.com/Health/teen-abortion-high-school/story?id=10189694.

205. Ibid.

206. Ibid.

207. Neale, Imogen. "Schools Arrange Secret Abortions." Stuff. May 15, 2011. Accessed November 6, 2020. https://www.stuff.co.nz/sunday-star-times/5005398/Schools-arrange-secret-abortions.

208. Ibid.

209. Wilkinson, Missy. "Hormones with Legs: Lessons from 40 Years Teaching Health to Teenagers." Thrillist. September 25, 2016. Accessed November 6, 2020. https://www.thrillist.com/health/nation/high-school-teacher-health-class.

210. Ibid.

211. Ibid.

212. Ibid.

213. Singer, Natasha. "How Google Took over the Classroom." *New York Times*. May 13, 2017. Accessed November 6, 2020. https://www.nytimes.com/2017/05/13/technology/google-education-chromebooks-schools.html.

214. Ibid.

215. Ibid.

216. Singer, Natasha. "How Google Took over the Classroom." *New York Times*. May 13, 2017. Accessed November 6, 2020. https://www.nytimes.com/2017/05/13/technology/google-education-chromebooks-schools.html.

217. Morrison, Sara. "Google's Education Tech Has a Privacy Problem." VOX. February 21, 2020. Accessed November 6, 2020. https://www.vox.com/recode/2020/2/21/21146998/google-new-mexico-children-privacy-school-chromebook-lawsuit.

218. Ibid.

219. Ibid.

220. Malkin, Michelle. "How to Protect Your Kids from Google Predators." Dallas News. March 14, 2019. https://www.dallasnews.com/opinion/commentary/2019/03/14/how-to-protect-your-kids-from-google-predators/.

221. Eisert, Caryn. "Online Predators Target Children's Devices." WANDTV. April 6, 2020. Accessed November 6, 2020. https://www.wandtv.com/news/online-predators-target-childrens-devices/article_d6264b28-7821-11ea-8530-d733a2474899.html.

222. "Education Technologies: Data Collection and Unsecured Systems Could Pose Risks to Students." Public Service Announcement: FBI. September 13, 2018. Accessed November 6, 2020. https://www.ic3.gov/Media/Y2018/PSA180913.

223. Gatto, John. *Dumbing Us Down: The Hidden Curriculum of Compulsory Schooling.* (Gabriola Island, BC, Canada: New Society Publishers; 2017), 16.

224. Bonnay, Juliet. "The Dumbing Down of America—By Design." Juliet Bonnay: Different Perspectives. February 19, 2019. Accessed November 6, 2020. https://by-julietbonnay.com/2019/02/the-dumbing-down-of-america-by-design/.

225. Ibid.

226. Ibid.

227. "Education and Socioeconomic Status." American Psychological Association. 2020 Accessed November 6, 2020. https://www.apa.org/pi/ses/resources/publications/education.

228. Ibid.

229. Mompremier, LaNina. "SPECIAL TOPIC: Socioeconomic Status and Higher Education Adjustment." American Psychological Association. April 2009. Accessed November 6, 2020. https://www.apa.org/pi/ses/resources/indicator/2009/04/adjustment.

230. Lynch, Matthew. "How Dumbed Down Education Is Creating A National Security Crisis." The Advocate. August 20, 2019. Accessed November 6, 2020. https://www.theedadvocate.org/how-dumbed-down-education-is-creating-a-national-security-crisis/.

231. Ibid.

232. Ibid.

233. Ibid.

234. Ibid.

235. "What Is Pedophilia?" WebMD. 2020. Accessed November 6, 2020. https://www.webmd.com/mental-health/features/explaining-pedophilia#1.

236. Denkinson, Katherine. "Outrage as Paedophiles Rebrand Themselves as 'Minor-Attracted Persons' in Chilling Online Propaganda Drive." *Daily Mail.* June 27, 2020. Accessed November 6, 2020. https://www.dailymail.co.uk/news/article-8466899/Paedophiles-rebrand-minor-attracted-persons-chilling-online-propaganda-drive.html.

237. Roemmele, M., & Messman-Moore, T. L. "Child Abuse, Early

Maladaptive Schemas, and Risky Sexual Behavior in College Women." *Journal of Child Sexual Abuse*, 2011. 20(3), 264-283. Doi:10.1080/105387 12.2011.575445.

238. Ibid.

239. Schraufnagel, T. J., Davis, K. C., George, W. H., & Norris, J. "Childhood Sexual Abuse in Males and Subsequent Risky Sexual Behavior: A Potential Alcohol-Use Pathway." 2010. *Child Abuse & Neglect, 34(5), 369-378.* Dio:10.1016,j.chiabu.2009.08.013.

240. Ibid.

241. Ibid.

242. Ibid.

243. Ibid.

244. Johnson, R. J., Ross, M. W., Taylor, W. C., Williams, M. L., Carvajal, R. I., Peters, R. J. "Prevalence of Childhood Sexual Abuse among Incarcerated Males in County Jail." Child Abuse Negl. 2006 Jan;30(1):75-86. doi: 10.1016/j.chiabu.2005.08.013. Epub 2006 Jan 18. PMID: 16412506.

245. Hall, M., & Hall, J. (2011). "The "Long-Term Effects of Childhood Sexual Abuse: Counseling Implications. Retrieved from http://counselingoutfitters.com/vistas/vistas11/Article_19.pdf.

246. King, A. R., Kuhn, S. K., Strege. C., Russell, T. D., Kolander, T. "Revisiting the Link Between Childhood Sexual Abuse and Adult Sexual Aggression." Child Abuse Negl. 2019 Aug; 94:104022. doi: 10.1016/j. chiabu.2019.104022. Epub 2019 Jun 12. PMID: 31200261.

247. Espinoza, Joshua. "Hasbro Pulls Trolls Doll from Shelves After Complaints of Feature Promoting Child Sex Abuse." Complex. August 7, 2020. https://www.complex.com/life/2020/08/hasbro-pulls-trolls-doll-from-shelves-after-complaints-of-inappropriate-feature.

248. Ibid.

249. Barnhart, Melissa. "Franklin Graham Lauds Parents for Protesting Drag Queen Story Hour at Libraries." *Christian Post*. September 8, 2018. Accessed November 6, 2020. https://www.christianpost.com/news/franklin-graham-praises-parents-protesting-drag-queen-story-hour.html.

250. Library MOMitors. "Drag Queen Strips for Kids in the King County Library." September 27, 2019. Accessed November 6, 2020. YouTube Video, 1:43. https://www.youtube.com/watch?v=Mb3JBbtpAMo.

251. LifeSiteNews. "Drag Queen Teaches Children to 'Twerk.'" August 7,

2019. Accessed November 6, 2020. YouTube Video, 0:42. https://www.youtube.com/watch?v=yDdckkn08VU.

252. Prestigiacomo, Amanda. "Photos Reveal Children Laid on Top of Drag Queens at Library 'Drag Queen Story Hour.'" Daily Wire. July 25, 2019. https://www.dailywire.com/news/photos-evidence-children-laid-top-drag-queens-amanda-prestigiacomo.

253. Du Cane, Lionel. "Drag Queen Accidentally Flashes Children at Story Hour." National File. March 10, 2020. Accessed November 6, 2020. https://nationalfile.com/drag-queen-accidentally-flashes-children-at-story-hour-event/.

254. Film Everything. "Drag Queen Story Time Grooming Your Children." November 5, 2019. Accessed November 6, 2020. YouTube Video, 5:38. https://www.youtube.com/watch?v=8CULHGeWVZA.

255. "Drag Queen Storytime Reader Once Charged with Child Sex Assault." ABC Eyewitness News. March 15, 2019. Accessed November 6, 2020. https://abc13.com/houston-public-library-drag-queen-story-time-albert-garza-reader-charged-with-child-sex-assault/5197176/.

256. Film Everything. "Drag Queen Story Time Grooming Your Children." November 5, 2019. Accessed November 6, 2020. YouTube Video, 5:38. https://www.youtube.com/watch?v=8CULHGeWVZA.

257. Ibid.

258. Fatherly. "Drag Kid Desmond Is a Ten-Year-Old Aspiring Drag Queen." March 20, 2018. Accessed November 6, 2020. YouTube Video, 9:12. https://www.youtube.com/watch?v=-w5X4aD6mo8.

259. "Church Vandalized with 'Satanic Symbols' after Pastor Opposed Drag Queen Story Hour." Instagram. September 23, 2019. Accessed November 6, 2020. https://www.instagram.com/p/B2xTgc-gd8P/?igshid=2lx0h84ec1oh.

260. Omega Frequency. "The New Normalization." August 23, 2020. Accessed November 6, 2020. YouTube Video, 1:11:30. https://www.youtube.com/watch?v=6WmKZT0Oiwo.

261. TEDx. "Pedophilia Is a Natural Sexual Orientation Mirjam Heine University of Wurzburg ugwbBgDOro." August 30, 2018. Accessed November 6, 2020. YouTube Video, 13:30. https://www.youtube.com/watch?v=knaxQPjHn2k.

262. Di, Kris. "Major Victory for Pedophiles as Baffling Law Is Passed That

Could See Rape and Sexual Assault Victims Thrown in PRISON Just for Telling Their Stories." *I Heart Intelligence*. August 26, 2020. Accessed November 20, 2020. https://iheartintelligence.com/victory-for-pedophiles-law-passed-rape-sexual-assault-victims/.

263. Ibid.

264. Ibid.

265. Henriques-Gomes, Luke. "Families of Deceased Sexual Assault Victims Would Need Court Order to Speak Out under Victoria Law." *The Guardian*. October 26, 2020. Accessed November 20, 2020. https://www.theguardian.com/australia-news/2020/oct/26/families-of-deceased-sexual-assault-victims-would-need-court-order-to-speak-out-under-victoria-law.

266. Blitzer, Ronn. "California Bill to Lower Penalties for Sexual Relations with Minor Heads to Newsom's Desk." *Fox News*. September 3, 2020. Accessed November 20, 2020. https://www.foxnews.com/politics/california-bill-lower-penalties-sexual-relations-with-minor-newsom.

267. Ibid.

268. Richmond, Todd. "Parents Sue Madison Schools over Transgender Policy." AP News. February 18, 2020. Accessed November 6, 2020. https://apnews.com/article/b339ee3eb623849659184af9fff49d7b.

269. Ibid.

270. Ibid.

271. Erin Brewer. "Teachers Trained to Assist Children with Transitioning… And Hide It from Parents." August 19, 2020. Accessed November 6, 2020. YouTube Video, 32:06. https://www.youtube.com/watch?v=E51wWpWv_e4.

272. Ibid.

273. Prestigiacomo, Amanda. "Transgender Puberty Blocking Drug Linked to Thousands Of Deaths, FDA Data Reveals." *Daily Wire*. September 26, 2019. Accessed November 20, 2020. https://www.dailywire.com/news/transgender-puberty-blocking-drug-linked-to-thousands-of-deaths-fda-data-reveals.

274. Ibid.

275. Ibid.

276. Prestigiacomo, Amanda. "Doctors Are Now Giving 8-Year-Old Girls Testosterone, Claiming They're 'Transgender'." *Daily Wire*. April 4, 2019. Accessed November 20, 2020. https://www.dailywire.com/news/doctors-are-giving-trans-8-year-old-girls-amanda-prestigiacomo.

277. Morse, Brandon. "The Normalization of Pedophilia Is Underway, and a California University Is Already Trying to Push It on Students." RedState. September 16, 2019. Accessed November 6, 2020. https://redstate.com/brandon_morse/2019/09/16/normalization-pedophilia-underway-california-university-already-trying-push-students-n115331.

278. Ibid.

279. Ibid.

280. "Minor Attracted Person vs.. Pedophile vs,. Sex Offender." Global Prevention Project. August 13, 2018. Accessed November 6, 2020. http://theglobalpreventionproject.org/blog/2018/8/2/what-is-a-minor-attracted-person.

281. Maykuth, Andrew. "Is COVID-19 Accelerating the Shift to a Cashless Society?" Government Technology. July 7, 2020. Accessed November 4, 2020. https://www.govtech.com/budget-finance/Is-COVID-19-Accelerating-the-Shift-to-a-Cashless-Society.html.

282. Ibid.

283. Ibid.

284. Ibid.

285. Villegas, Steve. "How COVID-19 Has Accelerated Digital Payments around the World." Digital Commerce. August 26, 2020. Accessed November 4, 2020. https://www.digitalcommerce360.com/2020/08/26/how-covid-19-has-accelerated-digital-payments-around-the-world/.

286. Maykuth, Andrew. "Is COVID-19 Accelerating the Shift to a Cashless Society?"

287. Miller, John. "Universal Basic Income Is Having a Moment. Can Advocates Convince a Skeptical Public?" *American Magazine*. October 2, 2020. Accessed November 4, 2020. https://www.americamagazine.org/politics-society/2019/10/02/universal-basic-income-having-moment-can-advocates-convince-skeptical.

288. Johnson. "How Long Until the Mark of the Beast?" *Bedford Gazette*. May 8, 2020. Accessed November 4, 2020. https://www.bedfordgazette.com/news/religion/how-long-until-the-mark-of-the-beast/article_78d480bd-54fe-5a81-9c39-7b4d2fbf86b9.html.

289. Tlaib, Rashida. "Automatic BOOST to Communities Act." Automatic Boost to Communities Act Proposal. American Government. 2020. Accessed November 4, 2020. https://tlaib.house.gov/sites/tlaib.house.gov/files/Automatic%20Boost%20to%20Communities%20Act%20.pdf.

290. Johnson. "How Long Until the Mark of the Beast?"

291. Tlaib, Rashida. "Automatic BOOST to Communities Act."

292. Johnson. "How Long Until the Mark of the Beast?"

293. Miller, John. "Universal Basic Income Is Having a Moment. Can Advocates Convince a Skeptical Public?" *American Magazine.* Oct. 2, 2020. Accessed November 4, 2020. https://www.americamagazine.org/politics-society/2019/10/02/universal-basic-income-having-moment-can-advocates-convince-skeptical.

294. Ibid.

295. Ibid.

296. Ibid.

297. Clarke, Kevin. "In Easter Message, Pope Francis Proposes 'Universal Basic Wage.'" *American Magazine.* April 12, 2020. Accessed November 4, 2020. https://www.americamagazine.org/faith/2020/04/12/easter-message-pope-francis-proposes-universal-basic-wage.

298. Ibid.

299. Caldera, Camille. "Fact Check: Americans Won't Have Microchips Implanted by End of 2020." August 1, 2020. Accessed November 4, 2020. https://www.usatoday.com/story/news/factcheck/2020/08/01/fact-check-americans-will-not-receive-microchips-end-2020/5413714002/.

300. "Desperate-times-call-for-desperate-measures." Your Dictionary Online. 2020. Accessed November 6, 2020. https://www.yourdictionary.com/desperate-times-call-for-desperate-measures.

301. Griggs, Richard A., *Psychology: A Concise Introduction: Fifth Edition* (New York: Worth Publishers, 2017), 399.

302. Ibid., 400.

303. Edwards, Phil. "The Cult That Inspired "Drink the Kool-Aid" Didn't Actually Drink Kool-Aid." VOX. May 23, 2015. https://www.vox.com/2015/5/23/8647095/kool-aid-jonestown-flavor-aid.

304. Wunrow, Rose. "The Psychological Massacre: Jim Jones and Peoples Temple: An Investigation." July 25, 2013. Accessed November 6, 2020. https://jonestown.sdsu.edu/?page_id=29478.

305. Ibid.

306. Brinton, Maurice. "Suicide for Socialism?" Libcom.org. July 25, 2005. Accessed November 6, 2020. http://libcom.org/library/suicide-for-socialism-jonestown-brinton.

307. Ibid.

308. Caldera, Camille. "Fact Check: Americans Won't Have Microchips Implanted by End of 2020." August 1, 2020. Accessed November 4, 2020. https://www.usatoday.com/story/news/factcheck/2020/08/01/fact-check-americans-will-not-receive-microchips-end-2020/5413714002/.

309. Ibid.

310. Horn, Tom. *The Messenger: It's Headed Towards Earth! It Cannot Be Stopped! And It's Carrying the Secret of America's, the Worlds, and Your Tomorrow!* (Crane, MO: Defender Publishing; 2020) 166.

311. "Oregon Senate Committee Votes Out SB 494, Endangers Patients with Mental Illness or Dementia." Oregon Right to Life. 2020. Accessed November 6, 2020. https://www.ortl.org/sb494vote/.

312. Kasprak, Alex. "Is An Oregon Bill Designed to 'Allow Starving Mentally Ill Patients to Death'?" March 5, 2019. Accessed November 6, 2020. https://www.snopes.com/fact-check/oregon-bill-starving-people/.

313. "Oregon Senate Committee Votes Out SB 494, Endangers Patients with Mental Illness or Dementia." Oregon Right to Life.

314. Ertelt, Steven. "Oregon Bill Would Allow Starving Mentally Ill Patients to Death." Life News. February 5, 2018. Accessed November 6, 2020. https://www.lifenews.com/2018/02/05/oregon-bill-would-allow-starving-mentally-ill-patients-to-death-2/.

315. Ibid.

316. Slayton, Scott. "Over 700 People in Ontario Died from Euthanasia or Assisted Suicide in 2019." Christian Headlines. July 18, 2019. Accessed November 6, 2020. https://www.christianheadlines.com/contributors/scott-slayton/over-700-people-in-ontario-died-from-euthanasia-or-assisted-suicide-in-2019.html.

317. Ibid.

318. "Australian State Legalizes Voluntary Euthanasia." DW. Online. June 16, 2019. Accessed November 6, 2020. https://www.dw.com/en/australian-state-legalizes-voluntary-euthanasia/a-49258193.

319. "Canada Opens Door to Expanding Assisted Dying." BBC Online. February 24, 2020. Accessed November 6, 2020. https://www.bbc.com/news/world-us-canada-51620021.

320. Ibid.

321. Srivastava, Vinod. "Euthanasia: A Regional Perspective." *Annals of Neurosciences,* vol. 21,3 (2014): 81–2. doi:10.5214/ans.0972.7531.210302.

322. Horn, Joe, & Belt, Daniel. *Unlocking Eden: Revolutionize Your Health, Maximize Your Immunity, Restore Your Vitality.* (Crane, MO: Defender Publishing; 2020) 34–35.

323. Griggs, Richard A., *Psychology: A Concise Introduction: Fifth Edition* (New York: Worth Publishers; 2017), 388.

324. Ibid., 388–389.

325. Zimbardo, Philip. "Stanford Prison Experiment." 1919–2020. Accessed November 18, 2020. https://www.prisonexp.org/.

326. Ibid.

327. Ibid.

328. Ibid.

329. Ibid.

330. Ibid.

331. Ibid.

332. Ibid.

333. Ibid.

334. Ibid.

335. Ibid.

336. Ibid.

337. Coast to Coast AM with George Noory. "Mock Prison Experiment / Consciousness." May 21, 2020. Archived retrieval, accessed November 18, 2020. https://www.coasttocoastam.com/guest/zimbardo-philip-64272/.

338. Wargo, Eric. "Bad Apples or Bad Barrels? Zimbardo on 'The Lucifer Effect.'" *Association for Psychological Science.* August 1, 2006. Accessed November 19, 2020. https://www.psychologicalscience.org/observer/bad-apples-or-bad-barrels-zimbardo-on-the-lucifer-effect.

339. Ibid.

340. "Cult," *Merriam-Webster's Collegiate Dictionary, 11th Edition* (Springfield, MA: Merriam-Webster, Inc.; Kindle ed.; 2014), locations 111635–111637.

341. Ayto, John, "cult," *Dictionary of Word Origins: The Histories of More than 8,000 English Language Words* (New York, NY: Arcade Publishing; 2011) 149.

342. "Cult," *Lexico*, by Oxford, last accessed March 16, 2020, https://www.lexico.com/en/definition/cult.

343. Zablocki, Benjamin, Thomas Robbins, eds., *Misunderstanding Cults:*

Searching for Objectivity in a Controversial Field (Toronto, Ontario, Canada: University of Toronto Press; 2001), preface.

344. Ibid.

345. France, R. T., *Matthew: An Introduction and Commentary: Vol. 1* (Downers Grove, IL: InterVarsity Press; 1985), 151–152.

346. Walls, D., & Anders, M., *I & II Peter, I, II & III John, Jude: Vol. 11* (Nashville, TN: Broadman & Holman Publishers; 1999), 208.

347. Stott, J. R. W., *The Letters of John: An Introduction and Commentary: Vol. 19* (Downers Grove, IL: InterVarsity Press; 1988), 153.

348. Anders, M., *Galatians-Colossians: Vol. 8* (Nashville, TN: Broadman & Holman Publishers: 1999), 4.

349. We've had a number of helpful resources to assist us in this area of study: Hassan, Steven, *Combating Cult Mind Control* (Newton, MA: Freedom of Mind Press, 2018; 30th Anniversary Ed.; 4th ed.); American Psychiatric Association, Marc Galanter, MD, editor, *Cults and New Religious Movements: A Report of the American Psychiatric Association from the Committee on Psychiatry and Religion* (Washington, DC: American Psychiatric Association Press, 1989); Clark, Jr., MD, John G., Michael D. Langone, PhD, Robert E. Schecter, PhD, Roger C. B. Daly, MDiv, "Destructive Cult Conversion: Theory, Research, and Treatment," *American Family Foundation*, Bonita Springs, FL, 1981; as well as information provided at ICSA (International Cultic Studies Association), last accessed February 10, 2020, https://www.icsahome.com/.

350. "Suicide Data," *World Health Organization*, last accessed November 2, 2020, https://www.who.int/mental_health/prevention/suicide/suicideprevent/en/.

351. Hassan, Steven, *Combating Cult Mind Control: The Guide to Protection, Rescue and Recovery from Destructive Cults* (Newton, MA: Freedom of Mind Press, 2018; 4th Ed.), 42.

352. Turner, Francis J.; Arnold Shanon Bloch, Ron Shor, "105: From Consultation to Therapy in Group Work with Parents of Cultists," *Differential Diagnosis & Treatment in Social Work* (Free Press: 4th ed., September 1, 1995), 1146; emphasis added.

353. "indoctrination," *Merriam-Webster's Collegiate…* locations 197919–197921.

354. "brainwashing," *Merriam-Webster's Collegiate…* locations 72617–72618.

355. "100 Most Frequently Challenged Books: 1990–1999," American Library Association, last accessed March 3, 2020, http://www.ala.org/advocacy/bbooks/100-most-frequently-challenged-books-1990%E2%80%931999; "Top 100 Banned/Challenged Books: 2000–2009," American Library Association, last accessed March 3, 2020, http://www.ala.org/advocacy/bbooks/top-100-bannedchallenged-books-2000-2009.

356. Jessica Crooke, "Is 'The Handmaid's Tale' Actually an Attack on Christianity?" June 14, 2019, *Christian Post*, last accessed March 3, 2020, https://www.christianpost.com/voices/is-the-handmaids-tale-actually-an-attack-on-christianity.html.

357. The bullet list referenced here involves information taken from the following two sources, which I will list once now, instead of adding an endnote to each item on the list: Hamilton, Amelia, and Alexa Moutevelis, "Easter Top 8: Which Shows Are the Worst to Christians?" March 29, 2018, *News Busters*, last accessed March 4, 2020, https://www.newsbusters.org/blogs/culture/amelia-hamilton/2018/03/29/easter-top-8-which-shows-are-worst-christians; Alexa Moutevelis, "Easter 2019: Top 10 Worst Shows for Christians," April 19, 2019, *News Busters*, last accessed March 4, 2020, https://www.newsbusters.org/blogs/culture/alexa-moutevelis-coombs/2019/04/19/10-worst-tv-shows-christians.

358. See last endnote for citation information regarding that which was said in this bullet list.

359. Avi Selk, "A Satanic Idol Goes to the Arkansas Capitol Building," August 17, 2018, *Washington Post*, last accessed January 14, 2020, https://www.washingtonpost.com/news/acts-of-faith/wp/2018/08/17/a-satanic-idols-3-year-journey-to-the-arkansas-capitol-building/.

360. Abby Phillip, "Oklahoma's Ten Commandments Statue Must Be Removed, State Supreme Court Says," June 30, 2015, *Washington Post*, last accessed January 14, 2020, https://www.washingtonpost.com/news/acts-of-faith/wp/2015/06/30/oklahomas-ten-commandments-statue-must-be-removed-state-supreme-court-says/?tid=lk_inline_manual_5.

361. Ibid.

362. "Ten Commandments Monument May Be Joined By Monkey God and Satanic Tribute at Oklahoma Capitol," December 16, 2013, *CBS News*, last accessed January 14, 2020, https://www.cbsnews.com/news/ten-commandments-monument-may-be-joined-by-monkey-god-and-satantic-tribute-at-okla-capitol/.

363. Sarah Pulliam Bailey, "Oklahoma's Controversial Ten Commandments Monument Was Quietly Removed Overnight," October 6, 2015, *Washington Post*, last accessed January 14, 2020, https://www. washingtonpost.com/news/acts-of-faith/wp/2015/10/06/oklahomas-controversial-ten-commandments-monument-was-quietly-removed-overnight/.

364. Abby Ohlheiser, "The Satanic Temple's Giant Statue of a Goat-headed God Is Looking for a Home," July 1, 2015, *Washington Post*, last accessed January 14, 2020, https://www.washingtonpost.com/news/acts-of-faith/wp/2015/07/01/the-satanic-temples-giant-statue-of-a-goat-headed-god-is-looking-for-a-home/.

365. "Bring Baphomet to Arkansas!" fundraiser, *ReasonAlliance*, last accessed January 14, 2020, https://www.flipcause.com/secure/cause_pdetails/Mzg4NTY=.

366. Max Brantley, "Satanic Temple Cleared to Enter the 10 Commandments Lawsuit," December 18, 2018, *Arkansas Times*, last accessed January 14, 2020, https://arktimes.com/arkansas-blog/2018/12/18/satanic-temple-cleared-to-enter-the-10-commandments-lawsuit.

367. Elisha Fieldstadt, "Satanic Statue Erected in Illinois State Capitol with Other Holiday Decorations," December 6, 2018, *NBC News*, last accessed January 14, 2020, https://www.nbcnews.com/news/us-news/satanic-statue-erected-illinois-state-capitol-other-holiday-decorations-n944706.

368. "Snaketivity" fundraiser, launched October 18, 2018, *GoFundMe*, last accessed January 14, 2020, https://www.gofundme.com/f/snaketivity.

369. Elisha Fieldstadt, "Satanic Statue Erected…," *NBC News*.

370. Ibid.

371. Bill Chappell, "Satanist and Christian Holiday Displays to Go Up at Michigan Capitol," December 17, 2014, *NPR News*, last accessed January 14, 2020, https://www.npr.org/sections/thetwo-way/2014/12/17/371503835/satanist-and-christian-holiday-displays-to-go-up-at-michigan-capitol.

372. Abby Ohlheiser, "The Florida Capitol's Holiday Display Will Include a Festive Message from the Satanic Temple," December 4, 2014, *Washington Post*, last accessed January 14, 2020, https://www.washingtonpost.com/news/post-nation/wp/2014/12/04/the-florida-capitols-holiday-display-will-include-a-festive-message-from-the-satanic-temple/.

373. Ibid.

374. Kristen Chapman, "Battle over Holiday Displays: Satanic Display Erected Next to Nativity Scene," December 6, 2016, *CBS 12 News*, last accessed January 14, 2020, https://cbs12.com/news/local/battle-over-holiday-displays-satanic-display-placed-next-to-nativity-scene.

375. Heck, Peter, "Satanist Assaults Pastor at D.C. Prayer Rally, Drenches Him in Blood," October 27, 2020, *Disrn*, last accessed October 27, 2020, https://disrn.com/news/satanist-assaults-pastor-at-dc-prayer-rally-drenches-him-in-blood.

376. "Obama: We Are No Longer a Christian Nation," YouTube Video, 0:00–0:04, uploaded by robxz on March 9, 2008, last accessed February 3, 2020, https://www.youtube.com/watch?v=tmC3IevZiik. Note that this was a part of the speech listed in the following endnote number, but the *New York Times* actually reported it incorrectly (likely to make his statement less offensive), as this video clip shows.

377. Photos of this monstrosity is all over the Internet. Many tourists have taken pictures of this "artwork" and added it to their own websites, articles, and Facebook and Pinterest accounts. Readers will not have a hard time finding news about this through a simpleGoogle search. However, as one example: "Lucifer in Westminster," August 16, 2014, last accessed February 3, 2020, https://enso6288.wordpress.com/2014/08/16/statue-of-lucifer/.

378. Similar to the last endnote regarding Fryer's "art," this is everywhere. One example: Olivia Cole, "London's Guerrilla Art," October 15, 2009, updated July 14, 2017, *The Beast*, last accessed February 3, 2020, https://www.thedailybeast.com/londons-guerrilla-art.

379. Similar to the last endnote regarding Fryer's "art," this is everywhere. One example: Andrew Hough, "Church Art Exhibition Includes Crucified Ape and Black Jesus on Electric Chair," October 14, 2009, *The Telegraph*, last accessed February 3, 2020, https://www.telegraph.co.uk/culture/art/art-news/6319258/Church-art-exhibition-includes-crucified-ape-and-black-Jesus-on-electric-chair.html.

380. This is an ongoing trend, actually, and readers will easily find countless stories of this occurring across our nation today simply by Googling it. One example is: Robert Spencer, "Canada: Church Takes Cross Off Wall to Avoid Offending Muslims," December 26, 2018, *Jihad Watch*, last accessed September 26, 2019, https://www.jihadwatch.org/2018/12/canada-church-takes-cross-off-wall-to-avoid-offending-muslims.

381. Groothuis, Douglas, *Truth Decay: Defending Christianity Against the Challenges of Postmodernism* (Downers Grove, IL: InterVarsity Press, 2000; Kindle edition), locations 999–1000.

382. Ibid., back cover.

383. Ibid., locations 2793–2794.

384. Pope Francis, in an encyclical released on October 3, 2020, translated and archived by the official Vatican website: "*FRATELLI TUTTI*: Of the Holy Father, Francis, On Fraternity and Social Friendship," *Vatican*, last accessed October 27, 2020, http://www.vatican.va/content/francesco/en/encyclicals/documents/papa-francesco_20201003_enciclica-fratelli-tutti.html.

385. Ibid.

386. Ibid.

387. Ibid.; note that internal quotation marks were removed to avoid confusion, since Pope Francis is here quoting an earlier document that he, himself, was author of.

388. Ibid.; last set of internal quotation marks were removed to avoid confusion, since Pope Francis is here quoting an earlier document that he, himself, was author of.

389. Both photos and videos of this incident can be found all over the web at this time, due to the fact that the controversy was so recent. However, as one close-up example showing the blessing of the idol by Pope Francis, see: "Video Shows Pope Francis Blessing Controversial 'Pachamama' Statue," YouTube, uploaded by LifeSiteNews on October 24, 2019, last accessed January 10, 2020, https://www.youtube.com/watch?v=2Wjdkrfj5OI.

390. Wilson, Andrew S., Timothy Taylor, Maria Constanza Ceruti, et al, "Stable Isotope and DNA Evidence for Ritual Sequences in Inca Child Sacrifice," October 16, 2007, *Proceedings of the National Academy of Sciences of the United States of America (PNAS)*, last accessed October 15, 2020, https://www.pnas.org/content/104/42/16456; quote taken from the abstract of the article.

391. Ibid.

392. Steven Mosher, "Not Even Pope Francis Can Deny the Pachamama is a Pagan Idol," October 28, 2019, *LifeSite News*, last accessed January 10, 2020, https://www.lifesitenews.com/blogs/not-even-pope-francis-can-deny-the-pachamama-is-a-pagan-idol.

393. John-Henry Weston, "Pope Calls Statues 'Pachamamas' and Apologizes for Their Removal from Church," October 25, 2019, *LifeSite News*, last accessed January 10, 2020, https://www.lifesitenews.com/news/pope-calls-statues-pachamamas-and-apologizes-for-their-removal-from-church?utm_source=LifeSiteNews.com&utm_campaign=15fdf5d6d6-Daily%2520Headlines%2520-%2520U.S._COPY_620&utm_medium=email&utm_term=0_12387f0e3e-15fdf5d6d6-401421241.

394. Strong, J., *A Concise Dictionary of the Words in the Greek Testament and The Hebrew Bible: Vol. 1* (Bellingham, WA: Logos Bible Software; 2009), 56.

395. Thayer, J. H., *A Greek-English Lexicon of the New Testament: Being Grimm's Wilke's Clavis Novi Testamenti* (New York: Harper & Brothers; 1889), 490.

396. Swanson, J., *Dictionary of Biblical Languages with Semantic Domains: Greek (New Testament)* (electronic ed., Oak Harbor: Logos Research Systems, Inc.; 1997), entry "4236."

397. For a bit more reflection, see: "Strong's G3947," *Blue Letter Bible*, last accessed October 16, 2020, https://www.blueletterbible.org/lang/lexicon/lexicon.cfm?Strongs=G3947&t=KJV; then, on this same page, follow the links near the top in the "Root Word (Etymology)" box to the roots G3844 and G3691 to study how *paroxuno* or *paroxyno* formed from a term that would have never applied itself to Pope Francis' "thrills" application.

398. Pope Francis, in a sermon delivered to the "general audience" at St. Peter's Square on Wednesday, November 6, 2019; translated and archived by the official Vatican website: "Catechesis on the Acts of the Apostles—15. '*Whom you adore without knowing him, I tell you*' (*Acts* 17:23). Paul at the Areopagus: an example of the inculturation of the faith in Athens," *Vatican*, last accessed October 16, 2020, http://w2.vatican.va/content/francesco/it/audiences/2019/documents/papa-francesco_20191106_udienza-generale.html.

399. Ibid; emphasis added.

400. "Pope Francis at Mass: Bishops Must Pray to Overcome 'Great Accuser,'" September 11, 2018, *Vatican News*, last accessed October 22, 2020, https://www.vaticannews.va/en/pope-francis/mass-casa-santa-marta/2018-09/pope-francis-mass-great-accuser-bishops-scandal.html.

401. Pope John Paull II, in a public homily on Sunday February 3, 1985; translated and archived by the official Vatican website: "Apostolic

Journey to Venezuela, Ecuador, Peru, Trinidad and Tobago: Liturgy of the Word in Cuzco," *Vatican*, last accessed October 16, 2020, http://w2.vatican.va/content/john-paul-ii/es/homilies/1985/documents/hf_jp-ii_hom_19850203_cuzco.html.

402. "Statue of Ancient God of Child Sacrifice Put on Display in Rome," November 6, 2019, *LifeSite News*, last accessed January 10, 2020, https://www.lifesitenews.com/news/statue-of-ancient-god-of-child-sacrifice-put-on-display-in-rome-days-before-amazon-synod.

403. Thomas Horn, "Visions, Chaos, and the Coming of Antichrist," 1:03:19–1:11:25; 1:27:47–1:29:48, *Stand 2020 Defender Conference*, presentation 4 on DVD Conference Collection released September, 2020. Available here: https://www.skywatchtvstore.com/products/stand-2020-defender-conference-dvd-6-disc-box-set?_pos=1&_sid=a8e8c4ebd&_ss=r.

404. "Competing Worldviews Influence Today's Christians," May 9, 2017, *Barna*, last accessed October 29, 2020, https://www.barna.com/research/competing-worldviews-influence-todays-christians/.

405. Ibid.

406. "American Worldview Inventory 2020—At a Glance…Release #3: Perceptions of God," April 21, 2020, *Cultural Research Center, Arizona Christian University*, last accessed October 29, 2020, https://www.arizonachristian.edu/wp-content/uploads/2020/04/CRC-AWVI-2020-Release-03_Perceptions-of-God.pdf.

407. "How We Got Here: Spiritual and Political Profiles of America," May 23, 2017, *Barna*, last accessed October 29, 2020, https://www.barna.com/research/got-spiritual-political-profiles-america/.

408. "A Snapshot of Faith Practice Across Age Groups," July 23, 2019, *Barna*, last accessed October 29, 2020, https://www.barna.com/research/faithview-on-faith-practice/.

409. "Sharing Faith Is Increasingly Optional to Christians," May 15, 2018, *Barna*, last accessed October 29, 2020, https://www.barna.com/research/sharing-faith-increasingly-optional-christians/.

410. "Almost Half of Practicing Christian Millennials Say Evangelism Is Wrong," February 5, 2019, *Barna*, last accessed October 29, 2020, https://www.barna.com/research/millennials-oppose-evangelism/.

411. "51% of Churchgoers Don't Know of the Great Commission," March 27, 2018, *Barna*, last accessed October 29, 2020, https://www.barna.com/research/half-churchgoers-not-heard-great-commission/.

412. Silent and Solo: How Americans Pray," August 15, 2017, *Barna*, last accessed October 29, 2020, https://www.barna.com/research/silent-solo-americans-pray/.

413. "American Worldview Inventory 2020—At a Glance…Release #11: Churches and Worldview," October 6, 2020, *Cultural Research Center*, *Arizona Christian University*, last accessed November 4, 2020, https://www.arizonachristian.edu/wp-content/uploads/2020/10/CRC_AWVI2020_Release11_Digital_04_20201006.pdf.

414. "The State of Theology," a survey conducted by Ligonier Ministries and LifeWay Research in March of 2020, findings released September 8, last accessed October 29, 2020, https://thestateoftheology.com/. Note that not all of these statistics are covered on the "Key Findings" tab. One wishing to observe the list in its entirety must click on the "Data Explorer" tab at the top right of the main study page.

415. Ibid.

416. Nichols, Stephen, as quoted in: Michael Foust, "'Drifting Away' from Scripture: 30 Percent of Evangelicals Say Jesus was Not God, Poll Shows," August 27, 2020, *Christian Headlines*, last accessed October 29, 2020, https://www.christianheadlines.com/contributors/michael-foust/drifting-away-from-scripture-30-percent-of-evangelicals-say-jesus-was-not-god-poll-shows.html.

417. Stonestreet, John and Shane Morris, "Self-Constructed, Build-a-Bear, Buffet-Style Christianity Is No Christianity At All," September 14, 2020, *Breakpoint*, last accessed October 29, 2020, https://www.breakpoint.org/self-constructed-build-a-bear-buffet-style-christianity-is-no-christianity-at-all/.

418. "Two-Thirds of Christians Face Doubt," July 25, 2017, *Barna*, last accessed October 29, 2020, https://www.barna.com/research/two-thirds-christians-face-doubt/.

419. "2013 Church Budget Allocations, Learning Priorities, and Quarterly Financial Trends," *Evangelical Christian Credit Union* (ECCU), https://www.eccu.org/resources/advisorypanel/2013/surveyreports20; preserved by *The Wayback Machine Internet Archive*, last accessed September 27, 2019, http://web.archive.org/web/20141019033209/https://www.eccu.org/resources/advisorypanel/2013/surveyreports20.

420. "Financial Score Conversions and Tables," *Charity Navigator*, last

accessed September 27, 2019, https://www.charitynavigator.org/index.
cfm?bay=content.view&cpid=48; emphasis added.

421. Aden, Josiah, "New York Presbyterian Church Hosts Pagan
Deity," September 12, 2019, *Juicy Ecumenism*, last accessed
January 10, 2020, https://juicyecumenism.com/2019/09/12/
binghamton-presbyterian-sviatovid/.

422. Kimberly Chastain, in an untitled, public response to Josiah Aden's
article over the United Presbyterian Church of Binghamton Facebook
account on September 13, 2019, at 5:38 in the evening. Last accessed
October 10, 2019, https://www.facebook.com/UPCBinghamton/
posts/1387642211411481.

423. Sherisse Pham, "Hallelujah! Christians Pole Dance for Jesus in Texas,"
March 22, 2011, *ABC News*, last accessed October 30, 2020, https://
abcnews.go.com/US/hallelujah-christians-pole-dance-jesus-texas/
story?id=13194891.

424. "'Pole Dancing for Jesus' Taking Off Among Churchgoing Women—and
Men" September 15, 2011, *Daily Mail*, last accessed October 30, 2020,
https://www.dailymail.co.uk/news/article-2037915/Pole-Dancing-Jesus-
taking-churchgoing-women--MEN.html.

425. "The Connected Generation" 2020 survey report conducted by the Barna
Group and World Vision, "Key Findings," last accessed October 29, 2020,
https://theconnectedgeneration.com/key-findings/.

426. "In U.S., Decline of Christianity Continues at Rapid Pace," *Pew
Research Center*, last accessed October 29, 2020, https://www.pewforum.
org/2019/10/17/in-u-s-decline-of-christianity-continues-at-rapid-pace/.

427. "State of the Church: One in Three Practicing Christians Has
Stopped Attending Church During COVID-19," July 8, 2020,
Barna, last accessed October 29, 2020, https://www.barna.com/
research/new-sunday-morning-part-2/?utm_source=Newsletter&utm_
medium=email&utm_content=Barna+Roundup%3A+One+in+Three+
Practicing+Christians+Has+Stopped+Attending+Church+During+CO
VID-19&utm_campaign=BU_07-08-20_Roundup.

428. "American Worldview Inventory 2020—At a Glance…Release #10:
Worldview in the Millennial Generation," September 22, 2020, *Cultural
Research Center, Arizona Christian University*, last accessed October 29,
2020, https://www.arizonachristian.edu/wp-content/uploads/2020/09/
CRC_AWVI2020_Release10_Digital_01_20200922.pdf.

429. Machen, J. Gresham, *Christianity and Liberalism* (New Edition; Grand Rapids, MI; Cambridge, UK: William B. Eerdmans Publishing Company; 2009), 113.

430. Ibid., 6.

431. Ibid.

432. "Global Christianity—A Report on the Size and Distribution of the World's Christian Population," December 19, 2011, *Pew Research Center*, last accessed October 29, 2020, https://www.pewforum.org/2011/12/19/global-christianity-exec/.

433. As quoted in: Poloma, Margaret M. and John C. Green, *The Assemblies of God: Godly Love and the Revitalization of American Pentecostalism* (New York and London; New York University Press, 2010), 1. Original source: Rabey, Steve, *Revival in Brownsville: [the Charisma Revival], Pentecostalism, and the Power of American Revivalism* (Nashville, TX: Thomas Nelson, 1998), 4–5.

434. Jones, Bob, "The [Charisma] Revival: Shaken or Stirred?" *World Magazine*, December 20 issue, 1997, accessed online February 28, 2020, https://world.wng.org/1997/12/the_pensacola_revival_shaken_or_stirred.

435. Ibid.

436. Joe Horn, *Everyday Champions: Unleash the Gifts God Gave You, Step into Your Purpose, and Fulfill Your Destiny* (Crane, MO: Defender Publishing; 2019), 90, 94–97.

437. Horn, Thomas, and Donna Howell, *Redeemed Unredeemable: When America's Most Notorious Criminals Came Face to Face with God* (Crane, MO: Defender Publishing, 2014), 118–120.

438. As quoted in: Exell, Joseph S. (n.d.), *The Biblical Illustrator: I. Corinthians Vol. 2* (New York, NY: Anson D. F. Randolph & Company, 1887), 365.

439. This is a small list, compiled from only two books: Steven Bancarz and Josh Peck, *The Second Coming of the New Age: The Hidden Dangers of Alternative Spirituality in Contemporary America and Its Churches* (Crane, MO: Defender Publishing, 2018); Dr. Thomas Horn, *Shadowland: From Jeffrey Epstein to the Clintons, from Obama and Biden to the Occult Elite: Exposing the Deep-State Actors at War with Christianity, Donald Trump, and America's Destiny* (Crane, MO: Defender Publishing, 2019). However, readers are encouraged to look beyond just these titles.

440. Steven Bancarz and Josh Peck, *The Second Coming of the New Age: The*

Hidden Dangers of Alternative Spirituality in Contemporary America and Its Churches (Crane, MO: Defender Publishing, 2018), 324.

441. "American Worldview...Release #11: Churches and Worldview."

442. Corduan, W., *Pocket Guide to World Religions* (Downers Grove, IL: InterVarsity Press; 2006), 39.

443. Laney, J. C., "Fishing the Sea of Galilee," from B. J. Beitzel & K. A. Lyle (Eds.), *Lexham Geographic Commentary on the Gospels* (Bellingham, WA: Lexham Press; 2016), 165.

444. Jaffe, M., *Great Commission Strategies, 2nd Ed.* (Springfield, MO: Global University; 2017), 20–26.

445. Bill Gaither, "The Church Triumphant," from the album "Reunited" by *Gaither Music Group*, track 11, "interlude," released September 8, 2009. Quoted with permission from Adam DeBolt, Music License Clearance Royalty Administrator for the Gaither Music Company, Alexandria, IN, via an archived email delivered to Donna Howell on September 23, 2019 at 9:07 AM; https://www.capitolcmglicensing.com/.